Strategic Data Warehousing Principles Using SAS® Software

Peter R. Welbrock

Comments or Questions?

The authors assume complete responsibility for the technical accuracy of the content of this book. If you have any questions about the material in this book, please write to the authors at this address:

SAS Institute Inc.
Books by Users
Attn: Peter Welbrock
SAS Campus Drive
Cary, NC 27513

If you prefer, you can send e-mail to sasbbu@sas.com with "comments for Peter Welbrock" as the subject line, or you can fax the Books by Users program at (919) 677-4444.

The correct bibliographic citation for this manual is as follows: Peter R. Welbrock, *Strategic Data Warehousing Principles Using SAS® Software*, Cary, NC: SAS Institute Inc., 1998. 384 pp.

Strategic Data Warehousing Principles Using SAS® Software

The SAS® System is an integrated system of software providing complete control over data access, management, analysis, and presentation. Base SAS software is the foundation of the SAS System. Products within the SAS System include SAS/ACCESS®, SAS/AF®, SAS/ASSIST®, SAS/CALC®, SAS/CONNECT®, SAS/CPE®, SAS/DMI®, SAS/EIS®, SAS/ENGLISH®, SAS/ETS®, SAS/FSP®, SAS/GRAPH®, SAS/IML®, SAS/IMS-DL/I®, SAS/INSIGHT®, SAS/IntrNet™, SAS/LAB®, SAS/MDDB™, SAS/NVISION®, SAS/OR®, SAS/PH-Clinical®, SAS/QC®, SAS/REPLAY-CICS®, SAS/SESSION®, SAS/SHARE®, SAS/SPECTRAVIEW, SAS/STAT®, SAS/TOOLKIT®, SAS/TUTOR®, SAS/Warehouse Administrator™, SAS/DB2™, SAS/GEO™, SAS/GIS®, SAS/PH-Kinetics™, SAS/SHARE*NET™, and SAS/SQL-DS™ software. Other SAS Institute products are SYSTEM 2000® Data Management Software, with basic SYSTEM 2000, CREATE™, Multi-User™, QueX™, Screen Writer™, and CICS interface software; InfoTap® software; JMP®, JMP IN® and JMP Serve® software; SAS/RTERM® software; the SAS/C® Compiler; Video Reality™ software; Warehouse Viewer™ software; Budget Vision™, Campaign Vision™, CFO Vision™, Enterprise Miner™, Enterprise Reporter™, HR Vision™ software, IT Charge Manager™ software, and IT Service Vision™ software; Scalable Performance Data Server™ software; SAS OnlineTutor™ software; and Emulus® software. MultiVendor Architecture™, MVA™, MultiEngine Architecture™, and MEA™ are trademarks of SAS Institute Inc. SAS Institute also offers SAS Consulting®, and SAS Video Productions® services. Authorline®, Books by UsersSM, The Encore Series®, *ExecSolutions®, JMPer Cable®, Observations®, SAS Communications®, sas.com™, SAS OnlineDoc™, SAS Professional Services™*, the SASware Ballot®, SelecText™, and Solutions@Work™ documentation are published by SAS Institute Inc. The SAS Video Productions logo, the Books by Users SAS Institute's Author Service logo, the SAS Online Samples logo, and The Encore Series logo are registered service marks or registered trademarks of SAS Institute Inc. The Helplus logo, the SelecText logo, the Video Reality logo, the Quality Partner logo, the SAS Business Solutions logo, the SAS Rapid Warehousing Program logo, the SAS Publications logo, the Instructor-based Training logo, the Online Training logo, the Trainer's Kit logo, and the Video-based Training logo are service marks or trademarks of SAS Institute Inc. All trademarks above are registered trademarks or trademarks of SAS Institute Inc. in the USA and other countries. ® indicates USA registration.

The Institute is a private company devoted to the support and further development of its software and related services.

IBM®, AIX®, DB2®, OS/390™, and SQL/DS™ are registered trademarks or trademarks of International Business Machines Corporation. ORACLE® is a registered trademark or trademark of Oracle Corporation. ® indicates USA registration.

Other brand and product names are registered trademarks or trademarks of their respective companies.

Acknowledgements

There are many people that have contributed both directly and indirectly to this book. In this field, completely original thoughts are very hard to come up with, which means that, obviously, I had to rely heavily and build on the work of others.

I would like to thank the following people for indirectly supporting this book: Malcolm Rhoades, in London, who went out on a limb for me when he really didn't need to, and Mike Durbin, in St. Louis, whose straight-forward, no-nonsense approach to data warehousing has inspired many of the thoughts contained within this book. Without these two people, I would not have had the opportunity or knowledge to write this book.

I would also like to thank the following for their direct input into the book: Pete Maher, in St. Louis, and all those at SAS Institute who took the time to review the technical content and to edit the text. I would especially like to thank Julie Platt of the Books By Users Program at SAS for her humor and patience over the past few months. She laughed when many would have cried!

Finally, I would like to thank my family, Ingela, Sean, and Nicholas who have had to live with restricted weekends and limited access to the family computer.

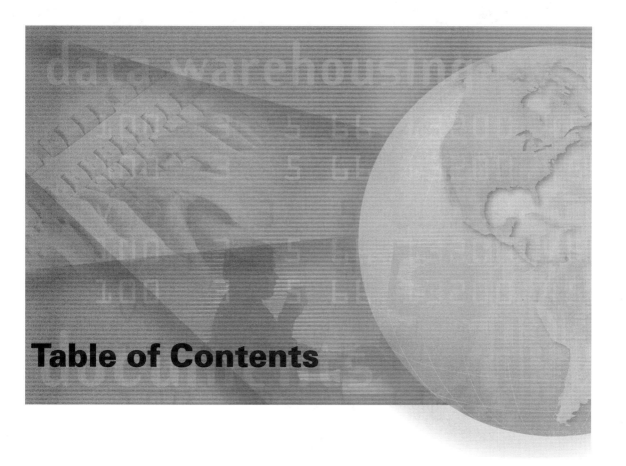

Table of Contents

Chapter 3:
Creating a Data Model for the Warehouse **41**

Chapter 4:
Effective Use of a Multi-Dimensional Model: SAS/MDDB™
and the Data Warehouse **81**

Chapter 5:
Data Storage within the Data Warehouse:
Using SAS/ACCESS® Software Effectively **103**

Chapter 1:
An Introduction to
Data Warehousing

Preface

Tackling the subject of Data Warehousing is a daunting task. Tackling the writing of a book about the subject is equally intimidating. Most textbooks about Data Warehousing take an easy course and specialize in a tiny portion of the topic. This leaves the reader more educated about one specific part but without the perspective necessary to put all the pieces of the puzzle together. In other words, this approach teaches us how to build each room of a house, with little regard as to whether the rooms will fit together as a cohesive building when finally constructed. This book will take an opposite approach. Although different topics will be broached in different chapters, they will all be tied together by continually referring to 'the big picture:' the entire Data Warehousing process.

Of course, what is referred to as 'the big picture' is not consistent across different organizations, or even within them. This is one of the problems in formulating generic Data Warehousing strategies: what are the common denominators that will make practical sense to all those who read a book about it? In the case of this book, it is SAS software, which can optionally be used in every step of the Data Warehousing process. For those of you who have only a passing acquaintance or no knowledge of SAS software, this book will still be of use to you in learning about the Data Warehousing process. It will also give you a bonus: an insight into one of the most robust, powerful, and flexible software products available.

Data Warehousing is not an academic exercise, but is a practical one that should have direct and measurable benefits to any organization that invests in it. This means that any writing about the topic should be grounded in the practical, as opposed to the academic. Sometimes what is logically the best approach is not always the most practical. In real data warehouse processes, there are often resource limitations or political realities that prevent the most logical approach from being used. This should not, however, ever prevent each data warehousing decision that has to be made from being put into a framework (or process). If the decision that has the best chance of leading to a successful implementation is not practical, then this should be documented.

Only through the careful consideration of each step within the data warehousing process can it lead to a responsive enterprise tool that is capable of responding to changes in the enterprise itself or the circumstance in which the enterprise finds itself. This book is intended to describe this framework so that a successful process can be formulated. Although this process will differ greatly in content from enterprise to enterprise, in all situations it will be the foundation upon which a successful Data Warehouse can be built.

1.1 Who Will Benefit from Reading this Book?

This book is primarily aimed at three different types of readers:

1. Those who are, or will be, involved in the administration and design of the Data Warehousing process (*Data Warehouse facilitators*).
2. Those who will be involved in the implementation of the Data Warehouse (*Data Warehouse developers*).
3. Those who will have a management responsibility or a stake in the outcome of the Data Warehousing process (*Data Warehouse Managers*).

Data Warehouse Facilitators

These people are absolutely essential to the successful implementation of a Data Warehousing project. They are the facilitators that turn just another Information Systems project into an enterprise that is responsive and successful. Although it is not necessary for these facilitators to be technical, they very often are, in a practical sense. They perform the role of a conduit between the enterprise goals and the physical implementation of the Warehouse itself.

Data Warehouse Facilitators have to mediate between the often outlandish desires of the business community and the inherent caution of the Information Systems folks. A practical knowledge of both the business and the technology available is therefore essential to successfully perform this role. Not only must the Warehouse Facilitators have the negotiating skills to keep the Warehousing project moving forward but they must be able to see the big picture at all times. This book will give the Warehouse Facilitators the framework within which the enterprise needs can be realized through the Data Warehouse process.

These people usually possess practical knowledge as well as an appreciation for technology. They understand how technology can be used to support and sometimes change business processes. Usually, this group of people has a clear vision of what is needed from the Data Warehouse process.

There is a good argument that suggests that this role can best be divided into two. First, the facilitators make sure that the enterprise needs are fully understood, so that the Data Warehouse can fully meet these needs. Second, part of the role translates these needs into a technological lexicon, so that the developers can understand fully what they are trying to achieve.

These Facilitators will benefit from reading this book by understanding the concepts and how different parts of the SAS System may be used to meet the very real technological challenges that Data Warehousing produces.

Data Warehouse Implementers

This book will give developers a firm grounding in how SAS software can be used to meet the goals that are set for them by enterprise needs that can be addressed through the Data Warehousing process. There is no inherent link between technical knowledge and conceptual understanding, so this book will help bridge that potential gap. Developers can use this book not only to gather the 'how to' but also the 'why', which will put them in a position where they can become more involved in the design as opposed to just the building of the implemented physical Data Warehouse.

In this day and age, building a database or a software application based upon a pre-defined specification is an anachronism, due to the phenomenal improvements made in both software and hardware. This is one of the principal reasons that Data Warehousing has gained in popularity: the nature of Data Warehousing, being both iterative and evolutionary, means that traditional software design techniques by definition could not work. It takes a new breed of developer, one that is willing to become involved in the entire process, not just the programming, to successfully implement a Data Warehouse. This means that the tools needed to implement a Data Warehouse go far beyond just the coding or database design. This book will address these needs. Alongside the many examples of SAS code and techniques, there will be a constant referral back to the big picture, explaining why and where the code and techniques fit into the entire Data Warehousing process.

Throughout the book, there will be references to other sources that the developer can use to gather more information about SAS. Both the topic of Data Warehousing and the SAS software are immense. This means that the code used within the book is there as an outline, an illustration of how it can be done. This does not mean that there are not alternative or better techniques to achieve the same results.

Data Warehouse Managers

Data Warehouse managers are people who might not actually take part in the design and building of the Data Warehouse process, but they have some form of responsibility toward its success. It is in their interests to understand the process of building the Warehouse so that they can be more responsive in managing the resources needed to make it successful. They take responsibility for educating the enterprise on the data warehouse process. It often falls into the hands of the Data Warehouse managers to 'sell' the concepts behind the data warehouse process that drive the delivery of the project.

This group of managers will come from both the business community and Information Systems. They all have a stake in the outcome of the Data Warehousing process. They all have some influence upon that outcome, but they might not be responsible for the actual implementation of the project. Understanding the Data Warehousing process will give these managers the information they need to make decisions that will result in a more responsive business tool.

Summary

To benefit from reading this book, all that is needed is an interest in Data Warehousing. Because the book is written from a Warehousing perspective, each topic is addressed at a high level. Instead of being bombarded with details and expecting the reader to fit them into the Warehousing process, every part of the book is tied back to the' big picture'. At no point should the details not be directly linked to the reason that the book is being read. This is primarily a book about Data Warehousing, not about SAS software. It is written, however, from the perspective of a Data Warehouse that is being constructed by using SAS software.

This book is not written with the assumption that you are a highly skilled technician, but that you are interested in the Data Warehousing process and have a desire to know how the different parts of this process fit together from both a conceptual and a technical level.

1.2 How to Read this Book

One of the major differences between life today, and that of ten, twenty, or fifty years ago is the amount of information we are asked to use in our everyday life. The technology for creating information has increased incredibly, without a corresponding increase in our ability to assimilate that information. This means that we have had to find ways to deal with this situation. At school, when expected to read several books a week, we learn to skim, pulling what we hope will be the key pieces of information to, at best, pass the test with flying colors, or at worst, escape public humiliation. When was the last time any of us read a technical book from cover to cover?

The temptation to ignore those chapters that don't immediately arouse our interest in favor of those that do is irresistible. To find out that understanding the interesting chapters is dependent upon reading the boring ones is always a huge disappointment. Readers of this book need not despair. There is only one chapter after this one that needs to be read: Chapter 2: "Planning the Data Warehousing Process." After that, you can use your random-number generator (with or without replacement) to select the next chapter to read, happy in the knowledge that it will stand alone. This does not mean that there will be no references to other chapters, but that, on a conceptual level, it is not necessary to read those chapters in order to understand the one you are reading.

The examples used within this book are extremely simple. Another frustration of reading a technical book is often the complexity of the examples. This means that the reader spends so much time trying to decipher what the example is actually trying to do, that the points the book is trying to elucidate are lost. The examples used in this book are far simpler than those tasks that you will come across in deploying a Data Warehouse in real life, but the real-life tasks will be a natural extension of the examples used within the book.

The book does not attempt to tell you how your Data Warehouse should be built (as many other books attempt) because no two Data Warehouses are alike. The concepts required to build a Warehouse are addressed, and then these concepts are available to you to help you design a Warehouse that works for your particular set of circumstances. From a technical, as opposed to a conceptual basis, the book will explain and demonstrate the use of SAS software in the Warehousing process.

1.3 Formatting Conventions

There are several formatting conventions in the layout that will make this book easier to read:

Key Concepts/Special Topics: Whenever special topics are addressed within the text, they will be reiterated within a box. This will help you to find topics that might be of particular interest to you. An example of a key concept follows:

 Key Concepts are those that are considered most important from a Data Warehousing standpoint, as opposed to a coding standpoint.

Syntax: There will be extensive sets of examples of SAS code to show how the Warehousing concepts can be practically applied. This code will often be one step within many, so it might not be complete and executable in itself. In every situation, however, the code will be put into perspective, and it will be explained how it could be used.

To keep in line with other publications, all SAS keywords will appear in uppercase. For example, the following lines of code for printing a SAS data set using the PRINT procedure are written as follows:

```
PROC PRINT DATA=libname.dataset ;
RUN ;
```

All the SAS keywords appear in uppercase letters. The code will be indented, whenever possible, to make it easier to read and to understand.

Glossary of Terms: There will be a glossary of terms included at the end of the book. *Any terms that are in the glossary will be distinguished in text because they will be in italics.*

Cross-references: This book is not intended to be an introduction to SAS programming or to replace current documentation. Many of the SAS software modules will be described in some detail, but references will always be made. For instance, the chapter dealing with Client/Server processes will be addressing SAS/CONNECT in detail and will therefore cross-reference the existing applicable documentation alongside any that is included.

For example, an excellent introduction to using SAS is *The Little SAS Book*, by Lora D. Delwiche and Susan J. Slaughter. If there is a specific reference in this book to a particular item in that book, the reference will be detailed in a footnote at the bottom of the page. For example:

It is possible that in this situation, your particular client might not handle the tasks you have asked of it. You might well receive a message that you have run out of memory or disk space,[1] in which case, given your current architectural limitations, another strategy will be required.

---

[1]See: Delwiche, Lora D., and Slaughter, Susan J., *The Little SAS Book: A Primer*, Cary, NC: SAS Institute Inc., 1995. 228pp., pp 186-187.

Chapter 2:
Planning the Data
Warehousing Process

2.1 Data Warehousing Definitions

A concise definition of Data Warehousing has proved more than elusive. There are many reasons for this, some acceptable and some that can only be described as a 'cop out.' The principal reason for the lack of a single definition is the fact that Data Warehousing has been primarily viewed as a way of storing data. It is instinctive to try to define Data Warehousing in terms of what it is, as opposed to what it does. For instance, one working definition of a Data Warehouse could be:

"The extraction, cleansing, and transformation of operational data for the purpose of Decision Support."

This is probably true, but it does not paint the entire picture: there is far too much 'white space.' The definition is rooted in the activities, rather than the function. Because the activities vary greatly among Data Warehousing projects, it has proved very difficult to create a catch-all concise definition. Is it necessary, for example, to cleanse data from the operational system for a Data Warehouse to be valid? Of course not! If the operational data is already 'clean,' then this part of the process is not needed. Indeed, is it even necessary to extract data from an operational system to create a Data Warehouse? The answer to this is less obvious, but the only reason we usually extract data to make the Data Warehouse is technological. Given current technology, there would be an enormous detrimental impact on the operational system if it was also used for data warehousing functions.

All the Data Warehouse allows us to do is create views into data that address the needs of the enterprise. It is by-and-by that we extract this data the vast majority of the time. We extract data not because it is an essential step to the implementation of the Data Warehouse, but to make it work given current technological limitations. These points are very important, not just as an excuse to annoy the traditionalists who think that data modeling is the key, instead of just one of many steps to a successful Warehouse, but because they form the basis for creating a successful Data Warehouse. This is not to say that the modeling of the data is not important, but that it is merely a means to an end, with that end being the fulfillment of enterprise needs.

The definition of Data Warehousing that we are going to use is

 Data Warehousing is a process of fulfilling Decision Support enterprise needs[1] through the availability of information.

Note that this definition does not even mention technology, although it is obviously implicit within the definition. To look at Data Warehousing from this perspective allows us to examine the subject without any preconceived limitations.

This definition allows us to approach the topic of data warehousing from a process-based, rather than implementation-based perspective. More specifically, this book will address data warehousing through the use of SAS Software and how SAS fits into the process. Many definitions of Data Warehouses use terms such as:[2]

- subject-oriented
- non-volatile
- integrated
- time-variant.

---

[1] An enterprise need is defined as an explicit requirement that can be addressed using the information contained within the Data Warehouse. It is not necessarily an enterprise-wide need, although it could well be. The set of enterprise needs is determined by the project scope (vision) of the Data Warehousing project.
[2] Inmon, W.H.: *Building the Data Warehouse*, John Wiley & Sons, Inc., 1993

All of these are typical features of a Data Warehouse. However, they define the Data Warehouse as a source of information, not as a process. Although it is likely that a Data Warehouse will have the above four features, it is only as a result of the process.

One of the keys to successfully implementing a Data Warehousing project is to ensure that it does not become a technological exercise, but a business exercise, utilizing any technology that is necessary to meet these ends. This means that it is the business, not the technology that should be the driving force behind the development of the data warehousing process.

> *The Data Warehousing process is a business process, as opposed to a technological exercise, that uses technological tools only inasmuch as they can directly help to achieve the stated enterprise needs.*

2.2 Data Warehousing Background

It has been only a few short years since Data Warehousing has become part of mainstream Information Technology. In this instance, mainstream means that it has become a subject addressed by both the Computer Press and the Industry itself. This is easy to see because almost every computer trade publication has articles dedicated to some aspect of Data Warehousing in every edition. Indeed, there are now publications dedicated to Data Warehousing itself, although they often come under the guise of Data Management.

For the casual observer, this high level of publicity might illustrate that Data Warehousing is new. This is, in fact, far from the truth. The very first time that data was used beyond its immediate reason for being was the day when Data Warehousing was born. The creation of data is usually for operational reasons (outside the Experimental Data environment). Orders are taken and the data stored so that the manufacturing process can take place and the customers can be billed. In other words, most data is collected as part of a transactional system that is necessary to keep the enterprise running (and, hopefully, profitable). Transactional Systems treat data in a very mono-dimensional manner: the data is created for a specific purpose and the use of that data is pre-defined based upon specific business requirements.[3] **The use of the data within a Transactional (Operational) System is predictable, as opposed to a Data Warehouse, where the use of the data is, by necessity, flexible.**

---

[3] For an excellent write-up of the differences between Operational Systems and Data Warehousing, see: Kimball, Ralph, *The Data Warehousing Toolkit*: John Wiley & Sons, Inc. , 1996, Chapter 1.

The more cynical amongst us see the movement of Data Warehousing into the mainstream as coinciding with the realization from the computer industry that there was money to be made. As with most cynicism, there is some fact to this. Indeed, this can be seen as a major factor in the brief history of Data Warehousing. Sometimes it takes a 'bandwagon' approach to inspire development. With this push from the computer industry (which includes software and hardware manufacturers, the computer press, and all associated consultants) came the move from the largely informal form of Data Warehousing, to a fast developing, yet still primitive, formal process. Is this a good thing? There is no one answer to this question, because many companies have thrown away millions of dollars following what they thought was a well-established formal methodology, purported by the computer industry. On the other hand, there are many very successful informal Data Warehousing projects. These tend to be on a small scale however, and do not, by-and-large, address enterprise-wide issues.

What is undoubtedly true, however, is that the best solution is a formal Data Warehouse that works. There are many reasons for this:

- The formal Data Warehouse will allow for longevity. The informal Data Warehouse is too subject to a particular individual. Metadata tends to be stored in the heads of key individuals, business rules are built into front-end applications, and the scheduling of refreshes are based upon key personnel remembering to start the job. A formal Data Warehousing approach, if properly executed, will internally store this information, and take the risk out of putting so much dependence on individuals, and therefore ultimately increasing flexibility.
- The formal Data Warehouse is more able to address enterprise-wide needs, which will lead to economies of scale that should, if properly managed, give an increased return on investment. Technology today is able to let us share information much more readily than a few years ago, so by addressing enterprise-level needs, there will be more shared information and therefore more educated decision making.
- The formal Data Warehouse is more likely to give access to greater resources. More resources will, if properly managed, lead to a more responsive Data Warehouse, which is able to change in accordance with the business as a whole.

So the last few years of Data Warehousing can be seen not so much in terms of development as much as an evolution in formal methodology. From the computer industry, we have not seen as much of new software technology dealing specifically with data warehousing (although there are exceptions), but in the repackaging of existing technologies, with some token enhancements to address specific Data Warehousing needs. This is because Data Warehousing is essentially a business process, rather than a new technological development, and therefore, it follows that if software and hardware already exist to meet the technological needs of Data Warehousing, then repackaging, rather than new development, is what the marketplace requires. This is not to say that there is no new development occurring (especially in metadata and read-only database technologies), but that most of the challenge of Data Warehousing comes in successfully responding to business needs, which can largely be addressed outside the needs for new technologies.

 The development of Data Warehousing over the past ten years can be measured in terms of the evolution of the process itself, rather than in any quantum leap in associated technology.

As the managers, designers, and implementers of the Data Warehousing process, this evolution of the formal methodology has a severe impact, most of it positive. For the first time, enterprises are investing both money and resources to allow enterprise-wide solutions. No longer is there a dependence upon 'underground' Data Warehouses, those that might not have complete enterprise-wide approval and support, but they have become a respectable part of Information Technology, with all of the associated advantages and disadvantages. The trick for those involved in Data Warehousing is to gather and manipulate these new resources to meet the needs of the enterprise!

2.3 Data Warehousing—a Perpetual Process

The term Data Warehousing is an unfortunate choice because it mistakenly suggests that the most important aspect is the storage of data. Although storage is a part of Data Warehousing, as the definition in section 2.1 illustrates, it is not the most important part. The process of Data Warehousing incorporates anything that is required to give the enterprise what it needs from an informational perspective.

The Data Warehousing process should be built around three major phases. These phases are part of a 'cyclical', rather than a 'waterfall' process. In other words, the development of a Data Warehouse is an iterative process, where each phase should be continually revisited to ensure that up-to-date enterprise needs are being addressed.

Figure 2.1 on page 14, illustrates the Data Warehousing process.

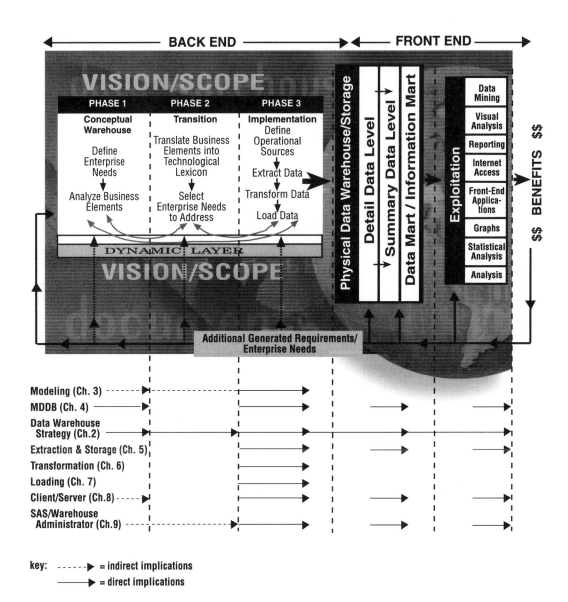

Figure 2.1

There are two distinct ways of looking at the Data Warehouse:

- From the back end, which includes the design and implementation of the warehouse.
- From the front end, which includes any aspect of the exploitation of the data.

This book is primarily concerned with the back end of the Data Warehouse. The front end is only of interest insomuch as it affects the design of the back end. For instance, if there are specific forms of analyses that are to take place on the data, then it makes sense to design the back end of the data warehouse so that the front-end analyses will be optimized.

The Data Warehouse Front End

The front end of the Data Warehouse mostly influences the Data Marts and Information Marts. This is because in an implementation that is directly responsive to the business needs of the organization, the design should reflect the expected access patterns. These patterns are directly related to the needs. In Figure 2.1, the front end is illustrated by the various types of anlyses: data mining, visual analysis, reporting, Internet access, statistical anlaysis, etc.

The Data Warehouse Back End

The back end of the Data Warehouse is every part of the process except the actual exploitation. In Figure 2.1, this is illustrated by the three phases:

- Conceptual Warehouse
- Transition
- Implementation

Each of these phases ride on a **dynamic layer**, which is essential for the Data Warehouse to be responsive to the needs of the enterprise both in the short and long term. This *dynamic layer* essentially means that inherent within the entire back-end process, there is the ability to move between the three different phrases during the entire life of the Data Warehouse.

Around each of these phases is the 'vision' or scope of the Data Warehouse. This is 'around' each phase because it is the principal driver that has the most influence on the development of the Data Warehouse. Each decision that will influence the development of the Data Warehouse should be made based upon its relevance to the 'vision.'

Figure 2.1 also illustrates that at any point in the development of the Data Warehouse, new enterprise needs can be recognized and incorporated into the process. These additional needs could be recognized as a direct result of exploitation or as part of a change in the 'vision' of the Data Warehouse.

Finally, the Figure illustrates the role each of the topics (as distinguished by each chapter) plays (or can play) in the development of the Data Warehouse. Often, each topic has direct implications to a particular stage in the development cycle (e.g., Transformation, which is discussed in Chapter 6, will have direct implications to the Implementation Phase). Sometimes the implications are indirect (e.g., using a multidimensional database model, as discussed in Chapter 4, can help in the design of the Conceptual Warehouse), which means that the techniques discussed within the chapter can optionally be used within the particular phase.

Each of the three phases included in the back end of the Data Warehouse has its own internal processes. For example, the first phase, the building of the Conceptual Warehouse contains the definition of the enterprise needs and the subsequent break down of these into business elements. These internal processes will tend to be less flexible than those between phases. In other words, it is possible to jump between phases during the development of the Data Warehouse, but it is less likely that steps jump across steps within a phase.

Without planning, the Data Warehouse might not bear any resemblance to what is actually required. The planning stage of the process uses the 'vision' of the project to determine what the Data Warehouse will address. Timing issues are essential. Understanding exactly what, from a data perspective, should be incorporated into the Data Warehouse and the order in which the data should be prepared should be decided during this planning phase. What is the key to ensuring that this actually happens? It is to fully understand the purpose of the Warehouse. Once again we come back to what should be the fundamental principle in the design of a Data Warehouse: that it is a user tool and a business tool, not a technological exercise. The success (or lack thereof) of the Data Warehouse should be gauged by looking at how the enterprise needs are met, not on the internal performance of the Warehouse itself.

> *Planning the Data Warehouse depends on understanding the needs of the enterprise based upon an* explicit *'vision'. Building the Warehouse before knowing the set of enterprise needs that are to be addressed will increase the probability of failure.*

Why Data Warehouse Requirements Change over Time

It is not, however, either realistic or practical to know everything that the Warehouse will be used for before it is initially built. On a practical level, to collect every requirement from the business community will, in all probability, lead to the project being stalled for months, maybe years. It is important that there is an agreed upon starting point for the project that contains a finite list of enterprise needs that the Data Warehouse will address. These needs, however, will change and develop over time. Two reasons for this are:

■ The nature of every enterprise changes over time, so it follows that the specific requirements are likely to change accordingly. Data Warehousing by its nature deals with a moving target. This should be an accepted part of the design, not a frustrating part of the Warehousing process.

■ Users do not necessarily know all of their requirements at the beginning of the project. Indeed, a successful Data Warehouse project is one that continues to develop over time. There is no real end to the project because a successful Warehouse will breed more requirements. This is another source of frustration for those who are involved in Data Warehousing projects but do not understand what they are doing on a strategic level. It is good that the users come back to the implementers to ask for additional requirements to be met, because it is an illustration that the Warehouse is working, not, (as is often thought) that it demonstrates scope creep.

> *Scope creep should not be necessarily viewed as undesirable. On the contrary, any growth or change, so long as it is justifiable from an enterprise perspective should be incorporated into the Warehouse design and managed accordingly.*

Establishing 'Vision' for the Data Warehouse

To begin the development of the Data Warehouse, there must be a conceptual understanding of what, from an enterprise perspective, is needed. One of the skills in developing a Data Warehouse is balancing the strategic needs at the enterprise level with the specific needs on a detail level. Too many Data Warehousing projects are undertaken without this high-level conceptual understanding, and therefore are prone to losing focus. The driving force behind the Warehouse development and the tool used to keep this development on target should be these high-level concepts.

As an example, let us assume that a high-level justification for the Warehouse is that it will be used as the informational tool to help the enterprise gain market share in new geographic regions. A new request is then submitted for the Warehouse to support a marketing project that is intended to ascertain how promotions are working for a specific product line. This request does not fit within the boundaries of the high-level justification and will therefore detract from the 'vision' of the Data Warehousing process. This is not to say that the specific request is not valid, but that these extraneous requests need to be managed: that there should be a balance between the high-level vision and the detail that is supplied within the Warehouse.[4]

---

[4] See Section 2.5 for a discussion on managing requests made of the Data Warehouse.

Vision is a key step in the planning process. Before any data is modeled, any hardware is purchased, any software is considered, there must be 'vision'. If the question: *What are we actually trying to achieve from an enterprise level through the use of Data Warehousing*? cannot be answered, then the chance of building a successful Data Warehouse is remote.

> *'Vision' is a major factor in determining the success of a Data Warehousing project. It is the guiding light for managing and implementing the Data Warehouse and is therefore essential to the process. A Data Warehouse without 'vision' will be harder to both justify and implement.*

Special Topic: Selling the Data Warehouse

To successfully create a Data Warehouse requires support from within the organization. This raises the question of how to garner this support. The mistake is often made to try to sell the Data Warehouse itself. This, in effect, is akin to selling a technological project, which will come against opposition (often justified) from the business community the Warehouse is designed to help.

A better approach is to sell the idea of solving the enterprise needs that would be contained within the Conceptual Warehouse. It is far easier to get support for the Data Warehouse by finding out what it is worth to the enterprise to more accurately target potential customers, for example, than to sell the concept of a vast database that could cost millions of dollars. This supports the argument that the Data Warehouse is, at heart, a business, not a technological project, and should be viewed as such.

Timing the Implementation of the Data Warehouse

Later in this chapter (Section 2.4) there will be a discussion about a Data Warehousing methodology that will suggest that the Planning Phase should be extended with an additional step before the Implementation Phase is started. This step is the Transition Phase that is designed to translate defined enterprise needs into technological solutions. The temptation is, however, to dive into implementation before the stage is correctly set. This pattern has been reflected in many Data Warehousing projects: key user requirements have been overlooked, or the data has been modeled in such a way that it does not meet the users' needs. This results in these projects being thrown away (or revamped), with the resultant loss of time and money, not to mention the opportunity loss associated with the enterprise needs not being met because the Data Warehouse was of no use.

The Implementation Phase of the Data Warehousing process is very often the only stage discussed by texts on the subject. Almost without exception, when the topic of Data Warehousing is written about, it begins with implementation. This oversight is compounded by both software and hardware vendors, but in this situation, the oversight is more understandable. The Implementation Phase of Data Warehousing is the part where computer software and hardware are both needed, and as such, the vendors are business bound to emphasize this part of the process.

2.4 Data Warehousing Methodology

Methodologies exist so that every action and decision can be made to ignore them. This one is no exception. The purpose of this methodology is to lay out a series of steps that should be addressed during the entire Data Warehousing process. It is not intended as a set of rules and regulations that, when followed, will guarantee a successful Data Warehouse. A generic methodology for Data Warehousing cannot work for all situations, because every enterprise has different needs and cultural morays that cannot be satisfied by a guideline. The advantage of using a methodology in this situation is that, if decisions are made to follow the guidelines (or any part of the guidelines), this is done at a conscious level rather than as a potentially expensive oversight. Omission might be justifiable, but at least it has been justified!

It is very easy when looking at a process as large as that inherent in Data Warehousing to get lost—to not 'see the forest for the trees.' A methodology can help avoid this problem because it can give a framework to reference the process and, therefore, keep it in perspective. The methodology outlined below starts at a simple level of looking at the entire process in three phases, each phase having sub-methodologies associated with them.

The methodology outlined below is a Data Warehousing Process Methodology that incorporates every aspect of many stages in that process, as opposed to being applicable to just one. Many texts on Data Warehousing convey methodologies that only apply to, for instance, the data modeling phase. For example, a Star Schema[5] is one way of modeling your data for incorporation into the Data Warehouse. This might be a perfectly valid methodology, but it is limited in terms of the entire process. There is often confusion between a Data Modeling and a complete Data Warehousing

---

[5] For a description of a Star-Schema model, see Chapter 3, Section 3.5.

methodology. A Star Schema methodology will be one of many potential techniques to store the data in the Warehouse, but it does not help when gathering and prioritizing enterprise requirements. Indeed, it may be justifiable to use more than one technique to store the data in the Warehouse. Although the Star Schema technique might be of value, it is only one piece of the puzzle.

The Need for a Three-Phase Methodology

This three-phase methodology is not a beginning-to-end of Data Warehousing design. The methodology is inherently an iterative process, where all components are revisited over-and-over again for the life of the Data Warehouse. There are three major reasons for this:

- To remain a useful business tool, the Data Warehouse process must stay in line with the requirements of the enterprise. It follows, therefore, that as long as the enterprise is changing, so must the Data Warehousing methodology be revisited.
- It is highly unlikely that an all-encompassing Data Warehouse will be created the first time. Incremental Data Warehousing is a more likely approach because it allows for experimentation without great risk. To try a new approach on a small scale is less risky than to 'put all the eggs in one basket' right from the beginning. This is why most successful Data Warehousing projects start small and grow. The 'Big Bang'[6] approach to Data Warehousing, where the entire enterprise is addressed all at once, is not usually a great success, mainly because it is developed without specifically addressing explicit enterprise needs. With an incremental approach to Data Warehousing, it is necessary to revisit the methodology with each iteration.
- The methodology itself might need to be modified based upon changes in the requirements of the Data Warehouse. This means that it might be necessary to go back to the methodology not because of adjustments to the Data Warehouse itself, but to adjust the way that the Data Warehouse is constructed. The physical Data Warehouse is dependent upon the methodology upon which it is built. If this foundation is faulty, then in all probability so will the resultant Data Warehouse be.

---

[6] See Dan Lutter's (Hewlett-Packard Company, Cary, NC) paper entitled: *SAS® Data Warehousing: Open Systems Designs for Enterprise Class Environments*, presented at the 1996 Midwest SAS Users Group Meeting.

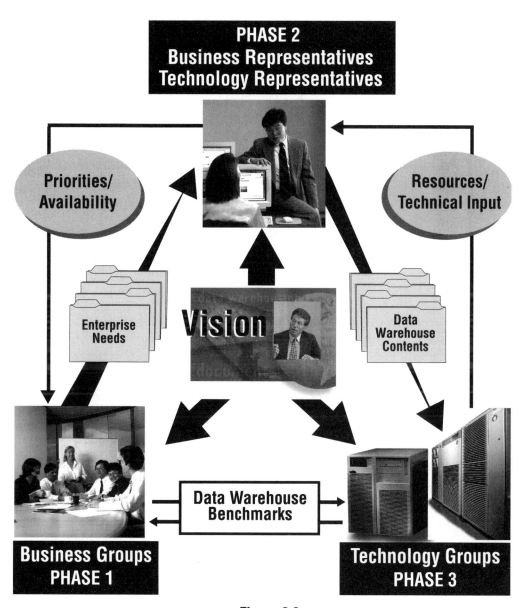

Figure 2.2

The basis for designing the Data Warehouse is outlined in Figure 2.2. This process, as outlined, is different from some of the more standard approaches taken by implementation-centric methodologies. Figure 2.2 shows a process held together by a standard 'vision', but which is broken up into three major steps. As mentioned before, each enterprise will approach Data Warehousing in a different way, so the way these three steps are approached will vary. There is no generic right or wrong way to approach these three steps because each enterprise has to find a way to incorporate each step in the way that suits it best. All three phases outlined in Figure 2.2 are necessary to implement a Data Warehouse that is not only going to perform the immediate enterprise needs, but one that will be positioned to both adapt as the enterprise changes and to grow in scope.

Figure 2.2 gives an overview of the entire Data Warehousing process. If we were to look at the Data Warehousing process in terms of building an arch, then the keystone (the piece that holds the entire structure together) is the figure in the middle. In many Data Warehousing processes, this person is a high-level executive from the business (not the technological) side. Without this 'vision', which encompasses the Data Warehouse's reason for being, the 'arch' will simply fall to pieces. What is so important about this 'vision' is not only that it exists in the first place, but that its influence is directly exerted in all the phases of implementation. In other words, it is not only important for the business units to understand what they are trying to achieve from a high-level aspect, but also the technology groups that carry out the implementation of the Data Warehouse. Without a single driver to the Data Warehousing process, fragmentation will result that will lead to a project without direction.

One of the major distinctions of this approach to the Data Warehousing process, which naturally derives from the methodology, is the abstraction of the design process (Phase 1) from the implementation process (Phase 3). This abstraction leads to a successful Data Warehouse because it allows for a more objective business (rather than a restrictive technological) approach that will ultimately pay off in terms of universal (enterprise-wide) functionality and flexibility.

From a SAS perspective, this three-phase approach works very well. As experienced SAS users know, the software is extremely flexible. In fact, it is so flexible that it is a rare circumstance when only one solution can be found to a problem. Indeed, it is not hard to find a solution with SAS software, but it may be hard to decide which one is most applicable for a given set of circumstances. What this means is that in using SAS as a fundamental tool within the Data Warehousing process, SAS will adapt itself to the methodology. The Data Warehousing process can be designed in isolation of the tools (as it should be) with the knowledge that SAS software will be able to adapt to both the initial design and any subsequent modifications. This is an extremely important point when thinking about tools that might be used to implement the Data Warehouse: the tools should not drive the process. The principal driver, as mentioned above, should be the 'vision'. This vision is a reflection of the way that the enterprise itself wants to advance, not the available technology.

The Three Phases of Building a Data Warehousing Process

There are three major phases to building a responsive Data Warehouse:

1. Conceptual Warehouse Phase: identifying the needs of the enterprise.
2. Transition Phase: guiding the contents of the Physical Warehouse.
3. Implementation Phase: building the Physical Warehouse.

All of these phases are essential, but in most Data Warehousing projects, the first two are either ignored (the technology department thinking it understands what the enterprise needs) or given a perfunctory regard. There is one further link that tends to be 'left by the wayside', and that is a link between the Conceptual Warehouse and the Physical Warehouse. In Figure 2.2, this is the Warehouse Benchmarks link. This is the step that keeps the Warehouse on target; the guide that lets the enterprise know if the Data Warehouse is responsive to the expressed enterprise needs outlined in Phase 1.

From a SAS software perspective, SAS has traditionally been utilized in both Phase 2 and especially Phase 3. This does not necessarily utilize the software to its full potential. Indeed, although Phase 1 does not need the direct intervention of the technology departments (in fact, it would be beneficial for them not to be involved during this phase), there is no reason why the outcome from this phase cannot be stored electronically. To do so would complete the loop, making benchmarking of the Warehouse far easier because the factors against which the Data Warehouse is being compared will be readily available. An example of using SAS software in the first phase of the process can be found in Chapter 10, Section 10.3.

2.5 The Conceptual Warehouse Phase[7]

It is generally accepted that a Data Warehouse process is not only specific to industries, but to different enterprises within those industries. It is arguable, but believable, that this process is also unique to departments within each enterprise, although this then gets into a Data Warehouse/Data Mart discussion. Given that the above is true, then obviously this Conceptual Phase of Data Warehouse development will also differ. Although true to a point, the intent of this phase will be consistent: the Conceptual Warehouse is the non-technological rubric for the Implemented Warehouse.

---

[7] For an example of constructing a Conceptual Data Warehouse, see Chapter 10, Section 10.3.

The progress and evolution of the Implemented Warehouse can be gauged upon comparisons to the Conceptual Warehouse.

This conceptual phase is the ultimate opportunity for the users to gather all of their requirements based upon business-need justification, as opposed to technological cost versus business-need justification. One of the confusing aspects of most current methods of developing a Data Warehousing process is that justification is often seen by looking at the ratio of business benefit to technological cost. Technological cost should not be a factor in deciding whether a requirement should be in the Conceptual Warehouse. This decision comes at a later stage.

 The inclusion of an enterprise requirement into the Conceptual Warehouse should not have to be technologically justified. The basis for inclusion should depend only upon the belief that the realization of that requirement will allow the business more control over its future.

The above point can best be explained by an example. Suppose that a Marketing Department predicts that it could increase sales of its line of squeaky gadgets if it could send direct mailings into the ZIP codes where their furry widgets sold well on Saturday mornings. In other words, they need a breakdown of sales by product, by ZIP code, and by time period. This is a perfectly valid need to include in the Conceptual Warehouse. The fact that, currently, sales data is not collected by time period and to do so would cost the company one million dollars is irrelevant at this time. The Marketing Department has a need that, if addressed, would benefit the company, and that is justification enough for its inclusion in the Conceptual Warehouse.

Including all business justifiable needs in the Conceptual Warehouse will act as the benchmark against which the implemented Data Warehouse can be judged. The basis to the benchmarking will be the proportion of enterprise needs that are addressed by the implemented Warehouse. A Data Warehouse that does not address many enterprise needs will be considered less successful than one that does.

High-Level Information

The Conceptual Warehouse therefore, by necessity, contains high-level information. It will contain enterprise requirements but will not state where this information resides, or in what form, or how it should be captured. That is entirely irrelevant to the Conceptual Warehouse.

High-Level Business Rules

High-level business rules also need to be included in the Conceptual Warehouse. In the above example, what exactly is a time period as the business (not the Computer Systems) requires it to be? In this case, a time period might be defined as either before or after 12 noon. If the Operational Systems were to currently collect time periods, the likelihood would be that the transaction would be time stamped, so one of the data transformations required would be a conversion from exact time to either morning or afternoon. These business rules will directly translate to the Implemented Warehouse if required (not so in the case of time period, because it is not currently collected). It is important to note that these business rules would also have an owner attached (this will be discussed later).

As a quick summary, the Conceptual Warehouse can be seen as the enterprise's wish list of requirements based not upon the narrow restrictions of current systems or resources, but entirely upon what is needed for the enterprise to control its future.

 The Conceptual Warehouse is a wish list of what is needed on an information level for the enterprise to have maximum control over its own destiny.

Ownership of Business Rules

As mentioned above, not only are high-level information requirements included in the Conceptual Warehouse, but also high-level business rules. A further piece of information should also be collected: the owner of the requirement. How many times in Data Warehouse development is a vast amount of time and money spent to make certain pieces of information available and not have them used? A level of accountability, which will flow through to the Implemented Warehouse, if applicable, should also therefore be built into the Conceptual Warehouse.

One of the major issues in Data Warehousing is data ownership, but this does not go far enough. It is also necessary to have requirement ownership, and therefore business-rule ownership. This naturally brings us to another classic problem with Data Warehouses: the inconsistency of business rules. Should the total sales of furry widgets include those sold by the stores belonging to the company that were recently taken over, or should these be tracked separately? Business rules become more important the more summarized the data becomes. These rules must be made and who owns these rules should be obvious, not part of some complex decision made by a person who left the enterprise three years ago.

Reporting Periods

One more piece of information that should be recognized and documented is the reporting period that the enterprise needs require. For instance, in the example that we have been using (where sales is reported information), would we want to see this on a daily basis, weekly basis, or monthly basis? This is a key piece of information because it will help in the design of the Data Warehouse Implementation by determining the level of data collected.

Priority of Requirements

Finally, the Conceptual Warehouse should contain information that gives a priority to different requirements. This is always a difficult topic to approach, because everyone is under the illusion that their requirements are of the highest importance. Very often, this assignment of priorities has to be made, not by those that requested them, but by someone at a higher level that is in a position to see the requirements from an enterprise-wide perspective. There will, of course, be disagreements, and each enterprise might even formulate some form of algorithm (scoring technique) to assign relative importance. Without this assignment, however, the creation of the Implemented Warehouse might well be developed in a random fashion, with little regard to broad enterprise needs.

Conceptual Warehouses in the Real World

Like the traditional Data Warehouse, the Conceptual Warehouse has to be dynamic. It should include as many enterprise requirements as possible to theoretically give the enterprise the best chance of control over its future. This is no small task. It has to be structured and organized. One of the continual challenges is to gain support from the users. They are the most vital source of information, whether building a Data Warehouse or an Operational System. As with any new development within a company, a project team has to be formed and support needs to be garnered at the very highest level to ensure continued and consistent support.

> *The Conceptual Warehouse contains metadata about the business. It contains no data itself. The contents of the Conceptual Warehouse can therefore be treated and stored as metadata.*

The Conceptual Warehouse contains no more than a set of high-level requirements, business rules, and owners. This is, in effect, metadata. It is metadata about the business: what information does the enterprise need to maximize control, what are the rules that determine that this information remains consistent, who defines the rules, and who needs this information. This is simply metadata, not about the data but about enterprise requirements. It is therefore possible to structure it as such. The tools that can be used to store this information can be as simple as a SAS data set, or it could be incorporated into a tool like the SAS/Warehouse Administrator. It can be structured as a Star Join Schema, where a fact table containing the requirements themselves will be linked to dimension tables that contain business rules, owners, and where it is addressed in the Implemented Warehouse (if at all). This final dimension, relating the enterprise requirement to the Implemented Warehouse, is very important. It is the link that will allow for the check on the progress and evolution of the Implemented Warehouse based upon comparisons to the Conceptual Warehouse.

One of the advantages of using the Conceptual approach is that requirements can be collected on a departmental basis, rather than having to look at the entire enterprise at one time. It is even possible to start with one department (or one high-level executive) and then move to others. This allows the size of the project to remain manageable, without decreasing its overall effectiveness. At all times, however, when specifically addressing the needs on a departmental level, it is important to consider the bigger, enterprise-wide picture. Without constantly addressing the broader enterprise-wide implications of approaching the Data Warehouse on a departmental basis, there is the danger of creating an 'island' of information that has no broad usefulness.

The Conceptual Warehouse will be a work-in-progress, as will the Implemented Warehouse. There are many less obvious uses that will make it a very important tool. If the Conceptual Warehouse is structured carefully then the following benefits should be achieved:

- Reports will be available to **let people know** what is available within the Implemented Warehouse, what is being worked on, and what data people deem as desirable to the business, with no restriction based on technical justification.
- It can be used to encourage an **open door** policy to the Data Warehouse, because suggestions can be incorporated without the need for lengthy justifications, and the suggestions will be available for all to see.
- It should, if structured correctly, **create a healthy breeding ground for discussions** about the business.
- It acts as a **continual reminder** of what the enterprise is not doing to control its own destiny, represented by the enterprise requirements that have not been included in the Implemented Warehouse.

These benefits are over and above those that will be directly related to the creation of the Implemented Warehouse, which will be discussed below.

A SAS Software Perspective on the Conceptual Warehouse

Although outside the traditional concerns of most software vendors, this phase of building a Conceptual Warehouse is very suited to the utilization of SAS software. Most of the work in this phase is involved in understanding the requirements of the enterprise through a 'trickle-down' approach. This means that the high-level information requirements are ascertained and then broken down into constituent needs. In the real world, this is not always possible, because in every large-scale project (Data Warehousing being one), there are short-term drivers. In other words, in an ideal world, a Data Warehouse is a completely proactive process, but in a real world it often becomes reactive. Controlling the latter is essential, because a reactive Data Warehouse lacks the overall vision that will allow it to become a long-term solution, instead of a short-term expensive folly.

SAS has the tools to help the formalization of this needs assessment phase of the Data Warehousing project. What is needed is not only a product that will allow for the storing of the data itself, but one that will have the analysis and planning tools to help with the entire Data Warehousing project. These tools are partly data storage, partly analytical, and partly visualization, but the bottom line is based not upon the features of the software, but on the techniques that will be needed to successfully implement the Data Warehouse. The skill to developing a Data Warehouse is eighty percent business, and twenty percent technical. If the eighty is right, then the twenty should fall into place without any trouble.

2.6 The Transition Phase: From Concept to Reality

At this stage, we have what we have termed a Conceptual Warehouse. It contains no data as such. However, it contains metadata pertaining to what the enterprise needs, to retain maximum control over its destiny. This metadata is in the form of business requirements that have associated business rules and owners of both the requirements and the rules. The metadata is stored in a structure that is self-contained (it does not pull information from other sources) and is linked to the Implemented Warehouse, inasmuch as it is possible to find any enterprise requirements in the Conceptual Warehouse that have actually been included in the Implemented Warehouse.

Up to this point, there has been little, if any, direct involvement from a technological standpoint. There has been no technological cost justification for including requirements that are in the Conceptual Warehouse into the

Implemented Warehouse, so that there is no confusion over the issue of what the enterprise needs as opposed to what can be sensibly supplied by current Operational Systems. As mentioned before, the two are entirely separate issues that should not be muddled when designing the Data Warehouse process.

 The cost effectiveness of obtaining information to meet enterprise needs should not be a factor in the decision to include it in the Conceptual Warehouse.

Indeed, this comes back to the classic problem that enterprises come up against time-and-time again: should software determine how the business is run, or vice-versa? There is no universal right or wrong answer to this question, because the answer depends on an enormous number of factors. Whatever the situation, in looking at the enterprise from a Decision Support (as opposed to an Operational) basis, isolating requirements from reality will open up far more options and therefore allow far more control.

Assuming we have reached the stage where at least part of the Conceptual Warehouse has been built, the project has to be broadened to allow for the involvement of those people who will actually be building the Implemented Warehouse. Very often, this will be an Information Systems (I.S.) Department, although this is not necessarily essential for a successful Warehouse process. For argument's sake, let's assume that it will be the I.S. Department. Along with the I.S. Department, there will have to be a Conceptual Warehouse liaison; the link to the enterprise, which is the single most important role because this liaison translates and interprets the enterprise requirements to the I.S. Department.

The transition phase involves the following steps:

- Breaking down each of the enterprise requirements into information needs.
- Documenting what data elements actually make up the information needs, and the Operational System (if any) from which these will be obtained.
- Deciding which of the enterprise requirements should be included in the Implemented Data Warehouse and in what order.

To successfully approach each of these three steps involves a great deal of work. The entire point of approaching the Data Warehousing process in this way is to ensure that it matches the real requirements of the enterprise, and also to streamline the Implementation phase of the process.

Analyzing Enterprise Needs in the Conceptual Warehouse

The first step is to take the Conceptual Warehouse and begin to break it down from high-level requirements into actual information needs from a computer system perspective. An example of this has already been given earlier. That is, if a user requires a report that will show the sales of furry widgets by ZIP code on a Saturday morning, then this could be changed to sales by product, by geographic region, and by time period.

Again, just like the Conceptual Warehouse, we are not just extending the metadata but are moving it from enterprise terminology to computer system terminology. This is an extremely important link, because if it is done correctly, then it will minimize the probability of a breakdown in communication between users and I.S. As with the Conceptual Warehouse, there are a variety of software tools that can be used to store this information. SAS has a number of options, from a straight forward SAS data set (using the broad definition), to the SAS/Warehouse Administrator, or, using one's imagination, a SAS/AF object similar to the Organizational Chart.

The key to this part of the process is to standardize all the computer system terminology. One of the major aims of this step is to ensure that in the future, as more enterprise requirements are considered, any potential overlaps with other requirements can be found. This will reduce the amount of effort it will take to move the enterprise requirements into the Implementation Phase.

> *Standardizing terminology will allow for streamlining in the Data Warehousing process by producing recognizable patterns, which will reduce both the work needed to recognize what needs to be loaded into the Warehouse and to maximize its use, after it's been loaded.*

As an aside, one of the major benefits of looking at the enterprise requirements in this way is that it allows for more structural thought from a systems standpoint. In a classic case, data is loaded into the Warehouse and then front-end tools are designed or supplied to use this information (a data-implementation approach). If the data and the use of that data are independent of each other, it should, if structured carefully, be possible to approach the Warehouse from an Object-Oriented approach. One of the key parts of Object-Oriented modeling is to look at your problem space. This can be a very difficult concept to implement given the classic data-implementation approach to designing a Data Warehousing process, but this is exactly what is being done in our concept-to-reality approach. An enterprise requirement can almost be viewed as an object, and if desired, this should lead to a situation where all the benefits of Object-Oriented techniques can be realized.[8]

---

[8] See Chapter 3, Section 3.4 for a brief overview of using an Object-Oriented approach to Data Warehousing.

Documenting Data Elements

Once the step of taking each of the enterprise requirements and turning them into more generalized computer terminology is completed, then the more detailed step of taking each of these terms and mapping them to data elements within a system (if possible) should be addressed.

> *The concept-to-reality approach to Data Warehousing will give you a working tool that not only controls what is actually being loaded into your Implemented Warehouse and for what purpose, but what is not being loaded and, therefore, which enterprise requirements are not being addressed.*

Just to reiterate, in our example, we have an enterprise requirement: generating a report that shows the sales of a specific product (furry widgets), by ZIP code and by time period. We have turned this into more generalized computer terminology as follows: sales, by product, by geographic region, and by time period. The next step is to take each of these four components and break them down even further. The breakdown must contain certain pieces of information that include (but not necessarily contain only) the following:

Using Sales as an example:

- **The source:** Accounts Receivable. It is important to note the importance of business rules being defined in the Conceptual Warehouse, because sales could potentially be obtained from Shipping if we define sales as shipped goods, or from Billing if we define sales as what is billed, not collected. Note also that there is a timing issue, because the time when the sales are made, accounts billed, the goods shipped, and the money collected could occur in different months. It is essential to explicitly define the business rule for sales, although it could differ from enterprise requirement to enterprise requirement. This does not matter so long as we can distinguish which rule is associated with which requirement and who is the owner of the rule.
- **The data element(s):** This will include both the file and the specific field within that file.
- **The level of data:** In this case, the sales amount will be obtained most probably from a line item on an invoice, so it could be collected on an invoice level (this is important because, although available on an invoice level, this might not be needed in the Implemented Data Warehouse).

Again, this information needs to be documented, because it should be possible to select any particular component of an enterprise requirement and find out each and every other requirement in which that component is contained. Indeed, let's assume that at a later date, a new enterprise require-ment is defined that requires a report on Salesperson profitability. One of the components of this requirement will have to be sales. If we manage this section of the process correctly, we will know that this has already been defined as part of another enterprise requirement and is already in the Implemented Warehouse.

The process outlined above is nothing new. There are many tools (the SAS/Warehouse Administrator, for example) that will help implement this process. However, what is different in this approach is that, traditionally, only those elements that are going to be loaded into the Data Warehouse are documented. This concept-to-reality approach also includes those data elements that will be needed to fulfill an enterprise requirement, but they might not yet be available or might be so expensive to obtain that they are not going to be loaded. This will then tell you what you don't currently have loaded in the Warehouse, but what you need if a particular enterprise requirement is deemed important enough to address.

Prioritize the Enterprise Needs

This leads to the final part of the Transition Phase: to take each of the needs in the context of the vision of the Data Warehouse and apply a priority to each. This is one of the most important steps because it will determine what is actually loaded into the Implemented Warehouse. Just to return to basics, the aim of the Data Warehousing process is to give the enterprise a tool to control its own future. It therefore follows that those enterprise requirements that are going to meet the above goal are the ones that should receive precedence. This should be determined by the priority that the particular enterprise requirement was given during the building of the Conceptual Warehouse. If only life were that simple! Deciding whether a particular enterprise requirement should be addressed within the Implemented Warehouse is also a factor of the mechanics of obtaining the information components that make up that requirement.

This decision is sometimes very easy to make. A given enterprise only has so many resources, and these should be used in the most effective manner possible to get the maximum benefit. Common sense comes into play as much as any complex algorithm, but the yes-or-no decision is nowhere as difficult to manage as the expectations of the users. Although a particular requirement is often currently (remember that a Data Warehouse process is dynamic) excluded from inclusion in the Implemented Data Warehouse on technical grounds (the Accounts Receivable system is still on an OS/390 (MVS) system to which we have no link), the decision should be a joint effort between the user and the technical staff. If the users are included in this decision, then they will feel part of the Data Warehousing process and are more likely to remain in support. They will understand what the components of their enterprise requirements are and why at the current time it is not being incorporated in the Implemented Data Warehouse. There is nothing worse than a Data Warehouse process that has no end-user support.

After these decisions have been made, then the Transition Phase of the Data Warehousing process is complete. This process will never be stagnant. Each and every enterprise need will be revisited to ensure that it should still be associated with its assigned priority. This will ensure that the Implemented Warehouse will remain in line with enterprise requirements.

Additional Benefits of the Transition Phase of the Data Warehousing Process

There are also other benefits that are associated with the concept-to-reality approach of the Data Warehousing process. These include the following:

- The structure of Data Marts will already, to a large degree, be formulated. Enterprise requirements will make it apparent the way that different users (departments) will want the information summarized. On the same grounds, if a multi-dimensional structure is required, these will be largely defined already.
- It forces the end-user community and the technical community to discuss, in terms that both can understand, the needs of the enterprise. This leads to less misunderstanding and, therefore, more realistic user expectations.
- All components of the Implemented Data Warehouse can be related back to one or many specific enterprise requirements. This leads to less redundancy and a more efficient data model (because the data can be modeled exactly to fit the need).

Summary of the Conceptual Warehouse

At this point, the implementation stage of the Data Warehouse process can proceed. Exactly what needs to be loaded, the business rules associated with the data, what the information will be needed for, and a myriad of other information will already be known. There are, of course, many other decisions still to be made: the structure of the data itself, the tools the end-users will be given, what should be the client/server configuration (if any). These issues are usually the ones that most architects of Data Warehouse processes begin with, and this is one of the major reasons that many projects fail.

The Data Warehousing process has been misunderstood due to the implementation-centric approach that has been foisted upon it by designers ill-prepared to move away from Operational Systems. The Data Warehouse process must reflect the enterprise requirements designed to give the organization maximum control over its future. The physical implementation of this process should not take place without checks and balances against the enterprise requirements. This is exactly what the concept-to-reality approach discussed earlier gives to the enterprise.

2.7 The Implementation Phase

When one reads articles or books about Data Warehousing, the Implementation Phase is where the process seems to begin. There is often mention of the needs analysis phase, but this is rarely given much thought. This is because it is easier to write about the Implementation Phase of the Data Warehousing process than about any other. The Implementation Phase includes some, or all of the following stages:

- Data Extraction
- Transformation
- Data Modeling.

Data Extraction [9]

Data Extraction encompasses the step where data is taken from Operational Systems and moved into the Data Warehouse. This stage can be very resource intensive, from both a time- and computer-usage perspective, because it often requires data to move from one internal format to another. The resultant extract is often on a different computer, so there is often a network overhead involved. In essence, however, the process is very simple. Because the data sources are already recognized and defined, all this stage involves is to grab data from one location in one format and move it to another location in possibly a different format.

With the software available today for the designer of the Data Warehouse, the Data Extraction stage of the process should be very simple indeed. The only potential problems that could arise are

- the timing of the data extraction.
- the possibility that only a subset of data, rather than entire data sources need extracting.
- the volume of data.

---

[9] See Chapter 5 for a full discussion on the extraction of data for the Data Warehouse and Chapter 8 for moving extracted data to its required host (computer).

Interestingly enough, the first two of these three potential difficulties require business-based responses, rather than technological ones. The timing of data extraction is dependent upon the data that is needed in the Data Warehouse from a business perspective. The need to subset the information is also a business-based dilemma, based upon whether the Data Warehouse needs a complete refresh or a partial refresh and update. From a technological perspective, after the required outcome is clear from the business, today's software tools are sophisticated enough to handle virtually every situation. SAS is certainly no exception to the above rule.

Transformation[10]

Transformation is the step where the extracted data is transformed from the way it looks within the Operational System, to the way it has to look in the Data Warehouse. This transformation is a very important part of the implementation of the Data Warehouse, because it transforms data that is optimized to run in an Online Transaction Processing System (an Operational System) to one that is optimized for the very different access patterns that are required of the Data Warehouse. This transformation might require that the data is denormalized (see Chapter 3, "Creating a Data Model for the Warehouse," later in this book for a discussion on denormalization) and combined with data from disparate systems. The transformation is a far more complex process than the extraction because, rather than just going and getting something, it requires that the underlying access patterns be thoroughly understood.

SAS is a very powerful tool to transform data. Not only does it contain a full Fourth Generation Language (4GL), but it has a multitude of procedures to aid in the process. Several sub-tasks within the general Transformation Phase are essential for its completion:

- Data Validation
- Scrubbing
- Integration
- Structuring
- Denormalization
- Creation of Business Metadata
- Creation of Summary Data

These subtasks are discussed in the following sections.

---

[10] Different aspects of the implementation of the Data Warehouse are discussed throughout this book, but Chapter 6 describes the Transformation Process.

Data Validation

One of the major reasons that Data Warehouses fail is because the users do not trust the data. Part of the Transformation Phase is to test the data, which is coming into the Data Warehouse, for potential problems. These validation rules are essentially business rules that should be constructed by the users of the Data Warehouse, not the implementers. Conversely, it is easy to over-validate the data, which slows down the data warehousing process and prevents the timely availability of information. It would be possible to develop an entire Quality Control project around the validation itself. This might be a worthwhile project for those enterprises that have resources. What is more important, however, is to instigate a process so that when problems are found with the data something can be done about the fact. There are three major choices:

- to correct the data in the Data Warehouse itself
- to correct the data in the source system from which it was extracted
- to load the invalid data and to record any of the known problems in the metadata.

This is largely a business decision, although in some cases it might not be technologically possible to clean the data in the source system. The key is to put the process in place and stick with it. How the data is modified is a business rule. All of the business rules that determine the definition of any element of data within the Data Warehouse should have an owner. This is usually a business (as opposed to technological) person who understands what the particular elements will be used for, and consequently how they should be created or transformed.

Scrubbing

This is a natural part of the Data Validation stage insomuch as it is the one where the data is actually recoded or removed. The same concerns arise in this stage as in the Data Validation stage. The rules for scrubbing the data should be explicit and the process for doing so should be known and adhered to. There is an argument that any scrubbing that is done on the data should be transparent to any audit of the Data Warehouse that might take place. In other words, any scrubbing that has been performed on the data should be logged so that the reasons for scrubbing and what actually happened are recorded. Another reason would be if the rules were to change and any scrubbing that had occurred should be undone. This logging of changes to data is rarely made in the Data Warehouse environment but should at least be considered. If the changes are made at the source system, instead of on the Data Warehouse itself, then it becomes the responsibility of the source system to track any changes that have been made.

Integration

Once clean, data must be altered so that diverse data attributes and data values are changed into a standard and consistent format. A good example of this is the handling of dates. Different source systems will handle dates in different ways. It is good Data Warehouse practice to ensure that all dates are dealt with in a similar way. Another example could be in the Healthcare Industry, where different sources might handle diagnostic codes in different ways. Each of these different ways of handling codes should come together into one consistent form. This integration makes Data Warehouse use much easier for both the users and any applications that need to run against it.

Structuring

Any new values that are needed within the Data Warehouse should be created during this phase. There should be a consistent set of business rules that are adhered to in the creation of these new data values.

Denormalization

Very often, the data extracted to be placed within the Data Warehouse is in a form that is not conducive to intuitive access to the data. For instance, for the user, which is easier to understand:

a) Two files, one of which contains a list of unique diagnostic codes with their associated descriptions, and the other, a list of claims made by the customers with just the diagnostic code.

b) A single file that contains the claim information along with both the diagnostic code and the description.

Although this is a simple example, it is obvious that option b) is intuitively easier to understand. From a data modeling perspective, this option is not as elegant, because it requires that diagnostic code descriptions be stored for every instance of a claim, rather than for every unique code. The disadvantages from this perspective are more than made up for in the extra use the Data Warehouse will get due to the users actually understanding the data structure. Additionally, the second option will save a join between the two different files every time the user wants to see a diagnostic code description, thus improving the performance of the Data Warehouse.

Creation of Business Metadata

During the transformation of the source data into Data Warehouse data, every item of data will be assessed based upon at least one business rule. Because all data will be read at this time, it is prudent to create any information about the data that could be needed by the users at this time. To do this at a later stage would just require that all the information to be re-read. The type of information that could be collected would be the range of values in a given column (especially useful for dates). Another example might be the creation of a list of unique categorical values for a given column (this is useful when the user might want a list of unique diagnostic codes, for instance).

Creation of Summary Data

It is very unusual in a Data Warehouse to only store detail information. This is especially the case when access patterns to data are understood. If the access patterns are known, even to a small degree, then it is often possible to create summary tables in anticipation of resource intensive requests that will almost certainly be made. These summary files are often of a very specific nature (and will therefore be placed in a specific Data Mart), but could also be of a more generic nature and might apply to broader based user requirements.

Transformation of data, therefore, covers a multitude of processes, all of which might be taking place concurrently. It is the heart of the implementation process insomuch as it takes into account the vast majority of the business rules that are established during the building of the Conceptual Warehouse. The actual transformations that the data will undergo are always to be revisited, and possibly modified, to stay in line with the enterprise needs of the business. Of course, if any changes in the transformation process change the underlying meaning of the data, then the impact of this change will have to be very carefully considered before it is implemented.

Data Modeling

The decisions have to be made after the transformations have taken place as to where the data should reside and in what form. This is almost the opposite of the Data Extraction Phase, because it moves the data from its staging area (where it resides whilst being transformed) into its final format and location. Note that the final format does not have to be the same as that used during transformation. For instance, SAS could be used to extract the data from a DB2 table on a mainframe and temporarily placed in SAS data files. The transformation of the data could then take place using all the SAS tools available. The transformed files could then be loaded into an ORACLE database as the final format for the Data Warehouse. In this situation, SAS was the tool of choice throughout the process, except for being the file format for the source system and the file format for the Data Warehouse.

The final choice for the Data Organization is only partially a technologically based decision. What is the real driver for the decision is the business needs of the organization. One of the key contributing factors in this case is the culture of the enterprise itself. If change is part of the culture of the organization, then this final format has to be flexible enough to account for continuous modifications. Not all data structures do this very well. What is most important is that, both in the present and in the future, the users of the Data Warehouse will be able to readily access the information they need to meet enterprise requirements. To meet this aim, there should be a list of essential needs that are required of the final data structure. This list is driven by business needs that are translated into technical answers. What this actually means, however, is that the decision as to the final structure of the data can only be made after the Conceptual Warehouse has been at least partially formulated. Data Warehouse implementations that select the tools and the data models before really knowing the needs are taking uninformed and unnecessary risks.

2.8 Summary

Building a successful Data Warehouse is not just grabbing the contents of a few Operational Systems, performing some data modeling, and letting the users 'have at it'. A carefully thought-out methodology that suits your particular organization is essential. This does not mean that every stage of the implementation has to be predefined before the project can be of use to the enterprise. What should be in place, however, is the structure for dealing with the implementation of the Data Warehouse. As part of this structure, there are several key pointers that will determine how well the Data Warehouse will work within the enterprise:

■ There should be a common high-level 'vision' for the Data Warehouse that has been explicitly communicated.

■ All participants, from both the business and the technological sides of the business, should be working together toward satisfying this common 'vision'.

■ The 'vision' should be business, not technologically, based.

■ Guidelines for what represents a successful Data Warehouse should be explicitly stated, so that true performance benchmarks can take place.

■ There must be a phase that defines what is needed from a business perspective, based only on business justification.

- There must be a phase that translates business requirements into a technological lexicon. This will act as a forum to:
  - ensure that business requirements are put into some form of priority
  - that enterprise requirements can be addressed by technology
  - that user expectations can be managed
  - act as a fulcrum around which the needs of the business and the reality of financially based technological limitations are balanced.
- The Implementation Phase should not be the driving force behind the Data Warehouse, but merely the tool to put it into operation (note that this is not downplaying the importance of the physical implementation of the Data Warehouse, but recognizing that it is one part of the entire process).

Chapter 3:
Creating a Data Model
for the Warehouse

3.1 Data Modeling within Data Warehouse Process

The model of a Data Warehouse is often thought of as the way the data itself is actually organized in terms of tables and columns within those tables. It is the way the physical data is laid out for the users to actually access it. This is true, to a point, but does not go far enough. There might well be more than one data model within the Data Warehouse. For instance, after data has been extracted from the operational systems, it is usually staged for the transformation process. This staged data also needs a sound model to ensure the efficiency of the transformations and loading into the Data Warehouse. In the first phase of the process, the design of the Conceptual Warehouse, there will also be a model (even though no actual data is discussed). Therefore in a three-phase Data Warehouse,[1] the data model is considered from the beginning of the process, not just as part of the implementation (Phase 3), as is often thought.

---

[1] See Chapter 2 for a detailed description of three-phase Data Warehousing.

In the three-phase Data Warehouse the phases are defined as:

- Phase 1 (the Conceptual Warehouse) contains modeling strictly from a business perspective, with no thought given either to the final content or to the organization of the data.
- Phase 2 (the Transition Phase) is the link that begins to determine the final content of the Implemented Data Warehouse and the way it should be organized.
- Phase 3 (Data Warehouse Implementation) actually determines the final physical model for the Data Warehouse, but it is not limited to just the final structure against which the users will obtain information. The model of the Staged Data is just as important, because this can determine the efficiency with which the Data Warehouse can be updated.

This chapter will address more than just the physical data model of the Data Warehouse. The actual way that the data is organized is part of a modeling process that involves converting the needs of the enterprise into a physical layout of the data. The approach to breaking down the needs so that they can be fully satisfied is addressed within this chapter. For instance, using an object-oriented approach to modeling the Data Warehouse requires a different thought process than does a Star-schema approach. This chapter addresses the approach to modeling the Data Warehouse, as opposed to the techniques of modeling data, which is a discipline unto itself.

SAS Software and Modeling the Data Warehouse

SAS software itself is not a modeling tool. This does not mean that it cannot help in the modeling of the Data Warehouse, but that in itself it will not take the designer through the process. What is important, however, is that it does not matter how the Data Warehouse is modeled, SAS will be able to implement that model. This is important because it means that SAS will conform to one of the principle rules of Data Warehousing: the tools that are used will be flexible enough to implement whatever the enterprise needs require. Because the model of the Data Warehouse should be based upon the enterprise needs, it follows that the software tools should be independent of the model.

If the Data Warehouse model has to be changed, either in the details (additions or changes) or fundamentally (a re-design), then SAS will be able to handle these changes. This is also an advantage of using an integrated software approach to Data Warehousing, as opposed to a 'best-of-breed' approach. Because a change in the model will require alterations at the implementation level, the more integrated the product, the less potential problems there will be.

Data Modeling within an OLTP Environment

There are many formal modeling approaches for OLTP (Operational) systems. A brief overview of one of these will help to put Data Warehouse modeling into perspective. A three-schema approach[2] is a good overall illustration of a Data Modeling process that can be directly compared to Data Warehousing situations. The three schemas within this approach are

Conceptual Schema Design
> deals with the definition and type of information to be made available from the database. It also deals with rules that control the state of and allowable changes to the information. This schema is entirely independent of any technology.

External (or Logical) Schema Design
> defines the way that the information is used and maintained by application systems or by users. Information is logically associated with tables with an implementation view in mind. This schema relates the business requirements outlined earlier to a technological lexicon.

Internal Schema Design
> determines the physical implementation of the data within the database.

This example of one methodology (directly dealing with Relational Databases) is not to suggest that this is the only (or even the best) method to build a data model. Indeed, there is a library of books dedicated to exactly the above process, and it is well beyond the scope of this book to cover the topic, except as it may help in understanding the Data Warehousing process. In many ways, these three stages parallel those within our three-phase Data Warehouse. The major difference, however, in the implementation of the above methodology is that the database modeled is usually (although not necessarily) the source system from which the Data Warehouse will be populated. In other words, the process is designed to specifically address the situation where data is being created (e.g., a new order, a new customer, a new billing) and the associated processes, rather than the reorganization of existing data. The processes defined within the three steps are also, by and large, finite. This means that, for example, when a new order is taken, there are a fixed number of consequences that have to be accounted for: the manufacturing process must be initiated, the billing process begun, and the myriad of financial systems must be kept in order. The rules and regulations for each of these different outcomes are definable, and therefore, the data can be modeled so that it is optimized for these predictable outcomes.

---

[2] This approach is loosely based on the ISO standard: ISO.TC97/SC5-N695.

The data modeling within an OLTP system, especially in schema 2 outlined above, can be very complex. The aim of the model is to maximize stability and this is done through a process called *normalization*.[3] This stability performs two major functions:

1. It ensures the integrity of the data through the use of rules (constraints) that control the admissibility of a specific row as being eligible for insertion into any given table. Only if these constraints are met can the row of data be allowed into the table. For example, suppose that there is a constraint that states that for an order to be taken from a customer, that customer must already exist within the system. The new order cannot be inserted into the order table until the customer name exists in the customer table. When an order is taken, the customer table will be accessed to find out if the customer name is there. If it is not, then the system will act accordingly, maybe by asking whether a new customer needs to be added.

2. Because the integrity is handled by the database, then it means that it can exist independently of any application that accesses that data. Therefore, it is not necessary to handle the integrity for any application that uses the data, but only once in the underlying database. The advantage this gives is that it is not necessary to coordinate each application in terms of data integrity, therefore reducing potential inconsistencies and increasing the stability of the data.

Modeling the Data Warehouse can certainly learn from the above process, but has many other problems associated with it:

- The rules (constraints) within the Data Warehouse must be explicit, but they will probably not be addressed as part of the database itself, but as part of the transformation process.[4] It would be possible to incorporate some of the transformation process into the database (maybe as a stored procedure), but the benefits of doing so would be few.
- The applications that are built against an OLTP system almost always update the data. In Data Warehousing, the applications (front ends) rarely have an update function. This means that the integrity of the data is less of a concern within the Data Warehouse because it is controlled by the transformation process. The integrity is therefore determined by ensuring that the rules controlling the transformation of the data are coordinated, which is largely performed by solid design of associated metadata.

---

[3] See Section 3.3.
[4] See Chapter 6 for a discussion about data transformations within the Data Warehouse.

■ The final model of the data needs to be a lot more flexible than it is in an OLTP system, because it should be designed for inconsistent access patterns by the users. There are a variety of techniques available to ensure this flexibility, two of which are the increased use of indexes (over-and-above the classic primary and foreign key design within a Relational System) and the denormalization of data.[5]

The key to successful modeling within the Data Warehouse is, as with many other aspects of the process, flexibility. The data model must be extensible and easily changed, without having an impact on current usage. A Data Warehouse, by its very nature of reflecting the needs of the enterprise, should be changing continually. Therefore, the model itself must be amenable to reflect that change.

The Data Warehouse Model should not be limited to just the final organization of the data, but must be integrated into every phase of the process. In the three major phases of Data Warehouse development, modeling (either the business or the data) is of key importance. It might not be of a formal nature, but each decision that is made will lead toward the final organization of the data.

In the first phase, considering enterprise needs, deciding upon the business elements that will be needed, and determining how they are interrelated will determine the final access patterns to the Data Warehouse and therefore influence its design.

In the second phase, (moving from Conceptual Warehouse to the Implemented Warehouse) decisions will be made about which enterprise needs will be addressed, and which specific data items will be needed to meet these needs. The data elements and the need will be directly linked (it will be possible to ascertain every enterprise need that a particular data item will help meet) and so, in an enterprise requirement driven Data Warehouse, these decisions will be fundamental in the final design and might indeed drive that design.

In the final phase, that of implementation, the involvement of modeling is more obvious. Most discussion about Data Warehouse modeling deals directly with this phase because this is where the final logical and physical model resides.

---

[5] See Section 3.3.

3.2 Will the Users Be Required to Understand the Structure of the Data?

This is a very important question that is often overlooked. The 'front end' and the 'back end'[6] of the Data Warehouse are often considered to be two different design processes. The optimal logical data model for the 'back end' is implemented only by looking at the data that needs to be incorporated, instead of considering how that data will be used. There might be a good reason for building the logical data model in this way, but the final physical model, the way the Data Warehouse is actually stored, should look far less like the logical than in a similar Operational System. Very often the point is forgotten that the Data Warehouse should be modeled to specifically address user access patterns. The outcome of this from a Data Warehousing perspective is potentially catastrophic. This illustrates the classic situation where a Data Warehouse is produced, the users are then given access tools after the fact and expected to successfully utilize the information. This rarely leads to a successful Data Warehouse. Separation of back-end and front-end design will lead to a limited use Data Warehouse that is only of use to technological experts. The Data Warehouse should be designed for business experts, independent of their technological capabilities.

 Separation of back-end and front-end Data Warehouse design will lead to a limited use Data Warehouse that will not fulfill its business potential.

This does not mean that the business expert should not need any technological skills, but that the Data Warehouse should be configured to help them reach their business goals, therefore minimizing the wasted time spent on struggling with an unfriendly data design. A degree of technical competence will always be needed to access a Data Warehouse. This should be addressed by continual user training.

Ideally, the data should be organized in a Data Warehouse based upon expected access patterns. This is far easier said than done. In a Data Warehousing environment, data access patterns will change over both the short and long term. They will change to align themselves with enterprise needs. This means there are two major influences: first of all, these changes can be fundamental because the nature and needs of the business have adjusted. Second, the changes can be contextual because, on a day-to-day basis,

---

[6] The *'back end'* of the Data Warehouse is every part of the design that does not involve actual access by the users. The *'front end'* is therefore any aspect of the Warehouse design that involves the use, as opposed to the design, of the data. See Chapter 2, Section 2.3.

different questions are asked from a business perspective, and accordingly data needs to be accessed in different ways.

This lack of a consistent access pattern is one of the major frustrations for Data Warehouse designers that move from an Operational Systems background. Access patterns in Operational Systems are by nature predictable, which explains the preponderance of static as opposed to dynamic SQL. The ways in which the data can be accessed is finite and defined, but this is never the case with a Data Warehouse. For example, in an Operational Order Entry System, when an order is taken, this starts a series of predictable actions that will culminate in the order being shipped, billed, and paid. Many systems will interact in a predictable and predefined way. Data Warehousing is the antithesis of this process because, to a large degree, it is unknown how, why, or when the data will be used. Because this access pattern is unpredictable, it is absolutely necessary to ensure robustness in the data structure that will allow for the 'unknown' as much as is feasible and practical.

This can be done in many ways. For example:

- Structure the data to the lowest common denominator, making the underlying structure as generic as possible and deal with specific needs on a Data Mart level.
- Keep as much detail as is possible[7], which will make changes possible, because there will be less chance that the required data has not been collected.
- Denormalize the data[8], which will add flexibility to the potential access patterns.
- Think about the enterprise, as opposed to individual projects, when structuring data. This will reduce the Data Warehouse becoming a series of independent data stores (a series of unrelated Data Marts) without underlying fundamental integrity.

---

[7] See Chapter 4 for a discussion on detail and summary data within the Data Warehouse.
[8] See Section 3.3.

Special Topic:
Reverse Engineering the Data Warehouse

A popular approach to creating an enterprise-wide Data Warehouse is to 'reverse engineer'. This approach is popular because of the natural evolution of a process within an enterprise. Very often, isolated departments within an organization will develop their own targeted Data Warehouse. This might not occur through a formal process, but as a direct result of the department's inability to access the information needed to successfully fulfill its function.

These small 'islands' of information often have to be incorporated into a more global Data Warehouse after they have been created. This is because the information stored within these Data Marts has to become accessible to the entire enterprise. This leads to 'reverse engineering' an enterprise-wide Data Warehouse based upon often very successful departmental models.

This kind of Data Warehouse design can benefit greatly from tools such as the SAS/Warehouse Administrator, described in Chapter 9.

It is fairly common in Data Warehouse projects that the requirements for the users, to either understand or not understand the underlying data structure, change over time. This is a normal and natural process that illustrates the growth in the scope of the Data Warehouse.[9] It is more likely that this change will occur in situations where the Data Warehouse was initially designed with the users having to understand the structure. This is part of the natural design process, where a group of more technologically proficient users begin the Data Warehouse, and because this information then becomes available to the enterprise, pressure is exerted to put it into the hands of less technological users.

Consider the following situation: two marketing research analysts have identified the data that they need on a continuing basis for them to fully track and analyze their projects. They are specifically looking into the excessively high return of goods that their retail shops are experiencing. The data they will need to look into this problem includes sales, product, time of sale, returns, time of return, type of sale (cash, credit card) and credit card number. All this is obtained from the point-of-sales system. This information is moved into the Data Warehouse and updated weekly, as is. In other words, there is no real transformation of the data as it moves from the point-of-sale system to the Data Warehouse because the analysts fully understand the intricacies of the data.

---

[9] See Chapter 10, Section 10.2, for a discussion on the importance of understanding the scope of the Data Warehousing initiative for its efficient design.

This arrangement works well until the company policy changes and sales representatives in the retail shops are to be paid based upon a commission on net sales. To calculate this commission rate, historical analysis of sales, by product and by salesperson, will be required. This analysis is also needed on a continuing basis to ensure that the commission scheme is affecting sales, and therefore that it is having a positive effect on company profits. It is known that most of the information that will be needed to calculate this amount is already available in the Data Warehouse, but additionally the Human Resources Department needs the salesperson number from the point-of-sales system. This information must then be cross-referenced to the Payroll and Personnel Information system as well as the Purchasing System to find out how much the product costs for the company to buy. Information from the four systems is now needed. What was once a simple enterprise need for the company has become very complex.

The alternatives open to the designers of the Data Warehouse are

- Incorporate the respective information into the Data Warehouse as is, and build a front-end to help the Human Resources Department complete the continuing analysis of compensation. This would mean that the users would **not** have to understand the structure of the data. The understanding of the structure would be inherent in the 'front end'. The advantage to this is that it does not require that the analysts become experts in the structure of the Data Warehouse. The disadvantages are that there will be a 'front end' to build and maintain, and that the degree of flexibility for the user will be limited to the flexibility of the Data Warehouse.
- Restructure the data so that it becomes intuitive for the Human Resources analysts. This will require considerable restructuring and will, at the same time, impact the Marketing Analysts who were perfectly happy with the way things were. The advantage of this method is that it does not limit the flexibility of the Data Warehouse for the users because they can access it outside a formal front-end application. The disadvantage is that a data structure might be intuitive to one group of users, but not for the next. This method also leads to a greater potential disadvantage because it sets the stage for a restructuring every time the Data Warehouse requires an expansion.
- Let the Marketing Analysts continue the way they are. Incorporate all the other information into the Data Warehouse as is, and then build an exclusive data source that is specifically designed for the Human Resources group (a Data Mart). This method probably has the least drawbacks because it will not impact the Marketing Group, and, it will give the Human Resources analysts the customized data they need. The

disadvantages are the increased amount of control necessary to ensure that the Data Mart has integrity, and it still doesn't really answer the question of whether the user should understand the structure of the data. A Data Mart is just another data structure, even though it addresses more finite needs than the entire Data Warehouse.

The best option is the one that suits the particular set of circumstances best. In other words, there is no generic 'black-or-white' correct answer. Truth be known, in most enterprises, a combination of both techniques will probably work best. If a group of users have the skills to directly access the information, then give them the tools to do so. For that group of users who do not have these skills, make sure that there are front ends designed to give them the access. The key, however, is to ensure that the needs of both groups are met. Do not expect a very technical user to be happy with an inherently restrictive front end that limits their access, and do not expect the less technical to learn how to perform a three-table join.

3.3 Is There a Place for a *Normal* Data Warehouse?

Relational database design methodology has preached the benefits of putting data into a normal form. There are several different levels of normalizing data, ranging from the first normal through the fifth normal. In typical operational systems, the data is usually modeled to the third normal form. We will discuss the definition of this below, along with the reasons for its apparent necessity.

A relational data model consists of a series of normalized tables. Each table is made up of rows and columns, and each column has a different name. Each row must be unique and is not in any intrinsic order. Every table must have a primary key. A *primary key* is a single or a combination of columns that make up a unique value for that table. This means that every row in the table can be uniquely and unambiguously recognized by its primary key. Tables are related by a column (or series of columns) in one table that means the same thing as a column (or series of columns) in another table. In other words, this column has an identical domain in each of the tables. If one table (A) has a primary key that will uniquely define each row in that table, and it can be linked (is related) to another table (B) where that key is not unique, then in table B a foreign key will be created. This way each of the tables is related, by the creation of primary and foreign keys.

These concepts are important to understand because both the advantages and disadvantages can be considered before such a model is used in a Data Warehouse. There are a series of formal stages to move through when normalizing data, but after the concept is understood, it is almost a natural process. The above concepts can best be looked at by considering two extremes: a data table that is completely denormalized and then the corresponding normalized form:

Invoice Number	Product	Customer	Region	Region Number	Salesman Number	Salesman Name	Amount Due
100	A1	SMITH	WEST	A12	10	JETHRO	97.23
100	A2	SMITH	WEST	A12	10	JETHRO	87.24
101	A1	BROWN	EAST	A16	11	ELVIS	99.00
101	A2	BROWN	EAST	A16	11	ELVIS	100.00

Table 3.1
Denormalized Data Table

Table 3.1 shows a simple extract from a denormalized data file. The data is related to invoices. According to classic Relational Modeling concepts, there are several problems with the above data. First of all, to update a Region name (which is a fairly common occurrence in most organizations), the column Region will have to be changed in every row. The same can be said for the Salesman Name. What would happen if Jethro left the company? This would mean that his replacement's name would have to be inserted into every row of the table. A normalized view of the above table would be as follows:

Salesman Name	Salesman Number
JETHRO	10
ELVIS	11

Table 3.2 Salesman

Region	Region Number
WEST	A12
EAST	A16

Table 3.3 Region

Invoice Number	Customer
100	SMITH
101	BROWN

Table 3.4 Customer Inventory

Invoice Number	Salesman Number
100	10
101	11

Table 3.5
Invoice Number and Salesman

Invoice Number	Product	Amount Due
100	A1	97.23
100	A2	87.24
101	A1	99.00
101	A2	100.00

Table 3.6 Invoice

From one simple table (3.1), we now have five. In all likelihood, if this were a real system, there would be many more. However, to illustrate how normalization fits into the Data Warehousing environment, the above will suit our purpose. It should now be possible to re-create Table 3.1 from the Tables 3.2–3.6. Table 3.1 can be re-created based upon relationship between the other five tables. For example, Table 3.2 and Table 3.5 are related because the 'primary' key in 3.2 (which would probably be Salesman Number) can be related to a 'foreign' key in table 3.5 (which would also be Salesman Number). Similar relationships can be determined among all the tables, so that the information that is in Table 3.1 can be reconstructed.

This process can be very confusing, but it has many advantages as outlined earlier. If a Region name changed, then it would only have to be altered once (in Table 3.3) rather than twice (in Table 3.1). If a Salesman were replaced, then the name would only have to be changed once (in Table 3.2) rather than twice (in Table 3.1). Although this might sound trivial with our small example, imagine if the file were several million records long. This normalization adds stability to the data. Referential Integrity would be easily enforced because, for example, it would be easy to check that a Salesman existed (by cross-referencing Table 3.2) before an invoice was created with his number. This is simpler than usually occurs in real systems, but certainly illustrates the point.

Weaknesses of a Normalized Structure for Data Warehousing

The above method of modeling data works well in situations where many small pieces of data are needed. A typical Operational System usually searches for small pieces of data: information pertaining to a single invoice or a single customer, for example. Data Warehouses usually request information on large blocks of data: all invoices between two dates, all invoices for any customer that bought product A16 on a Thursday afternoon. The type of access pattern to the data is very different than in a typical Operational System. This normalized data model does not respond well to such requests.

Very often, the normalized data model is changed for a physical implementation for performance reasons, but for an effective Data Warehouse implementation, Table 3.1 is the ideal situation. Extensive indexing will be needed to avoid the necessity to read the entire table every time information is requested. To many data modelers, Table 3.1 is anathema because it suggests that the control (stability) over the data is minimized. Table 3.1 would also be considered to have a high degree of data redundancy (see the Special Topic box on page 54) which is perceived to show weakness in a data model.

Data Warehousing is very different from the classic Operation System and should be treated as such. In the Data Warehousing process, the stability of the data is based upon the strength of the metadata. Stability does not need to be intrinsic in the data model itself. The rules and, therefore, the transformations that have to take place should all be in the metadata, and the stability of the data should be measured by how well it reflects these rules. In most Data Warehouses, there is not continual updating of existing data but, usually, periodic refreshes and additions (appends). For the information in the Data Warehouse to have both integrity and be 'stable' the following **must** be in place:

- The underlying metadata must be correct. This means that it should accurately reflect the explicit definitions (rules) approved by the enterprise.
- The transformations (that is, any actions performed upon the data as it moves from the Operational System into the Data Warehouse) must accurately reflect the underlying metadata.

At any point, it should be possible to take any data from the Warehouse and test it against the rules laid down in the metadata. Indeed, this is part of the integrity checking of the Data Warehouse. For instance, a rule might be that the total of all sales for a month should balance with the sum of five General Ledger Accounts. This check should be made to ensure that it is correct. This is a very obvious check of the integrity of the data, but it is exactly this process that is not instigated in the Data Warehouse process that leads to 'incorrect' data and a consequential loss of trust in the Data Warehouse. After this trust is lost, it is very hard to regain.

Special Topic
Data Redundancy within the Data Warehouse

Redundancy in the Data Warehouse is often misunderstood. There are two ways in which redundancy is traditionally viewed:

1. Having multiple copies of the same data.
2. Including data that is never used.

There is absolutely nothing wrong with having multiple copies of the same data so long as there is a sound business reason for doing so. If it helps the user to access the data faster, or in a different form, then why not have it duplicated? The fear of duplication is rooted in the anachronistic opinion that buying data storage is expensive (an opinion rooted firmly in the 1970s). In fact, if there is a major resistance to purchasing additional data storage, then maybe Data Warehousing isn't a good idea at all. The other objection to the storage of multiple copies of the same data is the more complex synchronization of disparate stores of data, and therefore it is more likely the Data Warehouse could lose its internal integrity. This objection is only valid in a situation where the Data Warehouse design and controls are weak. Therefore, removing the opportunity for multiple copies is treating the symptom rather than the cause.

Metadata is the basis for data integrity in the Data Warehouse. If the rules contained within the metadata are in accordance with the enterprise requirements and are correctly utilized, then the information will have integrity. There should be constant checking between the data within the Warehouse and the business rules identified within the metadata.

To add to the two points stated above, there is another very important factor in ensuring the integrity of the data within the Data Warehouse. If the data coming from the Operational System has no integrity, then the Data Warehouse faces an uphill battle. As soon as the Transformation Process includes rules to overcome the inadequacies of the Operational System, then the ultimate test cannot be enforced: the Data Warehouse will never match operational data. In many cases, this is just a fact of life and must be incorporated into the process. If during the Data Warehousing process, 'incorrect' data is found that has its roots in the Operational System, then ideally this should be corrected at the source. Unfortunately, this is very rarely possible, so it is up to the Data Warehouse itself to overcome these deficiencies. Incorrect data must be changed at some point in the process, somewhere between the point where the Operational System stores the data and the point where the users actually utilize the information. The closer the corrections are made to the source Operational System, the better. Although, after it has been decided where to make these corrections, this should become part of the Data Warehousing process and remain consistent. At least in this situation, the Data Warehouse can keep its own audit of changes, if they are required.

So the complexity of a fully normalized data model should not be needed within the Data Warehouse for data integrity purposes. There is, however, another major disadvantage of a normalized model in a Data Warehousing environment. To obtain even the simplest information, tables must be joined. Joining tables is very expensive, especially when it involves large chunks of data. For example, referring to the invoice example in Tables 3.1 through 3.6, suppose a user wanted to obtain a total Amount Due for the Customer SMITH if the Salesman is JETHRO.

Using the normalized model, the following SAS SQL program will do the job (note that the column names correspond to those in Tables 3.1–3.6 and do **not** conform to the pre-Version 7 SAS limit of eight characters):

```
PROC SQL;
 SELECT SUM(amount_due)
 FROM salesman, cust_inv, slse_inv, invoice
 WHERE salesman.salesman_name='JETHRO'
    AND cust_inv.customer='SMITH'
    AND cust_inv.invoice=slse_inv.invoice_number
    AND cust_inv.invoice_number=invoice.invoice_number
 ;
QUIT;
```

For a very simple request, four tables were needed. The joins, although not complex, are probably way beyond what should be expected from an analyst that needs the information. Remember that it is important that the Data Warehouse does not ask its users to become database experts, but to allow them to more efficiently spend their time on their specific enterprise requirements. If the users are asked to understand the underlying structure of the data[10] then the more normalized the data, the harder it will be to understand it. Even in a situation where views are created that pre-join tables, expensive joins will be needed every time a view is used.

Compare the above code to the code that will extract data from Table 3.1, which is the denormalized version:

```
PROC SQL;
 SELECT SUM(amount_due)
 FROM denorm
 WHERE customer='SMITH' and salesman_name='JETHRO';
QUIT;
```

Not only is the above code far easier to understand, but it does not require the need to join multiple tables. This example is fairly trivial, but if each of

---

[10] See Chapter 3, Section 3.2.

the tables is hundreds of thousand rows long, then the joins might become very expensive. Due to the unpredictability of requests made by the users of the data, creating indexes on each of the tables (which would help the speed of the processing) would be very difficult. It is true that the denormalized table contains data that could be considered redundant (for instance, the name of the salesman) but this disadvantage is more-than-made-up-for by the ease of use and, if correctly configured, the performance advantages. The denormalized table would also need multiple indexes to improve data access performance. These indexes will be based upon expected data access needs to the denormalized data, rather than as a means to joining tables. This is one factor that should affect the choice of a Data Warehouse storage product:[11] the speed with which indexes can be created.

3.4 Modeling and the Data Warehouse

Over the past few years, an Object-Oriented approach to designing systems has become more popular. Although this approach is often described as Object-Oriented Programming (OOP), the actual programming part is only a small piece of this pie. To address an enterprise requirement from an Object-Oriented Approach (OOA) involves far more than just the programming. It is a way of thinking about and dissecting a requirement into its component parts. The big picture is divided into many smaller parts and these, in turn, are dissected into even smaller components. These components are then analyzed so that it is fully understood what they do (their behavior), what data they contain to complete their function, and how they interrelate with other components (their properties).

One of the major problems with Object-Oriented Methodologies is that it has its own confusing terminology. After this terminology is understood, then the underlying thought process behind an OOA is very simple, in fact far simpler than most other methodologies.[12] One of the most elegant aspects of Object-Oriented Methodologies is that it allows the designer to actually directly relate real needs to a model that will be implemented. An 'object' actually solves a single or a set of problems that really exist, not just conceptually. This means that utilizing Object-Oriented techniques in solving enterprise needs can be a very rewarding task because the degree of conceptualization required is very low.

---

[11] See Chapter 5 for a full discussion on this topic.
[12] For an overview of Object-Oriented theory, see: Taylor, David A., *Object-Oriented Technology: A Manager's Guide*, Addison-Wesley, 1990.

In our three-phase approach to designing Data Warehouses, laid out in Chapter 2, the basis of success is to design a business-level Conceptual Warehouse (Phase 1), a physically Implemented Warehouse (Phase 3) and develop the processes to transition between one and the other (Phase 2). An Object-Oriented approach can help in Phase 1 and 3, and if begun, can certainly help in the development of Phase 2.

Because an exhaustive discussion of Object-Oriented Design and Analysis is beyond the scope of this book,[13] a brief outline of one methodology that can be directly incorporated into the Data Warehousing process is described below. This is not meant to illustrate how an Object-Oriented approach **should** be used, but an illustration of **how it can** be used to help in the design of the Data Warehouse process. It is not necessary to have an entire system (or Data Warehouse) design from an Object-Oriented standpoint, but use the techniques where they best fit.

Here are several steps that could be incorporated into a modeling process using an Object-Oriented methodology:

1. Define the Problem Domain(s).
2. Catalog objects within each Problem Domain.
3. Abstract the Objects, creating types (or classes, the implemented version of a type).

The Problem Domain

The initial key to understanding an Object-Oriented approach is to understand what is called the Problem Domain. The *Problem Domain* is the environment within which the problems that have to be solved actually exist. An example of a Problem Domain might be all the activities of a Marketing Department within a medical insurance company. Within a global Problem Domain, they could create two distinct subsets. The first is servicing the needs of existing clients (by supplying reports and analyses of all claims and associated costs, along with premium information). The second subset could be to support the sales effort by supplying information geared toward the creation of new business. These are two distinct Problem Domains for a single department, although there could well be overlap.

---

[13] An example of a useful source of detailed information on Object-Oriented Design is: Gamma, Erich, Helm, R., Johnson, R., Vlisides, J. (1995), *Design Patterns: Elements of Reusable Object-Oriented Software*. Reading, MA: Addison-Wesley Publishing Company.

Catalog the Objects within Each Problem Domain

With this very simple approach, we have started to help in the design of the Conceptual Warehouse by establishing the Problem Domains. Already there is structure within the Data Warehousing process. After each individual Problem Domain has been recognized, the next step is to break down each Problem Domain into 'object'. In this case, when we are dealing specifically with Data Warehousing, an 'object' could well be an enterprise (departmental) need. Using one of the Problem Domains in our example above, two examples of Objects could be:

- A semi-annual report (given to each client) that summarizes all claims by Diagnosis Code.
- An online need to access data down to the individual policy holder level, with the ability to cross-reference by Provider (e.g., hospital name, doctor name) and Provider Type.

This list of Objects could become very large indeed. An Object contains both behavior (actions, activities, changes to values) and properties (attributes and associated values), so both of these should be documented.

Defining both the Problem Domain and the Objects within that Problem Domain is included in the first phase of the Data Warehouse process, where the Conceptual Warehouse is built. At this stage, the Object will be partially described, only addressing the properties of each of the Objects. The behavior will be of more concern in Phase 2 of the Data Warehousing process, where not only the 'what' question, but also the 'how' question is addressed.

In our first Object mentioned, for the semi-annual report to be produced, the properties could include:

- Client Number
- Client Name
- Case Number
- Date of Service
- Provider Name
- Diagnosis Code
- Number of Claims
- Total amount of Co-payment
- Total amount covered.

What is interesting is that in creating each of these Objects, the actual enterprise needs are being directly referenced. In formulating this model, the business users are not being asked to conceptualize their business, but describe it directly. In Data Warehousing, it is also necessary not only to describe each of the attributes, but to also associate business rules and owners with each one.

After these Objects have been documented, then for all intents and purposes, the first stage of the Data Warehousing process has been performed. As outlined in Chapter 2, this does not mean that the process is completed, because there will be a continual process of creating new Objects as new needs arise.

Abstraction of the Objects

These Objects might well be complete from a strict business aspect, but at this stage, they will be incorporated into Phase 2 of the Data Warehousing process, where the enterprise needs are translated to a more technological lexicon. In Object-Oriented parlance, this means that there is abstraction of the Objects so that they can be classified by type. This is probably, from a Data Warehousing perspective, the most difficult part of the process.

> A useful Metadata hint: *whenever defining a data field to the Data Warehouse, have a rule about how missing data should be treated. If data exists, then at least it is possible for some form of verification, but this is not the case with missing data. There should be some form of predetermined action when a value is missing. Rules about what to do if there is an incorrect value are often included in the Metadata, but missing values are often overlooked.*

The first step is to complete each of the Objects that have been created. Two major activities have to be undertaken: the first is to break down each of the attributes of the Objects into the lowest level data. For instance, the Total Amount Covered attribute might well be made up of the total cost of the service minus the total co-payment amount. The second activity is to document the behavior of each object. For the report generation example mentioned above, possible behaviors could include

- extracting data
- generating reports
- printing reports.

At this point, it is then necessary to classify each of the 'objects' into types. This is a very interesting process because the classification process will produce many types, that is, groups of similar objects. The process for this follows:

1. Objects of similar characteristics and purposes are sorted into sets.
2. Within each set, there will be common behaviors (*operations*).
3. Within each set, Objects will share common characteristic properties (*attributes*).

In our example, where we had two 'objects' (in our case, an object being an enterprise need), there are seemingly two major types: one is a report, and the other is an online analysis of data. Both of these obvious types, have similar characteristics. First of all, they both need to extract or use data; they might share data transformations; and both will need the ability to print (with the online object printing a snapshot of the data). This means that we can start to list the different types (classes) that will be needed within the Data Warehouse.

Looking at a specific example (the creation of a Data Extraction class), many behaviors and attributes can be recognized.

Behaviors:

- Select specific rows of data.
- Select specific columns from the table.
- Perform joins between tables.
- Write out to a SAS data file.
- Write out to an external (non-SAS) data format.
- Send out messages when task is completed.

Attributes:

- Name of the input data source(s).
- Name of the output data source(s).
- Parameters specifying the subsetting of data.
- Parameters specifying required columns.
- Parameters defining the joins.

By creating these types, it means that as new needs are identified, the likelihood is that, over time, there will be a series of classes that will be able to directly address the specific need. The first few needs that are addressed will require the creation of new types (or classes when implemented). As more needs are addressed, the amount of work required to fulfill them will be reduced. There will already be a Data Extraction class defined, so any enterprise need that requires data to be extracted (all of them most probably) will already have a class available for that need. This class might need to be subclassed (altered in some way), but most of it should already be in place. This means that to directly address an enterprise need, it is not necessary to rebuild the wheel each time.

For instance suppose the Data Extraction class had been created. This class might have been subclassed so that there were four more classes as follows:

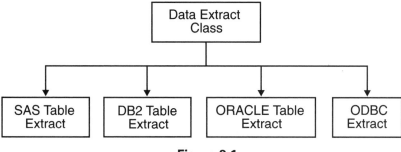

Figure 3.1

Figure 3.1 shows the Data Extraction class, and four subclasses. Each one of these has its own particular methods to extract data, but each one will share some features. Anything they share will be part of the generic Data Extraction class and they will *inherit* these features. In other words, they will not have to be re-programmed at the subclass level. Examples of the features the four subclasses might share are: the need to send out messages when the task is complete and the need to know the rules for subsetting the data. Each one will also have distinct properties: the access mode and maybe the platform upon which the data resides.

The key to this approach is that even if Object Oriented software tools are not employed to actually program the above classes, there is still a benefit from dissecting the enterprise needs into Objects. There will be an overall structure to the Data Warehouse that will allow for easy extensibility, and every time an enterprise need is addressed, commonality with other needs can be recognized and exploited.

SAS Object-Oriented Tools

An Object-Oriented approach to Data Warehouse design does not presuppose that corresponding Object-Oriented programming tools will be used. Object-Oriented programming is a specific form of structured programming. This means that it is not necessary to use Object-Oriented programming techniques to implement an Object-Oriented Model. Almost any software that will allow structured programming will be a candidate to implement the Object-Oriented Model. To take full advantage of the model, however, it follows that software that has Object-Oriented capabilities would be preferable. SAS has two specific modules that have Object-Oriented capabilities: SAS/AF and SAS/EIS.

SAS/AF is made up of two major parts: a set of generic classes[14] (implemented types in our modeling discussion above) that can be used as is. These classes contain a finite number of predefined methods (behaviors) and attributes (data). Every one of these classes can be subclassed (modified) in any way while conforming to the rules of Object-Oriented methodologies (inheritance, encapsulation, etc.). The second part of SAS/AF is SCL[15] (Screen Control Language). This language is becoming far more integrated within the SAS 4GL (Fourth Generation Language), thus many of the special features that SCL affords the programmer (e.g., additional functions) are now available to base SAS programming.

When thinking about Object-Oriented programming, many people tend to think of graphical user interfaces (GUIs). It is not, however, necessary for an Object to have a visual manifestation. Many of the classes available within SAS/AF are non-visual. This means that when they are used, they cannot actually be seen. For example, on a screen, there might be a graph (a visual object) that changes as the user makes a selection from a box that contains available variables. Every time the user selects a variable, new data needs to be extracted from a data file, and the graph needs to be re-drawn. For this to occur there will be at least three distinct Objects:

1. The graph on the screen will be an Object that has the task of visually representing the data. This graph will need to be re-drawn every time the user selects a new variable (from Object 2), and the data has been successfully extracted (see Object 3).

2. The box containing the list of possible variables to plot on the Graph Object will be an Object with tasks of giving the user possible options. It will also have the task of informing the third Object (see 3.) that a new variable has been selected.

3. The third Object has the task of actually extracting the data. After it has been informed that a new variable has been selected, it will inherently understand where that variable is located and will extract it. This Object also has another very important task: after the data has been extracted, it needs to tell the first Object (the graph) to re-draw itself because a new request has been made.

This is a very simple scenario that allows for easy extensibility. The obvious question to ask is why the first object, the graph, does not perform the

---

[14] For an extensive description of all classes available within SAS/AF, see: SAS Institute Inc., *SAS/AF® Software: FRAME Class Dictionary, Version 6, First Edition*, Cary, NC: SAS Institute Inc., 1996. 1158pp.
[15] For an introduction to SCL see: *SAS Screen Control Language: Reference, Version 6, Second Edition*, Cary, NC: SAS Institute Inc. 648pp. For examples of its use, see *Building Your Client/Server Solution with the SAS System*, Cary, NC: SAS Institute Inc. Alternatively, see: Stanley, Don, *Beyond the Obvious with SAS Screen Control Language*, Cary, NC: SAS Institute Inc. 347pp.

extraction itself. Why does the third object (a non-visual object) have to perform the task? The reason for this is quite simple. What would happen if another method of displaying the data were needed? Maybe a report or a map has to be displayed, based upon the same data. For example, suppose the data was demographic information that is broken down by geographic regions. The Graph Object could display a vertical bar chart that shows demographic data by State. If the application were to be extended and a Map (chloropleth) Object were created that should be refilled dependent upon the selected variable, then given the three-object approach discussed earlier this would be very simple.

To extend the application, there would have to be absolutely no changes to the three Objects discussed earlier. Not one line of code would need to be changed. The Map Object would be created that would automatically re-draw when it was informed by the non-visual data extraction Object that the data had changed. This non-visual data extraction Object will send a single message when the data has changed. This message might be CHANGED. Both the Graph Object and the Map Object would be programmed to perform a task (re-draw) when it hears the message. A single message can therefore impact different objects in different ways.[16]

If the Graph Object itself were designed to extract data, then when a new Map Object is created, it would also have to include code to extract data. This means that if this extraction process changed, then changes would have to be made in any Object that extracted data. This would lead to obvious problems and far more maintenance than is acceptable.

For any Object to work, it has to perform many tasks. These tasks are in the form of programs that in SAS will be written using SCL. The user or application will often need to utilize these tasks (in which case, they are called *methods*), and often these tasks are part of the set-up of the object and will automatically be used whenever the Object is required. SCL, as the primary language used to create all of these tasks, is a very important part of the process of utilizing an Object-Oriented approach within the Data Warehouse process. It is also likely that many of the objects available within SAS/AF will be used as is (without any modification).

SAS/EIS began its existence as an *Executive Information System*.[17] It was originally designed as a tool to design high-level information delivery

[16] For a detailed discussion on Object-Oriented techniques using SAS, see: SAS Institute Inc., *SAS/AF® Software: FRAME Application Development Concepts, Version 6, First Edition*, Cary, NC: SAS Institute Inc., 1997. 216pp.
[17] For an overview of SAS/EIS basics, see: SAS Institute Inc., *Getting Started with SAS/EIS®, Version 6, Second Edition*, Cary NC: SAS Institute Inc., 1995. 62pp.

systems specifically geared to highly summarized data. It has long since become far more than this. Now it gives the developer and user alike a set of specific Objects that can easily be configured to build a front end on a Data Warehouse.

SAS/EIS software is written using SAS/AF software. This means that to use SAS/EIS, SAS/AF must also be licensed, along with SAS/GRAPH. SAS/EIS consists of a series of Objects that are already pre-defined to perform specific tasks. Here are a series of categories under which these Objects are listed:

- Business Graphs
- Business Reports
- Data Access
- Menus
- Presentation Tools
- Utilities
- Viewers.

As these seven categories suggest, the Objects are designed to get to data and then report upon it. It is possible to build entire front-end applications with the SAS/EIS software. The capability exists to link between different Objects and even build in some of the SAS/AF capabilities for communicating between them. It is also possible to extend the existing objects,[18] using SCL, so if the Objects do not quite meet all the needs, these can be included without starting over. SAS/EIS has the advantage over the SAS/AF module of being far quicker to develop. This means that in a very short period of time, quite complex and elegant exploitation of the Data Warehouse can be implemented without the user needing to understand the model of the underlying data.

Although building an application using SAS/EIS will take a lot less time than using the generic Objects in SAS/AF, SAS/EIS applications are not as flexible. From a Data Warehousing perspective, most of the Objects are suited to front-end, rather than back-end, design. Primarily, SAS/EIS is a tool that can be used in the exploitation of the Data Warehouse, rather than in the building process.

---

[18] See *Getting Started with the FRAME Entry: Developing Object-Oriented Applications, Second Edition*, Cary, NC: SAS Institute Inc. for an explanation of extending object.

Fitting SAS Object-Oriented Tools into the Data Warehousing Process

The above discussion on Object-Oriented modeling and the associated SAS tools is a very limited overview of the approach. It is not necessary, however, to be an expert in Object-Oriented Design to fully appreciate or understand how it can be incorporated into the Data Warehousing Process.[19] There are two key points to remember:

- An Object-Oriented approach means that real-life (as opposed to conceptual) requirements can be modeled, especially in the formative Conceptual Warehouse phase in the Data Warehousing process. This means that it is easier for the business needs and definitions to be modeled because they do not have to be conceptualized. An enterprise need as an object also means that the Data Warehouse will directly address specific enterprise needs because the model is based upon these needs.
- Object-Oriented methodology does not have to be used for the entire Data Warehouse. Objects are best utilized in situations where there is potential re-use. In other words, if an Object can be defined that will be needed in numerous situations, then there is a case for going through the process. Use the Object-Oriented methodology where it best fits, but don't try to force a fit.

3.5 Star and Snowflake Data Warehouse Models

Due to the nature of Data Warehousing, especially the lack of predictability in the patterns of data access to data structures, a form of modeling that creates a Dimensional Warehouse has been developed. This technique has been made popular by Ralph Kimball and is described in great detail in his book: *The Data Warehouse Toolkit*.[20] This technique essentially takes the enterprise needs of an organization and, through a series of steps, breaks them down into facts and dimensions. The process for this break down of enterprise needs into facts and dimensions is to develop the following:

1. The Business Process Model
2. The Logical Model
3. The Physical Model.

---

[19] See: McNee, Amy Turske; "An Evolutionary Data Warehouse—An Object-Oriented Approach," SAS Institute Inc., *Proceedings of the Twenty-Second Annual SAS® Users Group International Conference*, pp 542-547.
[20] Kimball, Ralph: *The Data Warehouse Toolkit: Practical Techniques for Building Dimensional Data Warehouses*. John Wiley & Sons, Inc. 1996. 388pp.

These three steps are in line with almost any form of modeling. From a Dimensional Warehouse perspective, each step must be addressed with the intent of breaking down the business needs into the facts and dimensions necessary for the final physical implementation.

The Business Process Model

In a classic Relational model (described briefly in "Data Modeling within an OLTP Environment" in this Chapter), this is akin to the first stage of the three-schema approach. The purpose of the Data Warehouse must be ascertained, and then the information available is modeled. For instance, assume one of the aims of a Data Warehouse within a medical insurance company is to monitor Emergency Room claims to see the overall effect of rejecting those claims. The Dimensional Warehouse requires from this stage that, given our stated purpose, relevant questions are asked. Such questions could include:

- Which insurance groups are the predominant Emergency Room treatment users?
- Which hospitals are mostly used for Emergency Room treatment?
- Which hospitals claim more money based upon similar Diagnosis Codes?
- Over time, are the costs increasing based upon similar Diagnosis Codes?
- Is there an actual savings by rejecting facility claims?

These questions lead directly to recognizing attributes and the relationship among them. For example, looking at the four questions presented earlier, the following attributes could be recognized:

- Providers (hospitals)
- Insurance Groups
- Claims
- Diagnosis Codes
- Time.

These attributes will be among the major subject areas for the Data Warehouse.

The Logical Model

Already, each of the subjects (dimensions) of the Data Warehouse have started to be recognized. Each of these subjects might have internal structures that can also be addressed. Taking Insurance Groups as an example, Figure 3.2 shows the subjects that might be addressed.

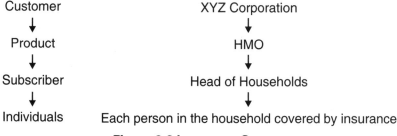

Figure 3.2 Insurance Groups

These levels should be addressed because it will be very important to determine the *granularity* (the level to which the data is required). In the above example, if the enterprise need requires only an analysis to the subscriber level (meaning there is no interest in each individual in the household that is covered by insurance), then the data would only be needed to the subscriber level.

There are some interesting points about this stage in the development of a model:

- There is a distinct similarity between this technique and the technique suggested for implementing a Multi-Dimensional Database (see Chapter 4, Section 4.3 "MDDB and the Data Warehouse").
- This technique asks that the availability of data be considered when looking at a *measure* (analysis variable). In the example above, one of the key measures will be the amount of the claim, and this should be looked at in context of the dimensions. To determine the level of granularity, it follows that the level upon which the data is stored must be addressed. This approach is different from the three-tier approach to the Data Warehouse process outlined in Chapter 2. This is because of a fundamental difference in approach. The methodology as outlined in Chapter 2 assumes that the success of the Warehouse should be based upon its ability to meet the needs of the enterprise. To ascertain this, a Conceptual Warehouse must be developed with no thought given to the availability of data. This Dimensional-Warehouse methodology is geared directly toward implementation so, naturally, will need to address the availability of data at an early stage.
- This technique has a fundamental difference from the Object-Oriented Methodologies discussed earlier in this chapter, because these methodologies ask that conceptualization happen very early in the modeling process. In this case, the actual real enterprise need is abstracted immediately into its constituent subjects. In the Object-Oriented example, what is actually modeled is what is programmed.

Breaking down the enterprise needs into subjects means that the 'dimensions' of the Data Warehouse can be determined. In our example, we have several different 'Dimensions': Providers, Insurance Groups, Claims, etc. We also have what are called 'Facts'. In the case of the example above, a 'Fact' would be the amount of the claim. It might also be a co-payment amount or the number of days spent in a hospital. 'Facts' are usually numeric, and as can be seen from the example, of a continuous nature, whereas 'Dimensions' are by their nature categorical.

The Physical Model

The physical model of the Data Warehouse is how the data will actually be stored. The physical storage of the Data Warehouse should be a direct reflection of the expected data access patterns. This means that it cannot be fully addressed before fully understanding the way that the data will be used. This is where this technique comes 'full circle'. Early in the design of the Business Model (see "The Business Process Model" in this chapter), the actual needs of the enterprise were conceptualized, thus isolating the access needs. It is now necessary to revisit those needs to find out exactly how the data will be used, and therefore the most optimal physical storage organization.

The Dimensional Warehouse is physically designed so that the questions that are likely to be asked can be easily answered. In the first two stages of this process, the questions were gathered and broken down into 'Dimensions' and 'Facts'. The granularity of the data required to answer each of the questions was also ascertained. These pieces of information supply the constructs for the implemented Dimensional Warehouse. The physical layout of the Data Warehouse at its simplest will be a single table that contains all the Facts, and multiple tables that contain the Dimensions.

In our example of the medical insurance company needing questions answered with regard to Emergency Room treatment, a simple physical model could be as shown in Table 3.7:

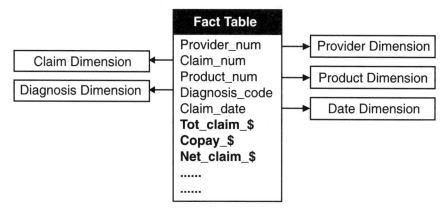

Table 3.7 Medical Insurance Model

In Table 3.7, the 'facts' are in bold; the 'dimensions' are not. Each of the dimensions will link to another table or to a series of tables (in the snow-flake schema). The key to this design is that the needs of the enterprise have been fully understood and broken down into the correct 'Facts' and 'Dimensions'. The Dimension Tables will be much **shorter** (have far fewer rows) than the Fact Table. Each of the Dimension Tables will have a primary key that will link it to a foreign key in the Fact Table. For instance, Diagnosis_Code in the Fact Table will link to a Dimension Table that will have a unique index on a field that will probably also be named Diagnosis_Code. This table could look like the following:

Diagnosis Dimension
Diagnosis_Code
Diagnosis_description
Diagnosis_Category

Table 3.8 Diagnosis Code and Fact Table

This technique of organizing the data borrows heavily from traditional relational modeling techniques. It has a heavy reliance on the joining of tables on primary and foreign keys. The Dimensional Warehouse constantly fights with the issue of over-normalizing the data. For instance, in the Diagnosis Dimension Table (Table 3.8), there is more information required about the Diagnosis Code. It is likely that each diagnosis will be categorized into additional groups and categories for analysis. The categories could include such items as heart conditions, asthma, and pregnancy. Indeed, these categories might well be industry standard and are required for reporting to research groups or government agencies. This makes these categories essential for the Data Warehouse.

The problem this gives is that following the model, another sub-dimension table will be needed that is linked to the Diagnosis Table above. This would make the tables look as follows:

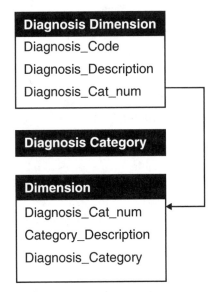

Table 3.9 Diagnosis Sub-Dimension Table

This creation of a new table moves the model away from being a star schema to being a snowflake schema. The implications of this are fairly obvious:

- The data model becomes more complex.
- Complicated joins will be needed for even the simplest requests.
- Computer performance will be sacrificed for the sake of the elegance of the model.

For these reasons, it is highly unlikely that the final physical model will fully reflect the model outlined above. If the Data Warehouse has been designed so that the users must understand the structure of the data, then in all likelihood a star-shaped or a snowflake schema will be too complex to understand. It would be more feasible to implement if the structure of the data were to be hidden behind a friendly Data Warehouse front end or if a series of views that pre-define the joins were created to make the data far easier to use. This would not, however, overcome the performance problems such a model will inherently pose, due to the reliance on potentially expensive joins between tables.

The more complex the needs of the Data Warehouse, then the more complex the star schema will become. As the number of dimensions and facts increase, then so will the overall complexity of the model. This is true whatever modeling technique is used, but in the case of a Data Warehouse, where there is usually access to large amounts of data, as opposed to many smaller pieces of data, then the repercussions will be on a performance level. This means that it is unlikely that a star schema would be physically implemented 'as is', but that it will be denormalized to the extent needed to meet performance requirements.

Accepting the fact that the star-shaped/snowflake schema might not be the most efficient from an implementation perspective, then the question is raised as to what part of the Data Warehousing process it has relevance toward. The likelihood is that this model will be an integral part of the development because it lends itself to various parts of this phase in the Data Warehousing process. The following are the major steps in the implementation of a Data Warehouse:[21]

1. extraction
2. transformation
3. validation
4. scrubbing
5. integration
6. structuring
7. denormalization
8. summary data creation.

The star-schema approach to modeling the Data Warehouse is especially beneficial in the staging of the data, which encompasses steps 2-7 above. The reason being that the creation of dimension tables will allow for efficient validation and scrubbing because, if the dimensional model is utilized, this will be performed upon normalized data. For example, if an incorrect Diagnosis Code were to be extracted from the operational system, then this would become part of a dimensional table during the staging phase of implementation. To validate the Diagnosis Codes would mean running procedures against the dimensional table, rather than running the validation against a very large denormalized table. This would make this process far quicker, and any changes that had to be made would be far more efficient because they would only have to be made once, rather than potentially multiple times if a denormalized table were to be scrubbed.

---

[21] For a detailed explanation of each of these stages in the implementation of the Data Warehouse, see Chapter 7.

Integration of data would also be far more efficient against these more normalized tables. This stage takes data from operational systems and, when necessary, changes it to a consistent Data Warehouse view. For instance, if data for a Warehouse were to come from a variety of different companies, each one might use different coding schemes. To avoid any confusion, these would have to be changed so that the Data Warehouse has one consistent coding scheme. This would be a far easier process to manage in situations where the tables were normalized because the number of physical changes that would have to be made would be reduced.

The break down of the enterprise needs into 'Dimensions' and 'Facts' will also help the strategy of data summarization. As already mentioned, this break down is very similar in some ways to that of using the multi-dimensional model (see Chapter 4) to understand the needs of the enterprise. By analyzing the 'Dimensions', the organization of summary data will be far easier to ascertain. In the same way as with the multi-dimensional model, the business will be interested in 'crossings' of data. For example, following the Emergency-Room claim example discussed earlier, it becomes obvious that there will be interest in seeing the amount of claims for every Diagnosis Code by every provider. This means that through the model, summary strategies can more easily be discerned.

SAS Software and the Star-Schema Model

SAS has all the tools necessary to implement a full star-schema, or snowflake-schema model. The model is essentially a modified normalized system that depends upon the efficiency of joining tables by the use of common indexes (keys).[22] There are many SAS tools that will aid in this process, but as already mentioned, SAS is not a modeling tool. It will not actually perform the modeling, but it can implement any star-schema model that has been created.

There are a variety of SAS tools that will be of use during the implementation of a star-schema model. These are the same tools that will be used during any implementation of a Data Warehouse that uses SAS and are outlined more thoroughly in Chapter 6 in which Data Transformation is discussed.

---

[22] To see an excellent example of using SAS to implement a star-schema design, see: Barnes-Nelson, Greg; "Implementing a Dimensional Data Warehouse with the SAS® System," in SAS Institute Inc., *Proceedings of the Twenty-Second Annual SAS Users Group International Conference.* pp 582-591.

However, the following is a short list of some of the more obvious tools that can be used:

SAS Procedures:[23]

SQL
SUMMARY and MEANS
FREQ
SORT
FORMAT
DATASETS
COMPARE
PRINT
TABULATE

Other SAS Tools:

DATA step
Indexing
Data compression
MODIFY statement

These basic (they all exist within base SAS software) SAS capabilities will fulfill most of the needs when implementing a star-schema model. There are more complex capabilities that might well come in use in implementing the Data Warehouse. While these are not directly related to this particular model, they would be of use in any schema. For instance, you could use visualization tools such as, SAS/INSIGHT and SAS/SPECTRAVIEW for complex data validation. For fitting expected distributions to data you could use SAS/STAT, but these could also be used in any data model, star-schema or not.

Star-Schema Summary

One of the dichotomies of the star schema is that in the Data Warehouse implementations where it would be of most use, it is least practical. In a small Data Warehouse, where the size of the Fact Table is not enormous, it might be practical to actually implement the star schema on a physical level. Because the Fact Table is not large, however, there is a good reason for just denormalizing the data completely, which would be the simplest model for the business to understand. A large Data Warehouse, however, could benefit greatly from the internal structure and organization that a star-schema

---

[23] Basic procedures are documented in: SAS Institute Inc., *SAS® Procedures Guide, Version 6, Third Edition*, Cary, NC: SAS Institute Inc., 1990. 705 pp.

approach would afford, but because of the size of the joins, if it were to be physically implemented, then the response time would, in all likelihood, be too slow. This means that for large Data Warehouses that would benefit from the formal structure, it is less practical to implement.

The basis for a star-schema approach is that it is a technique for changing business needs (in the form of questions that are asked) into subjects and facts. These subjects are then further analyzed so that they can be clearly understood from a data perspective. What actually makes up the subject, and how can this be further categorized? From this point onward, the actual needs of the enterprise have been conceptualized, and any direct link to the data has been lost. This is a potential problem of using this technique because it means that there is no direct link between enterprise needs and the Data Warehouse, therefore, there is a limitation in benchmarking capabilities.[24]

However, the star-schema approach is an excellent way to start to address the needs of the enterprise and convert them to a technical lexicon. Data warehousing can be intimidating, especially when addressed from an enterprise (as opposed to a departmental) level, and so any approach that can formalize this process is useful. Because it is essentially a very simple technique, there is no problem in explaining it to the business users, so it will help them put their Data Warehouse needs into perspective. They will more easily be able to look at their needs and succinctly define their component pieces, as 'Facts' and 'Dimensions'.

3.6 The Impact of End-User Interfaces on Data Warehouse Modeling

Very often, the access that users have to the Data Warehouse is a combination of front-end interfaces and direct access to the tables (detail and summary). The front-end interfaces will deal with requests that are largely known and understood, whereas the direct access to data will be in more ad-hoc situations. There are Data Warehouses that do not have a front end built. These will work in a situation where the users are very knowledgeable but will not be as effective if there is a range of technical skill in the user base.

In a situation where the users will be accessing the data directly, they might not be asked to create actual programs to extract and analyze the data, but they are more likely given some form of guidance. In a SAS environment,

---

[24] See Chapter 10, Special Topic: "How do I know if my Data Warehouse is successful?"

this might be the Query window, which will help to build simple to moderately difficult queries. In the case of the Query window, the users will be given a list of available tables, which can be in any format that SAS can read.[25] They will be able to select columns of information that they require (without needing to know the type of the data) and to join between tables. As the user builds the query, the SQL code itself will be generated and optionally stored for later use. Although this technique will ensure that the syntax (as opposed to the logic) is correct, it does not minimize the fact that the users will need to fully understand both the contents and structure of the available tables.

If a front end is developed, then this has implications for the data model, because it is possible to physically organize the data to suit the front end. This might mean making the internal organization of the data very complex, so that the front-end application will be able to fully exploit the data. In other words, the data model can be far more complex in a situation where a front end is built because it does not ask for the user to understand the structure. This should improve the efficiency of the Data Warehouse because the front end will presumably be addressing specific business needs. So the data will be structured to this end.

In most Data Warehouse models, the data should be kept 'long and thin' as opposed to 'short and fat'.[26] In a situation where a company might have 50 products, the data should be stored in a table where there is a PRODUCT column, as opposed to there being 50 columns (one for every product). This is important because, if a new product is added, then the structure of the table does not have to be changed (i.e., a 51st column for the new product). However, this is fine unless the sales for combinations of products need to be calculated, but these combinations cannot be pre-summarized. It might not be possible to summarize these values because the combinations might not be known ahead of time. This situation might occur if a 'what-if' analysis is being undertaken.

> *There is often confusion between* summarization *and* aggregation *in a Data Warehouse.* Summarization *is the act of creating a statistic (sum, mean, standard deviation, etc.) across rows in a table.* Aggregation *is the act of creating a statistic across columns in the same row. From a performance consideration, aggregation tends to be quicker, but summarization is logically simpler to understand.*

---

[25] See Chapter 5 for a discussion on accessing external data.
[26] See: McNee, Amy Turske; "An Evolutionary Data Warehouse—An Object Oriented Approach," SAS Institute Inc., *Proceedings of the Twenty-Second Annual SAS® Users Group International Conference*, p 543.

For example, consider a situation where a General Ledger is being extracted into a Data Warehouse. The General Ledger is made up of account numbers that have values for each month. It would usually be sensible to have an ACCOUNT, a DATE, and a VALUE column. As an experiment, the following snippet of SAS code could create such a file:

```
DATA acct(keep=account month year value);
 LENGTH account $8;
  DO year=1990 to 1997;            *Create data for every year from 1990 to 1997;
  DO month=1 to 12;                *Create data for each month;
   DO a=1 to 1000;                 *Create Accounts from 1 to 1000;
    account='A' || TRIM(LEFT(a));  *Create the Account number;
    value=month*month*a;           *Generate a pseudo amount for each account;
   OUTPUT;
   END;
  END;
 END;
RUN;
```

This simple SAS DATA step will create a file that is 96,000 records long. It will contain a value for each year between 1990 and 1997 and for each month of the year. Each of the accounts A1-A1000 will have a single entry for every year and every month. Although not real data, this will have some of the features that will be included in a Data Warehouse file. For the users, it is very easy to understand, and for most queries, it will be very simple to perform.

The resultant data file would look like this:

Account	Month	Year	Value
A1	1	1990	1
A2	1	1990	2
A3	1	1990	3
A4	1	1990	4

Table 3.10 Query Table

What happens, however, in a situation where the users might want to combine the values of certain accounts by each month. In most General Ledgers, accounts are created for 'roll-ups', but situations might occur where a combination of accounts will be needed. Suppose a situation arises where the following analysis is needed: (A99+A158)–A987. This might be a situation where a figure is needed for:

Total Product Sales(A99)+Total Services Sales(A158)–Total Sales Expenses(A987)

Although from a financial perspective, this might be very naive, it will serve to illustrate a point. This data is needed for every month.

If the data were to be structured as in the ACCT table shown in Table 3.10, then the following code is one of many ways that the information could be calculated:

```
/***********************************************************************
* Sort the file, although in a real Data Warehouse, the index created should *
* make this unnecessary.                                              *
***********************************************************************/

PROC SORT DATA=acct;
 BY year month account;
RUN;


/***********************************************************************
* Use a SAS DATA step to find out the values required.                *
***********************************************************************/
DATA newacct;
 SET acct;
 BY year month;
 SELECT (account);
 WHEN ('A99') reta99=value;
 WHEN ('A158') reta158=value;
 WHEN ('A987') reta987=value;
 OTHERWISE;
END;
IF last.month THEN DO;
 newval=SUM(reta99,reta158,-reta987);
 OUTPUT;
 reta99=0;
 reta158=0;
 reta987=0;
 END;
 RETAIN reta99 reta158 reta987;
 WHERE account IN('a99','a158','a987');
RUN;
```

The above DATA step is quite complex. It requires some fairly advanced understanding of not only the data but also of SAS programming techniques. There are many other ways the same result can be programmed, but what is required from a logical standpoint is quite complex, so any code will reflect this. The above code reads the file and retains the values required for the final calculation for every month the calculation is made and the results are stored in a new file named NEWACCT.

There are two major problems with the preceding approach: first, it is complex to perform, and second, it is very difficult to program generically. This is just one example of one specific request, but there are millions of potential permutations to the requests that the users might have. Building a front end to perform the above task would be very difficult.

However, if the data were to be restructured both the complexity of the code required to create the necessary information and the complexity of the program would be reduced. For instance, the data could be transformed using the following code:

```
PROC TRANSPOSE DATA=acct @code:OUT=tranacct(DROP=_name_);
 ID account;
 BY year month;
 VAR value;
RUN;
```

This code would change the way the data is actually organized by turning the account numbers into column names, while retaining the year and the months as rows. This means that if there are one thousand unique account numbers, then each account number would be a column in the output data file TRANACCT, along with two named YEAR and MONTH. This means that a very 'wide' data table has been created, but one that is far shorter (in this case, only the number of years (8) multiplied by the number of months (12)). Note that using this technique, there is a limit to the number of columns that can be stored in a SAS data file. In the Windows environment, the limit is 32,767. (The limit will be operating system dependent.) This technique also assumes that there is never more than one row for each account for each month and year.

The data table TRANACCT will have 1002 columns: one for each account, one for year, and one for month. The names of the columns will be YEAR, MONTH, A1, A2, A3, etc. What does this transformation actually give us? It certainly goes against the usual advice given on structuring tables within a Data Warehouse, so why would there be any real benefit?

To understand this, consider the same question as was raised above. What if we wanted to create a calculated value based on the formula A99+A158– A987. If the data were transformed as described above, then the following code would work:

```
PROC SQL;
 CREATE TABLE results AS
 SELECT SUM(a99,a158,-a987) AS newval, a99, a158, a987
 FROM tranacct(KEEP=a99 a158 a987);
QUIT;
```

Or, if a SAS DATA step is preferred,

```
DATA select;
 SET tranacct(KEEP=a99 a158 a987);
 newval=SUM(a99,a158,-a987);
RUN;
```

there would be performance gains. On a Pentium PC running Windows 95, there was an enormous improvement in performance (approximately 6 seconds against 0.5 seconds) between the two techniques. Not only does the performance improve, but the complexity of the code that is required decreased considerably. The four-line program above is far preferable to the 19-line program required in the first example. Of course, there is the fixed cost of transforming the data, but this will become insignificant over time.

If this technique has so many benefits, then why is it not used all the time? The answer is that it is a very unwieldy structure for the end user. To ask the user of the information to understand over one thousand (it could be far more in other situations) columns is beyond being reasonable. The number of columns would also vary by the addition of new accounts, so there could be considerable differences in the data structure from month to month. This structure is, however, extremely friendly for an application: it is easy to build an application around the structure, especially if the metadata were well defined. The users could be prompted for a formula using account descriptions (part of the metadata) and then this would be easy to translate into a working query.

This use of PROC TRANSPOSE is one way that the structure of the data can be affected by the incorporation of a front end. If the users are shielded from the actual data, then the internal structure of that data can be far more complex and designed for efficiency rather than easy understandability.

> **Front-end applications can improve performance of the Data Warehouse. The front end will shield the users from the underlying structure of the data so it can be modeled to suit the application instead of the users.**

Another disadvantage of the modeling of data to suit the front-end application is that there is a possibility that the structure will only benefit that specific front end and will not have generic use. This means that the data is being modeled specifically for a single enterprise need. This is okay so long as the resources needed are justified by the satisfaction of that need, but this should be fully addressed in the second phase of the Data Warehouse process, the transformation of the Conceptual Warehouse to the Implemented Warehouse.[27]

---

[27] See Chapter 2 for an explanation of the three stages of a Data Warehouse process.

3.7 Modeling the Data Warehouse: Summary

The modeling of the Data Warehouse is not a SAS issue. The flexible nature of SAS software means that the design of the Data Warehouse data model can be addressed independently of the software. This should be true of any software that is being considered for the Data Warehousing project. The data model of the Data Warehouse is not, however, independent of other concerns: Client/Server[28] being an example. In the case of Client/Server, the model of the data might be affected based on the architecture or vice-versa. Either way, the model of the Data Warehouse will be dependent upon factors other than just the enterprise needs, as reflected by the 'dimensions' and 'facts' in the dimensional, or the Object in the Object-Oriented model.

A single modeling approach to the Data Warehouse is not essential. There might be situations where a star-schema approach will apply because the enterprise easily conforms to the creation of dimensions. In other situations, maybe an Object-Oriented approach will be preferable because the enterprise needs are very defined and finite. A situation might occur where a star-schema approach could be used with the Data Warehouse detail, and Data Marts could be designed using an Object-Oriented approach. The model should be dependent upon best meeting the needs of the enterprise, and therefore it is essential that the Data Warehousing tools should be flexible enough to ensure that they are model independent.

Modeling of the Data Warehouse should follow the same rules as other aspects of the process: ensure that the model is flexible enough to allow for the inevitable changes that will occur. Do not commit to a model that cannot be easily extended or modified. When each decision is made as to the model of the data within the Warehouse, make sure the question is asked as to what would happen if (when) things change. How will this impact the model? Secondly, and for the same reason, do not model the data based upon a specific data product: ensure that the products fit the needs. This means that it is imperative to model the Data Warehouse around the enterprise needs that are driving the project, not around the available data itself.

---

[28] See Chapter 8 for a discussion about Client/Server architecture within the Data Warehousing process.

Chapter 4:
Effective Use of a
Multi-Dimensional Model:
SAS/MDDB™ and the
Data Warehouse

4.1 MDDB and OLAP

What Are MDDB and OLAP?

MDDB is an abbreviation for *Multi-Dimensional Database* and OLAP is an acronym for *Online Analytical Processing*. An MDDB is a way that pre-summarized data can be stored. *OLAP* is a technique for exploiting the information contained within an MDDB. Both an MDDB and OLAP owe their existence to the need of the users to efficiently view and analyze summary-level information.

MDDB and OLAP are often mistakenly used interchangeably. The reason for this confusion is very understandable on one level, but the distinction between the two is very important within Data Warehousing. The reason for the confusion between the two is that they are often intertwined in terms of their functions, but they are at the same time mutually exclusive. It is possible to have an MDDB without OLAP and vice-versa. Essentially, an MDDB represents a noun and OLAP a verb. An MDDB is something (a particular data structure) and OLAP is doing something (a technique for navigating data).

OLAP is predominantly a data exploitation tool and is therefore firmly ensconced in the front end of the Data Warehouse. SAS software literally has hundreds of ways that the data residing within the Data Warehouse can be exploited. OLAP is one of these techniques. Exploitation of the Data Warehouse is largely outside the scope of this book, but OLAP is briefly discussed in the next section. Understanding OLAP on a high level can assist the design of the Data Warehouse in two ways:

1. It can enable a more proficient and efficient creation of Multi-Dimensional Databases. This will improve the back end of the Data Warehouse by ensuring that its structure will reflect the access patterns required by the enterprise.

2. It can help in the process of turning enterprise requirements into an effective Data Warehouse.[1]

Although both points are important, from a strategic, Data Warehouse design perspective, the second is most crucial. This will be discussed in the Special Topic entitled "Report Vs. Information Centric Design" later in this chapter.

> **MDDB (Multi-Dimensional Databases) and OLAP (Online Analytical Processing) are related but independent facets in the design of the Data Warehouse. OLAP is part of the front-end *exploitation of the Data Warehouse and MDDB is part of the* back-end *design.***

4.2 OLAP and the Data Warehouse

Online Analytical Processing is a method of viewing data. The computer industry has termed this technique of viewing the data as 'slicing and dicing'. Essentially, data can be seen as a series of levels that make up hierarchies. Hierarchies and analysis variables,[2] which are the measures of performance, reflect the ways that an enterprise can be viewed. Hierarchies are made up of levels,[3] such as: sales regions, sales people, products, time periods, insurance claims, financial transactions, General Ledger accounts, manufacturing plants, warehouse bin numbers. Examples of analysis variables are: sales,

---

[1] This process is discussed in Chapter 2, as the 'Transition Phase' in the three-phase Data Warehouse design.
[2] Kimball refers to these as 'Dimensions' and 'Facts', respectively, in his book: Kimball, Ralph, *The Data Warehousing Toolkit*: John Wiley & Sons, Inc. 1996.
[3] The term 'level' can be used synonymously with 'dimension'. Hierarchies are therefore made up of levels, or dimensions, depending on your preference.

delivery times, manufacturing costs, purchasing costs, salaries, co-payment amounts, and amount of time stored in warehouse.

Hierarchies allow for the organization of levels in a natural drill-down relationship that makes sense to the enterprise. For example, a hierarchy might contain manufacturing plant, sales people, and product, but is unlikely to contain warehouse bin number and General Ledger account.

The analysis variables will usually be closely tied to the hierarchy. For example, if the hierarchy contained sales people, then it would be likely that an analysis variable might be sales or business expenses. In this situation, it is unlikely that a good candidate for an analysis variable would be purchase cost because this is largely unrelated to the sales function.

Assuming a simple hierarchy with three levels (Manufacturing Plant, Sales People, and Product); each will have internal domains. This means that there might be 5 manufacturing plants, 50 sales people, and 2000 products. The number of internal domains can also be referred to as its *cardinality*. Each level in a hierarchy could have a low cardinality (the Manufacturing Plant) or high cardinality (the Products). If the analysis variable is sales, then it is possible to see half a million (5*50*2000) different sales figures if one were to systematically look at a report of each manufacturing plant and break each report down by every sales person and by every product. This figure increases if, for instance, every manufacturing plant by sales person is considered. OLAP will allow the user to easily view this kind of information.

This kind of analysis can take place without using an MDDB. In Data Warehousing terms, OLAP is merely a method by which the data can be exploited. The key factor to the enterprise when using OLAP is that it allows users to analyze figures as they work. It is true that it would be relatively easy to programmatically produce half a million reports, but these would be largely redundant except in situations where the specific combination of manufacturing plant, sales people, and product were already known. Giving users the tool to see what they want, when they want, reduces the amount of unnecessary pre-processing that is likely to end up with analyses that are never used.

OLAP allows the user to easily see results and act upon them to further isolate the analysis process. For instance, the user could look at sales at the highest level (by manufacturing plant) and determine that the Tallahassee plant has the lowest sales figures. The user would then drill-down to the Tallahassee plant to see how the sales people were performing at that plant. Then the user would drill-down to particular (or series of) sales people to find out the performance of each of the products. OLAP software products are usually flexible enough for the user to ignore particular levels within the hierarchy, so that it is possible, for example, to drill directly from manufacturing plant to products.

The software industry has had a field day in inventing new acronyms for OLAP based upon the way that the products have to access the underlying data. Examples of these are: ROLAP (Relational Online Analytical Processing), MOLAP(Multi-dimensional OLAP), HOLAP (a hybrid of ROLAP and MOLAP), and DOLAP (a desk-top only version). Whether these acronyms have been created to confuse or amuse is largely irrelevant and should not be taken into consideration when contemplating their use. However, what is important from a Data Warehouse perspective is the performance of OLAP tools. A Data Warehouse lives or dies on its *perceived* performance by the business users (in terms of response from the computer). Therefore, it is of primary importance to select a product that will match the expectations and needs of the users.

Well used, OLAP tools can bring information to light that would otherwise be hidden. Like all computer tools, it can also be an expensive toy. Although OLAP tools are very flexible in terms of how they can manipulate data and consequently perform any corresponding analysis, this should not be confused with having flexibility in their purpose. To effectively use an OLAP tool, it should be configured with sound business reasons in mind. In other words, it is necessary to know **why** the OLAP tool is being used, even though it is not always necessary to know **how** it is being used. This relates back to our essential rules: OLAP use within the Data Warehouse should explicitly reflect the enterprise needs of the organization to be successful.[4]

Where Does OLAP Fit into the Data Warehousing Process?

OLAP is part of the front end of the Data Warehouse. It can be a very important tool in the exploitation of the data within the Warehouse. Although in itself, it is probably not pivotal in the design of the Data Warehouse, it might have a certain degree of influence.

One of the key aspects to successfully designing a Data Warehouse is to ensure that it will be able to solve real and defined enterprise needs. If the designer of the Data Warehouse can thoroughly understand applied OLAP access patterns to the data that is required by the enterprise, then a large

---

[4] See Chapter 2 for a full discussion on the importance of specifying explicit enterprise needs to help in the successful design of a Data Warehouse.

step has been taken in knowing both the Data Warehouse's contents and its structure.

A major complaint Data Warehouse designers have is the difficulty of extracting enterprise needs from the users. Designers complain that the users are not specific enough, and the users complain that the designers are too limiting. Therefore, they are afraid when documenting their needs that they will commit themselves to too small a scope. This problem is a good argument for the integration of an Iterative Application Development Model, where the needs of the users are not necessarily pre-defined, but are slowly developed alongside that of the Warehouse itself. As the users see the development of the Warehouse, they can take this knowledge to further define their own needs, leading to a spiral (as opposed to a waterfall) development that can suit both user and developer.

One of the ways around this frustrating dichotomy is to guide the users. An inherent part of guidance is education. If the users can be educated to start to think about their requirements in terms of an OLAP model, then there is enough implicit flexibility for the users and enough specific detail for the designers. There is little difference between thinking of the business in terms of a series of OLAP designs and trying to think through a star-schema design.[5] In fact, to use an OLAP model as a design tool does not mean that an OLAP product should necessarily be available. It would obviously be nice if it were, but this approach to the design does not inherently pre-suppose its existence. To think of the business needs in terms of an OLAP approach (hierarchies, levels, analysis variables, etc.) means that the process of translating these needs into a technological lexicon will be made easier. The conversion of the enterprise needs (the Conceptual Warehouse) into technological solutions (the Implemented Warehouse) is the pivotal phase in the Data Warehousing process. Looking at the enterprise in terms of an OLAP model can help this pivotal phase in the process, thus leading to a more successful implementation.

To use the OLAP model as a design tool, the users must be educated in terms of hierarchies, levels, analysis variables, and statistics. For some users, this is a natural approach, but to others it will be difficult. It can certainly help to bridge the gap between users thinking in terms of reports rather than information which, in turn, will lead to a more flexible and robust Data Warehouse.

---

[5] See Chapter 3 for a discussion on the Star-Schema Model.

Special Topic:
Report Vs. Information Centric Design

One of the major problems in designing a Data Warehouse is when the users are **Report Centric** as opposed to **Information Centric**. Many job functions within an organization depend upon the production of reports. The timely manner and accuracy of these reports are the factors upon which job performance is measured. The problem with a Report Centric approach is that it is short-sighted and usually illustrates an enterprise or job function that is not geared to change. It represents a reactive, rather than a proactive approach, which might work well in some organizations. The Data Warehouse itself, however, cannot afford to be Report Centric because it will be intrinsically inflexible and, therefore, have a limited life span.

The problem is how to help the users move beyond the reports they have to produce and look at the underlying information, which they might need to fulfill their function. This is not an easy move for many people, but the good Data Warehouse designer should have a set of tools and skills available to help make this shift in approach easier. One of these tools can be to ask the users to visualize their business in terms of hierarchies and levels. Analysis variables and statistics are easier to understand and tend to fit automatically.

The key to presenting this approach is to ensure that the education is complete (that the users fully understand what a hierarchy is) and that the benefits are fully presented. Presenting benefits to the users is a sales skill. To get the most out of the users, it is often necessary to approach the process in terms of selling the potential benefits so that support is garnered. The users that resist the design of the Data Warehouse must be involved in the process, not placed on the outside. Involvement will lead to a degree of ownership, which will naturally lead to support. Data Warehousing design is far more than a technological exercise in implementation. It is a full sales process that must bring together, if not the entire enterprise, then the departments that will have some potential payback.

The Report Centric users must be coerced into looking at their function in a different way. This new way must include their current report needs, or else support will not be forthcoming. In other words, if they are asked to look at their needs from an OLAP perspective (hierarchies, levels, etc.) then it must be emphasized that they will not be losing their existing reports but gaining far more. For the Data Warehouse designer, it will be obvious in many cases that those reports will soon become superfluous given the new sources of information. This does not detract from the fact that the insecurities of the users must be addressed as a means to extracting information that will help in the design of the Data Warehouse.

SAS Software and OLAP

There are two major ways that OLAP can be exploited through SAS software:

- Through the use of SAS/EIS, which includes a series of pre-programmed multi-dimensional objects specifically designed for OLAP.[6] This should be the default way of using SAS for OLAP because it is easy to set up, and it is fully documented from both a designer's and a user's perspective.
- Through the use of SAS/AF, the SAS application design tool.

Which method to use is dependent upon the particular application, but the recommendation is to use the SAS/EIS objects if at all possible. If these objects do not entirely suit a specific situation, then look into extending their capabilities[7] before using SAS/AF. Remember that the SAS/EIS objects have been designed using SAS/AF as the tool, so why re-invent the wheel? Building an OLAP front end is not a small undertaking and should only be attempted after exhausting all other options.

> *SAS/EIS is predominantly a tool used to exploit the Data Warehouse, rather than to build it. It is, therefore, not discussed in detail in this book but only referenced. SAS/EIS software is a set of objects that will make up applications. The designer will define, through a point-and-click environment, what data an object will use and other details that will result in the objects making up an application. Any data that is used by an object must be registered in a central database, which contains metadata, called a metabase. This means that, in a very short period of time, a designer can create complex applications very simply. For a list of available objects, see SAS Institute Inc.,* SAS/EIS Software: Reference, Version 6, Second Edition, *Cary, NC: SAS Institute Inc., 1997.*

Which SAS Products Are Needed for OLAP?

As already mentioned, there is often confusion between OLAP and MDDB. There are two key distinctions that should be drawn when looking at SAS software and OLAP:

- It is possible to use the OLAP viewers within SAS/EIS without an underlying MDDB. The OLAP viewers that exist within SAS/EIS do not need SAS/MDDB to run. This is not necessarily an advisable path to follow

---

[6] For an introduction, see SAS Institute Inc., *Getting Started with SAS/EIS® Software, Third Edition*, Cary, NC: SAS Institute Inc., 1997. 80pp, pages 47–53, or SAS Institute Inc., *SAS/EIS® Software: Reference, Version 6, Second Edition*, Cary, NC: SAS Institute Inc., 280 pp.

[7] See SAS Institute Inc., *Extending SAS/EIS® Software Capabilities*, Cary, NC: SAS Institute Inc., 1997.

because, without an underlying MDDB, in all likelihood, the performance will not be as fast. Far more processing will be required at run time because the summary information will have to be created upon request.

- SAS/MDDB software does not come packaged with viewers for the data. Therefore, it is necessary to use the viewers that exist within SAS/EIS software or to write them using SAS/AF software. SAS/MDDB software is an engine to create and maintain the database, and is independent of the viewer into the data.

Further details on the SAS OLAP tools can best be found on the SAS World Wide Web site (www.sas.com). This is a very dynamic topic that is not necessarily current in published books. Therefore, it is always best to go to the most dynamic source of information to ensure that it is the most current available.

4.3 MDDB and the Data Warehouse

In the OLAP discussion earlier, it was mentioned that users can 'slice and dice' information so that they can see it based upon hierarchies, levels, analysis variables, and statistics. Without an MDDB, each time an item of information is required, it must be calculated. For instance, suppose a user wants to see the total sales from the Tallahassee Plant, for a particular sales person, for a particular product in the month of March. The underlying file that contains this data, depending on its granularity, could be immense. The OLAP tool would have to identify what data would be needed to calculate the specific item, extract that data, and then perform the calculations. The request from the user might be for a series of products or time periods. The time it takes to perform these actions might first of all be outside the acceptable limits determined by the users, and secondly might be so resource intensive that overall computer performance might be affected.

What if the item that the user wants to see is already calculated? There are obvious benefits to this. The OLAP tool would then just have to understand what the user needs, have pointers that tell it exactly where that information resides, then go and get it. There would be major benefits because the computer would have to do less work. Therefore, the information could be returned to the user more expediently. This is the essence of a Multidimensional Database. It is not a single file but a series of files that contain pre-summarized information and pointers to locate that information.

It is very easy to become confused with MDDBs, partially because, unlike a traditional SAS data file or an Excel spreadsheet, it cannot be directly printed. It is possible to perform a straight print on either the SAS data file or Excel Spreadsheet, but the MDDB needs some form of a viewer to access it. The second reason it is easy to be confused by MDDBs, is the way that they are often described in associated literature. Very often, an MDDB is represented by a cube, which is only a three-dimensional object. Using SAS/MDDB, it is possible to have an unlimited number of dimensions (unlike many other MDDBs), so the cube analogy quickly falls apart, and it is more likely to confuse than help. When thinking MDDB, do not think 'cube'. In fact, do not think of any geometric structure but think in business terms. The MDDB is made up of data elements (calculated summaries) wherever levels cross (e.g., with the two levels, Sales people and Product a crossing will be whenever a particular salesperson sells a particular prod-uct). These elements might well be physically stored in different tables, but it is far easier to understand an MDDB by referencing the business model, rather than the physical model (the way in which the data is organized).

An MDDB from a conceptual standpoint is very easy to understand, so long as it is thought of in business, rather than technological terms. The MDDB reflects the enterprise needs directly and is constructed using business defin-itions (hierarchies, levels etc.), rather than in abstract terms. This is why the potential benefits of an MDDB exceed just providing the user access to com-plex summary information very quickly. It can also be used as a design tool, allowing the business users to express their needs in business terms, and also, coincidentally, it will help the physical design of the Data Warehouse.

Creating a SAS MDDB

There are four basic ways that an MDDB can be built using SAS tools:

1. The MDDB procedure: This is a programmatic method that produces the MDDB. Within a Data Warehousing environment, this will proba-bly be the primary method used.

2. SAS/EIS software: The MDDB is created through a point-and-click environment. This will reduce potential syntactical errors and will help guide the designer through each step. Other than being a point-and-click interface for designing the MDDB, there is one other major difference between this method and using PROC MDDB. With SAS/EIS software, the source data (the table that contains the detail from which the summary information is calculated) must be pre-registered in an EIS metabase.[8]

---

[8] See: SAS Institute Inc., *Getting Started with SAS/EIS® Software, Third Edition*, Cary, NC: SAS Institute Inc., 1997. 80pp, pp 10–17.

One of the benefits to using SAS/EIS software is that it forces the designer to create metadata, which is stored in a metabase. To use data within SAS/EIS, each table and any column of information that will be used has to be registered. To create an MDDB is no exception. The down side of this is that there are several steps to creating an MDDB using SAS/EIS, but the advantage is that once the table is registered with the metabase (this registration can be easily updated if needed), then it may easily be used by any applicable EIS object.

3. SAS/AF software: The MDDB is a class within SAS/AF. Therefore, it can be created and manipulated by using Object-Oriented techniques.[9] It is possible to create an MDDB from within a custom-built application. Indeed, because it is a class within an application design package, it is possible to custom build an entire application that will dynamically link the MDDB creation directly to specific Data Warehouse requirements. From a Data Warehousing perspective, this has some repercussions:

- It is possible to design a full process to build, design, and maintain a Data Warehouse using SAS/AF, including the creation of MDDBs. (This has already been accomplished with SAS/Warehouse Administrator software[10]).

- There might be situations where having pre-defined MDDBs throughout the Data Warehouse is not feasible. Certain users and functions might not be able to thoroughly pre-define a set of hierarchies, levels, analysis variables, and statistics, so this must be done at run time.

- Another situation might be where the structure of the MDDB might be predictable, but the underlying data might be very dynamic. Therefore, it might be most efficient to create MDDBs as required (through an application) rather than continually rebuilding them based on changes to the data. Although unusual in a Data Warehousing environment where the data should be as static as possible, volatile data sources are a possibility.

  In all of these cases, creating the required MDDBs within an application built with SAS/AF might well make sense.

4. SAS/Warehouse Administrator software: More information on this can be found in Chapter 8, but the process is, in principle, very similar

---

[9] See Chapter 3 for more information about Object-Oriented Modeling within the Data Warehousing process.
[10] See Chapter 8 for more information.

to using SAS/EIS. The heart of the system is the creation of metadata upon which data structures can be based.

Example of Creating an MDDB Using SAS/MDDB

The code below is an example of creating an MDDB using the first method outlined earlier (PROC MDDB.) Assume that the source detail data for the MDDB is in a SAS data file (although the source data could be in any data format that SAS can access[11]) with the following structure:

PLANT	REGION	PRODUCT	QUARTER	SALESMAN	SALES
MO	MW	R65X	1	55	998.65
WA	NW	P78X	1	88	97.00
CA	WC	F87P	2	78	1098.78

The file shown is a very simple example of detail data that might be found in a Data Warehouse for a manufacturing company. There are plants located in different regions around the country. Sales people work in different regions and can sell products from different plants. Products may be manufactured at different plants. This file could well be loaded into the Data Warehouse from an Accounts Receivable system, so that the sales amount reflects the amount that the customer has paid, and the quarter report will reflect the paid date, not the billed date. There might well be more information in this file (e.g., Customer, Sub-Products, Sales Manager, Sales Expenses), but this is enough to illustrate the creation of an MDDB. Let's suppose this is located in a SAS data file on a UNIX machine in the directory: **/dw/data/sales/** in a SAS file named SALESDAT.[12]

In constructing this file, one of the direct business requirements was wanting to track sales performance. The following code would create an MDDB in the same directory in which the detail data resides.

```
❶ LIBNAME detdata '/dw/data/sales';
❷ PROC MDDB DATA=detdata.salesdat OUT=detdata.salesmdb;
❸ CLASS region plant quarter product salesman;
❹ VAR sales / sum;
❺ HIERARCHY product salesman;
❻ HIERARCHY region plant product / display=yes name='Region Breakdown';
❼ RUN;
```

This shows how to create a very simple MDDB, and illustrates some very important features that need to be considered. The explanation of the above code will incorporate discussions of these features.

---

[11] See Chapter 5 for information regarding the extraction of external file formats.

[12] Note that this file could be stored in any format that SAS can access. It does not need to be in a SAS data file format. For instance, it could be a view into a Relational Database table, such as DB2 or ORACLE, or it could be a VSAM file.

❶ This simply assigns a libname so that SAS knows where the data resides physically.

❷ This tells SAS that the MDDB procedure is going to be used, using detail data that resides in the file SALESDAT within the library DETDATA. The resultant MDDB will be created in the same library but will be called SALESMDB.

❸ In **every** creation of an MDDB, an *NWAY* table is created, which contains summarized information for every combination of values within each of the columns listed in the CLASS statement. Each of the columns specified must contain categorical data. The NWAY table is the **only** summarized table created by default. In the example above, it means that for every value of region, plant, quarter, product and salesman, the sum of sales (see ❹) will be created, **unless the value does not exist**. Each one of these unique intersections, where a summary value will be stored, is called a crossing.

Note: The order of the columns in the CLASS statement is not critical.

❹ The VAR statement will list the columns that are to be used as the analysis variables and will list the required statistic(s). There is no limit to the number of columns that can be selected, but there is a limit of eight statistics for each column. This means that it is possible to **store** eight statistics, but the EIS viewers can calculate many more upon request.

❺ Each HIERARCHY statement represents additional summary tables. For a discussion on creating additional summary tables, see ❻. Line 5 essentially instructs SAS to create a summary table (in addition to the NWAY table) that contains the sum of sales by product and by salesman.

Note: The order of the columns in the HIERARCHY statement is critical.

❻ Another summary table will be built, but it will have additional information that may be used by the data viewer (within SAS/EIS) to recognize this combination of categorical columns as a drill-down hierarchy. In this case, the user of the viewer will be able to see a drill-down hierarchy named "Region Breakdown" and can automatically drill from regions to plants to products, and see the sum of sales in each case.

❼ The RUN statement completes the program and tells SAS to perform the processing.

It doesn't matter which of the four techniques, presented in the first part of this section, is used to create the MDDB, the thought process must be the same. In reading through the code in this section, it becomes apparent how closely tied the creation of an MDDB is to the actual enterprise needs. Not only is it necessary to fully understand what is required of the Data Warehouse from an analysis variable perspective (in this case, it is paid sales based on payment date), but also the expected access patterns that will be required. If an MDDB can be designed, it means that there is a business understanding of the data. Going through the MDDB design process, even if there is no immediate intent to physically create one, will result in ensuring that the enterprise needs have been successfully interpreted on the technology side.

MDDB within the Data Warehouse

There are several specific features and points that should be considered in the creation of an MDDB. These are largely related to the use of SAS/MDDB within the larger SAS software picture, and then as additional features of the product itself.

No Limitations on the Computer Platform upon Which the MDDB Is Built and Resides

SAS/MDDB is not limited to a single platform. It conforms to all the multi-platform/multi-vendor support consistent across SAS software. This means that the Data Warehouse designer can select the most advantageous platform on which to create and store the MDDB. Remember, also, that the MDDB need not be stored on the same platform upon which it was created. For instance, it might be beneficial to have all MDDBs created on an OS/390 (MVS) mainframe (because this could be where the detail data residing within the Data Warehouse is), and then have them stored either on Windows or UNIX based computers where it best suits the users. Note that the SAS implementation of an MDDB, unlike most products, is supported on the IBM OS/390 mainframe environment.

The MDDB Should Fit into a Client/Server Architecture

It is possible to utilize all of the Client/Server[13] capabilities of SAS software in using SAS/MDDB. This means that, not only is it possible to create and to store the MDDBs wherever they are best suited (see ❶ in the example code discussion), but like any other data source accessible to SAS software, it can be used in a Client/Server architecture. Many MDDB products allow for a local model only. This will inherently limit the Data Warehouse architecture thus reducing future Data Warehouse options. SAS/MDDB supports the following operating systems: Windows, Windows NT, UNIX, OS/390 and

---

[13] See Chapter 8 for a full discussion on Client/Server architecture using SAS.

VMS. This does not only mean that the MDDB can be created and exploited on each of these platforms, but that it is possible to move it between any of them, based upon your data storage and processing needs.

Because the MDDB can be created and stored on almost all platforms, it follows that the underlying detail data should also have this ability. A SAS MDDB does not need to reside on the same platform as the underlying detail data. Indeed, it is not even necessary to have the MDDB created on the same platform that the detail data resides on (although it is highly unlikely that this would ever happen). A key benefit of SAS/MDDB is that it has the ability to 'reach-through' to the detail data. The Remote Library Services capabilities of SAS/CONNECT[14] may be used to obtain 'reach-through' detail information if the detail data resides on a different computer or platform from the MDDB.

In situations where an MDDB might be needed on a different computer or platform than the one it was created on, it can only be moved by using the Data Transfer capabilities of SAS/CONNECT if the Versions and Releases of SAS Software on each platform are similar. This might not always be the case. If the MDDB was created on a mainframe running SAS Release 6.09, and it is to be transferred to a PC running SAS Release 6.12, then the transfer would have to be made by using PROC COPY after the MDDB had been made available to the local session through Remote Library Services. In either situation, it will obviously be necessary to have SAS/CONNECT available on both computers. If the platform is the same but the MDDB must be moved to another computer, then it would be possible to just copy the MDDB to the new computer.

MDDB Access Speed Should Suit the Needs of the Data Warehouse

The MDDB can be stored in Scalable Performance Data Server (SPDS) software,[15] which will allow the access to data to take advantage of parallel processing. There are, in this situation, two performance enhancements working together to improve over-all Data Warehouse information access speeds. In those Data Warehouse implementations that require an extremely fast response time, this alignment of an MDDB and parallel processing can be a very important option. Moving the MDDB to the SPDS server is a simple process (identical to moving any standard SAS data file). There are additional benefits that can be obtained if the underlying detail data is also

---

[14] See Chapter 8, Section 8.4 for detail on using Remote Library Services within a Data Warehousing environment.
[15] See Chapter 5, Section 5.4.

stored within an SPDS server, especially if this detail is often needed. (See Section "No Limit on Viewing Detail Data" later in this chapter.)

Use of Information Should Not Be Limited to MDDB Viewers

Although SAS/MDDB must have a viewer to navigate the data, at any point, the information that is being used can be moved out of the MDDB for further analysis by using any of the available SAS analysis and presentation tools. This is a return to one of the basic Data Warehouse needs—that of flexibility. One of the major problems that users have when dealing with data is when they are told that, because of a technological limitation, they cannot use the data they can see. There is a cut-and-paste ability through the MDDB viewers that opens up the data structure not only to other SAS tools, but any other tools the users might require.

There are a series of report templates (approximately 35 in number) that are supplied with SAS/EIS that will allow the user of the MDDB to drag-and-drop information directly into the templates without any further setup being needed. This effectively means that the multi-dimensionality of the data can be very easily translated to a relational format that has the more traditional row-and-column format, for further analysis and presentation. This opens up the multi-dimensional data to classic analysis and presentation tools, including SAS itself.

The MDDB Must Be Tunable to Meet Varying Data Warehouse Situations

The SAS/MDDB is a tunable data structure. In our earlier example, there are only two hierarchies requested. The number of summary tables will therefore be three: the NWAY table, plus two more tables that represent summaries based on the categorical variables (levels) specified in each of the hierarchy statements. This does not mean that the user can only access the information stored in these three tables (which would be very limiting), but that if any data elements of crossings that were not pre-calculated were required, then they would have to be pre-calculated at run time. These calculations would usually, but not necessarily, be based upon the data in the NWAY table. Deciding upon the number of hierarchies (summary tables) is the major way the MDDB can be tuned:

■ More hierarchies will result in more summary tables. This will mean that more disk space will be needed to store the MDDB and longer times needed to create or to update it.

■ Fewer hierarchies will save disk space and decrease the time it takes to create or to update the MDDB, but they will lead to potentially longer response times for the users because, if there is no pre-calculated value for any required crossing of two levels, then it will have to be calculated.

Experimentation will probably be needed to find out the optimum configuration of any particular MDDB. As the Data Warehouse usage changes over time, this configuration will also need to be adjusted accordingly.

 A tunable MDDB will be able to stay in line with any changes in the access patterns to the Data Warehouse, based upon new or modified needs of the enterprise.

No Limit on Viewing Detail Data

One of the nightmare situations for the users of a Data Warehouse is being unable to obtain the detail data behind the summaries. One of the weaknesses of early Executive Information Systems (EIS), which were designed to give a very high level of information to the users, was their inability to scale to incorporating detail data. The ability to drill-down into other, more detailed levels of information was limited and so, therefore, were the applications. These early EIS systems were quickly replaced because of the erroneous underlying assumption that high-level data will meet the needs of the business.

MDDBs, because they do not contain the smallest pieces of information (e.g., a transaction from a General Ledger or a claim in the Insurance industry), could well fall into the same trap as did the early EIS products. SAS/MDDB allows the user to dynamically drill-down beyond the scope of the MDDB itself and then move back into the structure from which the summarized data was collected. One particular feature that will be of use in this 'reach-through' capability is that the Data Warehouse designers do not have to pre-define the code needed to retrieve the pertinent information. Many products require that this code (to 'reach-through' to the detail) be pre-defined (and therefore be pre-determined). SAS will automatically generate this code (which happens to be SQL) at the time the user wishes to go deeper than the summary levels stored within the MDDB.

Multiple Options to Store a Wide Variety of Statistics for Each Analysis Variable

One of the major strengths of SAS software is its broad analysis capability. For each of the analysis variables defined for the MDDB, there is a wide choice of statistics available. One of the major misconceptions, which many software vendors fall into, is that they see the world in terms of sums, counts, maximums, and minimums. Availability of information breeds sophistication in the user because, as the major hurdle of data access is overcome, so more time can be spent on analysis. Therefore, this means that having the option to both pre-summarize and request additional statistics, over-and-above the very basic, is essential.

SAS/MDDB has many other statistics that are possible to store with the MDDB (in other words, they are pre-calculated): number of missing values, uncorrected sum of squares, sum of weighted variables, and uncorrected sum. There are other statistics that can be calculated at run time if they are needed. These can be calculated on an as-needed basis depending on the requirements of the users. These additional statistics include: range, variance, standard deviation, standard error, co-efficient of variance, *t*-value, probability of greater absolute value, lower confidence limit, upper confidence limit, corrected sum of squares, and average.

With SAS/MDDB, it is possible to have a maximum of 8 statistics that are stored for each analysis variable, and an additional 13 statistics available at run time, when the user is actually viewing the information.

The MDDB Should Be Integrated into the Wider Data Warehouse Architecture

One of the key points, when designing a Data Warehouse, is that the tools selected must both be flexible (so they can easily be realigned when the requirements change) and that they must be integrated. An MDDB should be capable of being implemented within a cohesive Data Warehouse design, rather than as an add-on. As already mentioned, the MDDB can be a strategic tool to help design both the contents of the Data Warehouse and the structure that the data will take. SAS/MDDB is not an add-on in terms of functionality. It is another tool that fits into the larger Data Warehousing picture. It can be built and maintained from within a planned Data Warehouse implementation because it can **share metadata with the other parts of that Data Warehouse**. This is of primary importance if the MDDB is to stay in line with any changes. Data Warehouses should be metadata driven, when at all possible. If the MDDB shares that metadata, then maintenance and enhancements will be easier.

The MDDB Should Be Easy to Maintain

SAS/MDDB does not require an entire re-build when the data within it needs updating. In a Data Warehouse, where data can be voluminous, this feature is absolutely essential. Imagine a situation where the source detail data from which the MDDB is created comes from a DB2 table that is stored on an IBM mainframe that contains 25 million rows of information. This table is updated monthly, which means that the MDDB will also need updating. If each month the MDDB needed to be re-created, then it is possible that an immense amount of processing will have to take place. Incremental updates or 'drip feeding' is therefore possible.

With SAS/MDDB, the updates to the base detail file will be stored in a separate file. This is then used to update the original MDDB. What actually happens is that a new MDDB is created to be used as needed. Very probably, this new MDDB will be copied over the old version, unless for some reason old versions are required. From a coding perspective, this is a very simple process:

```
PROC MDDB DATA=detdata.updtdata IN=detdata.salesmdb OUT=work.salesupd;
RUN;
```

The above code simply states that the new MDDB SALESUPD stored in the library WORK be created from the existing MDDB SALESMDB stored in the library DETDATA. New detail data is incorporated into the new MDDB from the SAS file (which could be a view of any external data format) UPDTDATA stored in the library DETDATA. This technique obviously means that at some point there will be two MDDBs, so disk space must be available for both of them. The advantage of not updating the MDDB in place is that, if there were to be a problem during the update process, the original MDDB will remain intact. After this new MDDB is created, if it needs to replace the original, then it can be moved using the SAS COPY procedure as follows:

```
PROC COPY INLIB=work OUTLIB=detdata MEMTYPE=mddb;
 SELECT salesupd;
RUN;
```

This code will copy the new MDDB SALESUPD from the library WORK to the library DETDATA, thus overwriting the existing MDDB.

The SAS/MDDB in the Data Warehouse

OLAP is often positioned as a Data Warehouse exploitation tool only. However, to thoroughly take advantage of this technology, it can also be incorporated into the design of the Data Warehouse. To only use an MDDB and associated OLAP applications to exploit the data in the Warehouse is a very limited perspective. It lacks the foresight to follow the two key factors in the design of a Data Warehouse: **Flexibility** and **Integration**.

The design of the MDDB (as determined by the OLAP needs of the enterprise) is a gateway through which the Data Warehouse is designed, as well as exploited. It is not just a means by which summarized information can be

Special Topic: Sparsity

One of the great potential benefits of an MDDB is that it is capable of helping in the process of managing large data files.[16] If the MDDB is correctly constructed, then the need for continued sequential access to very large data files will be reduced. For any given request from a user of an MDDB, the amount of work that the computer will need to perform will be far less with an MDDB than if the data were to reside in a 'relational' style data file.

One of the key concepts, to ensure that the above point is in fact the case, is that of 'sparsity'. Consider a situation where the crossings of all values of sales people, product, and customer were requested. In other words, it is expected that the user will want to look at particular (or group of) sales people to find out the sales they made by each product, for each customer. What would happen in a situation where sales person A never sells a product B to a customer C? In SAS/MDDB, this particular crossing would not be stored. This is especially important in data files that are *sparse*. This could happen in the situation when both the sales people and the customers were very specialized in the products they either sell or buy respectively. If the MDDB were to calculate and store every potential crossing, then the size of the MDDB could very quickly become immense and reduce many of the potential benefits they can provide.

The way in which the MDDB handles sparse data is the primary control over the physical size. Two different MDDB products could contain the same information, but one needs far less physical space. If this is true, then the most probable explanation lies in the way that sparse data is handled. In the case of the smaller MDDB, sparse data is probably not stored.

*SAS/MDDB will not store sparse data cells but **is aware of them and will report on them**. This means that from a design perspective, it is possible to get the best of both worlds: information from a source where no data is actually stored!*

easily accessed. It is a strategic Data Warehouse planning tool that should be used to its full extent in the design of the process.

The MDDB server directly acts in two ways:

1. It fulfills requests for summarized information from the Data Warehouse.

2. It acts as the engine through which detail information can be extracted from the Data Warehouse.

---

[16] See: Moorman, Mark, "Getting a Grip on a Growing Concern: Managing Large Data Sets with a Multidimensional Database", *Observations®*, 1Q, 1997.

There are a series of other ways that the MDDB can be of use to a Data Warehousing process.

1. Because the MDDB by its nature deals with pre-summarized data, it is a tool that allows users very fast access to data that would otherwise have to be summarized upon request. It is, therefore, a tool to manage very large data stores within the Data Warehouse.

2. Successful design of an MDDB requires a very good understanding of the data access patterns needed by the users of the Data Warehouse. This means that the design of the MDDB can be used as a tool to help define and model the data within the Data Warehouse. Of all the data structures, the MDDB most closely resembles the direct requirements of the enterprise. Indeed there is a strong argument to suggest that the model of detail data within the Data Warehouse should be determined by working back from the MDDB model, instead of vice-versa.

3. The MDDB allows for efficient use of information. This is because patterns in data can be seen at the summary level and further explored by isolating the pertinent detail data. Although there is often the need for extensive exploratory analysis on detail data (thus the need for Data Mining), most enterprise requirements have more mundane use of the data.[17]

   For instance, consider a requirement that gives a Sales Manager the ability to see trends from one quarter to the next within each sales region and to concentrate on those doing the worst. The Sales Manager would benefit greatly by seeing the summarized data of the lowest selling regions and then requesting the relevant detail data. If that summary data did not exist, then it would have to be either calculated upon request (which would be both time consuming and expensive from a computer resource perspective) or the Sales Manager would have to deal with volumes of detail data to extract what was needed. The MDDB would fulfill this enterprise requirement quite easily through efficient pre-calculation of summary data.

---

[17] See Special Topic: 'Data Integrity—Summary or Detail Data?' later in this chapter.

Special Topic:
Data Integrity—Summary or Detail Data?

One of the major problems that a Data Warehouse often has to overcome is one of trust in its integrity. Integrity is acknowledged by the information that comes from the data within the Data Warehouse being trusted by the enterprise in general. This means that the process of moving the data into the Warehouse should include many data integrity tests, plus associated scrubbing and transformations. If this process of ensuring data integrity is not thoroughly defined and implemented, then as soon as the users find fault with the data, they will naturally require that the detail data be thoroughly investigated before any summary information is disseminated.

The pattern of analyzing detail data, rather than trusting summary data is not an ideal situation for either the users or the Data Warehouse. The detail extracts or analyses will involve large amounts of data and will require both computer resources and time. After the pattern has been set, where users work from detail to summary, it is very hard to break. This is because the Data Warehouse will be in a position where its integrity has to overcome the doubts of the users, which will not happen overnight. The integrity of the data need only be compromised once for trust to be lost, but it will take a long time before this trust can be regained.

Analysis of data, where possible, will be more efficient moving from the highest level of summary to detail, not vice-versa. This is why the term *drill-down*, and not *drill-up* is the usual description when moving through data. The aim should be for the users to only need access to the smallest, most targeted, section of detail data, but this is only possible if the users believe in the integrity of the data.

Chapter 5:
Data Storage within the Data Warehouse: Using SAS/ACCESS® Software Effectively

5.1 The Implications of the Internal Structure of the Data Warehouse

The internal structure of the Data Warehouse is the actual format that is used to contain the data. This internal structure need not be limited to a single choice but could be several, depending on the needs and the stage in the Data Warehousing process. When this topic is usually discussed, only the final storage format is usually considered: where the cleansed and transformed data is made available to the users or to the front end of the Data Warehouse. From an extraction and storage perspective, there are other stages in the Data Warehousing process that need to be considered.

To discuss the internal data format (storage) of the Data Warehouse, it is also necessary to consider how it can be accessed because a format is only as good as its access capabilities. For example, an ORACLE database could be considered as an internal data structure for the Data Warehouse, and the access techniques could be SAS/ACCESS views. To make a decision upon the structure (ORACLE) without the access methods (SAS/ACCESS views) does not make sense because the former cannot be of use without the latter.

This chapter deals explicitly with the internal data storage format and the access to that format both from a Data Warehousing and a SAS perspective.

The internal data structure of the Data Warehouse is an important decision because there are several stages of the Data Warehousing process where it has relevance:

1. The source systems from which the Warehouse data will be extracted.
2. The staging of the data after it has been extracted.
3. The storage of the detail Data Warehouse data.
4. The storage of any summarized detail Data Warehouse data.

All four of these steps are firmly based in the Implementation Stage of the Data Warehouse process, which is outlined in Chapter 2. The other two major stages, the design of the Conceptual Warehouse and the transfer into implementation are not concerned with the way the data is stored or accessed.

> *The only pre-determined data storage formats within the Data Warehouse process are the ones associated with the source (Operational) data systems. Although the designer of the Data Warehouse might not have complete control over the Operational Systems, there is usually a degree of flexibility. To make a determination on a storage format, it is essential to consider the data access tool(s) that will be used. It, therefore, follows that the storage format is dependent upon the access tool(s). To this end, it is necessary, when possible, to determine the front-end tools to the Data Warehouse and their associated access technique (e.g., ODBC, SQL).*
>
> *SAS as a front-end tool is largely unlimited in the data formats that it can access. However, it is most effective against a SAS data format (as opposed to ORACLE or DB2 formats). If the data manipulation, analysis, and presentation abilities of SAS are required for the front end, then it is important to incorporate this into the decision on the storage format of the Data Warehouse.*

Between each of these four stages, there must be the ability to, at least, access the data and, in many cases, to modify that data. For instance, to move between steps 1 and 2 will require software that can read and manipulate the staged data and be able to write to the 'Final' detail storage format. In some cases, this format might be the same (it could be a SAS data file in both cases), but this is not necessarily so.

Both the internal data structures and the available access methods in combination must be, at least,

1. flexible enough to allow for any changes that might be necessary. For instance, if the source system (e.g., a General Ledger) is moved from an IMS database to an ORACLE database, then the access methods should allow for these changes. In this case, there is a severe change in the OLTP system that will impact the Data Warehouse. We would be fooling ourselves if we were to think that the Data Warehouse would be a factor in the decision to alter the General Ledger, so the capabilities of the Data Warehouse data extraction tools must allow for such changes.

2. fast enough to meet the needs of the enterprise. It is fairly common to hear of Data Warehouses where the monthly refresh takes days to complete. This is fine if the enterprise's needs allow that much time, but usually, the faster this can be performed, the better. Performing a Data Warehouse update through an ODBC connection might not give the same performance results as using pass-through SQL,[1] so ensuring that the combination of data structure and access techniques will meet enterprise needs is extremely important.

The internal structure and the data model are important to the success of a Data Warehouse implementation, but alone they do not ensure its success. As outlined in Chapter 2, to be concerned about the structure of the data, at the expense of the remainder of the process, leads to an implementation centric Data Warehouse that is inherently flawed. The structure of the data has to be carefully considered, based on technology, enterprise needs, internal enterprise politics, and budget, but certainly it should not be considered the heart of the project. The key to successful Data Warehousing is the reflection of enterprise needs to information availability. The successful transformation of enterprise requirements from a business lexicon to a technological lexicon is the heart of a Data Warehouse. This transformation is what 'makes or breaks' the Data Warehouse from the perspective of meeting enterprise requirements. What follows after the technical lexicon has been defined, including the selection data structure, is part of the implementation of the Data Warehouse, not part of the planning and design process.

There is a bewildering array of options open to the Data Warehouse designer in deciding what data structure to use. The past few years has seen a move by the traditional Relational Database Management Systems to claim that their products are now optimized for Data Warehousing.

---

[1] See Chapter 5 for a discussion about Pass-Through SQL.

Along with these claims, there are software companies that have developed products strictly for Data Warehousing, based upon extremely fast access to data. Alongside these two broad groups are a variety of other options that should not be disregarded, for instance, spreadsheets and PC-based Database products. Any form of electronic storage of data is a candidate to be included in a Data Warehousing strategy. What is most important, however, is that the selection must allow for complete access by the front-end tools. It is no good selecting a data structure that cannot be used by the front end.

Users of SAS software are in a very good position from a data structure aspect. Not only does SAS have its own internal structure (actually, several different structures all designed for different purposes), but it can read virtually any other. This means that from a SAS perspective, the selection of the internal format of the data does not matter. The Data Warehouse can have data residing in any of the major Relational Database Management Systems (e.g., ORACLE, INFORMIX, SYBASE), in any ODBC compliant structure, or in a SAS format. One of the important aspects of Data Warehouse design is to make the structure of the data flexible enough to anticipate changes in the requirements of the enterprise. This makes SAS an excellent choice because it is highly unlikely that SAS tools will not be able to accommodate any changes in format that are required.

 Two key rules are absolutely essential to remember when considering the use of data storage products:

1. *Never commit to a product that will not allow you to grow and change. If you select a certain storage product, ensure that, if you were to need to change tomorrow, that change would not endanger the Data Warehousing project.*

2. *Do not commit to a single storage product in the Data Warehouse. Use each product for which it is best suited. Many Data Warehouse projects use an RDBMS to store the detail data, and then use SAS for their Data Marts and summary-level information. This is a perfectly acceptable approach, so long as Rule 1 is not transgressed.*

   There might well be a sound case for different formats and access techniques in each stage of the Data Warehousing process. For instance, using a SAS format to stage the data after extraction from the Operational System might make sense, especially if the data validation and manipulation tools available within SAS will be used. The detail data within the Warehouse might then be stored in an ORACLE structure and summary tables within a SAS format. As long as the format best suits the access needs for the particular phase in the process, using different formats is perfectly acceptable.

5.2 Choosing the Data Structure of the Data Warehouse

Factors that affect the choice of the Data Warehouse data structure are discussed in the next four sections.

The Data Access Tools That Will Be Used within the Data Warehouse Process

The prime question that should be asked before deciding upon an internal data storage format for any part of the Data Warehouse is:

 What are the principal data access tools that will be used to access the data?

It is more important before selecting the data storage tools, to select the data access tools. Two major reasons for this decision are

1. The Data Warehouse is only as good as the way it can be used. Many Data Warehouses are designed without giving more than a perfunctory thought to the way it will be accessed by the users, yet this is the single most critical factor that will determine its perceived usefulness. To ensure that the users have the right access tool can be done before and independently of the decision about the storage tool.

2. If the data access tool is decided upon, then the back end of the Data Warehouse can be designed to optimize the requirements of this tool. In other words, if a specific data access tool has been selected due to its statistical analysis and reporting tools, then the physical organization of the Data Warehouse can be optimized to align itself to these requirements. Not only the back-end tools need to be considered before really deciding on the structure of the data, but so should, as far as possible, the ways that the access tool will be acting on the data.[2]

Very often, the format of the Data Warehouse is pre-determined. One of the very common, and often neglected, rationales for selecting a certain set of products is the fact that the organization already has them in-house, along with the skills to use them. This, of course, neglects the fact that although the technical skills might be available, the Data Warehousing skills may not be available. A top-notch data modeler in an Operational System environment is not necessarily equipped to deal with a Data Warehouse. The reality of the situation is that very often the selection of a data structure for the

---

[2] See Chapter 3, for an example of structuring the data to suit the access pattern.

Data Warehouse is based upon 'Grandfathering' rather than upon a rational, objective set of guidelines. Just because the source systems for the data are in a certain Relational Database Management System, why should the Data Warehouse also be in the same structure? This is not to imply that the Data Warehouse should not be constructed in the same Relational Database as the source Operational System, but that it does not necessarily follow that it should.

Openness of the Data Structure

Openness is the degree to which a variety of external tools can access the data in the Warehouse. The degree of openness of the data structure is very much a concern to the designers of Data Warehouses because it reduces the risk of the Data Warehouse in the long-term. Predicting what the Data Warehouse will be needed for in the years to come is an almost impossible task, so ensuring that it can be used for as much as possible will 'hedge your bets'.

Data Warehouses that do not display openness are often designed for a specific purpose. Software vendors who sell *vertical* products, those that are designed for a specific industry, where the front end and the back end are sold as a package, are very restricted in openness. What often happens in this situation is that the enterprise outgrows the front end very quickly and finds that it is left with a back end that is virtually impossible to use. The answer that many enterprises use in this situation is to build a working Data Warehouse off the existing, inactive back end. Another problem with this situation is that the rules for creating the back end are often proprietary and cannot be extracted. This is obviously a situation that needs to be avoided.

Although in Chapter 3, we discussed the importance of understanding the front end and building the structure of the back end accordingly, this did not mean that the Data Warehouse should be built along the narrow confines of current access patterns. What was meant was that the efficiency of the front-end tool can be leveraged by back-end design. Specific design of data structure to a narrow user requirement is almost always implemented through the use of a Data Mart, and, as such, should have less of a strategic impact on the actual Data Warehouse design.

Openness can be discussed on many levels. The SAS data structure, for instance, is ODBC[3] compliant, which means that it can be 'front-ended' by any tool that is also ODBC compliant. This means that if SAS data sets are

---

[3] ODBC is an acronym for Open Data Base Connectivity and is an industry standard by which any two products that are compliant can understand and use each other's data structure.

used as the physical store for some or all of your Data Warehouse, the access to the data will not be restricted to just using SAS. At the same time, when SAS is used as a front-end access tool to the Warehouse, due to its ability to read just about any data format on any computer platform, a degree of openness is automatically ensured. The format of the physical storage of the data can be changed without extensive changes to the front end of the Data Warehouse. This is a fantastic advantage for the Data Warehouse designer because it ensures that the 'unknown' can be accounted for.

Budget Implications

One of the frustrations of reading about Data Warehousing (maybe including this book) is the assumption that resources are limitless. Although it seems to be this way in many enterprises as illustrated by the way that these resources are often squandered needlessly, budget concerns are, nevertheless, often a restriction on Data Warehousing activities. This budget limitation essentially means that it is necessary for the Data Warehouse designers to leverage the resources that they can realistically expect from the enterprise. To this end, spending money on mono-dimensional products can become more expensive than first perceived. Data Warehousing is not just a Database project, or a Client/Server project, or a Data Analysis and Reporting project, or a data transformation project, it is all of those things and many more. Data Warehousing is not a mono-dimensional project, so neither should the technological tools be.

A 'best-of-breed' approach to Data Warehousing, where the perceived best solution for each different segment of the project, is one option that might work for companies where the resources exist to purchase, support, and train personnel for multiple products. This might especially work on the Data Warehouse back end where there is usually more control over activities than on the front end. Multiple front-end products is more risky, however, because it is hard enough to design a Data Warehouse to anticipate fluctuating access patterns, without adding the additional burden of multiple products (all with their own strengths and weaknesses) using different access techniques.

Users of SAS software are again in a very strong position to leverage their investment because the broad range of products fit very closely with all aspects of the Data Warehousing process. Although the decision might be reached, for instance, not to use the SAS file structure as the physical storage for the Data Warehouse, there is always the option to do so. From a budget perspective there has to be two main objectives, assuming finite resources:

1. Get the most out of the resources by using each product to its limit before considering another product. In other words, a 'best-of-breed' approach should only be used out of necessity, rather than by choice. Why use different products for each part of the Data Warehouse process if they are not needed?

2. Do not expend resources on products that take the Data Warehouse down a 'dead-end'. When considering how to spend the finite resources available, ensure that they are expended on products that work well with other products. If their limits are reached, then there must be a 'natural' next step, instead of frantic 'back peddling'. In the design of the Data Warehouse, always be thinking of the 'natural' next step, so that if it is not actually planned for, it is at least considered.

In-House Skills

Never underestimate the cost of training. There are two costs involved here: money and time. If need be, start the structure of the Data Warehouse using products that are already known to the technical implementers of the Data Warehouse because this saves the costs of training, in the short run. Even if the long-term plan is to move to other, less familiar products, there is a lot to be said for starting a new and unfamiliar project with tools that are understood.

One reason for taking advantage of existing skills, above-and-beyond the obvious savings in time and money in the short term, is that in the majority of cases, the first try at a Data Warehousing project ends up being a learning exercise. Enterprises very often backtrack after learning many lessons from their first experience with Data Warehousing. By using familiar tools, there will not be any confusion over which lessons are being learned about Data Warehousing, and those that are being learned through the use of a new product.

5.3 Using SAS/ACCESS Tools for Data Extraction

One of the most powerful and convenient features of SAS software is its ability to use almost any format of data on any computer platform. Note that the key concept here is not that it can access almost any format of data, but that it can use that data. It is absolutely essential in a Data Warehouse environment that the designers understand that access in itself is not enough. The Data Warehouse design process goes beyond the access, into the use of data. SAS software has a multitude of tools that give the designer of the Data Warehouse the options to ensure, as much as possible, that the users will be able to fulfill their enterprise needs. The access to data cannot be viewed in isolation of the use of that data because the former is of no benefit without the latter.

The benefits of SAS having this flexibility in reading external file formats on almost any platform are felt both from a Data Warehouse front-end and back-end perspective. Indeed, SAS goes beyond being able to just read these external formats. It can usually manipulate them in place or write out to them. This means that not only does SAS give the Data Warehouse designer the option of using the software's native file structure and associated analysis and data manipulation tools, but it can act as the glue that holds the Data Warehouse together.

From a Data Warehousing back-end perspective, this means that SAS can be used to extract data from the source system, validate, scrub, and transform that data, then write it out to the required Data Warehouse storage format. To put this into perspective, consider the following situation: SAS can read data from an IMS Database on an IBM mainframe, convert it to a SAS format, and move it directly to a UNIX platform for validation, scrubbing, and transformation. The detail information can then be moved into an ORACLE Database format, numerous Multi-Dimensional Databases can be created within SAS, and moved to Windows NT servers for individual departments to use. Three platforms and four different file structures, while leaving all options open for the inevitable changes that are par-for-the-course in Data Warehousing environments. This is part of the SAS Multiple Engine Architecture (MEA) that allows the users of the software to use and exploit data from virtually any external format.

From a Data Warehousing front-end perspective, it is possible to use all the extensive analysis and presentation tools that SAS offers without the data necessarily residing in the SAS native file structure. If the format of the back end of the Data Warehouse changes, then all that will be needed from the front end perspective is to change the pointers that reference the data. For instance, suppose a custom front end is built to run a series of parameterized reports on data from a DB2 Database that resides on an IBM mainframe. The situation then changes and it becomes necessary to move that structure to a UNIX platform. The only things that need to change in the front end are the pointers to the remote computer (i.e., from the IBM to the UNIX machine) and the name of the tables (assuming the internal layout of each of the tables remains constant). The skill in Data Warehousing is as much anticipating the future as it is in solving the present.

Special Topic:
Should the Native SAS File Structure Be Used in the Data Warehouse?

This topic is one that evokes many emotional responses. Users of SAS tend to become defensive about the use of the SAS file format, and non-users tend to downplay its Database features. There are three major issues that should be considered when addressing this question:

1. What are the Database Management features that are needed in the Data Warehouse that SAS does not have?
2. What are the performance issues of using SAS instead of other data structures?
3. What are the budget constraints?

The first question, one of features, cannot be answered easily. It is unusual in a Data Warehousing environment, for instance, to need rollback, recovery, and locking, which SAS currently does not support. Other database products, however, have features that might be of use in the design of the Data Warehouse: ORACLE, for instance, has a feature that will automatically log any changes made to an Operational System. The Log can then be used to update the Data Warehouse, therefore ensuring that only items that have changed will be refreshed. This feature is inherent within the software and could easily reduce load times into the Data Warehouse. There are, however, severe overheads to a full-blown RDBMS (Relational Data Base Management System), one being that they definitely need dedicated Database Administrators to make them effective. The SAS structure is far easier to administer and tune than the majority of RDBMS products currently available. SAS is, in most cases, a very good option to consider. In making this decision, it is essential to consider the features that an RDBMS will give you that SAS cannot (and vice-versa), and then decide upon whether these features are needed.

The second issue, one of performance, is also not clear-cut. Performance depends on a multitude of factors including hardware, database design, and the access patterns required by the users. One factor to consider, along with the above, is that if SAS is being used as the front-end tool to access the Data Warehouse, then it naturally follows that SAS running against a SAS structure will be faster than SAS running against an external data structure. Most RDBMS packages were originally designed for use in transaction based systems, where very fast access to isolated, minute pieces of data is needed. RDBMS are not explicitly designed for fast, sequential access, which is in essence what is needed in a Data Warehousing environment. There are currently several products available that are specifically designed for fast sequential access, but many of these tend to be read-only structures. In many cases, this is not of any concern, but it should be looked at strategically before committing to them.

The third question, that of budget, is also important. Remember that if you have SAS as an access tool to your Data Warehouse, you automatically have all the features of its native data structure. This means that if there are no extenuating reasons to use another structure, then why bother? All implementations of a Data Warehouse have resource limitations, and so, it makes sense to use these finite resources effectively. Leveraging the use of each software component to use it to its maximum effect and capabilities makes perfect financial sense. Why buy a tractor to pull the plough when a horse you already own will perform the job equally as well?

Actually, from a SAS perspective, the answer to the question is that it really doesn't matter. SAS handles almost any file format on any platform, so the SAS vs. external SAS file-format argument is largely irrelevant and time consuming. Instead, look at what the data will be used for, the best tool available to perform the task, and finally, look at which file format will best suit the analysis tool. If it happens to be a SAS format, then fine, and if not .... then also, fine.

One of the products that SAS software offers is SAS/ACCESS. There are many different SAS/ACCESS engines, depending on what kind of external data needs to be accessed. All the engines, from a user's perspective, work in very much the same way. Behind the scenes, there are many differences because each distinct data structure will require very different techniques to be accessed. These differences are not of importance when using SAS/ACCESS within a Data Warehouse environment. The important part is that after it is understood how to use SAS/ACCESS when looking at one data source, then a new set of techniques does not have to be learned to access subsequent data sources.[4]

> **One of the key benefits within a Data Warehouse environment for using the native SAS structure is that the data stored on any medium (e.g., tape, disk) is accessed using exactly the same code, except for the libname. That is not the case with the major Relational Database products. This means that data archived from the Data Warehouse can be accessed using the same code as that still online. The benefits of this are the reduction of code design and maintenance, and improved access to data for the Warehouse users.**

Installing SAS/ACCESS

As with any situation where more than one product is dependent upon another to work, there is a degree of understanding and configuration that has to take place to successfully install SAS/ACCESS software. This installation process is similar (up-to-a-point) with every different access mode, but due to the divergence of each one, there has to be some customized set-up. This is always described in the installation instructions that are sent with SAS software, but there are many additional sources available to ensure that this installation is made as efficiently as possible.[5] It is usual that there is some set-up at the Operating System level and the Database level, especially for the non-PC data access methods.

As with most software products that require between-product communication, correct set-up is essential and unavoidable. The resources that are available for successful SAS/ACCESS installation and use are extensive (in

---

[4] Note that in Version 7 of SAS, using SAS/ACCESS will become easier because the need to build explicit 'access' information and 'views' into data tables in external formats will no longer be necessary.

[5] On the SAS Web site, Technical Support has a series of excellent technical articles that are a resource for all kinds of product installation. These can be found at the following address: www.sas.com/techsup/download/techsup.

terms of installation notes, documentation, user papers[6] and SAS Institute Technical Support), which can all lead to an informed and therefore smooth product installation.

The Three Methods of Using SAS/ACCESS

Three principal ways that SAS/ACCESS can be used within a Data Warehouse environment are to read, write, or extract information from a data source external to SAS.

Using SQL[7]

SAS will allow the user to create SQL that is specific to the external file format. This external product can then resolve the SQL, and only the results are returned to SAS for further processing. It is easier to understand this process by example. Consider the following:

```
❶ PROC SQL;
❷   CONNECT TO DB2(SSID=db2db);
❸   CREATE TABLE sastable AS
❹   SELECT * FROM CONNECTION TO DB2(
❺   SELECT * FROM db2.db2table);
❻   %PUT &SQLXRC &SQLXMSG;
❼   DISCONNECT FROM DB2;
❽ QUIT;
```

❶   This tells SAS that SQL code will follow and begins the procedure.

❷   The connection is made to an IBM DB2 database. This tells SAS that a connection will be necessary, and that the specific DB2 subsystem (SSID) in which the data resides is '**db2db**'. Connections to other external formats obviously require different parameters because these are dependent upon the data source itself. Other examples for line 2 are

CONNECT TO ODBC(DSN=datasrce);

where the connection is to an ODBC data source. This, in effect, gives the SAS user access to any ODBC compliant data sources that have a driver installed. Remember that just because you have a product that might be ODBC compliant does not mean that you have the associated ODBC driver. Often, drivers are obtained from third-party vendors

---

[6] The Proceedings from the SUGI (SAS USER GROUP INTERNATIONAL) conference (SAS Institute Inc., *Proceedings of the Twenty-Second Annual SAS® User Group International Conference*) alone has 15 indexed references to SAS/ACCESS, all of which will be valuable background.

[7] SQL stands for Structured Query Language. It is a standardized, high-level language for extracting, altering, creating, and manipulating data files that reside in a relational database.

rather than the manufacturers of the data source itself. [8] For a discussion of ODBC drivers, see Special Topic "ODBC" at the end of this chapter.

Or

```
CONNECT TO ORACLE    (USER=myuser
                     PASS=password
                     PATH='oracle based physical reference');
```

In this situation, the ensuing access will be to ORACLE tables. The USER and PASS are security options required by the ORACLE Database and must be set-up by your ORACLE administrator. The PATH= option references not only the physical location of the tables being accessed, but also the communication method. With ORACLE, the tables you need to access need not be on the same computer on which SAS is running. Indeed, it is possible and, from a Data Warehouse perspective, potentially desirable to have SAS running on one computer and ORACLE on another.[9] This can be achieved as long as ORACLE SQL*NET is installed on the same computer as SAS.

The three different **CONNECT TO** options presented here are not intended as a 'how to', but to illustrate how different data access modes need different and specific parameters for a successful connection.

❸ Line 3 in the code is native SAS SQL that will create a SAS data file from the result set created by the query.

❹ Line 4 tells SAS to use everything (**SELECT ***) from the data returned from the **CONNECTION TO DB2**. All the processing being performed up to this point in the query is done by SAS.

❺ After the **CONNECTION TO DB2** code in line 4, the subsequent code is passed through to DB2 for processing. All the code contained within the parentheses must be DB2 compliant SQL. In other words, the SQL must reference the DB2 tables as though it were DB2 doing it itself. DB2 column names and table names are therefore used, and only the SQL features that DB2 supports will be understood. For instance, in Version 3 of DB2, only inner joins are supported, so if an outer join were asked for, the query would be rejected by DB2 (even though SAS does support outer joins). In the example (line 5), all that is asked of the DB2 engine is to return (pass back) everything that is contained in the **db2.db2table** to SAS.

---

[8] For more information about ODBC in Data Warehousing, see the Special Topic, "ODBC," at the end of this chapter.

[9] This would mean that the application processing (e.g., SAS performing a complex statistical analysis) and the database processing (e.g., ORACLE extracting the 100,000 records from a 4 million-record file) would be performed by different computers. The ORACLE computer could be optimized for Database processing and the SAS computer for CPU intensive calculations.

⑥ The **%PUT** statement will write out to the Log any return codes (messages) from the native database (in this case DB2). These messages will be contained in the SAS macro variables **SQLXMSG** and **SQLXRC**. Without this line of code, if the request to the native database were to fail, there would be no way to know why.

⑦ The connection to the DB2 database is ended.

⑧ The SQL procedure is ended.

This method of using data from an external data source is very elegant. This is a form of Client/Server computing, with SAS being the Client, and the underlying database being the Server. Only the data that SAS needs to complete its tasks are returned (passed back) to SAS. This reduces the amount of translation that must be done to change the external data files into a SAS format. Consider the following snippet of code:

```
⑨   PROC SQL;
⑩     CONNECT TO DB2(SSID=db2db);
⑪     CREATE TABLE sastable AS
⑫     SELECT DISTINCT col1 col2 col3
⑬     FROM CONNECTION TO DB2(
⑭     SELECT * FROM db2.db2table);
⑮     %PUT &SQLXRC &SQLXMSG;
⑯     DISCONNECT FROM DB2;
⑰   QUIT;
```

This code is almost identical to the code in the first example, except for line 12. An explanation for the lines 9-11 and 13-17 can be found in 1-8 above. Line 12, however, specifies that only the three columns **COL1-COL3** are actually needed. Line 14 (which is part of the code actually passed through to DB2) specifies that the DB2 engine retrieve every column from the table **db2.db2table**. What would actually happen, is that the DB2 engine would get every column and pass it to SAS. SAS would then look at its own SELECT statement and use only the three columns named. This means that there are potentially extensive wasted resources because more data is being passed to SAS than is needed. A better way to write this code would be

```
⑱   PROC SQL;
⑲     CONNECT TO DB2(SSID=db2db);
⑳     CREATE TABLE sastable AS
㉑     SELECT *
㉒     FROM CONNECTION TO DB2(
㉓     SELECT DISTINCT db2col1,db2col2,db2col3
㉔     FROM db2.db2table);
㉕     %PUT &SQLXRC &SQLXMSG;
㉖     DISCONNECT FROM DB2;
㉗   QUIT;
```

The difference here is that the request for the distinct three columns is made to DB2 because that information is within the parentheses (between lines 22 and 24). This forces the DB2 engine to perform more processing (creating the distinct values of the three columns) and minimizes the data that has to be passed to SAS. One of the major aims in using any of the tools available within SAS for access to external file formats is to minimize the volume of data that needs to be converted into the SAS format. This also holds true when using a SAS view of an external file format (see the Section "Creating SAS Views of the External Data Source" later in this chapter). Sometimes, the native database engine will not be able to perform some of the tasks that are needed, so it will be necessary for SAS to do the work.

This pass-through technique illustrated above by accessing DB2 data is very similar in concept and execution to almost all formats of data. To use Pass-Through SQL, it is necessary to have the relevant SAS/ACCESS module, even though the SQL procedure within SAS is part of base SAS software. Although the concept will be identical for accessing different data sources, there could well be a big difference in the code that is actually passed-through to the external data engine. This is because each engine has its own peculiarities that must be conformed to. This means that to use Pass-Through SQL, it is necessary to understand the syntax required by the external data source. This is not as big a problem as it sounds because in the SAS Query Window, which is part of base SAS, this code is automatically gener-ated if alternative access modes are requested.[10] Most products do have a fairly similar 'flavor' of SQL, but there are often subtle differences that can lead to problems.

Where Might Pass-Through SQL Be Used in the Data Warehouse?

This technique of accessing data residing in an external format will almost always be used in a Data Warehouse where it is advantageous to use the data source's native engine as much as possible. This is usually the case (as in the example above). If SAS were used to perform the entire query, then all the data would have to be converted into a SAS format for the query to be completed. Another obvious problem is that if the data is passed to SAS, then the indexing[11] that might be inherent in the external database will not be available for use. The alternative to this situation is to index the tables in SAS after the data has been converted, which might or might not (depend-ing on the query), result in a faster resolution of the query.

---

[10] See: SAS Institute Inc. *SAS® Guide to the SQL Query Window: Usage and Reference, Version 6, First Edition,* Cary, NC: SAS Institute Inc., 1995. 167pp., pages 124-125.
[11] See the Special Topic, "Indexing in the Data Warehouse," in Chapter 6 for a discussion on indexes and their use in Data Warehousing.

> *It is advisable, unless there are definite mitigating circumstances, to use the native data engine of the data source as much as possible. When using SAS/ACCESS, make it a rule to only pass to SAS the data it needs to perform the analysis. If the native engine can do the work, then that is where it should be performed.*

Pass-through SQL is useful in both the back end and the front end of the Data Warehouse. It can be used when loading the data into the Warehouse from the Operational System, and it can be used to extract information for manipulation, analysis, and presentation. One of the big advantages of pass-through SQL is that the designer has complete control over which engine completes the processing. There is no ambiguity. Therefore, it is easier to configure the database engines accordingly.

In the back end, the SQL used will tend to be static. This means that because the extraction process will remain fairly constant each time it occurs (thus making the Data Warehouse itself consistent) then this SQL will not change. Static SQL can be thoroughly tested to ensure that it is efficient. Most databases have a process for testing SQL (e.g., in DB2, an 'explain' can be performed), so that the passed-through portion of the code should be tested before being implemented. This usually needs the assistance of database administrators.

In the front-end of the Data Warehouse, the SQL is rarely static. Dynamic SQL by its nature does not go through an efficiency optimization process. It is therefore very difficult to ensure that the pass-through SQL is as efficient as it could be. In Data Warehouses where access to the data is controlled by an application (where the users do not directly access the tables, but do so through a custom front-end) then the inherent design can ensure that there is some degree of control over the SQL. In a Data Warehouse where the users access the data directly, by referencing table names and columns, it is virtually impossible to ensure efficient SQL. This is where the importance of training the users comes into play. The more flexibility, then the more training that will be needed, to ensure, as much as is possible, that the requests for access to the Data Warehouse are formulated efficiently.

Creating SAS Views of the External Data Source

Understanding the concept of a 'view' is essential when designing a Data Warehouse:

- A view contains no data.
- A view is purely a description of a single access into data. Not until the view is actually used is any of the data actually accessed.

- Views can be as simple or as complex as the designer of the Data Warehouse needs them to be.
- Views can be generic (where it contains a description of an entire table) or specific (where it contains a description containing certain columns from a table subset by predefined criteria).

Because views define a 'roadmap' into the data, rather than the data itself, they can have a very large role in the design of a Data Warehouse. For instance, a view, or a series of views could be considered as a *virtual Data Mart*. Views could be created that give a specific department the access patterns to data that they require, without actually extracting that data. The enormous advantage to this is that, if the access pattern changes (as it invariably will), the data in the Data Mart does not need to be re-created, only the views would need to be changed. The disadvantage of this approach and, one that very often makes this approach untenable, is that to resolve a view can be very expensive from a computer resource perspective. For instance, if a view is created that joins four tables together, one of which might be in a data format external to SAS, then every single time the view is used, the tables have to be joined. This might be impractical if the view has to be used multiple times, but maybe not if its use is very infrequent.

Types of Views Created in SAS

SAS creates three major types of views:

- DATA Step Views:[12] These views are simply stored DATA step[13] programs that result in the creation of a data file. Every time the view is used, it is as if the DATA step is being run. This is the most flexible form of SAS view because it is not limited to a single input source, and it can actually update the underlying input data.
- SQL Views: These views contain the virtual result set from an SQL query. Although very powerful, they cannot, in the current release of SAS, update the input source.
- SAS/ACCESS Views: This is a view into a single table from a data source external to SAS. It is possible to update the underlying data using this type of view, but it is restricted to only one table.

---

[12] For examples and advantages of DATA Step Views, see: First, Steven, "Faster SAS® Jobs and Fewer Passes Via DATA Step Views" contained in SAS Institute Inc., *Proceedings of the Twenty-Second Annual SAS® User Group International Conference*, p.1474.

[13] A SAS DATA step is a series of actions performed on one or multiple SAS files (which are from any data source that has been pre-defined to SAS) using the SAS language. For a further discussion, see: Delwiche, Lora D., and Slaughter, Susan J., *The Little SAS Book: A Primer*, Cary, NC: SAS Institute Inc., 1995. 228pp., pages 14-17.

Although the first two types of views are very useful (given the correct situation) for accessing external data, the SAS/ACCESS view is the most important. It is possible to use Pass-Through SQL to perform the same function as a SAS/ACCESS view, except that it will not be possible to change the underlying data.

Creating a SAS/ACCESS View

Creating a SAS/ACCESS view is a two-part process. An Access Descriptor must first be created. This *Access Descriptor* contains a generic description of the table that is being used in the view. With the majority of the different access modes that SAS can facilitate, creating an Access Descriptor is very simple indeed. In a Data Warehouse environment, this Access Descriptor might describe a table in an Operational System. For instance, it might describe a General Ledger that is stored in an IMS-DL/I hierarchical format on an IIBM OS/390 (MVS) system. Another example would be a table that is part of an Order Entry system, which contains a unique list of customers that is contained in an ORACLE table on a UNIX system. After an Access Descriptor is created, an unlimited number of views can be built based upon this one descriptor.

The Access Descriptor

There are two ways to create the Access Descriptor. It can be done by using a full-screen entry mode or by using code. In a Data Warehousing environment, it is more likely that the descriptor will be created by using code. It is unlikely that an end-user would be creating Access Descriptors because Descriptors are part of the design of the Data Warehouse. If a full-screen mode were to be used, then the Access Descriptor would be created in the Access Window, which can be reached from within SAS by selecting **Globals ➤ Access ➤ Access database files**. The following code could also be used:

```
❶ PROC ACCESS DBMS=oracle;
❷   CREATE myfile.customer.ACCESS;
❸   USER=myname;
❹   PASS=mypw;
❺   TABLE=customers;
❻   PATH="@oracust";
❼   RENAME customer_id=cust_id;
❽ RUN;
```

This is a very simple example of how to create an Access Descriptor. Certain parameters are needed by the external database (in this case lines 4, 5, and 6 all contain information that is specific to ORACLE). Other databases need different information. With most databases, simple code as shown in lines 1-8 will be enough to create the Access Descriptor, however, some databases need much more information. For instance, the IBM IMS-DL/I is not relational but has a hierarchical structured data organization, and each item of data will need to be explicitly stated in the creation of the descriptor.[14] The SAS/Warehouse Administrator will automatically generate code to create the Access Descriptors that are needed. The Access Descriptor definition itself is contained in a SAS library, but it cannot be used for any purpose other than to create a view.

Each different access mode (e.g., ORACLE, ODBC, SYBASE, INFORMIX) will require that the code above differs in some or many ways. The particular differences required by each access mode are very well outlined in the documentation that comes with the SAS/ACCESS product,[15] but the principle in each case is identical. The Access Descriptor is simply an underlying definition of the source data so that views can then be built to actually access the data.

Creating the View from the Access Descriptor

After the Access Descriptor has been created, creating a view is a very simple process. This can be done in a full-screen interactive mode or, as is more likely, will be done with code. To create a view in interactive mode, the same process of moving to the ACCESS procedure window will be used because the view is created from the same set of screens as the Access Descriptor.

Assuming that the Access Descriptor has been created already (using the code shown in the previous example) then the following example would create a view:

```
❶ PROC ACCESS DBMS=oracle
❷   ACCDESC=myfile.customer.ACCESS;
❸   CREATE myfile.custview1.VIEW;
❹   SELECT custname cust_id custaddr custzip;
❺   SUBSET WHERE custzip =: '91';
❻   RUN;
```

This code will create a view named **myfile.custview1.VIEW** based upon the Access Descriptor **myfile.customer.access**. Only four columns are to be selected and the data, when converted from the ORACLE table, will be automatically subset where the column **custzip** starts with '91'.

There are many other options available to create both Access Descriptors and associated views, but for the purpose of illustrating their use within the Data Warehouse environment, the above example illustrates the major points.

---

[14] See: Jacobs, Charles A. and Willis, Kimberly, "Tips and Tricks for Using SAS/ACCESS DATA Step Interface to IMS-DL/I," *Observations: The Technical Journal for SAS Software Users*, First Quarter, 1997.

[15] For example, see: SAS Institute Inc., *SAS/ACCESS® Software for Relational Databases: Reference, Version 6, First Edition*, Cary, NC: SAS Institute Inc., 1994. 196pp.

Guidelines for Creating Views

When designing the Data Warehouse, there are several very important considerations to take into account.

1. When SAS/ACCESS views are being used in the back end of the Data Warehouse, the RENAME= option should be used to its maximum capability.

2. After a view has been created, then the underlying Access Descriptor is no longer needed. This means that after a view has been created, the Access Descriptor can be deleted.

3. Views should contain only the columns that are actually going to be needed.

Using the RENAME=Option

One of the key factors in the success of the Data Warehouse is to ensure that there is a consistent naming convention. SAS will automatically rename the columns from the external database to fit its own conventions.[16] Very often, this renaming is adequate, but there is nothing to ensure that it is. It is best to explicitly rename every column being defined to the Access Descriptor. The same rules should be applied to the front end of the Data Warehouse, but if the users are creating their own views, this will be a great deal harder to enforce.

Deleting the Access Descriptor

There are obvious reasons why deleting the Access Descriptor is not advisable. For instance, if new views were needed, then the Access Descriptor would need to be re-created. However, there is a far more important implication to be resolved than the view not being dependent upon the Access Descriptor: that is, if the underlying structure of the external database table changes, then every single view will need to be changed.

Creating Access Descriptors and Views Dynamically

A very good reason for the argument to create Access Descriptors and views dynamically is presented below. The following code illustrates one technique of creating Access Descriptors and views dynamically. In this situation, SCL (Screen Control Language[17]) is being used, but it could just have been as easily constructed using Macro Language.

---

[16] This will become less important with Version 7 of SAS because it will have the ability to store 32 character column names, and the need to explicitly create Access Descriptors will no longer be necessary.

[17] Screen Control Language is part of SAS/AF that is the application design component of SAS, which enables the construction of graphical user front ends.

This simple example assumes that the underlying external database table has only three columns, and that we have a metadata file in a SAS format that contains the database names for the columns in the table and the associated SAS column names. This table looks like this:

DBNAME	SASNAME	TABLENUM
name_of_client	cli_name	1
number_of_employees	emp_num	1
annual-revenue	annl_rev	1
product_number	prod_num	2
product_name	prod_nme	2
sales_amount	slse_amt	3
sales_volume	slse_vol	3

Table=SASALIAS

There is also a metadata table that contains the list of all tables that are available to the Data Warehouse. This table looks like this:

DBTABLE	SASTABLE	TABLENUM
creator.client_information	cli_info	1
creator.product_list	prodlist	2
creator.sales_info	slseinfo	3

Table=TABALIAS

In this example, let's suppose that the user has the ability to access the tables through a front end that has been developed using SAS/AF software. The users can select the table that they want to use from the file `tabalias`, and the columns that they want to use from the file `sasalias`. This is done by the users selecting their requirements from lists in a SAS frame,[18] and the parameters they select being passed through to the labeled section of code that will automatically create the Access Descriptor and view.

In our example, assume that a user has selected the table `client_information` and the columns `name_of_client` and `annual_revenue` from that table. The table name will be passed to the code below as the variable `dbtable`, the corresponding SAS name for the table will be in the SCL

---

[18] Designing SAS/AF applications is outside the scope of this book. An introduction to the SAS application facility can be found in: SAS Institute Inc., *SAS/AF® Software: FRAME Application Development Concepts, Version 6, First Edition,* Cary, NC: SAS Institute Inc., 1995.

variable **sastable**, and the column selections will be in the SCL list **collist**. This SCL list will contain the DB2 column name as the item and the corresponding SAS name for the column as the item name.

```
VIEWCRT:                              * Begin labeled section of code;

SUBMIT;                               *Submit code to SAS;
 PROC ACCESS DBMS=DB2;
 CREATE work.&sastable.ACCESS;
 SSID=db2a;
 TABLE=&dbtable;
 ASSIGN=YES;
 RENAME
ENDSUBMIT;

DO I=1 TO LISTLEN(collist);           *Loop over all columns selected;
 DBNAME=GETVARC(COLLIST,I);
 SASNAME=NAMEITEM(COLLIST,I);
 SUBMIT;
  &DBNAME=&SASNAME
 ENDSUBMIT;
END;

SUBMIT ;
 ;
 CREATE work.&sastable.VIEW;
 SELECT
ENDSUBMIT;
DO I=1 TO LISTLEN(collist);
 DBNAME=GETVARC(COLLIST,I);
 SUBMIT;
 &DBNAME
 ENDSUBMIT;
END;

SUBMIT CONTINUE;
 ;
 RUN;
 ENDSUBMIT;
return;
```

For those already familiar with SCL, the preceding is a simple program that allows for the interaction of SAS/AF capabilities with those of the other SAS products. The program presented is simple because all it does is to use the SAS/AF facility to collect parameters (in this case, the DB2 table and columns that are required) and pass those through to a SAS/ACCESS procedure so that the user can dynamically create a view into a DB2 table. Understanding the code itself is less important than understanding the concept. Views are more efficient when they are built for a specific situation. Because situations are not always predictable, it follows that views must be dynamically created. Within SAS, there are a myriad of options available to do this. The SCL code above is one of those techniques.

After the SCL code is run, it creates the following, which is submitted to the ACCESS procedure for execution by SAS. The shaded items show the parameterized options that could change every time the user requests a different table and columns.

```
PROC ACCESS DBMS=db2;
CREATE work.cli_info.ACCESS;
 SSID=db2a;
 TABLE=creator.client_information;
 ASSIGN=YES;
 RENAME
name_of client=cli_name
annual_revenue=annl_rev
 ;
 CREATE work.cli_info.VIEW;
SELECT
 name_of_client
annual_revenue
 ;
 RUN;
```

This dynamic view can then be used within SAS for any reporting and analysis that needs to be completed by the user. Note that both the Access Descriptor and the associated view are stored in WORK files, so they will be deleted when the user's SAS session ends.

There are two very important advantages that dynamic creation of views have:

- Reduction in Maintenance Overhead: The first of these advantages is that it is not necessary to create beforehand all the views that users need. Let them dynamically create them themselves. This reduces maintenance overhead and makes the Data Warehouse more adaptable to change. All that needs to be adjusted is the metadata itself. If any of the underlying metadata tables change, then the options the users are given should also change automatically. Additionally, metadata itself should be generated automatically. For example, the column dbname in the table sasalias (used in the above example) could be populated automatically from the DB2 system catalog, which would be updated whenever the Data Warehouse is refreshed.

> *As much as is viable, let the Data Warehouse depend on the underlying metadata. Changes to metadata should automatically be seen from the front end of the Data Warehouse without any maintenance to those systems.*

- **Creation of Views That Fit Particular Specific Requirements**: The second advantage to creating dynamic views is one of efficiency. It would have been possible to create a view containing all the columns from the table `creator.client_information` and let the user access this. Although a simple option, this is not a good one. If a view contains all the columns from an external database, then all the data contained within every column will have to be passed to SAS for processing **even if that column is not needed in the specific analysis**. Therefore, the amount of unnecessary overhead could be vast. If the view only contains the columns needed for the analysis, then this makes it very efficient.

If possible, the SUBSET option should also be used with the view. Whenever possible, SAS asks the native database engine (in this case, the DB2 engine) to perform the subsetting, thus saving again the amount of data that SAS has to actually receive. The next version of SAS (Version 7) will display marked improvement in its use of the native database engine.

Note that the creation of Access Descriptors and associated views takes up minimal computer resources, so this dynamic approach does not effectively impact the user of the view.

Summary: Putting SAS/ACCESS Views into a Data Warehousing Perspective

SAS/ACCESS views are easy to create and easy to use because they look just like SAS data files. They are a nice way to hide complex underlying structures from the Data Warehouse itself or from the users of the Data Warehouse.

There are two major roles that SAS/ACCESS views can play. They can be used in the back end of the Data Warehouse as a means to accessing the source systems from which the Data Warehouse is populated. This capability will mean that the views could be used as one of the techniques to load the Data Warehouse. This role, however, is probably better filled by using Pass-Through SQL (see above), because it is of primary importance to have complete control over which engine (SAS or the native database) should perform which task.

The second role that SAS/ACCESS views can fulfill is in the front end of the Data Warehouse, to give SAS users a transparent technique to access data that is stored in a format external to SAS itself. This is a far more likely candidate for usage of SAS/ACCESS views, especially in a situation where they can be created dynamically, based upon the specific access pattern that is currently needed. These views in this context are especially useful because they can then be applied to any of the thousands of analysis options that SAS affords its users. In this situation, Pass-Through SQL is less useful, due to the inherent limitation of SQL in the analysis of data.

Writing Data to an External File Format

To round out the flexibility that SAS/ACCESS contains, there is also the ability to write data out to external file formats. In the previous sections, there were examples of the way SAS can incorporate external formats by using them in place or by moving them into a native SAS format. This means, within a Data Warehousing environment, that SAS has the ability to act as the 'data format broker'. It is very important in the Data Warehouse to not only have the data physically residing in the most optimal location, but to have this data in the most optimal format for the role it has to fulfill. It is not, and should not, be necessary to limit the Data Warehouse to one data format. It should be possible to use the correct format for the correct situation.

To illustrate this point, consider a situation where data from a General Ledger residing in an ORACLE database on an IBM OS/390 mainframe is required so that multiple time-series analyses can be run. The results are then selectively made available in a Microsoft Excel spreadsheet format for financial modeling. One of the many routes that could be taken here is to replicate the General Ledger every month and move this, as is, into the Data Warehouse. Pass-Through SQL is then run against the replicated General Ledger, which will extract the information into SAS data files within the Data Warehouse. Every month the Pass-Through SQL is run to refresh this part of the Data Warehouse, and then a batch job is scheduled to run the multiple time-series analyses using SAS/ETS.[19] It has been determined that it is more efficient to extract the ORACLE data into a SAS format so the time-series analyses can run against a native SAS format. The output from the analyses are then moved to a Windows NT server where they are converted to Excel spreadsheets ready for the financial modeling.

In this situation, SAS could be used to transform the ORACLE data into SAS data for the analyses. SAS would then perform the analyses and through SAS/CONNECT,[20] upload the information to the Windows NT server. SAS running on the server would then convert the resultant data into the Excel format. Except for the ORACLE replication piece that moved the Operational General Ledger into the Data Warehouse (a piece that SAS

---

[19] SAS/ETS is the Econometric Time Series module that is specifically designed for all types of temporal analyses.

[20] See Chapter 8 on Client/Server computing in a Data Warehouse environment.

could have performed if necessary) all the other tasks were completed by using SAS. The only piece that has not yet been covered is the conversion from the SAS format to the Excel spreadsheet. In this case, using SAS/ACCESS software, we would use the DBLOAD procedure. This is the final part of SAS/ACCESS; the piece that will allow conversion into an external file format.

The DBLOAD procedure is very straightforward and does not need much explanation. As with many sophisticated tools that are now available, the skill is not so much in knowing how to use them, but when to use them. Using the situation outlined above where a SAS file needs to be converted to a Microsoft Excel format, the following snippet of code will fulfill that function:[21]

```
❶ PROC DBLOAD DBMS=xls DATA=warehse.sasdata;
❷ PATH='s:\windows\directory\name\excelnme.xls';
❸ VERSION=5;
❹ PUTNAMES=YES;
❺ RUN;
```

❶ This tells SAS that you want to load a Microsoft Excel spreadsheet from the data currently stored in the file `warehse.sasdata`. Note that this file could be a view (either a SAS/ACCESS, a DATA step, or an SQL view) into yet another external file format.

❷ Contains the name of the Excel file that will be created.

❸ Tells SAS which version of Excel is being used.

❹ The `PUTNAMES=YES` option tells SAS to write the names of each column into the first row of the spreadsheet.

As with other SAS/ACCESS products, there are a multitude of different parameters, based upon the file format to which the data is being moved. Not only is it possible (using the DBLOAD procedure) to move data from one file structure to another but also from one storage format to another, without using any disk (DASD) whatsoever.

The use of the DBLOAD procedure is easy to understand. It is one of the ways that SAS supports the movement of data from one structure to another. From a Data Warehouse perspective, it is another tool that the Data Warehouse designer has to ensure that the data is in the correct format for the particular processing that needs to be performed.

---

[21] For more information on the parameters needed to write out to external file formats, see the product associated documentation. More detail about writing out to Excel files can be found in: SAS Institute Inc., *SAS/ACCESS® Software for PC File Formats: Reference, Version 6, First Edition*, Cary, NC: SAS Institute Inc., 1995. 226pp., p. 8-19.

The key to the data design within the Data Warehouse is more than just the modeling from an organizational aspect; the data should be modeled from an internal structure aspect also. The designer should not be limited by artificial technical limitations that restrict this structural modeling. The structure of the data should be dependent upon what it will be used for, and not restricted by a shortsighted, inflexible decision that is usually made before the real requirements are fully assessed. Time and time again, we address one of the basic rules of Data Warehousing: if the enterprise requires information in one way today, it can be guaranteed that tomorrow, it will need it in a totally different way. This means that flexibility should be the fulcrum around which the design of the Data Warehouse should take place. The *What happens if.... ?* question is the one that should most frequently be asked when designing the Data Warehouse. Whatever design decisions are made, there should be answers to the *What happens if ....?* question to ensure that the current decision will not lead down an expensive and time-consuming 'blind alley'.

5.4 Other SAS Structures Available to the Data Warehouse

The discussion so far in this chapter has been concentrated around the native SAS file format and how SAS can read other formats. SAS has two other formats that can be used within the Data Warehouse.

The Multi-Dimensional Database

The first of these is the *Multi-Dimensional Database,* which is a way that information can be stored in a summarized fashion to enable extremely fast and flexible access. This format is best used in situations where information will be used for specific purposes. This does not mean that there should necessarily be limits to the way the data can be accessed, but that there is some knowledge as to the expected purpose to which the data will be put. SAS/MDDB will not be covered in this chapter, but details on its function and how it is created can be found in Chapter 4.

The SAS Scalable Performance Data Server

The second alternative file format that is especially designed for a Data Warehouse environment is the Scalable Performance Data Server, which is a separate SAS product to take advantage of parallel processing. To understand the Scalable Performance Data Server it is necessary to understand a little about why it might be worth incorporating the Scalable Performance Data Server into the Data Warehouse and secondly the architecture it incorporates.

Any data that is stored in the Scalable Performance Data Server format will be referred to as *Scalable Performance Data Server data* and any data stored in a native SAS format will be referred to as *SAS data*, to avoid any confusion between the two.

Scalable Performance Data Server Features and Benefits in the Data Warehouse Environment

1. Scalable Performance Data Server will store massive amounts of data. *This will give the Data Warehouse designer more flexibility in creating extremely large denormalized files required to meet the enterprise needs demanded of the Warehouse.*

2. Scalable Performance Data Server is designed for fast access to data. *Fast access not only means that individual requests from the Data Warehouse can be processed more quickly, but also means that more requests can be processed.*

3. Scalable Performance Data Server effectively uses the Client/Server model[22] so that each platform is used to its best advantage. *This increases the flexibility for the designer, so that the Data Warehouse can be flexibly configured to balance computer loads with user requirements.*

4. Scalable Performance Data Server can reduce network traffic. *As an extension to the Client/Server architecture of Scalable Performance Data Server, only information that the user actually needs is extracted and passed through the network. Scalable Performance Data Server reduces the need for unnecessary large files to be moved across the network.*

The Scalable Performance Data Server Architecture

Scalable Performance Data Server is a unique type of server that has one sole purpose: to allow extremely fast access to the data that it has under its control. Multiple users can access this server at the same time, so it does handle concurrency. This is very important in Data Warehousing due to the potential for multiple concurrent requests. There are major differences, however, between the SPDS and another type of SAS server, the SAS/SHARE server. The two should not be confused. First of all, the data in the Scalable Performance Data Server is not developed architecturally for updating of data. A SAS/SHARE server has as one of its reasons for being its ability to

---

[22] See Chapter 8.

allow multiple users to update the same file at the same time. Scalable Performance Data Server is not designed for users to update the files, let alone multiple users. It is possible to update the data in the Scalable Performance Data Server server, but this is not why it is designed. Version 2. 0 of Scalable Performance Data Server will, however, support record-level locking. The second major difference is that Scalable Performance Data Server has been designed to take advantage of parallel processing.

Parallel processing is easy to understand by using an analogy: suppose that Spring has arrived and the local garden center has dumped 50 yards of mulch (data) outside your house (computer). It is necessary to take that mulch to the other end of the garden and distribute it over the flowerbeds (reports). There might be a variety of limitations that will prevent this happening quickly. For example, you might only own one wheelbarrow (processor) or, even if you own multiple wheelbarrows, if you are the only one doing the moving, then you might just as well put the extra wheelbarrows back in the shed. The fastest way to move the mulch to the other end of the garden is to get out all the wheelbarrows, bribe the neighbors, and have each take one load. This, in very simple terms, is what happens with the parallel processing capabilities of Scalable Performance Data Server. Consequently, Scalable Performance Data Server is only of use where you have a parallel processing computer and the correct software (in this case, a combination of the Operating System[23] and Scalable Performance Data Server) to run on the computer. Scalable Performance Data Server is analogous to bringing all the neighbors around to move the mulch. They are no good if you only own one wheelbarrow or if there is not enough mulch for them all to move (in which case, they will invariably still come around to help, but drink your beer instead).

It is important to note that there are overheads (fixed costs) to parallel processing that require that the data being accessed is large enough to warrant this cost. Although there are no hard-and-fast rules, it is necessary to benchmark the use of parallel versus regular access to similar data to ensure that there are true benefits to the parallel access.

Therefore, Scalable Performance Data Server uses multiple processors to expedite any single request. It physically resides on one machine that can be accessed from any other machine that is running SAS or from any application that is ODBC compliant. This means that Scalable Performance Data Server has its own ODBC driver and, therefore, fits in with one of the guidelines we look for when designing a Data Warehouse, the characteristic

---

[23]The current release of SAS (6. 12) supports Solaris and AIX operating systems.

of being a flexible product. The access needs to the Data Warehouse will change over time, so make sure that the technical products selected are not 'dead-end' ones. In this situation, Scalable Performance Data Server has the inherent capabilities of being able to act as a server to any ODBC compliant application, giving it the flexible attributes that are needed.

The way that Scalable Performance Data Server works is that it interacts with an operating system that is capable of scheduling code segments to execute in parallel. Not only must these segments run in parallel, but for performance to be truly enhanced, these threads must not be allowed to run in contention with each other. These two factors allow a request to be divided into smaller parts, each of which can be fulfilled using a different processor without getting in each other's way.

How Is the Structure of the SPDS Data Different than other SAS Data Formats?

Although it is not necessary to understand exactly how the data is structured, one key point to understand is that data within Scalable Performance Data Server is not in a native SAS format. It is not a SAS data file with a fancy access engine slapped around it to make it faster. To the user, it looks like SAS data, and the process to move the data into Scalable Performance Data Server is very simple, but it is not what is traditionally considered to be a SAS data file.

A SAS file is stored as a single table that contains both the data and some descriptors that tell the software what is contained in each of the data columns. In other words, a single table contains both the data and the metadata about that table.

A Scalable Performance Data Server file has four distinct components:

- One component contains the data in the form of a single stream. It is essentially a long 'snake' made up of the data.
- The second component contains the metadata for the first file.
- The third and fourth components are index files. A major difference between SAS files and those within Scalable Performance Data Server is the structure of the indexes. With SAS files, index information is stored in a separate physical file, but this is tightly linked to the data file. With a Scalable Performance Data Server file, there are two *index* files, one of which stores the actual index data, and the other which stores for each of the indexed columns a sorted list of all the keys and associated row numbers.[24]

---

[24] For detailed information on the structure and use of SPDS, see: SAS Institute Inc., *Scalable Performance Data Server™ User's Guide, Version 1, First Edition*, Cary, NC: SAS Institute Inc,. 1996. 92pp.

Another key difference is that Scalable Performance Data Server does not discriminate between component types. With SAS files, the associated index file is stored along with the data file and is intrinsically tied to that data. This is not the case within Scalable Performance Data Server. The different files can be stored based upon system requirements (adding flexibility).

There are some other essential differences between Scalable Performance Data Server files and SAS files. Scalable Performance Data Server files can span storage devices and are not restricted to the two-gigabyte limit imposed by many operating systems. The designer of the data also has flexibility over the type of indexes that are being created. SAS files use B-tree indexing,[25] but Scalable Performance Data Server has a further option; bitmap indexing. There is one simple reason for this option: in certain circumstances, one indexing method will out-perform the other. It is up to the designer of the data to decide which is the better choice. One of the factors that determine which type of index should be used is the cardinality of the column or columns being indexed. In other words, how many unique values the column has. The lower the cardinality, the more likely that a bitmap, as opposed to a B-tree index, will work faster. In Version 2.0 of Scalable Performance Data Server, this choice will become more complex because it will be possible to support high cardinality with a hybrid bitmap index.

Another major difference with the Scalable Performance Data Server files is the way that they can be sorted. Although it is possible to specify different types of sorts with SAS files (e.g., TAGSORT or by using an external sorting program), there are more options with Scalable Performance Data Server. Different sorts can be specified: *Quicksort* and *Heapsort*.[26] These, along with the different types of indexes that are available, mean that it is essential to understand the data to get the best out of the software product. Using the wrong indexing or sorting technique can lead to a detrimental effect on performance. Understanding the data can also improve Data Warehouse performance immensely however. The key to using Scalable Performance Data Server is two-fold: to understand in which situations different options are most effective (understanding the software product) and thoroughly knowing the data. The two have to be matched to really gain the vast benefits Scalable Performance Data Server is capable of producing.

---

[25] For an excellent description of indexes, how they work, and how they are created, see: Raithel, Michael A., *Tuning SAS® Applications in the MVS Environment*, Cary, NC: SAS Institute Inc., 1995. 303pp., Chapter 6, pp. 147–172. This chapter is essential reading for anyone involved in optimizing SAS data files to run within a Data Warehousing environment, on any operating system.
[26] See: *Scalable Performance Data Server™ User's Guide*, p 37-38.

Special Topic: ODBC

ODBC (Open Database Connectivity) is an industry standard interface that provides a common application programming interface (API) for accessing databases. What this really means is that from within SAS, it is possible to read and update data that is in an external format, and, from other applications (e.g., Microsoft Excel, Lotus,Paradox), it is possible to directly access SAS data files.

This sounds wonderful because in principle, it gives a freedom and openness to where data can reside. This is especially useful within a Data Warehouse in which the data should reside; where it is most convenient for access. Unfortunately, there is always a cost associated with any benefit. In the case of ODBC, the costs are the complexity and overhead of installation and performance.

It would be ideal if there were one ODBC server that acted as the master controller that would perform all the translations required for one application to use the data residing in another. This is not the case. In a Data Warehouse, if there were data residing in ORACLE, SAS, Microsoft Excel, and Paradox, then there would have to be four drivers, one for each product. Each of these drivers has their own particular quirks and each would have to be installed on the client's computer. During installation, the drivers will be registered with the Windows ODBC manager. It acts as the driver information broker that lets any application that wishes to use them know the file information that is required for the external data access that the particular driver supplies. The bottom line here, from a Data Warehousing perspective, is that ODBC can be a useful (though awkward) tool to deal with specific situations that might arise. It is probably not a good choice within a Data Warehouse from an architectural perspective due to the high installation and maintenance overheads. ODBC is a useful tool, but there should be great care in depending upon it on a fundamental architectural level.

The second drawback of ODBC is the performance. Although there are now drivers that claim to be high performance, it would still be doubtful if ODBC would be a prudent selection as the medium by which data is accessed across a Data Warehouse.

From a SAS perspective, although the ODBC driver to allow SAS files to be accessed by other products is free, there is a cost associated with using SAS to access other ODBC compliant applications (SAS/ACCESS to ODBC software will be needed). It is possible through use of the SAS ODBC driver to allow PC based ODBC compliant applications (like Excel) to access SAS data on a remote platform (e.g., in a UNIX based SAS data file). In this situation, however, both SAS/SHARE and SAS/SHARE*NET will be required on the remote computer.

One other factor to consider is that when an ODBC compliant application is accessing a SAS file, then a dedicated SAS session will be needed to handle the requests through the driver. This session does not need all the overhead of a 'full-blown' SAS session, but anytime an extra process is needed, performance concerns must be considered.

Security within SPDS

Another difference between SAS files and Scalable Performance Data Server files is the amount of security available. SAS files can be password protected, but more traditionally, the security has been a function of the underlying Operating System. There are two levels of security within Scalable Performance Data Server: the first of these is on the name-server level that controls access to the server itself. Scalable Performance Data Server when installed comes with a component called the Scalable Performance Data Server name server. Whenever Scalable Performance Data Server is active, it registers itself with this name server. It registers its network address and a list of domains it has under its control. A domain in this case is analogous to a SAS libname and is set-up by an administrator. In the case of the Scalable Performance Data Server, the libname domain is more that just a directory or a file (under OS/390) pointer as it is in native SAS. It also contains other information such as the owner of the library. This means that users only need to know the domain they want to use, and the name server can determine from this information which server that domain is controlled by, thereby automatically pointing users to the correct Scalable Performance Data Server.

This means that the name server controls the initial access to the domain. There is a second level of security within Scalable Performance Data Server called ACLs (Access Control Lists) that control the access to tables within a domain. The owner of the table can grant different permissions to other users to access this table. There are four different permissions: read, write, alter, and control. The first two options speak for themselves. *Alter* means that the actual structure of the table can be changed, and *Control* means that ACLs can be defined or changed for the table.

How Can Scalable Performance Data Server Help in Data Warehouse Performance

Some of the benefits that Scalable Performance Data Server can give have already been mentioned. There are several key features of Scale Performance Data Server that can indicate how much it can help an individual Data Warehouse. These key factors are completely dependent upon access patterns. Again, this takes us back to one of the essential parts of implementing a successful Data Warehouse: to understand as much as possible about the access patterns to data. If access patterns can be predicted, then there is no excuse for a sloppy data model. These access patterns are going to change over time, and this is good because it means that the business of the enterprise is moving. This also means, however, that the design of the Data Warehouse has to be flexible enough to stay in line with potential changes.

Scalable Performance Data Server will in many cases fit exactly with the data access patterns that traditionally are associated with Data Warehouses. Scalable Performance Data Server is designed to optimize performance when an access pattern is required that will

- **Sort** the underlying data
- **Query** the underlying data
- Utilize **WHERE clauses** or **SQL Select** syntax
- **Appends** new data to the Data Warehouse
- **Index** columns in the Data Warehouse.

All of these activities will be considerably faster under the parallel processing options that Scalable Performance Data Server uses. Both front end and back end performance can be enhanced by intelligent use of Scalable Performance Data Server, but it is completely dependent upon the particular Data Warehouse implementation. The best Data Warehouses are those that are designed to meet specific needs, and because these reasons vary between different organizations, there can be no 'typical' Data Warehouse implementation. This means that a product like Scalable Performance Data Server will suit certain Data Warehouses but not others. One important factor is that the types of access patterns that Scalable Performance Data Server is designed to optimize tend to be those that are common across most Data Warehouses. Therefore, it is likely that Scalable Performance Data Server will enhance performance. The question is really whether it is actually needed, not whether it will fit into the Data Warehouse architecture. This is a question that can only be answered within the framework of a particular Data Warehouse, rather than on a generic level.

Chapter 6:
Data Transformation within the Data Warehousing Process

6.1 Data Transformation in the Data Warehousing Process

Transformation in the Data Warehousing process is considered to be an umbrella term for everything that goes on between the data being extracted from the source system and its placement in the implemented Warehouse. This stage of the process is firmly ensconced in the third of the three stages in the Data Warehousing process: the implementation.

What does it actually take, after the data is extracted, to move it into the implemented Data Warehouse? There are a series of stages, all of which need to be addressed during transformation, to ensure that the Data Warehousing process is thoroughly defined. As with many of the other topics covered in this book, the transformation of data is specific to every particular Data Warehouse implementation, and as such there is no generic right or wrong approach. This does not mean that any of the stages in the transformation process can be disregarded, but rather that the way they are treated, and the relative importance of each, will vary from implementation to implementation.

Example of the Transformation Process

A very common situation is for a Data Warehouse to act as a central repository for business information for an organization that is comprised of several other companies. An example of this might be a financial institution (a bank) that merges with other banks. Each of these other banks will have their own unique operational systems. They will each have their own loan approval systems. When the banks merge, the loan approval system will change to comply with the purchasing bank. The old loan portfolios will still exist, however, based upon the old operational system. This gives the Data Warehouse a very challenging situation: it should still be possible to track the old portfolios to see how they behave separately from all other portfolios. At the same time, it should also be possible to ensure that the measures for portfolio performance are similar to those of other portfolios, to ensure that comparisons can be made, and that it is possible to combine the old portfolios with the new so that overall performance tracking can take place.

These challenges of analyzing old and new loan portfolios should be incorporated into the Data Warehousing process. When a new bank is purchased, there should already be rules in place that ensure that the purchased bank's portfolios will conform to all the analysis demands of the bank. The transformation process handles this conversion of operational system to Data Warehouse information. It is very important to realize that most of the problems such a situation creates should be handled first on a business level: exactly how does the bank want to track portfolios it has purchased? These rules should remain constant over all purchased portfolios, but how they are enforced might vary from portfolio to portfolio. The implication is that the transformation process will vary depending on the portfolio, and the process will be, by necessity, different for each one. Although this situation is unavoidable, it can be incorporated into the Data Warehousing process so that each new portfolio will not be treated as a brand new problem.

Approaches to the Transformation of Data

Many approaches to Data Warehousing have a very simplified approach to the transformation of data because there is an underlying assumption that for a single subject,[1] there is one source system. One source system means one transformation process per subject. If there are several data sources for a single subject, then there will obviously be a proliferation of transforma-

---

[1] See Chapter 3 under the section on Star-Schema modeling for a discussion on *subjects* within a Data Warehouse

tion processes because each one will need a different conversion process to become an integrated information source.

> *Inherent in the design of the Data Warehousing process should be the appreciation that a single subject need not be entirely derived from a single source system. A single subject may therefore be constructed from a number of transformation processes. This proliferation of transformation processes should be a part of the Data Warehousing process and not seen as isolated instances.*

An Object-Oriented approach[2] can elegantly handle the situation of transforming the source data into the Data Warehouse in many different ways to reach the same end. A class could be defined that would be a generic transformation process for moving source system data into a specific Data Warehouse subject. For instance, if an area of interest in the Data Warehouse is the total population of insurance policy holders. This might be a key indicator of business performance. How the numbers are actually reported (based upon specified enterprise needs) would be intrinsic in this Population Class. This information might well be made up from a variety of different source systems (possibly pertaining to different insurance products in different divisions of the company). It is possible that the Population Class could be sub-classed to account for the differences in source systems and the transformations they would go under so that a unified subject can be defined for the Data Warehouse. This use of objects would mean that if new companies were purchased or new insurance products were added, then including them in the Data Warehouse would possibly mean adding a new sub-class that incorporates all the rules already established in the parent class.

Considering Data Transformation as Part of the Entire Data Warehousing Process

It is not necessary to use this Object-Oriented approach, but a key part to the design of the transformation process is the understanding from a macro level as to what is actually happening. Designing an isolated transformation process without really looking at the big picture can lead to the necessity to redesign large portions of the entire Data Warehousing process at a later date. This is one of the dangers of building a series of Data Marts and then

---

[2] See Chapter 3, Section 3.4 for a discussion on using an Object-Oriented approach within the Data Warehousing process.

backing into a Data Warehouse. The Data-Mart approach has many benefits:

- direct response to enterprise (or often, departmental) needs
- relatively short implementation period
- less investment in hardware and software.

However, there is the danger of each Data Mart being an island unto itself. When building Data Marts, as with the design of the transformation process, there should be a consistent referral back to the bigger picture. Each part of the transformation should be looked at in terms of the entire enterprise. In the case of Data Marts, the micro level is usually departmental, so it is important to constantly refer back to how the department fits into the entire organization. Hopefully, this will reduce the possibility of creating Data Mart 'islands'. The transformation process is usually based on a subject area, so it is necessary to constantly refer to how the subject relates to other subjects to avoid subject 'islands'.

Therefore, the transformation process is not a single set of related and consecutive actions on source data that will make it compliant with the design needs of the implemented Data Warehouse. It is a series of possibly concurrent processes that could well transform a variety of source systems into a single coherent informational repository. For each subject in the Data Warehouse, the transformation of source data should not be approached as a single-threaded process (although it could well be in a simple situation), but as a multi-threaded process designed to reach a common objective (a coherent and consistent subject). As with every other part of the Data Warehousing process, the transformation of the data should be viewed and designed with flexibility as one of the fundamental decision drivers. What would happen in a situation where another source system was to be added? How would this affect the transformation process, and could it easily be integrated?

SAS Software and the Transformation Process

SAS software has a natural fit in the transformation of the source data into the Data Warehouse. This is because the transformation process requires that many of the features are extremely well developed within the software. SAS software has at its heart the understanding that data is there to be used, and therefore its design and development has been based around the reading, manipulation, and analysis of data. In the transformation process, both the manipulation and analysis are very key factors.

The ability to manipulate data is extremely important in the data transformation process. It is often essential to compare values against other values in the data validation stage. The ability to readily manipulate the data so that it is programmatically possible to perform a variety of comparisons is essential. SAS software has many tools that will allow data to be manipulated, ranging from pre-defined procedures (e.g., PROC TRANSPOSE, PROC SQL) to programming languages (base SAS software and SCL). The final physical layout (model) of the data in the Warehouse will probably bear little resemblance to the way it is when extracted from the source operational system. The software that performs all the transformations will need to be very flexible in its abilities to handle this data.

Analysis tools are one of the fundamental strengths of SAS software. For the transformation process, these tools range from such procedures as FREQ and MEANS to very complex statistical techniques such as PROC GLM, time-series analysis (SAS/ETS) and SAS/INSIGHT.

Stages in the Transformation Process

There are several stages in the transformation process. These can be summarized as follows:

- Data Validation
- Data Scrubbing
- Data Integration
- Data Derivation
- Data Denormalization
- Data Summarization
- Metadata Creation

Each one of these will be discussed in detail, both in terms of how they fit into the Data Warehousing process, and how they can be addressed using SAS software. Each Data Warehouse implementation poses a unique set of problems that not only have to be solved as they arise but must also be incorporated into the process. Although each of these different stages in the data Transformation Phase of the Data Warehouse process are treated separately, in practical terms they are often closely associated. It is likely, for instance that the *scrubbing* of data will take place directly alongside the validation because, as an invalid value is found, it might also be possible to automatically resolve the problem. It would make no sense to go through the validation and then have to find the incorrect value again to scrub it.

The following sections will discuss each of the parts of the transformation process. It is assumed that the data is already extracted from the source systems,[3] so the following sections will cover what will happen between this extraction and the final loading into the implemented Data Warehouse.

---

[3] See Chapter 5 for a discussion on Data Extraction within the Data Warehousing process.

6.2 Data Validation

In a perfect world, data validation should not be necessary. Wouldn't it be marvelous if all the data that was to be exported from an operational system was already fully validated? This rarely happens, for a variety of reasons:

- The source operational system does not have the internal data validation checks that would prevent incorrect data being input.
- Data is still updated by people, making human error a possibility.
- Data can be valid for the system but incorrect in context. In other words, data that is a valid option might not be correct for the particular situation.
- Data might not be invalid, but missing.[4] This is a special case that is difficult to handle and needs comprehensive business-based decisions as to the actions that should be taken.

It would be possible to ignore all data validation issues within the Data Warehousing process on the grounds that, if data is invalid in the source systems, then it should remain so in the Warehouse, so as to be consistent. Although on one level this is an attractive argument (wouldn't it be nice not to have to perform any validation?) it actually does little for the enterprise. The Data Warehouse is the window through which the enterprise looks to find out the information upon which short- and long-term decisions can be made. These decisions can only be rational if the underlying belief in the data is unquestionable. It is the job of the source data systems to effectively keep the enterprise operational. It is the job of the Data Warehouse to help in the decisions to make it successful. It is not always necessary for the data to be validated for the operational system to work correctly (if a ZIP code is incorrect, then the package will still get to the right address). It is, however, always essential for the Data Warehouse to be completely valid (if the ZIP code is incorrect, then business decisions based upon ZIP code will be flawed).

Different Forms of Invalid Data

Given that data validation is a necessary evil, then what should the process be for uncovering potential problems in the source data? There are several different types of invalid data, so the process for handling each will be different (but possibly overlapping). Invalid data most commonly includes

---

4 This topic is briefly discussed in Chapter 3, Section 3.4 as a Special Topic.

- data that is 'inadmissable'. This means that the piece of data cannot possibly be correct in context. For instance, a two-digit State code of MU is not possible in the U.S. Because there are only 50 options for a State code and MU does not fall within that set, it cannot be correct.
- data that is missing. This is a particularly annoying form of invalid data because it is not always possible to remedy the situation.
- data that is out of the possible range. This data is fairly easy to discover, as long as the expected range is known.
- data that has been duplicated. Duplicated data is usually a quirk of the extraction process that reads the data from the source system, in which case the extraction methodology needs to be revisited. It is highly unlikely that duplicated data will exist within the source system, so if it does turn up during the Transformation Phase of the Data Warehousing process, then it is likely that it is a problem with the process itself. In this case, the process should be revisited.

 There are four major forms of validation, each of which poses a different set of problems for the designer of the Data Warehouse.

Exploratory Validation: *is very common and is used in a situation where values are looked at in terms of their relationship with the rest of the values. For instance, outliers might be found by using SAS/INSIGHT, or unusual values might be discovered by using PROC FREQ.*

Finite Validation: *is the simplest form of validation. It states that a given value should be part of a pre-defined set of possible values. It is easy to use this form of validation because all it takes is some form of look-up against the universe of potential values.*

Derived Validation: *is validation based upon a set of predetermined rules. A very simple example would be in medical insurance where the gender of a person could be validated against diagnoses that are gender specific (pregnancy).*

Statistical Validation: *is a more complex form of validation. It will look at particular values as to where they fall within an expected distribution. For instance, if the distribution were expected to be normal, then any values outside a 95% confidence interval could be candidates for further validation.*

Data Warehousing is a continually developing process. This means that, over time, the data validation process is likely to be enhanced. This change could be based on new data being added to the Data Warehouse or new knowledge about the data itself. Either way, it is important to remember that if changes are made to the validation process, then the data already loaded in the Data Warehouse should also be re-verified. One of the key reasons to create a Data Warehouse is for the enterprise to have a source of information that is consistent over time. The verification process is usually applied against new data as it moves from the source system to the Warehouse itself. If that verification process changes, then it follows that the entire Data Warehouse will need re-verification.

6.3 SAS Software and Data Validation

There are countless ways in which SAS software can help in the data validation process. To comprehensively outline each of the possible techniques is beyond the scope of this book, but to outline a few of these methods will put the process into a real-world perspective. The techniques below all use SAS tools that are available within base SAS software, as opposed to those within other modules (e.g., SAS/ETS, SAS/QC, SAS/OR) that are less generic in nature. The validation techniques discussed below are based on the four different types outlined earlier.

Exploratory Validation

Exploratory Validation is used in situations where inconsistencies within the data are recognized. This type of validation essentially shows, that given the internal distribution of values in a particular column or set of columns, which values can be considered unusual. This does not necessarily mean that the 'unusual' values are necessarily invalid, but only that they require further investigation. One way to do this, when using SAS software to perform this type of validation, is by using the FREQ procedure.

SAS Tools for Exploratory Validation

The FREQ procedure is ideal for assessing the validity of the domains within a particular column in a table or the domains of combinations of columns. The domain is the set of all the existing values for a particular column. The FREQ procedure is ideal for creating summary data that can be visually analyzed in a report or passed to other procedures for further analysis. This is best illustrated by example.

Suppose the source data was extracted from a medical claims operational system. Each row of the extracted record represents a claim for a service processed by a medical provider (e.g., a doctor, a hospital, a nursing home). Each row of information contains multiple items (columns) of data which include a Provider Number and a Diagnosis Code. Other data might include the amount of the claim and the co-payment amount, but for validation purposes a check is incorporated into the process to look for invalid Diagnosis Codes. The table will look like this:

PROVIDER_NUMBER	DIAGNOSIS_CODE	CLAIM_AMOUNT	COPAY_AMOUNT
A100	250	150.00	10.00
A101	724	340.00	5.00
B8	493	50.00	10.00

Table 6.1

A Simple Exploratory Validation Test

A simple validation test for the data (using PROC FREQ) could be

```
PROC FREQ DATA=claims;
 TABLES diagnosis_code;
 TITLE 'List of Diagnosis Codes and Associated Statistics';
RUN;
```

This code will create a list of all the unique values of DIAG (`diagnosis_code`) with the number of rows in which that particular code is referenced. It will also give the percentage of the total number that this frequency represents and additional information as shown in Table 6.2.

DIAG	FREQUENCY	PERCENT	CUMULATIVE FREQUENCY	CUMULATIVE PERCENT
493	2	0.1	2	0.1
250	151	8.0	153	8.1
724	89	4.7	242	12.8

Table 6.2
List of Diagnosis Codes and Associated Statistics

Table 6.2 shows a small portion of the complete report. It would be as long as the number of unique values of **diagnosis_code**. This analysis will quickly show the diagnosis codes that are either over- or under-represented in the source data. This is using SAS software at its very basic level, learned almost at the beginning of any SAS programming class,[5] With a few basic modifications, this technique can be extended to be quite sophisticated. It is

---

[5] For a nice introduction to PROC FREQ, see Delwiche, Lora D., and Slaughter, Susan J., *The Little SAS Book: A Primer*, Cary, NC: SAS Institute Inc., 1995. 228 pp., pages 110-111.

possible to create very complex cross-tabulations based upon values from more than one column.

Analyzing Validation Testing Output Programmatically

It is not necessary to stop at just printing the output from procedures such as FREQ. If the output is stored as a data table, then it is possible to start to analyze the output programmatically. In a large Data Warehouse implementation, it might be necessary to validate hundreds of columns to ensure that the incoming data makes sense. In this case, it might not be a reasonable option to 'eye-ball' all of the results, but to programmatically access the resultant tables to select only those items that are outside a pre-specified range. For example, only print those diagnosis codes that occur in the extracted source file less than five times.

This could be done with simple extensions to the preceding code:

```
PROC FREQ DATA=claims NOPRINT;
 TABLES diagnosis_code / OUT=diagfreq (where=(count lt 5));
 RUN;

PROC PRINT DATA=diagfreq;
 TITLE 'List of Diagnosis Codes and Associated Statistics';
 TITLE2 'where frequency count is less than 5';
RUN;
```

This code produces an elementary form of an exception report, as seen in Table 6.3. The major difference in the preceding code is that the FREQ procedure does not actually print a report, but it produces an output file (`diagfreq`) that only contains those Diagnosis Codes that occur less than 5 times in the input file (`claims`).

OBS	DIAG	COUNT	PERCENT
1	493	2	0.10616

Table 6.3
List of Diagnosis Codes and Associated Statistics
where frequency count is less than 5

The FREQ procedure is an extremely useful tool in the development of validation techniques. It can also be an integral part of the metadata as described in Section 6.8. The FREQ procedure can be used as part of the Exploratory Validation technique. Some of the more complex statistical options within the procedure[6] can be used with the Statistical Validation technique. It is

---

[6] For a full description of the FREQ procedure, see: SAS Institute Inc., *SAS® Procedures Guide, Version 6, Third Edition,* Cary, NC: SAS Institute Inc., 1990. 705pp, Chapter 20.

unlikely, although possible, that the FREQ procedure will be used to validate against external values (Finite Validation). This could be easily done, however, using the FORMAT procedure described later in the Section "Finite Validation."

Using Exception Reports for Exploratory Validation

A simple example of an Exception Report was illustrated in Table 6.3. An exception report is also another way to perform Exploratory Validation. Exception Reports can help to find unexpected domains within a distribution of values for a particular column. They are more targeted than the PROC FREQ example shown earlier, because it is necessary to have some kind of idea as to what is unusual. For instance, in Table 6.3, any Diagnosis Code that occurred less than 5 times was selected for further exploration. Just because the Diagnosis Code only occurred less than 5 times does not, in itself, mean that it is invalid.

Exception reports are heavily dependent upon the use of WHERE clauses[7] that are used to select certain rows from a table, based upon a set of specified criteria. Those familiar with SQL or base SAS programming techniques should be very familiar with the WHERE clause, but in Data Warehousing its use is extensive, both in the back end and the front end. One of the major keys to Data Warehousing is efficiently obtaining the information that is needed to fulfill a particular enterprise need. The WHERE clause is one efficient way of doing this.

There are numerous tools within SAS software that will perform Exploratory Validation. Such tools include:

The DATA step (base SAS software)
PROC SQL (base SAS software)
PROC UNIVARIATE (base SAS software)
PROC MEANS (base SAS software)
PROC SUMMARY (base SAS software)
PROC FSBROWSE (base SAS software)
PROC GCHART (SAS/GRAPH)
PROC GPLOT (SAS/GRAPH)
SAS/INSIGHT.

---

[7] The WHERE clause is succinctly described in: Delwiche, Lora D., and Slaughter, Susan J., *The Little SAS Book: A Primer*, Cary, NC: SAS Institute Inc., 1995. 228pp. pages 207-209.

Finite Validation

Finite Validation is when there are a known number of possibilities for a given value in a given row. Conceptually, this is the easiest form of validation. The set of all the possible values must be stored in some form and then the existing values from the extracted source data should be cross-referenced to this list.

The options available within SAS for table lookups are immense.[8] From a Data Warehousing perspective, Finite Validation is an important technique and will certainly be part of the Transformation Phase in the Data Warehouse implementation process. There are two important factors, however, in deciding on techniques for Finite Validation. First, the look-up technique must be efficient. There is no easy answer to finding the most efficient look-up technique because there are many factors involved. However, it might be necessary to implement different look-up techniques depending upon the situation. The other important factor is ease of maintenance. Whenever there is a list of valid values against which new values need to be compared, this list will need to be maintained. Make sure that a technique is selected that will allow for easy maintenance. New valid values must be added, and existing valid values removed or re-coded. Although this is, in principle, fairly simple, there should be a process to ensure that it is actually done. This is more of a metadata issue (see Section 6.8), but has direct relevance to the Finite Validation of data.

SAS Tools for Finite Validation

Within SAS there are many ways to perform this look-up. One of the more flexible procedures available is PROC FORMAT, which is part of the base/SAS module. Using this procedure, the set of valid values are stored as a format, and when that format is used against the column being validated, any values that cannot be formatted will, by definition, be invalid. This can be best illustrated by using a simple example:

```
PROC FORMAT LIBRARY=dwformat;
 VALUE $ diag
  '250'='Diabetes'
  '724'='Back Pain'
  OTHER='Invalid Value';
RUN;
```

---

[8] Look-up techniques have been a continual topic for discussion for many years and have been featured heavily in all SAS User Group conferences. Any of the *Proceedings* will contain references to this subject. A specific example is: Rafiee, Dana, "No More Merge—Alternative Table Lookup Techniques," SAS Institute Inc., *Proceedings of the Twenty-Second Annual SAS® Users Group International Conference.*

This piece of SAS code will create a format named **diag** that will be stored in the SAS library **dwformat**. The format contains the two valid values 250 and 724 and their associated descriptions. The following piece of code will take our extracted source data and print out a report displaying only the invalid values.

```
DATA check;
 SET claims;
 LENGTH desc $40.;
 desc=PUT(diag,$diag.);
RUN;

PROC PRINT DATA=check;
 WHERE desc='Invalid Value';
RUN;
```

This code will create a new column named **desc**. The value of **desc** will be the formatted value based upon the format **$diag** that is already created. For the Diagnosis Code 493, the value of **desc** will be **Invalid Value**. It is then a simple matter to print out any row that has an invalid value as the Diagnosis Code.

Using Formats for Finite Validation

This is using the FORMAT procedure in its simplest form. There are many complex ways to use this procedure. Their discussion is beyond the scope of this book.[9] However, using PROC FORMAT is a very efficient way to perform a look-up because it uses an efficient binary search technique. Some features of PROC FORMAT are worthwhile mentioning: first of all, if the list of potential valid values is very long, then if possible, order the way the values are included in the format so that the most common valid values are included first. Because the format is searched from top-to-bottom and the search ends after the correct format has been found, it makes sense to include the most likely value first. Secondly, values can be grouped together in the format, so each individual valid value does not have to be listed as a separate item.

It is also possible to create a format from an external file (using the CNTLIN option). This means that a file of any format that SAS can read could be the basis for creating a format within SAS. It would therefore be possible, only using the techniques discussed in this chapter, to create a SAS data file of valid values for a column in an existing SAS file and create a format from it.

---

[9] SAS Institute Inc., *SAS® Procedures Guide, Version 6, Third Edition*, Cary, NC: SAS Institute Inc., 1990. 750pp. See Chapter 18 for full documentation on PROC FORMAT.

Creating a format from an existing file has many uses in a Data Warehousing environment. Given our examples in the earlier Section "Exploratory Validation," suppose we run a PROC FREQ on the DIAG column in the CLAIMS file that is loaded into the Data Warehouse. Instead of printing the results, we save them as a SAS data file (by using the OUT= option), which we then use as a basis for creating a format, making the assumption that all the values are valid. When new data is subsequently extracted from the source system, all the new DIAG values can be checked against this format. Any that do not have a specific format will be new Diagnosis Codes that are not currently in the Data Warehouse. These codes could then be printed and assessed for validity.

Additional Tools for Finite Validation

There are many other techniques within SAS that can be used to look-up a set of values against a list of valid values. This can be performed using both base/SAS and PROC SQL, by joining tables (one containing the column to be validated and the other a column of valid values). In SCL (Screen Control Language), valid values could be stored as lists that could then act as pseudo-formats and could programmatically be used to validate against new data.

Derived Validation

Derived Validation is a very simple form of validation to perform, but a much harder one to maintain. In Derived Validation, the validity of a specific value is based upon a series of tests. These tests might range from the very simple, to the very complex. For example, suppose, using the same Diagnosis Code example shown earlier, that a specific code is only valid based upon other criteria. It makes sense that for Diagnosis Code 250, the visit should be an outpatient, not an inpatient, visit. It would then be easy to set up a program to check for this derived validation.

SAS Tools for Derived Validation

Derived Validation typically will use Exception Reports to display those values that do not meet specific criteria. In SAS, this will almost certainly be performed using a DATA step. For example, the following code is a very simple example of a program that will print such a report.

```
DATA invalid;
 SET claims;
 IF diag='250' and in_out='IN' THEN OUTPUT;
RUN;
```

Special Topic:
Validating Dimension and Fact Data

In a dimensional Data Warehouse (see Chapter 3 for details), columns of information are either Dimensions (or part of a Dimension) or Facts. Dimensions are ways the enterprise determines information should be viewed, and Facts are the actual measures. For example, Diagnosis Code would be a Dimension. The enterprise will want to look at the business based upon Diagnosis Codes. The amount of the claim will be a Fact because this is a measure. Usually (although not always), a Dimension is categorical and a Fact is continuous.

Validation for **Dimensions** and **Facts** tend to take on a different look. A Dimension can more easily be validated using **Finite** or **Exploratory Validation**, but a **Fact** can only be validated based upon an expected range of values. Usually, there are no finite set of valid values for a **Fact** column, which makes the validation process less precise. For instance, it is possible to flag a claim that is greater than $250 if it is an outpatient claim.

Generally, however, the source Operational Systems are more attuned to incorrect **Fact** information. They usually deal with the amount that is paid or the number delivered and therefore, by necessity, have to be more precise. There are usually (although not always) more problems with **Dimension** rather than **Fact** data coming from source systems.

The code that immediately precedes the Special Topic box is the bare minimum. All it does is create a new table named **invalid** that will contain only the rows in the input file **claims** where the Diagnosis Code has a value of 250 and the **in_out** column (which flags whether the claim is an inpatient or outpatient) is IN (meaning inpatient). The file **invalid** can then be printed or analyzed further.

The way the preceeding program is constructed is a maintenance nightmare. This is one small example of one validation test on one column. There might be thousands of possible values for Diagnosis Code, each of which could potentially have different tests. There might also be thousands of columns of data within the Data Warehouse, all or some of which might need checking.

This small program could become very large, very quickly. In a very short period of time, it would become unmaintainable, and generations of programmers and business users will curse it forever. There really is no absolutely elegant way of dealing with Derived Validations. The problem is one of metadata control, rather than validation. This is because the rules for validating a certain domain within a certain column are business issues. The validation rules should be part of the metadata, not hidden away in a multi-thousand line program.

There are some techniques that can be of use in such a situation. The first of these is to make the validation process table driven,[10] which will essentially place all of the rules into tables that can easily be maintained. These tables would then be used in a program that would validate the data. Another option, which is probably simpler (but is not free of problems) would be to take each column that needed validating and create a SAS macro that would contain all of the code and the business descriptions of all of the necessary rules. This would be easier to maintain because all validation pertaining to a particular column would be in one place (in this case in a single macro), but it is no more than taking the single long program and compartmentalizing it into manageable units. Depending upon the columns that need to be validated, the correct macro could be called (run), thus allowing for selective validation. For example, a macro named `diag_mac` could be created that would look like this:

```
%MACRO diag_mac;
/ *************************************************************************
* This macro contains all the rules pertaining to the validation of the  *
* Diagnosis_Code column in the CLAIMS file.                               *
************************************************************************** /
* Rule: A Diagnosis Code of 250 can only be in an outpatient claim;

IF diag='250' and in_out='IN' THEN OUTPUT;

%MEND diag_mac;
```

This again would be a very simple example. Each of the rules might also have an owner, or there might be an owner at the column (in this case, macro) level. This macro could then be used in the following way:

```
DATA invalid;
 SET claims;
 %MACRO diag_mac;
RUN;
```

There could possibly be a macro for each of the columns in the `claims` file, so each one could optionally be called within this same DATA step. This would be far more efficient than running a new DATA step for each macro, which would require as many reads of the data as there are macros.

SAS has all of the tools that would be needed for Derived Validation, but the major challenges are in the handling of the metadata. Derived Valida-

---

[10] The entire topic of data validation and especially how it pertains to a table-driven approach is discussed at great length in: Kolosova, Tanya and Berestizhevsky, Samuel, *Table-Driven Strategies for Rapid SAS® Applications Development*, Cary NC: SAS Institute Inc., 1995. 259 pp.

tion tends to become more complex over time, so ensure that the design of the process will allow for this growth.

Statistical Validation

Statistical Validation will validate values based upon an expected distribution instead of validating values against other values, or against each other. SAS has more statistical techniques and books available than can possibly be referenced here. The use of statistical techniques to test the validity of data within the Data Warehouse has not been fully developed. Most of the uses of statistical techniques have been applied to the exploitation of the Data Warehouse (e.g., Data Mining), but many of these same techniques could be used to determine data that is not in line with other data or with a set of pre-determined hypotheses.

A very simple example of the use of Statistical Validation could be calculating the standard deviation of the values in a particular column and extracting any that do not fall within the 95th percentile. Another example could be to use the GLM (General Linear Model) procedure (part of SAS/STAT software) where the data in the Data Warehouse could be tested against the incoming, recently extracted data. There are a variety of tests to find out if the new data is statistically different from the old data. This could be easily extended. For example, the volume of claims for Diagnosis Code 250 is not significantly different in the data being validated from the data already validated within the Data Warehouse. One of the benefits to such a validation test is that it will not be necessary to know anything about the data beforehand, except an expected distribution.

It would also be possible to use very advanced techniques, such as Artificial Intelligence or fuzzy logic, to perform the validation. However, incorporating these techniques into the Data Warehousing process would require a great deal of resources. Deciding whether to go to the lengths required to incorporate Artificial Intelligence or fuzzy logic would require assessing where the finite and valuable resources would best be placed: in the validation of data or elsewhere in the Data Warehousing process.

Duplicate Data

Duplicate data is a very annoying occurrence in a Data Warehouse. It usually shows a weakness in the extraction methodology from the source system. It is highly unlikely (although possible) that the source system could contain duplicate data, but it often occurs usually because data is being extracted more than once, and there is nothing in the process to prevent this from happening. In any case, a check for duplicate data should occur during the validation process.

SAS Tools to Test for Duplicate Data

Using SAS there are a variety of techniques to do this. Two of these techniques are outlined briefly in the next sections, but in all reality, the checking for duplicate data will not occur as a separate process in the validation stage, but while the other checks are being made.

Using the FREQ Procedure to Recognize Duplicate Data

The first technique is to use the FREQ procedure:

```
PROC FREQ DATA=claims noprint;
 TABLES diagnosis_code / out=dupes (where=(count ne 1));
RUN;
```

This procedure will run a frequency for **diagnosis_code** in the table **claims**. The results will not be printed but will be output to a file named **dupes**. Only values of Diagnosis Code will be output if **count** is more than one. In our case, this probably does not tell us much. We expect that there will be more than one occurrence of each Diagnosis Code. What we probably do not expect, however, is more than one occurrence of a Diagnosis Code on the same day for the same person (unless they went for a second opinion!).

This code could then be modified as follows:

```
PROC FREQ DATA=claims noprint;
 TABLES diagnosis_code*person*claim_date / out=dupes (where=(count ne 1));
RUN;
```

Obviously, the TABLES statement can be expanded to as many columns as is necessary. The output file **dupes** can then be analyzed and reported upon.

Using SQL to Recognize Duplicate Data

A similar result can be obtained by using SQL as follows:

```
PROC SQL;
 CREATE TABLE dupes AS
 SELECT * , COUNT(*) as count
 FROM CLAIMS
 GROUP BY diagnosis_code, person, claim_date
 HAVING count GT 1;
QUIT;
```

This SQL will produce a report showing any duplicates and the number of times they are duplicated (as denoted by the column **count**).

These two techniques do not, however, actually indicate where the duplicates are located within the table **claims**, just that they exist. It is probable that not only would the above report be necessary, but also another report (or data file) that contains the actual locations of the duplicates within the file. There are a variety of ways to do this, but one of these would be to use an additional SQL step as follows:

```
PROC SQL;
 CREATE TABLE dupe_obs AS
 SELECT a.diagnosis_code,a.person,a.claim_date
 FROM claims a, dupes b
 WHERE a.diagnosis_code=b.diagnosis_code AND a.person=b.person
      AND a.claim_date=b.claim_date;
QUIT;
```

This uses two different steps. There are other options available using just the tools within base SAS. There are a variety of programming techniques that can be utilized to meet the same ends. One very popular technique is to use a DATA step with the options FIRST.BYVARIABLE and LAST.BYVARIABLE.[11] Another is to use the RETAIN statement that allows for comparison of values across rows in a data file. These programming techniques are often more efficient and are especially valuable in situations where multiple tasks are being performed with only a single read of the data. For instance, in a single read of the data it would be possible to check for duplicates and run all the other validation tests against the data. This will reduce the number of reads of the data it will take to perform the validation, thus improving performance.

6.4 Scrubbing the Data

Validation in itself does nothing for the Data Warehouse except raise real and potential problems with the data. Alongside the validation process, there is the scrubbing (or cleansing) of the data. This stage in the Transformation Process is usually run alongside the validation of the data. It makes sense, from an efficiency standpoint, to scrub the data as incorrect values are found.

There are, however, very fundamental questions that need to be answered before scrubbing is performed:

- Should the invalid data be scrubbed as it moves into the Data Warehouse, or should it be changed in the source Operational System?
- If an item is scrubbed, should there be an audit trail, so that it will be possible to balance Data Warehouse information and information in the source Operational System?

---

[11] This technique assumes that the data file is sorted (or indexed) by the columns that are being checked for duplicate values. A description of this technique can be found in: Delwiche, Lora D., and Slaughter, Susan J., *The Little SAS Book: A Primer*, Cary, NC: SAS Institute Inc., 1995. 228pp. pages 142-143.

- If the pertinent table in the Data Warehouse is refreshed every period (as opposed to updated), then there is a chance that the invalid data will be reloaded. How will this be handled?

There is no right or wrong answer to any of these three questions. The key to successfully scrubbing is consistency. If a specific value is changed one way in one month, then an identical value should be changed in exactly the same way the following month. The Data Warehouse in most situations is designed to be a consistent view of business measures over time. If any of these measures change, which may impact the validation and, therefore, the scrubbing, they should also be changed in the existing data in the Warehouse. For instance, if it is discovered that a certain Diagnosis Code has been verified by using derived techniques (see the Section "Derived Validation" earlier in this chapter), but one of the rules changes, then it will be necessary to re-verify the entire Data Warehouse based upon the new rules. Any invalid data within the existing implemented Data Warehouse will also need to be scrubbed.

Special Topic:
Changing Data Already Loaded into the Warehouse

There are two major schools of thought on changing data within the Warehouse:

- After data is loaded, then it is effectively frozen. This means that there will always be consistency in the analyses generated from the Data Warehouse.

- The data within the Warehouse should be subject to modification based upon new or modified rules. This might mean that the results of similar analyses might change over time, but that the Data Warehouse will comply to the most recent enterprise rules.

From a technological perspective, it does not matter which of these two camps is predominant. The former is technologically preferable because it requires less maintenance, but updating existing data should not, if the Data Warehouse is efficiently modeled, overtax the system.

However, the decision should not be a technological issue, but a business issue. It should be dependent upon the uses of the Data Warehouse. So any decision should be deferred to the business units it will impact.

Given a choice between deleting information or re-coding it, choose the latter every time. After the data is deleted, then so is any record of it ever having existed.

Unless absolutely positive that there will be no unexpected results, avoid using inner joins when denormalizing data. It is better to be safe than sorry, so default to outer joins.

The validation process will isolate the invalid values in the data. These can often be programmatically replaced with valid data. Very often, however, each case needs to be taken and assessed independently. This sometimes means generating a report that is passed to the owners of the data. It is then up to them to decide what should be done. This report need not be in the form of paper. It could be a data file that needs modifying. The scrubbing process would then take this modified file, re-join it with the invalid data and replace it with the new valid data. If these modifications are performed on a paper report (as is often the case), then the new data will have to be manually modified.

Ideally, as much of the invalid data should be modified programmatically as is possible. Human intervention, although often necessary, slows down the process of loading the new data into the Warehouse, so this should be avoided when possible. Again, the key is to ensure that there is a process in place for deciding on valid values. This process should be designed for both efficiency and accuracy. If at all possible, avoid the dreaded paper reports. Updating the data from a file will be preferable because it will be possible to store a history (audit) of modified data. If needed at a later date, it will then be possible to re-create the original data. It will also be possible to track who has decided that a specific value should be changed, so if there are questions at a later date, they can be answered. This process obviously involves up-front work, but it will lead to confidence in the Data Warehouse. If the information from the Data Warehouse is not believed, it can at least be explained!

SAS Techniques for Scrubbing Data

At its very simplest level, scrubbing data involves locating the invalid value and changing it. The validation process should have already determined what is valid and invalid, then it is a case of performing the actual change. The change will either be a re-coding or a removal of data.

If the number of changes that are needed are few, then it will be possible to use the VIEWTABLE or FSEDIT (part of SAS/FSP) to update the data. These editing choices can be embedded into an application (written using SAS/AF) that will give more control over the editing process and have the ability to create an audit of the changes.

This manual process of scrubbing the data is less preferable than a programming technique. Using a DATA step, changes are easy to make. Note that many of these changes can be made at the same time as the validation is being made. Very often, the validation and scrubbing of data are part of the same physical process. An example of using a DATA step to update data follows:[12]

```
DATA valid;
 SET claims;
 IF diagnosis_code='879' THEN diagnosis_code='880';
 ELSE IF diagnosis_code='X999' THEN diagnosis_code='X099';
RUN;
```

This technique is fraught with the same problems that occur in the validation process. The program shown could become very long, very quickly. What would happen in a situation where 879 became a valid code? The scrubbing of this value would be hidden away in a program, maybe never to be discovered. For this reason, it is essential that the scrubbing process be very methodical. As with the validation rules, they could become table-driven or segmented into macros, which would at least make them manageable.

Scrubbing Duplicate Data

As with validating duplicate data, the scrubbing can become an immense problem. The issue is very much the same: why are there duplicate values appearing in the extracted data from the source system? Removing duplicate values in SAS is a very simple process. There are many techniques that can be used. If SQL is preferred, then the following piece of code will remove any duplicate values from a data file:

```
PROC SQL;
 CREATE TABLE valid AS
 SELECT DISTINCT *
 FROM claims;
QUIT;
```

This will remove any completely similar rows from the file **claims**, and create the new validated file **valid**, which will be devoid of any duplicates.

Sometimes, it might be necessary to remove rows from a table based only on certain columns being duplicated. This can be done using the SAS SORT procedure as follows:

```
PROC SORT DATA=claims OUT=valid NODUPKEY;
 BY diagnosis_code person claim_date;
RUN;
```

---

[12] If SQL is preferred to the DATA step, then the same code could be created using the CASE expression in the SQL procedure. The CASE expression is a SAS extension to ANSII standard SQL. It allows for an action (a reassignment of a column value) based upon a condition being met. For a full description, see: SAS Institute Inc., *SAS® Guide to the SQL Procedure: Usage and Reference*, Version 6, First Edition, Cary, NC: SAS Institute Inc., 1989, 210 pp. pages 121-123

The NODUPKEY option tells SAS to remove any row if there are duplicates of the columns specified in the BY statement. In this case, if there are any duplicate rows with identical values of `diagnosis_code`, `person`, and `claim_date`, then they will be removed.

Both of these techniques are very destructive. It is essential to ensure that these duplicate rows really do need to be removed. After they are gone, because there is no internal record in the data file that they ever existed, unless other pre-cautions (e.g., some form of audit trail) are in effect, then the data cannot be re-created. It might well be preferable to mark the duplicate records as such. This goes along with the basic rule: **re-code** rather than **delete** if at all possible. It might well be possible to have a column that represents a flag to indicate whether or not a row should be used.

 Given a choice between deleting information or re-coding it, choose the latter every time. After the data is deleted, so is any record of it ever having existed.

There are other features within SAS that can help in the scrubbing process. These include the following:

- MODIFY statement (base SAS sofware)
- UPDATE statement (base SAS sofware)
- SELECT statement (base SAS sofware)
- FORMAT procedure (base SAS sofware)

6.5 Integration of Data

Integration of data is a very important step in the Transformation Process, when preparing extracted data so that it can be loaded into the Data Warehouse. Integration of the data is the single most important phase in making the Data Warehouse a usable, consistent tool for the business users. There are instances of Data Warehouses that contain perfectly valid data. Data has been extracted from the source system, has been validated, scrubbed, and fully prepared to load into the Warehouse. Unfortunately, the Data Warehouse is virtually unusable because the *integration* of the data was largely ignored. Integration is the single most important stage in the Transformation Phase. It turns the Data Warehouse from a store of relevant data into a store of relevant information.

The integration of data is the step that adds consistency across the data in the Warehouse. It means that a date in one table has the same internal representation as a date in another. It means that if two tables need to be joined on specific columns, each will be of the same data type (numeric or character, if SAS is being used). It means that, if gender is contained in many tables in the Data Warehouse, it will always be represented the same way (e.g., 'M' or 'F').

Consistency should be actively sought within the Data Warehouse in three major ways. Each of these three topics contain metadata level information that needs to be applied to the internal structure of the Warehouse.

Consistency across Column Attributes

It is highly likely that across a Data Warehouse, there will be columns in different tables that contain the same data. Examples that are very common include: gender, age, product number, salesman number. It is highly advantageous for each of these columns to have the same attributes. Access to the Data Warehouse will take three major forms: direct access by a technologically proficient user, guided access using a tool like the SAS Query window, or from a front end. In every one of these situations, having similar columns with similar attributes will add to the efficiency of access. If the attributes are similar, then there is less to learn for the users and less to program if the access is through a front end.

The column attributes should be similar so that there is less to learn for the end-users. Another reason is that very often, joins will be necessary between tables in the Data Warehouse. Ensuring that column attributes are similar will help ensure that the joins will work. For instance, if a product number is stored as a numeric variable in one table and a character variable in another, then a join between these two tables using product number as the key will not work. This is an extreme example of the importance of consistency in column attributes, but illustrates its importance.

Consistency across Column Attributes when Using SAS Software

Using SAS, the tables within the Data Warehouse will either be SAS data files or SAS views. In either case, there are four main attributes that should be made consistent among columns across the Data Warehouse:

- the column name
- the column label
- the column format
- the column informat.

In most cases, if consistency does not already exist (this can be done by prudent naming during the extraction of the data), this can be performed by using the DATASETS procedure, which is part of base SAS. An example of using the DATASETS procedure follows:

```
PROC DATASETS LIBRARY=dw;
  MODIFY claims;
  RENAME person=member_num;
  LABEL claim_amount='Amount of Claim';
  FORMAT claim_amount DOLLAR12.2;
  INFORMAT diagnosis_code $CHAR25.;
RUN;
QUIT;
```

In this example, PROC DATASETS modifies the table `claims` that is stored in the SAS data library `dw`. It trenames the column `person` to `member_num`. It then establishes a permanent label for the column `claim_amount` so that whenever the column is visually displayed, the label will appear instead of the variable name. The FORMAT statement then assigns the DOLLAR12.2[13] format to the column `claim_amount`. This means that whenever a value of `claim_amount` is displayed, it will be preceded by a $, will contain commas, and will only be displayed to 2 decimal places. Finally, the informat `$char25.` is assigned to the column `diagnosis_code`. This means that when the column is read (as opposed to being displayed) only the first 25 characters will be used.

This information about each of the columns should be part of the metadata of the Data Warehouse. During the design of the Data Warehouse, there should be a concerted effort to ensure that these attributes are common across tables, so that the direct assignment, as performed in the DATASETS procedure above are not necessary. If planning takes place, then the attributes of each of the columns can be determined when they are extracted from the source system, as opposed to when they are ready to load.

To find the attributes of columns in a SAS data file or a SAS view, the CONTENTS procedure can be used. An example follows:

```
PROC CONTENTS DATA=wh.claims;
RUN;
```

This will create a report that will display all the characteristics of the specified data file. An example is shown in Table 6.4.

The information contained in Table 6.4 holds key information pertaining to the data. It is information that should be available to both the users of the

---

[13] SAS® has at its disposal vast numbers of both FORMATS and INFORMATS. To use the software effectively, it is advisable to become familiar with at least the basic options. These are documented in: SAS Institute Inc., *SAS® Language: Reference, Version 6, First Edition*, Cary, NC: SAS Institute Inc., 1990. 1042 pp, pages 635-714. The use of formats and informats are also described in: Delwiche, Lora D., and Slaughter, Susan J., *The Little SAS Book: A Primer*, Cary, NC: SAS Institute Inc., 1995. 228pp. pages 52-53.

```
                          CONTENTS PROCEDURE

Data Set Name:  WH.CLAIMS           Observations:          151,098
Member Type:    DATA                Variables:             5
Engine:         V612                Indexes:               0
Created:        7:42 Wed, 10/31/98  Observation Length:    38
Last Modified:  7:42 Tu, 11/30/98   Deleted Observations:  0
Protection:                         Compressed:            NO
Data Set Type:                      Sorted:                NO
Label:


            -----Engine/Host Dependent Information-----

            Data Set Page Size:              8192
            Number of Data Set Pages:        854
            File Format:                     607
            First Data Page:                 1
            Max Obs per Page:                177
            Obs in First Data Page:          154


            -----Alphabetic List of Variables and Attributes-----
```

#	Variable	Type	Len	Pos	Format	Label
4	CLAIM_DT	Num	6	24	DATE8	Date of Service
3	CLM_AMT	Num	8	16	DOLLAR12.2	Claim Amount
1	DIAG	Char	10	0	$CHAR10.	Diagnosis Code
2	PERSON	Num	6	10	10.	Insurance Holder
5	PROV_NUM	Num	8	30	10.	Provider Number

Table 6.4

Data Warehouse and the designers. The same information can be stored in a data file that can become part of the metadata for the Data Warehouse. This file can be created using the same CONTENTS procedure.

```
PROC CONTENTS DATA=wh.claims OUT=metadata.claims;
RUN;
```

This will create a SAS data file named `claims` in the SAS library `metadata`. This file will contain all the information pertaining to the data file `claims` in the library `wh`. This file can then be stored with the metadata and accessed programmatically when needed.

For experienced SAS users, both CONTENTS and DATASETS are basic procedures that are used time and time again.[14] Together with the SQL procedure, they can control and report upon the structure of the data files or views within the Data Warehouse. For this reason, they are absolutely essential to both reporting upon the attributes of the columns and keeping them consistent.

> *If the values of a column are only made up of numbers, then it is good practice to store them as numeric. Manipulating numeric data is far easier than with strings (character) data, so this benefit should be incorporated if at all possible. Making the column numeric will also create a built-in validation check, because it will not be possible to load it with incorrect character data.*
>
> *A special case is a column whose values contain leading zeros. Technically, these could be stored as numeric but the leading zeros would be lost. In this situation, the ramifications of losing the leading zeros should be thoroughly investigated before a decision is made.*
>
> *SAS has a variety of techniques that can be used to change a character column to a numeric column and vice-versa. It will automatically be performed when some form of character operation (e.g., a concatenation) is performed on the column. It can also be achieved by using the PUT function. However, it is not good practice in a Data Warehousing environment to let this automatic assignment happen. The column type should be explicitly stated and stored in the metadata. If a column is to be character, then it should be specified as such in a LENGTH statement or created as such in the MODIFY options in SQL.*

Consistency across the Values of Data

In the earlier Section, "Consistency across Column Attributes," the consistency of the structure of the tables within the Data Warehouse was discussed. The structure of the tables does not take into account any consistency that the data itself might have. It is as important for the data itself to show consistency, as the structure itself. A feature of almost every single Data Warehouse is dates (see Special Topic, "Dates within the Warehouse"). Different Relational Database Systems internally store dates in a variety of ways. If a Data Warehouse contains data extracted from a variety of data sources, then each of the ways the dates are represented should be changed

---

[14] Information about system catalogs for SAS files can also be obtained using Dictionary Tables. These are a set of SQL objects that are generated at run time to retrieve information about SAS data libraries, SAS data sets, SAS catalogs, SAS system options, and external files that have been associated with the SAS session. Specific information can be found in: SAS Institute Inc., SAS® Technical Report P-222, *Changes and Enhancements to Base SAS® Software, Release 6.07*, Cary, NC: SAS Institute Inc., 1991. 344pp. Pages 286-295.

so that there is complete consistency across the entire Warehouse. Another good example, which is very common, is gender. There are a variety of ways that this can be stored. Some example are: M or F, 1 and 2, Male and Female. The point is that wherever gender appears in the Data Warehouse, the internal coding should always be the same.

The reasons for data value consistency are the same as for the consistency of column attributes discussed in the previous section. First, there will be less for the users of the Data Warehouse to learn, and secondly, when joining tables that use like columns as keys, if the internal representation of the data is not consistent, then the join will be flawed.

There are two parts to actually creating consistency across data values. The first is probably the most difficult:

- The standard convention should be decided upon. Although the repercussions of this decision are principally technological, the internal values should mimic, as closely as practical, the way the business would like to see the values. For example, it is easier for a user to understand M for male and F for female, so there is an argument to standardize on this convention. The M and F convention is preferable because its meaning is obvious from a business perspective. However, there are good technological reasons to use numeric coding (1 and 2). Numbers are easier to manipulate. After the standard convention is decided upon, it should be strictly adhered to and should become part of the metadata for every similar column in every table.
- Each column from the extracted source data that has these standards should then be re-coded to incorporate the benefits of data value consistency.

Consistency across Data Values When Using SAS Software

The first of the two phases to creating consistent data values is a Data Warehouse design issue that is largely irrelevant to the second phase. SAS has many ways to change the values of particular columns. The most flexible and most used is the DATA step. The following is a simple illustration of how a DATA step can be used to re-code data. This example assumes that, in the extracted file, there is a character field named `date` that has the internal representation of the form: 'YYYY-MM-DD'. It has been decided that all dates should be converted to a SAS internal representation.[15]

---

[15] See Special Topic: "Dates within the Warehouse" later in this chapter.

Special Topic:
Dates within the Warehouse

One of the most difficult aspects of Data Warehouse design is how to deal with dates. Dates are an integral part of virtually every Data Warehouse. There is no industry standard as to the internal representation of dates between different database products. This means that, as far as the Data Warehouse is concerned, dates are an open field. This makes it doubly important that they are treated in a consistent manner within the Data Warehouse. Planning for consistent treatment of dates should be a key part of the design process.

Ensure that parts of dates are represented as full dates, so they can be handled in the same way as full dates. For example, suppose monthly data is to be loaded into the Warehouse. This data does not have a specific day of the month. It might be in the format 'YYYY-MM'. A decision should be made as to whether such a date should have the start, middle, or end of the month associated with it, and then stored as such. This column can then be treated as and compared to any other date column.

In SAS, always store a date as a SAS date. The way that SAS deals with dates is that it stores them as an integer with a column attribute of numeric. This makes it very easy to perform calculations using dates. Many other software products have a special date type, which can be limiting in a Data Warehouse environment.

A SAS date value has a value of 0 for 1 January 1960. This value is increased by one for every subsequent day. This means that the value for 1 February 1960 would be 31 because there are 31 days in January. SAS has a myriad of formats, informats, and functions that handle virtually anything that can be done with a date.[16] This means that it is very easy to extract information for very specific time periods.

```
PROC PRINT DATA=claims;
 WHERE DAY(date)=1 AND MONTH(date)=2;
RUN;
```

The example above would print any row from the file **claims** where the column **date** (which is stored as a SAS date) is a Monday (day(date)=1) and in February (month(date)=2). This is a simple example, but it shows how easy it is to extract quite complex requests from a SAS date.

It also raises another question: if the day of the week is important, should it be extracted from the date and stored permanently? From a logical perspective, the answer to this question should be "no" because, as the example above shows, it is very easy to extract that information upon request. There might, however, be an enterprise need that would make the extraction of day of the week advantageous. If the need required heavy analysis on day of the week, then the continual cost of extracting it from the date might be more expensive than storing it permanently. This is mainly a business decision, however, it should not be done as a matter of course but as each need is assessed.

---

[16] See: Aster, Rick and Seidman, Rhena *Professional SAS Programming Secrets*, Updated with New Features of Releases 6.08-6-10, 1997. 588pp.

```
DATA wh.recoded;
 SET wh.claims;
 newdate=INPUT(date,MMDDYY10.);
 FORMAT newdate MMDDYY8.;
 DROP date;
RUN;
```

This DATA step will take the column **date** and using the INPUT function and the **MMDDYY10** informat will convert it to a SAS date. To stay consistent with all the column attributes (see Section "Consistency across Column Attributes"), a format is assigned to the new variable so that whenever the date is viewed, it will be seen in an MM/DD/YY form. Finally, the old column **date** is discarded, so it will not be stored in the new file **wh.recoded.** It is likely that a program to convert values of data would be much longer because of the number of conversions that would realistically be required. Ideally, you would want to handle all of the conversions for the **wh.claims** file in one program.

There are a multitude of techniques within SAS to re-code data. Along with the simple DATA step, the following could be used:

- PROC SQL (base SAS, with use of the CASE statement)
- PROC FORMAT (base SAS)
- DATA step using IF/THEN/ELSE logic (base SAS)
- DATA step using SELECT (base SAS)
- SCL (SAS/AF).

Consistency in Measurement of Columns

There is little, more annoying, than not understanding the units that a particular column might be stored in. This is particularly applicable to columns that store such information as: weight, distance, or volume.

An example of a situation where this problem could arise is in a manufacturing company. Some of the products are sold by the bag, and others are sold loose, by weight. In the billing system, the **amount_sold** might be in units (number of bags) or weight. To further complicate matters, there are different size bags, depending on the product. In addition to this, the weight could be in tons or in pounds, depending upon the product. This means that a single column will have many potential measurements. For the Data Warehouse, this situation will lead to misunderstanding and make any analysis on the data in **amount_sold** potentially disasterous.

What needs to be done in this situation is for this column to be converted to an actual weight **before** loading into the Warehouse. At the same time, the information about the bags must not be lost, but stored elsewhere. The final column that is ready for the Data Warehouse should have a single measurement. In the example above, this will probably be in pounds, but that is a business decision.

Consistency of Measurement When Using SAS Software

Converting to consistent measurements can be approached within SAS in very much the same way that consistency of values is achieved (See "Consistency across Data Values" earlier in this chapter). Again, the hardest part of the process is deciding upon a common measure, and then creating the algorithms to ensure that they are enforced.

The example outlined in the previous section could be approached in the following way:

```
DATA measure;
 SET billing;
  IF product='A1' THEN DO;
  weight=amount_sold * 2000;          *amount_sold in tons;
  END;
  ELSE IF product='A2' THEN DO;       *product A2 sold in bags;
  IF bag_type=1 THEN DO;
  weight=amount_sold * 50;            *bag_type=1 contains 50 lbs.;
  END;
  ELSE DO;
  weight=amount_sold * 10;            * all other bags contain 10 lbs.;
 END;
END;
RUN;
```

This is an example of how to deal with the inconsistency of **measurement** in the column **amount_sold**. In all likelihood, this program would be driven by a table that would cross-reference **product** with **bag_type** and **measurement**. If there were a large number of products, the above program will become very unwieldy.

The look-up table would look like this:

PRODUCT	BAG_TYPE	MEASUREMENT	CONVERSION_FACTOR
A2	1	50lb Bag	50
A2	2	10lb Bag	10
A1		Tons	2000

Table 6.5 Table name=FACTORS

This table would be relatively easy to maintain. If a **bag_type** changed, then only the table would need changing. The column **weight** in the data file would always remain consistent, it would represent the true weight that was sold.

The other big benefit to standardizing the measurement is that, if at some point the non-standard measurements changed, then there would only need to be minor changes to the driving look-up table. For example, suppose that for product A2 in Table 6.5, `bag_type` 1 was changed to 20 lbs. If the data was moved to the Data Warehouse without being converted to a consistent measure, then not only would the weight each bag holds need to be known, but also the date that the bag weight changed would be a factor. Over a period of time, this would become a nightmare for those using the data.

If a driving table were used (Table 6.5) then to create the new values, the SQL procedure could be used:

```
DATA measures;
 MERGE billing factors;
 BY product bag_type; *assumes both files sorted (or indexed) by product and bag_type;
 weight=amount_sold*factor;
 DROP factor measurement;
RUN;
```

This DATA step would join the table `factors` (see Table 6.5) with the table `billing` and create a new column named `weight`, which would represent the consistent measurement.

6.6 Data Derivation

One of the key reasons to create a Data Warehouse is that it is an opportunity to take data that is used for operational reasons and re-organize it so that its use can be more for strategic purposes. Very often in this process, it is necessary to create new information based upon existing data. This can be done in two ways:

- Create the new information before the data is loaded into the Data Warehouse.
- Load the data into the Data Warehouse and then let the new information be created by the users or front-end applications that access the data.

The first of these two options means that there is more control over the creation of this new information. During the Transformation Phase of the Data Warehousing process, the new information will be defined and will be entered into the general metadata. If this information were to be used by an enterprise unit, the precise definition would be known and the results would be consistent.

In the second situation, the creation of the new information is left up to the foibles of the users or of each individual application. This means that there need not be any consistency in terms of the way the information is created. This will eventually manifest itself as a lack of consistency in analyses across time or across different parts of the enterprise. Unfortunately, this lack of trust will then be aimed at the Data Warehouse in general, rather than at the specific inconsistent generation of derived data.

This does not mean that the users should not be allowed to generate derived data from the Warehouse; try and stop them! What it does mean is that in situations where derived data is required to meet a specific enterprise need, this should be formally addressed in the Transformation Phase of the Data Warehouse process. Consistency of business definitions is one of the major problems in any Data Warehouse. By putting the onus of responsibility on the users to create their own derived data, there will be an inevitable decline in the consistency of business definitions, and therefore in the derived data that results from them.

As part of the Transformation Phase of the Data Warehousing process, it is therefore necessary to include the ability to create derived data. This is often called structuring data. The new information that is created will be derived from existing data. This means that before this stage can be completed, the data will have to be both validated and scrubbed. If this is not already performed, then a situation will arise where the derived data will also need validating. The only situation where this might not be the case is where the derived data is a good measure for validity. Therefore, it makes sense to validate the derived data, which will automatically validate the underlying data from which it was created.

It is just as important to include information about derived data within the metadata, as with any other data. Derived data has its own format, rules, and algorithms. It is very important that these be documented.

Data Derivation and SAS Software

As with most of the Transformation Phase and the utilization of SAS software, it is not a question of whether SAS can perform the task, but which of the multitude of different available methods should be used. For every one technique that is illustrated, there will be another ten waiting in the wings. The decision as to which one to use is based upon the skills of the designers, the relative efficiency of each (which will be dependent upon each situation), and personal preference. From a Data Warehousing perspective, an important factor is that, as with the other stages in the Transformation Phase, the algorithms should not be hidden in a program. Although this might work in the short term, remember that a good Data Warehouse is continually changing and evolving. This means that these underlying algorithms will need to change accordingly. If they are embedded as part of a vast program, then maintenance will, over a period of time, become unwieldy.

Creating Derived Columns by Using PROC FORMAT

One of the techniques that can be used to create derived columns within SAS is the use of the FORMAT procedure. The FORMAT procedure has more than one function. It not only can be used to validate data, as illustrated in the Section, "SAS Tools for Finite Validation" earlier in this chapter, but it also can be used as the basis for assigning values to a new column.

Using the example of the table **claims**, there might be thousands of different Diagnosis Codes. These could be clustered into logical groupings: for instance, there could be Diagnosis Codes that refer to heart problems, or Diagnosis Codes that are specific to outpatient treatment. Very often, an enterprise need will require that these Diagnosis Codes are grouped, which will save the user analysts from having to do this work. These groupings could be defined as a format or a series of formats (if there are a series of different groupings). A format could be created as follows:

```
PROC FORMAT LIBRARY=wh_fmat;
 VALUE $diag_f1
   'A100', 'A101', 'A102'        ='Heart'
   'A103', 'A104', 'A105'        ='Lungs'



   'Z876'                        ='ENT';
RUN;
```

This would create a format named **diag_f1** that would be stored in the library **wh_fmat**. Note that it is not always necessary to explicitly state each of the values on the left-hand side of the '=' assignment. This procedure will accept ranges. This could then be used to create a derived field as follows:

```
DATA derived;
 SET claims;
 LENGTH diag_grp $ 40;
 diag_grp=put(diag_grp,$diag_f1.);
RUN;
```

Again, this DATA step creates one, new derived column **diag_grp**. In the Transformation Phase in the Data Warehousing process, it is likely that all the new columns would be derived in a single DATA step (if possible). One of the advantages of this technique is that it is essentially table-driven. The format `diag_f1` can be extracted into a control SAS file very easily, modified, and then written back out to the format. This can be done as follows:

```
PROC FORMAT LIBRARY=wh_fmat CNTLOUT=edit_fmt;
 SELECT $diag_f1;
RUN;
```

The SAS data file `edit_fmt` would be created and if any changes were needed to the groupings (maybe new Diagnosis Codes added) these can be made. The updated values could then be read back from this file into the format as follows:

```
PROC FORMAT LIBRARY=wh_fmat CNTLIN=edit_fmt;
RUN;
```

Creating the formats in the first place can be a lengthy process, especially if the number of groupings is very large. If these values are already available in a SAS file, then by using the CNTLIN= option, the format could be programmatically created. For a data file to be eligible to be included in the CNTLIN= option, it must have, at a minimum, the following columns: `fmtname`, `start`, `label` and `type`. `fmtname` should be the name of the format, `start` will be the value to be formatted, `label` will be the format that will be assigned to `start`, and `type` will be either C or N depending on whether it is a character or a numeric value.

The following file could be used as the input to the FORMAT procedure to create the format `diag_f1` as illustrated earlier:

FMTNAME	START	LABEL	TYPE
DIAG_F1	A100	Heart	C
DIAG_F1	A101	Heart	C
DIAG_F1	A104	Lungs	C

Table 6.6

Creating Derived Columns by Using PROC SQL

Using straight assignments either in a DATA step or in the SQL procedure can create new derived columns. In both cases, there is a vast array of operators and functions that can be used to expedite the derivation of the new columns. To discuss all of these operators or functions is beyond the scope of this book, and they are well explained in all the SAS documentation that refers to the DATA step and PROC SQL.

Creating Summary Data

Along with derivations of data based upon other values in the same row of information, it is often necessary within a Data Warehouse to include summary data alongside detail data. This is especially important if an enterprise need requires, for instance, that a particular value be compared against normative data. For example, using the file `claims`, it might be necessary to report on a claim basis how a claim amount for a specific diagnosis is compared to the average amount of all the claims for that diagnosis. It would be possible to create a summary file, and then either ask the users to perform the join so that the summarized information could be viewed alongside the detail data, or a view could be created for the user that would perform the same thing. There might be situations where it might be more efficient to store the summarized information with the detail information. It would certainly use less computer resources when the information was needed. The decision as to the best action is based upon the sophistication of the users, and the number of times such requests will be processed.

If it were decided that it would be worthwhile to store the summary data with the detail data, then the following is a technique that could be used:

```
PROC SQL;
 CREATE TABLE summary AS
 SELECT diagnosis_code, SUM(claim_amount) AS diag_avg
 FROM claim
 GROUP BY diagnosis_code;

 CREATE TABLE det_avg AS
 SELECT a.diagnosis_code, a.claim_amount, diag_avg
 FROM claim a, summary b
 WHERE a..diagnosis_code=b.diagnosis_code;
QUIT;
```

There are two steps involved because the summary amounts must be known before they can be combined with the detail amounts. The first step in this SQL procedure takes the data file `claims`, and summarizes it by `diagnosis_code`. A calculated field named `diag_avg` is created, which is the average of all the `claim_amounts` for each `diagnosis_code`.

The second stage takes the file **summary** and merges (joins) it back with the file `claims`. This step creates a new data file named `det_avg`. It will have one more column (named `diag_avg`) than the original file (`claims`).

Storing Summary Data

This concept of storing summarized data alongside detail data requires a lot of thought. It should not be done unless there are direct needs and associated benefits. It is usually only of use if the data needs to be analyzed at the detail level. If the data does not need analysis at the detail level, then it makes more sense to store the summarized data separately (see Section 6.9), or if at all possible, create a Multi-Dimensional database.[17]

---

[17] See Chapter 4 for a discussion on the Multi-Dimensional Database structure.

6.7 Denormalization of Data

When data is extracted from the source Operational System, it is usually in a normalized form.[18] This is not always an ideal form for the Data Warehouse because:

- For even the simplest request, it is possible that multiple data tables must be accessed. This leads to multiple table joins that are very costly in computer resources.
- The users of the Data Warehouse must understand the structure of many tables and the concepts of joins. Depending on the knowledge of the users, this might discourage usage of the Data Warehouse.

Denormalizing extracted data sources is, in essence, taking all the joins that would be necessary if the tables were to remain in their normal form, and performing these joins ahead of time. This means that denormalization techniques are no more than carefully constructed pre-joins between selected tables.

Denormalizing data also has disadvantages. The primary problems are

- the lack of referential integrity
- possible redundancy in the data[19]
- increased usage of storage space for data.

The advantages in a Data Warehouse environment to denormalizing the data usually far outweigh the disadvantages.

Denormalizing Data by Using SAS Software

The are two principle tools that are used in the denormalization of data when using SAS software. These are the SQL procedure and using match-merge techniques in the DATA step.

Using PROC SQL to Denormalize Data

The SAS flavor of SQL will allow for four types of joins.[20] These are

- The Inner Join: this will join tables and only result in output where there is a match between them. This is the default join type in PROC SQL and will always attempt a many-to-many match.

---

[18] Normalization and its implications to Data Warehousing is discussed in Chapter 3, Section 3.3.

[19] See Special Topic: Data Redundancy with the Data Warehouse, Chapter 3.

[20] Any book on SQL will describe the types of joins available and their implications on the resultant output. The SAS flavor of SQL is fully described in: SAS Institute Inc., *SAS® Guide to the SQL Procedure: Usage and Reference* , Version 6, First Edition, Cary, NC: SAS Institute Inc., 1989, 210 pp.

The three other types of joins have to be explicitly requested in the PROC SQL code. The description is taken directly from the SAS online help facility:

An outer join combines rows of data from two tables. Three types of outer joins are

- Left Join: returns all matching rows in both tables, in addition to rows in the left table that have no matching rows in the right table.
- Right Join: returns all matching rows in both tables, in addition to rows in the right table that have no matching rows in the left table.
- Full Join: returns all matching and unmatching rows from both tables.

If SQL is to used to denormalize the data, then these concepts must be thoroughly understood. SQL is extremely good at merging information from different tables, but it is very easy to obtain erratic results. When dealing with very large data files, these erratic results might not be apparent, so, as with any code, it should be thoroughly tested for reliability before being trusted.

The key to denormalizing when using SQL (or other techniques) is to understand exactly what is required in the result set (the output). If this cannot be fully documented, then it is unlikely that any denormalization technique will help. Although this sounds obvious, this preparation is important not only so the joining techniques can be optimized, but also because it is part of the design of the Data Warehouse. Don't denormalize for the sake of it, but because there are enterprise needs that can more readily be met because of the technique. This goes back to one of the basic rules we have in Data Warehousing: if it isn't doing anything directly for the enterprise, then don't bother!

Using SQL to denormalize data is a book topic in itself, but a basic example is shown in Table 6.7. These techniques are thoroughly documented elsewhere,[21] and it is well worth reading as much as possible on the topic before deciding upon specific techniques. One important factor is that in Data Warehousing, there is far more likely to be an emphasis on outer, rather than inner joins. In an Operational System, because of referential integrity,[22] an inner join will usually return a result set. This cannot be assumed in a Data Warehouse. When designing the denormalization process, it should be assumed that there will be missing information. If an inner join is used, then

---

[21] See SAS Institute Inc., *Proceedings of the Twenty-Second Annual SAS® Users Group International Conference,* Cary, NC: SAS Institute Inc., 1997. 1642 pp. There are several papers discussing SQL and table joining. A specific example of a paper that is directly related to the denormalization of data is: Bahler, Caroline: "It Takes at Least Two to Tango—A Data Set Joining Primer" (*Paper 38*).

[22] See Chapter 3, Section 3.3

it is possible that information will be lost. Consider the following example:

CUSTOMER_NUMBER	PRODUCT	AMOUNT_SOLD
A1	34	45.54
A2	45	67.76
A3	98	75.43
A1	55	99.87

Table 6.7 DATA FILE=BILLING

PRODUCT	PRODUCT_GROUP
34	Rubber
45	Plastic
98	Metal

Table 6.8 DATA FILE=GROUP

In this first example, an inner join is used to denormalize the two tables (6.7 and 6.8). The idea in the Data Warehouse design is that the PRODUCT GROUP should be stored with the detail information. This is because the enterprise needs dictate that product groups are needed in the analysis of sales.

```
PROC SQL;
 CREATE TABLE denorm_i AS
 SELECT a.customer_number, a.product, a.amount_sold, b.product_group
 FROM billing a, group b
 WHERE a.product=b.product;
QUIT;
```

The resultant table **denorm_i** will look like this:

CUSTOMER_NUMBER	PRODUCT	AMOUNT_SOLD	PRODUCT_GROUP
A1	34	45.54	Rubber
A2	45	67.76	Plastic
A3	98	75.43	Metal

Table 6.9 DATA FILE=DENORM_I

Now, instead of using the default inner join in the Table 6.9, let's use a left join.

```
PROC SQL;
 CREATE TABLE denorm_l AS
 SELECT a.customer_number, a.product, a.amount_sold, b.product_group
 FROM billing a left join group b
 ON a.product=b.product;
QUIT;
```

CUSTOMER_NUMBER	PRODUCT	AMOUNT_SOLD	PRODUCT_GROUP
A1	34	45.54	Rubber
A2	45	67.76	Plastic
A1	55	99.87	
A3	98	75.43	Metal

Table 6.10 DATA FILE=DENORM_L

The difference in the code is fairly subtle, but the difference and repercussions of the resultant file are immense. Note that in Table 6.10, there is an extra row that corresponds to a **product** value of 55. This value does not have a corresponding entry in the file **group** (Table 6.8). There is an argument that says that the table **group** should have this entry because it should not be possible for a product to be sold that does not apparently exist. On one level (a logical one), this might be the case, but by the time this argument is disproved, it might be too late: the data might be gone.

This problem has a direct link to the validation and scrubbing process. One of the checks on the **product** should be to cross-reference it with the file **group**. This illustrates another point, that the denormalization of the data can also be used as part of the validation process. If the tables are denormalized, then it is easier to check for the validity of the data.

 Unless absolutely positive that there will be no unexpected results, avoid using inner joins when denormalizing data. It is better to be safe than sorry, so default to outer joins.

Using Match-Merging to Denormalize Data

Match-Merging is a technique that is used with the SAS DATA step. Any number of data files can be joined in a single match-merge, but each one must be either sorted or indexed on the columns that will be used within, as the joining criteria. This can best be illustrated by using an example:

```
DATA denorm;
 MERGE billing group;
 BY product; *assumes that product is indexed or sorted in both billing and group;
RUN;
```

The table **denorm** will look exactly like the table **denorm_1** shown in Table 6.10. Note that both the data files **billing** and **group** should be either sorted or indexed by the columns in the BY statement (**product**). The Match-Merge technique has very much the same capabilities to join tables as the SQL procedure has.

There is one situation where the SQL procedure is definitely preferable: when joining tables in a *many-to-many* instance. This means that there might be more than one instance of a specific value in the columns that are used to join the two tables (in the situation above, this would be **product**). For instance, in our example, if the tables **group** and **billing** had **product** 34 more than once, then this would be a many-to-many join. In the denormalization of tables, this should be a very unusual situation, but one that should be looked for.

It is possible to re-create the output in Table 6.10 using the match-merge technique, as follows:

```
DATA denorm;
 MERGE billing(IN=a) group(IN=b);
 BY product; *assumes that product is indexed or sorted in both billing and group;
 IF. a AND b;
RUN;
```

In this situation a row is only output to the data file **denorm** if a match is found (if it can be found in both **billing** and **group**). The use of the IN= option is a very powerful technique to determine exactly which rows should be written to the output data file.

PROC SQL or Match-Merge?

Both techniques have strengths and weaknesses. There is always discussion as to which one is the best to use, and there seem to be strong proponents on both sides. By-and-large, these discussions are technical and generic in nature, whereas we are concerned directly with how each will apply within the Data Warehousing environment. The truth is that both of them have their place, and the relative merits should be determined in every individual situation. However, there are a few basic rules and advice that can be applied:

■ Default to PROC SQL. The code can be understood and optimized by individuals who do not know any SAS programming whatsoever.
■ PROC SQL does not require that the data files be sorted or indexed before they are joined. This could save resources.
■ There is the danger with PROC SQL that a large intermediate data file is created (a Cartesian Product). When dealing with large data files, this can become a resource problem. Clever SQL programming can reduce the size of this intermediate data file but not if two tables are to be joined without any prior subsetting.
■ The Match-Merge technique is probably preferable if there is complex data validation, scrubbing, data derivation, or integration occurring at the same time. The base SAS code is far more able to deal with manipulation of data than SQL.
■ SQL will be preferable in situations where there is a *many-to-many* match.

Special Topic:
Time-Stamping Data

Time-Stamping is the process of tagging every row in the Data Warehouse. Tagging means that there will be a column (or a series of columns) that will contain a date. This date will correspond to the date the row underwent some form of activity. This activity could be: created, loaded, or modified.

Not all Data Warehouse implementations use Time-Stamping. It takes valuable storage space and, if it is never going to be used, is superfluous. It definitely has its place in Data Warehouses that use a Changed Data Capture technique. The Time-Stamp will let the Data Warehouse administrators know exactly in which Refresh Cycle an update was performed for any row in the Data Warehouse.

Time-stamping is an easy process when using SAS. It can best be achieved by using either of the functions **TODAY** or **DATETIME**. The choice depends on whether the time as well as the date are to be stored. An example of creating a Time-Stamp follows:

```
DATA denorm;
 MERGE billing(IN=a) group(IN=b);
 BY product;
 IF a AND b;
 datestmp=TODAY();
 timestmp=DATETIME();
RUN;
```

The function **TODAY** will return a SAS date value, and the function **DATETIME** will return a SAS datetime value.

6.8 Summarizing Data

The summarizing of data logically comes toward the end of the Transformation Phase in the Data Warehousing process. One of the essential features of summarized data is that it should tie back to the detail. Only after the detail data is deemed correct can the summarized data be created. This means that the validation, scrubbing, integration, and derivation will almost certainly have to be completed for the summarization to take place. If the detail data is still being worked on while the summarized data is being created, then the likelihood is that it will have to be re-created.

It is possible to have a full Data Warehouse implementation without any summarization of data. This is a highly unusual situation because it depends on the ability of the business users to summarize on demand (at run time). This will be very expensive on computer resources. One of the major reasons why there might be limited summarization of data is that the enterprise needs have not been fully defined. This means that the Data Warehouse designers do not know how the data should be summarized.

Generic summarization of data, without specific business needs in mind can be a pointless activity. As in the Data Warehouse implementations that are completed before the users have been fully consulted (the *limited-use* Data Warehouse),[23] the summarized data might never be used. Ideally, the detail data should only be summarized with a specific enterprise need in mind. If a data file containing summarized data can be used to either completely or partially help fulfill multiple enterprise needs, then so much the better.

The creation of Data Marts (data extracted from the Warehouse for specific purposes) is usually, but not necessarily, summarized. It is very unlikely that a Data Mart will only contain detail data, but in some situations that might be the case (e.g., when the department that needs the information requires it on a detail level, but it is not practical for them to use the full Data Warehouse). This means that the summarization of data is one of the key stages in ensuring that the Data Warehouse will actually be used. If the summarization is performed to reflect enterprise needs, then it increases the likelihood of Data Warehouse utilization. Get the summaries wrong, and it is likely to turn the users away from the Data Warehouse.

Pre-summarization of data is performed for two major reasons:

- It increases efficiency by reducing the number of times the large detail data in the Warehouse will need to be accessed.
- It puts the data in a form that is easier for the users to both analyze and report upon.

Summarizing Data When Using SAS Software

Summarization of data is a form of data manipulation, which is a strength of SAS software. There are many techniques available to summarize data, but of these, three are most commonly used:

- Create a Multi-Dimensional Database.[24]
- Use the SUMMARY (or the MEANS) procedure.
- Use the SQL procedure.

In any of these three cases, it is necessary to understand not only the requirements (needs) that make summarization an attractive option but also the actual data itself. Whichever option is used, Facts will be summarized by one, or a series of, Dimensions.[25] Distinguishing between the two, however,

---

[23] See Chapter 3, Section 3.2 for a discussion on *limited-use* Data Warehouses.
[24] See Chapter 4 for full information about SAS/MDDB.
[25] See Chapter 3, Section 3.5 for a discussion on Dimensions and Facts.

is not part of the Transformation Phase of the Data Warehousing process. This information should be fully understood before the implementation of the Data Warehouse even takes place. It is part of the design of the Conceptual Data Warehouse where the enterprise needs are broken down in terms of business, so that the Dimensions and Facts are fully recognized. The summarization stage when transforming data in the Warehouse is merely the implementation of what is already known, not part of the design. If it becomes part of the design, then it will be necessary to take a few steps back and really assess the overall strategy of the Data Warehouse Process.

CUSTOMER_NUMBER	AMOUNT_SOLD	PRODUCT	PRODUCT_GROUP
A1	45.54	34	Rubber
A2	67.76	45	Plastic
A1	99.87	55	
A3	75.43	98	Metal
A1	88.00	34	Rubber
A2	86.23	45	Plastic
A1	120.00	55	

Table 6.11 DATA FILE=DETAIL

Example: Using PROC SUMMARY to Summarize Data

The SUMMARY procedure is especially advantageous when multiple summary levels are required.

For example, consider the following code which uses the denormalized data in Table 6.11:

```
PROC SUMMARY DATA=detail;
 CLASS customer_number product;
 VAR amount_sold;
 ID product_group;
 OUTPUT OUT=sumdata SUM=;
RUN;
```

This procedure will take Table 6.10 (**denorm_1**) and sum all the values of **product** for every unique combination of **customer_number** and **product**. It will also, at the same time, create a **sum** of all the values of **product** for each unique value of **customer_number** and every unique value of **product**. Additionally, a grand total of the sum of all values of **product** will be created. All of these summaries will be contained within the new file **sumdata**. Because there are different levels of summaries, and they are all in the same output data file (**sumdata**), there must be some way to distinguish between them. This is done by looking at the column **_type_**. This is automatically created by the procedure and has a value that corresponds to the summary level.

Contains the level of the summary	Contains the number of detail records	Contains the sum of the column `amount_sold`

PRODUCT_ GROUP	CUSTOMER_ NUMBER	PRODUCT	_TYPE_	_FREQ_	AMOUNT_ SOLD
Rubber			0	7	582.83
Rubber			1	2	133.54
Plastic		34	1	2	153.99
		45	1	2	219.87
Metal		55	1	1	75.43
Rubber	A1	98	2	4	353.41
Plastic	A2		2	2	153.99
Metal	A3		2	1	75.43
Rubber	A1	34	3	2	133.54
	A1	55	3	2	219.87
Plastic	A2	45	3	2	153.99
Metal	A3	98	3	1	75.43

Table 6.12 DATAFILE=SUMDATA

The data file **sumdata** can be seen in Table 6.12. Note that there are four levels of summary, and that they can be distinguished by looking at the values of the variable **_type_**. The column **_freq_** is also added by the procedure. The value of this column denotes the number of rows from the table DETAIL that make up the summary.

Note also that the column **product_group** has also been included in the data file **sumdata** because it was referenced in the ID statement. The value of **product_group** will be the value of this column in the detail data file (**detail**) on the final row used in making up the particular summary level.

Example: Obtaining the Lowest Level of Summary

It is often not necessary to obtain every level of summary. Very often, only the highest level of summary is required (in Table 6.12, this would be when **_type_**=3). This can easily be achieved by modifying the procedure code slightly, adding the option NWAY to the PROC SUMMARY line, as follows:

```
PROC SUMMARY DATA=detail NWAY;
 CLASS customer_number product;
 VAR amount_sold;
 ID product_group;
 OUTPUT OUT=sumdata SUM=;
RUN;
```

In this case, the data file SUMDATA would only contain the final four rows from the Table 6.12, where `_type_`=3.

Additional Feature of PROC SUMMARY

The SUMMARY procedure does not limit the Fact columns to be summed. There are a variety of statistics available. All of these statistics are documented in the *SAS Procedures Guide Version 6, Third Edition*. They include: mean, the number of observations with nonmissing values, standard deviation, minimum, and maximum. The SUMMARY procedure is also capable of including or excluding missing values in the calculations, so how missing values are to be treated for the particular Fact column should be known.

Using PROC SQL to Summarize Data

The SQL procedure is capable of performing many of the same tasks as the SUMMARY procedure, but it cannot easily create multiple levels of summary. An example of using the SQL procedure to achieve the same results as the SUMMARY procedure follows:

```
PROC SQL;
 CREATE TABLE sumdata
 AS SELECT SUM(amount_sold) as amount_sold, customer_number, product
 FROM detail
 GROUP BY customer_number, product;
QUIT;
```

This produces the same results as the SUMMARY procedure, with the NWAY option shown earlier. Note also that SQL will not handle an ID column as the SUMMARY procedure does.

Summarizing Large Data Files

Summarizing very large files is often a problem in the Data Warehouse environment. There are various ways to avoid this: first, break up the summaries into smaller jobs, and then bring all the pieces together after these jobs have finished.[26] Using the SUMMARY procedure, it is often quicker to pre-sort (or index) the data file by the columns that would be used in the CLASS statement, and then replacing the CLASS statement with a BY statement.

---

[26] An excellent paper addressing this technique is: Raithel, Michael A., "Summarizing Impossibly Large SAS® Data Sets for the Data Warehouse Server Using Horizontal Summarization," SAS Institute Inc., *Proceedings of the Twenty-Second Annual SAS® Users Group International Conference*, Cary, NC: SAS Institute Inc., 1997. 1642pp. Pages 514-518.

Additional Tools for Summarizing Data

There are also other ways that data can be summarized when using SAS software. Some of these have already been illustrated. They include

- the DATA step
- PROC FREQ
- PROC TABULATE.

6.9 The Creation of Business Metadata

One of the key parts of the Transformation Phase in the Data Warehousing process is that it is an opportunity to create metadata. The collection of metadata is a key activity to ensure that the warehouse can be both used and maintained. It acts as both information for the users to understand the contents and as storage for parameters that drive the maintenance process. The reason that this phase is a good place to collect the metadata is that at some point in the process, all of the data is being read. While it is being

Special Topic:
Indexing in the Data Warehouse

Indexing data files within the Warehouse is very important for performance considerations. In traditional Operational Systems, indexing was seen as a way to improve joins between normalized tables (see Chapter 3, Section 3.3), but they play a very different role in the Data Warehouse environment.

Like summarizing data, the creation of indexes can only be successfully performed if the enterprise needs are thoroughly understood. This will lead to an understanding of the way the data needs to be accessed, and therefore, how best to index that data.

Although there is often the need to join tables with a Data Warehouse, the primary use of indexes is for fast subsetting/extraction of data. The primary way by which data will be subset in a Data Warehouse is based upon the defined **Dimensions**. In the design of the Data Warehouse, it is therefore necessary to look at each of these **Dimensions** and make a decision as to whether an index will improve performance. Very often, access to data is based upon a combination of different **Dimensions**, in which case there might be a case for the creation of composite indexes.

Be prepared in the Data Warehouse to experience the strange situation of an index file being larger than the underlying data file. This could well happen, especially on summarized data. This is not necessarily a bad thing, as long as the indexes are being used, and it does not slow down the loading of the Data Warehouse significantly.

Using SAS, indexes can be built using the SQL procedure, the DATASETS procedure, and as part of the data set option.

read, the extra tasks of collecting information about the data (the metadata) can be efficiently completed.

What metadata should be collected is based upon the individual needs of each Data Warehouse implementation. However, the data can be divided into two major groups:

- Metadata pertaining to Dimension data.
- Metadata pertaining to Fact data.

There is general metadata that should be collected for both Dimension and Fact data when the column is first registered in the Data Warehouse. This includes:

- Column Name
- Business Name (should be stored as a label)
- Column type (character or numeric)
- Column length
- Table it will be contained within
- Business definition (rule)
- Business owner[27]
- Format
- Informat
- Whether the column is an index or part of an index
- How to handle missing information.

Some of this information will be inherent in the dictionary of the table itself (e.g., format, informat, column type, column length) but many will not. A mechanism should be set up for this information to be stored.

Metadata for Dimension Data

One of the problems with collecting metadata is that it can become an end in itself. There is no point in collecting it unless it will be used in some way. This means for each column in the Data Warehouse that can be considered Dimension data, decisions should be made as to what is useful. However, there are some basics that should always be collected:

- For each column, there should be a list of all the values that make up its domain.

---

[27]Assigning business owners on a column basis is not commonly practiced. However, it is a good idea, because it is usually columns of information that are questioned, rather than a table. If it is possible to register a business owner on a table (as opposed to a column) basis, then this is preferable, mainly because it is less work.

- The number of instances of each item within the domain should be collected.
- The date that an item within the domain was first found should also be collected.

Each of these can be collected very easily during the Transformation Phase, using techniques that have already been discussed in this chapter.

It should not be necessary to read the entire Data Warehouse to update metadata. It should be possible to create this metadata on the new data, and then incorporate it with the existing metadata. The following is a simple technique for doing this. This program will look at a column named **product** in the file **billing**. It uses the FREQ procedure to extract the information, and then creates a new consolidated metadata file.

```
PROC FREQ DATA=billing NOPRINT;
 TABLES product / OUT=billmeta;
RUN;
```

This first step will create a list of possible values in the column **product** in the data file **billing** and save it in the new data file **billmeta** . There exists an 'old' metadata file, named **oldmeta**, that contains the metadata from previous loads. The following step will incorporate the old (**oldmeta**) with the new (**billmeta**) to create updated metadata without reading the entire column already loaded into the Warehouse.

```
PROC APPEND BASE=oldmeta DATA=billmeta;
RUN;

PROC FREQ DATA=oldmeta NOPRINT;
 TABLES product /OUT=modmeta;
 WEIGHT count;
RUN;
```

The new metadata, **billmeta**, is first appended to the existing metadata (**oldmeta**) using the APPEND procedure. Another PROC FREQ is then run, using the column **count** as a weight. This will result in the new data file **modmeta** containing all the existing values of the column **product**. It will also mean that the statistics collected by the FREQ procedure will be correct, for **count** and **percent**. This metadata has therefore been updated without having to re-read both the incoming data and the data already loaded in the Data Warehouse.

Collecting such information will be of great use in the Data Warehouse. If specific values of a Dimension are needed, then this table could be used as the lookup list. If the SAS Query Window is being used, then without much manipulation, it could be incorporated as a lookup table.[28] Users, without knowing it, often ask for metadata, as opposed to data itself. This metadata can be created as needed, but this could become very expensive. If the table `billing` were 20 million rows, then to find all the unique values of the column `product` would take immense resources (a full table scan if the column were not indexed). To have such information at hand and available, would answer many of the questions that are asked of the data.

Metadata for Fact Data

Fact data requires a different type of metadata than Dimension data. Usually, this is of a statistical rather than a categorical nature (as one would expect). This means that the type of metadata that is needed is

- Maximum value
- Minimum value
- Range
- Mean
- Standard deviation.

This kind of data can be collected using either the SUMMARY or the SQL procedure. If the statistic is additive, then the same technique, as illustrated in the earlier section, "Metadata for Dimension Data," could be used to combined metadata from incoming data with that already collected for the Data Warehouse.

In all of the examples given, only single Dimension or Fact columns have been used in a single procedure. This was done because the aim was to illustrate techniques. In nearly every case, multiple columns could be analyzed in the same step. This should be encouraged because one of the major costs of the Transformation Phase in the Data Warehousing process is that of reading and writing data (Input/Output). The entire phase should be designed to reduce this cost, so it is essential that as much as possible is achieved with each I/O.

---

[28] SAS Institute Inc., *SAS® Guide to the SQL Query Window: Usage and Reference, Version 6, first Edition*, Cary, NC: SAS Institute Inc., 1995. 167pp., pages 102-106.

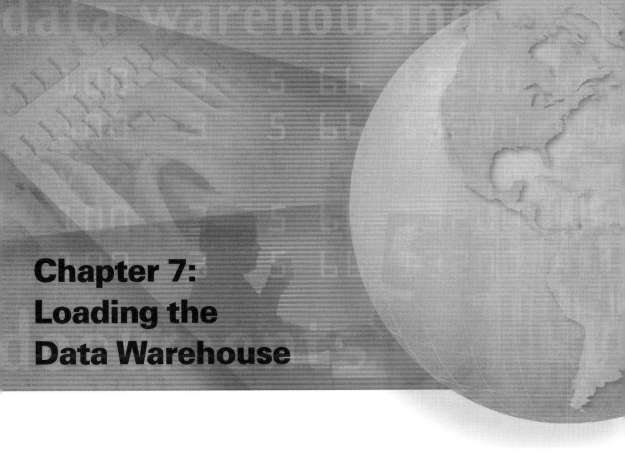

Chapter 7:
Loading the
Data Warehouse

7.1 Loading the Data Warehouse

Loading the Data Warehouse occurs after the Transformation Phase has been completed. The vast majority of Data Warehouses are refreshed on a monthly basis, although this is a business, not a technological decision. In situations where the Data Warehouse is loaded monthly, there is often a problem with resource contention from the Operational Systems. This is because most Operational Systems work on a monthly cycle to meet the needs of the enterprise. The mayhem that surrounds 'month-end' in most enterprises creates a resource problem for all Operational Systems that will 'spill over' into the Data Warehouse environment. Even if the Data Warehouse is not running on the same computer or environment as the Operational System, there will still be the problem of coordination with the Operational System. There is, unfortunately, no easy solution to this conundrum. In mainframe environments, the end-of-month process is usually run by the utilization of a *job stream*. This is a series of programs that are designed to run, one after another, based upon the success of the previous job. Extract programs for Data Warehouses are not usually part of this job stream. This means that the Data Warehouse extract programs usually have to wait until the complete month-end process has ended before they can begin.

Several enterprise-wide operational software products now claim that there is no actual month-end process. This means that the job streams of old do not exist as such. As the data is entered during the month, there is a perpetual, iterative month-end process. There are two major repercussions to this from a Data Warehousing perspective:

- First of all, even if the software doesn't work on a monthly cycle, the business still does. End-of-month performance is still essential to ensure that the company is on target. It also helps to gauge quarterly and annual results. The Data Warehouse will still be required to freeze data monthly, so there will still be a conflict of resources during a key business period.

- In situations where there is no true month-end, it will be especially important in the Data Warehouse process to ensure that the correct data is being extracted. One of the beauties of a month-end is that the books are usually closed. On the one hand, this means that the data will not be revisited (which is good because no data will be changed), but on the other hand, revisions for the previous period (month) will be made in the current period. This gives the Data Warehouse designers a business question: should revisions made to the previous period in the current period be reflected in the month they actually refer to, or in the month where the revision is made? For example, suppose that in a General Ledger, a particular expense item was incorrectly entered into the wrong account number. The books were closed for the month, and then the mistake was discovered. This would mean that the entries would have to be backed out of the incorrect account and re-entered in the correct one in the current period (because the old one was closed). This leads to a Data Warehouse problem because there will be incorrect data for two accounts for two months. When the data is averaged over the months, this will not matter, but if monthly analysis is performed, then it will. The decision as to how to handle such situations is a business one, but the repercussions are technical.

Process for Loading the Data Warehouse

Assuming that the data has been extracted and has successfully been transformed, then the next job in the process is to load the Data Warehouse. There are different parts of the Data Warehouse that usually need to be loaded. The data that will be loaded is either in a detail or a summary format. What often happens is that only detail data is loaded, and then summary data (for the Data Marts) is created. This will lead to a two-stage loading process:

- The loading of the detail data
- The loading of the summary data after it has been calculated.

The timing for both of these will be independent. Depending on the size of the Data Warehouse, the loading process can be very lengthy. One of the often-ignored aspects of deciding upon the Data Warehouse architecture is the speed with which a data repository can be loaded. Some products are faster than others, and the process should be designed with this in mind. If the loading process runs into days (as is often the case with large implementations), this is obviously a weakness in the process and one that should be addressed. Another key factor is whether it is necessary to take the Data Warehouse 'off-line' during the loading process. Technically, this is not always necessary, but from a business perspective, it might be a good idea. As the Data Warehouse is being refreshed, the results will be dynamic (because the data will be in a state of change), which, depending upon the business question being answered, could lead to incorrect (or incomplete) analyses.

Storing Data for the Data Warehouse

The actual repository for the data within a Data Warehouse is often a Relational Database Management System. The reason for this is that designers tend to be caught in the trap of assuming that products designed for extremely fast retrieval of small bits of data will also be able to handle the sequential retrieval and analysis of large amounts of data. Many of these Relational Database products bring with them excess baggage to the Data Warehousing environment. Referential integrity, audit trails, two-phase commits, and roll-back capabilities common to Relational Database systems are not commonly needed in the Data Warehousing environmen. They bring with them an overhead that could detrimentally affect performance.

Decisions Affecting Loading of the Data Warehouse

The key factors to decide upon in loading the Data Warehouse are as follows:

- Should the Data Warehouse be shut down during the loading?
- Is the loading process optimized for performance? (This is often overlooked in the design process because Warehouse performance is seen as the speed in which users can access already loaded data.)
- Will the entire Data Warehouse (including the Data Marts) be loaded simultaneously or consecutively?

- Is it possible to spread out the loading of the Data Warehouse over longer time periods, instead of over-utilizing resources during a very short period of time? The answer to this is probably a resounding NO, but it is worth asking anyway.

7.2 Three Different Loading Strategies

Three different strategies in loading data into the warehouse are

- Full Production Load
- Full Refresh Cycle
- Changed Data Capture.

 Three strategies used to update a Data Warehouse are

- *Full Production Load: Every time new data is available, the entire Data Warehouse is re-loaded. This can be effective in a small Data Warehouse or in the initial creation, but it is of limited use otherwise.*

- *Full Refresh Cycle: Every time the Warehouse is updated, only data between two specific points in time is used.*

- *Changed Data Capture: Every time the Warehouse is updated, only data that has changed since the last update will be incorporated.*

Full Production Load

The first of these is always the easiest to deal with from a loading perspective. With the Full Production Load, it is just a question of taking the data from the Transformation Process and writing it out to the data repository.

Full Refresh Cycle

The Full Refresh Cycle is a little more complex because it means that the newly transformed data is to be appended to the external structure. This is quite similar to the third option.

Changed Data Capture

In this case, the new data is combined with the existing Data Warehouse data, based upon pre-set conditions. In both of these latter strategies, it is usual for relatively small amounts of data to be added to the pre-existing data within the warehouse.

7.3 Using SAS to Load the Data Warehouse

For users of SAS, the repository for the data within the warehouse will either be in a SAS or an external file format.[1] From a SAS perspective, however, the final decision as to the data repository is not an issue because SAS can write to virtually any other format. Two different situations are

- Using SAS to load transformed data into an external file format.
- Using SAS to load transformed data into a SAS file format.

Using SAS to Load Data into a Data Repository other than SAS

Assuming that SAS has been used as the Data Transformation tool, then the issue becomes creating a new external file from a SAS data file. This can be done using the DBLOAD procedure. This is described in Chapter 5, Section 5.2, and is essentially a very easy process. Remember that, to use PROC DBLOAD, the authority to write to the external source must be granted.

Joining SAS data files with those in another structure is always a topic of great debate, but the simplest way is to create SAS views of the external data table. The data can then be joined using either SQL or match-merge in the DATA step,[2] or in the case of the Full Refresh Cycle (where none of the existing information in the Data Warehouse will be affected by the load), the APPEND procedure may be used. These techniques are described later in this chapter.

In a situation where a large amount of data is to be joined with a large external data structure, the following strategy should be considered. First, load the SAS file into the external data format by using the DBLOAD procedure. Then using the native SQL abilities of the external software, this converted data can be incorporated into the Data Warehouse. This entire process could be managed using SAS, by using the DBLOAD procedure alongside pass-through SQL to perform the merge. It is always necessary to experiment to find the file-joining strategy that works best in any given Data Warehouse implementation.

This would be an example of the preceding situation:

```
PROC DBLOAD DBMS=ORACLE DATA=billing;
 USER=youruser;
 PASS=yourpass;
 TABLE='warehse.updt_billing';
 PATH="@p:";
 LOAD;
RUN;
```

---

[1] This topic is addressed in detail in Chapter 5.
[2] See Chapter 6, Section 6.6.

This step would take the SAS data file BILLING and create an ORACLE table called `warehse.updt_billing`. Note that using SAS/ACCESS to ORACLE the user name (USER=) and password (PASS=) are both required. The PATH= option specifies some internal ORACLE information, such as the driver and the physical location of the database.[3] After this has been completed, then the actual update of the Data Warehouse can take place using Pass-Through SQL:

```
PROC SQL;
 CONNECT TO ORACLE(PASS=yourpass, USER=youruser);
 EXECUTE (CREATE TABLE warehse.billing AS
         SELECT



 Other ORACLE SQL statements



         ) BY ORACLE;
 QUIT;
```

The above SQL pass-through is similar to that illustrated in Chapter 6, but this one uses the EXECUTE statement. The EXECUTE statement sends SQL statements directly to the DBMS for processing (in this case, it is ORACLE). As with all Pass-Through SQL, the statements within the parentheses following the EXECUTE statement should be compatible with the database that is being connected to (in this case, ORACLE).

An alternative to using this technique is to use the MODIFY statement with a BY statement in a SAS DATA step.[4] This will join the SAS data file and a view of the ORACLE table very efficiently. In this situation, there will be a SAS/ACCESS view of the base ORACLE table. There are some warnings to using the MODIFY alternative, however: first of all, it is only applicable in situations where there is a one-to-one match. When joining the SAS data file, it will take each row in turn and find the first available join. It will then look no further. This shouldn't matter as long as there is a one-to-one match between the base data file and the new, updated data. In a Data Warehousing environment, this is usually the case, but it should not be assumed. The other major concern is that the MODIFY alternative will update the ORACLE table in place, so if something untoward happened during the process, there is a potential of corrupted data.

---

[3] Each file format external to SAS that is supported with SAS/ACCESS software will have its own set of parameters. This information is best found in the documentation specific to the particular database.
[4] The MODIFY statement is best documented in the Online SAS help facility but can also be found in: SAS Institute Inc., SAS® Technical Report P-222, *Changes and Enhancements to Base SAS® Software, Release 6.07,* Cary, NC: SAS Institute Inc., 1991. 344pp, pages 36–42

Joining a SAS table with an external data file will become far easier in Version 7 of SAS software. The entire process will become far easier because the concept of SAS/ACCESS views will become outmoded. External databases will be defined in a LIBNAME statement, and there will be extended use of the native (in our situation above, ORACLE) database engine.

Using Changed Data Capture

The third situation, Changed Data Capture, is the most difficult to deal with. Changed data will have been extracted from the source Operational System and will have gone through the Transformation Process. This then has to be incorporated into the Data Warehouse. The only way this can be done is if a unique identifier is in every row. The files can then be joined on this unique identifier (key). A variety of techniques can be used to perform this join, all of which have been previously discussed.[5] Using either the SQL procedure or a match-merge in the DATA step are the most commonly used options. The use of the MODIFY statement in the DATA step is also a very efficient option to updating an existing table based upon the data in another data file. From a strict efficiency perspective, the MODIFY option is probably the most efficient, but it also has the most risks involved. Because the data file being updated is changed 'in-place', if there is any problem during the update, then the results could be untrustworthy. The MODIFY statement does have one other benefit insomuch as it does not lock an entire file during update. This means that other users can access the data during update. Whether or not this is a good idea is really a business based decision, but the choice is available.

Loading Data into a SAS Data Warehouse Repository

There are a variety of techniques for incorporating new, transformed data into the existing Data Warehouse data when the data repository is in a SAS format. Many of these techniques have already been discussed, but they include the following SAS techniques.

Using PROC COPY

The COPY procedure will do exactly as one would think. It takes the transformed data and moves it, as is, to another location and retains all of the

---

[5] See Chapter 6.

existing features of the data (including column formats, column informats, and indexes). An example of using PROC COPY follows:

```
PROC COPY IN=transfrm OUT=warehse;
 SELECT billing
        claims;
RUN;
```

This program will take the two SAS files BILLING and CLAIMS and move them from the data library TRANSFRM, which contains the transformed data, to the library WAREHSE, where the Data Warehouse resides. This technique of using the COPY procedure will work in a full production load where the transformed data will be replacing the existing Data Warehouse data (if it currently exists).

Using PROC APPEND

If a full refresh cycle were to be undertaken (where the incoming data was to be appended to the existing Data Warehouse tables, rather than replacing or updating them), then the APPEND procedure would be applicable. An example follows:

```
PROC APPEND BASE=warehse.billing DATA=transfrm.billing;
RUN;
```

This will take the incoming data file **billing**, which resides in the SAS library **transfrm** and will append it to the existing Warehouse data, which resides in the library **warehse**. This is very efficient because it does not require the BASE=data file (**warehse.billing**), which might be very large, to be read. Only the data referenced in the DATA=data file (**transfrm.billing**) is read. Note that, when using the APPEND procedure, any indexes in the BASE data will remain intact, and that the structure of the two files should be identical. You can work around this by using the FORCE option after the APPEND statement. If the FORCE option is required, there is probably an adjustment needed in the transformation process to ensure that the column names and attributes match those in the existing warehoused data.

7.4 Verifying the Loading of the Data Warehouse

When possible, the data loaded into the Data Warehouse should be verified to ensure that the process was completed successfully. This is easiest to achieve when the data loaded is in a full production load because the loaded data should be exactly the same as the transformed data. In this situation, the verification tests are simple because both sources should be identical. To perform this test the COMPARE procedure can be used.

```
PROC COMPARE BASE=warehse.billing
           COMPARE=transfrm.billing
           LISTALL;
RUN;
```

This program will perform the following comparisons:

- It will compare the contents of the two data files.
- It will compare the actual values of each of the different columns across the two data files.
- It can create either reports or an output data file from the results.

Of course, the data file referenced in either the BASE= or the COMPARE= options need not be in a SAS data structure. This could reference a SAS/ACCESS view of an external database table. This way, it is possible to compare, for instance, a SAS data file with an ORACLE table.

This method of verification, although very powerful, is very limited in its application. In a mature Data Warehouse, the loaded data and the transformed data will rarely be the same. In this situation, it is necessary to create other forms of verifications. When a Full Cycle Refresh or a Changed Data Capture strategy is used it will be necessary to capture the updated rows from the Data Warehouse table and compare them to the transformed data. It might be possible to perform counts and calculate statistics on only the updated rows in the Data Warehouse and run similar reports on the transformed data, then compare the two. An easier option would be to use the COMPARE procedure with a WHERE clause. For example:

```
PROC COMPARE BASE=warehse.claim
           COMPARE=transfrm.claim
           LISTALL;
 WHERE dataupdt > mdy(10,16,98);
RUN;
```

The situation above will compare the data file **warehse.claim** with the data file **transfrm.claim** only where **dataupdt** is after 16 October 1998. This situation would work where the rows were date stamped and the data loaded to the Warehouse had a stamp of 16 October 1998 or after.

7.5 Client/Server Implications

In most Data Warehouse implementations, there is an element of Client/ Server technology involved. This does not only pertain to the front end of the Warehouse, where users might be accessing data residing on other computers or platforms, but also on the back end. The source operational systems might be located on one platform, the transformation process might take place on another, and then this data might be dispersed to a variety of other computers. Using SAS in a Client/Server environment is covered in detail in Chapter 8.

The loading of the Data Warehouse in a Client/Server environment should be very carefully thought out. Loading, by its very nature, requires that the computer perform a large amount of input/output activity and that large amounts of data be moved across platforms. Understanding and working with the underlying architecture is of prime importance. If network traffic is a concern, then the loading process should ensure that it is not competing with itself for a fixed amount of resource. This means that it might be advantageous to consider a consecutive loading strategy. Instead of trying to update multiple tables at once, which would require many data files to be moving across the network at a single time, trying to schedule the loads consecutively might improve performance (and keep the network administrators happy). There is no rule as to what is wrong or right in this situation, it is a question of working within the architecture that exists.

The following issues have to be addressed in deciding upon the Client/Server strategy in the loading of the warehouse:

- Network resources.
- Competing traffic on the network.
- The best platform for performing the actual load (this will impact the movement of transformed data across the network).

Sometimes the optimal answer is not the practical one. Both network and computing capabilities change over time and to reflect this, the client/ server loading process must be fluid. If updates in capabilities result in the opportunity for a more efficient load, then it should be possible to easily revisit the current configuration to make changes and enhancements.

The implications of a Client/Server architecture to the loading of the Data Warehouse can be addressed during the scheduling of the loading process (see Section 7.7).

7.6 Re-summarization of Data

In Chapter 6, Section 6.7, the summarization of data was discussed as to how it relates to the transformation process. Very often, it is not possible to create summary data during the transformation phase. This is especially the case when Full Cycle Refresh or Changed Data Capture is used. This is because the existing Data Warehouse data will be needed for the summarization to take place.

If at all possible, the complete re-creation of summary data should be avoided. If SAS/MDDB is being used,[6] then this is accounted for by the concept of 'drip feeding' the database. If the Changed Data Capture approach is used, then re-summarization of the complete Data Warehouse tables might be unavoidable. This is because with Changed Data Capture there is the possibility for extensive changes to the existing warehoused data. This would mean that any summary data derived from this detail data would be invalid. This would require a complete refresh of the summarized data to ensure that it is in line with the most recent detail data.

Performing Full Cycle Refresh with PROC SUMMARY

The most common form of Data Warehouse updating is using the Full Cycle Refresh. Hopefully this will allow for summarization to take place on the smaller (hopefully) update file. This summary file can then be appended to the existing summary file. This technique, in principle, is described (Chapter 6, Section 6.8) by using the FREQ procedure. For this example the following file is used:

CUSTOMER_NUMBER	AMOUNT_SOLD	PRODUCT	PRODUCT_GROUP
A1	45.54	34	Rubber
A2	67.76	45	Plastic
A1	99.87	55	
A3	75.43	98	Metal
A1	88.00	34	Rubber
A2	86.23	45	Plastic
A1	120.00	55	

Table 7.1 DATA FILE=TRANSFRM.BILLING

```
PROC SUMMARY DATA=transfrm.billing NWAY;
 CLASS customer_number product;
 VAR amount_sold;
 ID product_group;
 OUTPUT OUT=transfrm.billsum (DROP=_FREQ_ _TYPE_)
        N=amount_sold_n
        SUM=amount_sold_sum;
RUN;
```

As shown PROC SUMMARY takes the transformed data in the file **billing** that is stored in the SAS library **transfrm**. It then creates the new data file BILLSUM stored in the same library. Both SUM and N (the number of observations in the sub-group with a non-missing value) are stored for each combination of values for **customer_number** and **product**. Both of the

---

[6] See Chapter 4, Section 4.3.

columns **_freq_** and **_type_**, which are automatically generated by the procedure, are dropped from the output file.

Table 7.2, is the existing summarized file that results from the SUMMARY procedure illustrated in the program above.

PRODUCT_GROUP	CUSTOMER_NUMBER	PRODUCT	AMOUNT_SOLD_N	AMOUNT_SOLD_SUM
Rubber	A1	34	2	133.54
	A1	55	2	219.87
Plastic	A2	45	2	153.99
Metal	A3	98	1	75.43

TABLE 7.2 DATA FILE=TRANSFRM.BILLSUM

The output from this procedure (seen in Table 7.2) can then be appended to the existing summary file that applies to the data previously loaded into the Data Warehouse. So long as the statistics created are additive (as in most cases in a Data Warehouse), the resultant file can be summarized to create a new summary file. This will be achieved without actually reading the entire existing row in the BILLING table in the Data Warehouse.

Assume the existing summary file looks like this:

PRODUCT_GROUP	CUSTOMER_NUMBER	PRODUCT	AMOUNT_SOLD_N	AMOUNT_SOLD_SUM
Rubber	A1	34	9222	104188.66
	A1	55	89087	1103265.67
Plastic	A2	45	67542	43183.21
Metal	A3	98	198	3279.65

TABLE 7.3 DATA FILE=WAREHSE.BILLSUM

```
PROC APPEND BASE=warehse.billsum DATA=transfrm.billsum;
RUN;

PROC SUMMARY DATA=warehse.billsum NWAY;
 CLASS customer_number product;
 VAR amount_sold_sum amount_sold_n;
 ID product_group;
 OUTPUT OUT=warehse.billsum (DROP=_FREQ_ _TYPE_)
      SUM=amount_sold_sum amount_sold_n;
RUN;
```

This step will append the summary data file that is created from the new data to the existing summary data. This data will then be summarized, but in this case, by just using the SUM= option. The resultant output file will look like Table 7.4.

PRODUCT_GROUP	CUSTOMER_NUMBER	PRODUCT	AMOUNT_SOLD_N	AMOUNT_SOLD_SUM
Rubber	A1	34	9224	104322.20
	A1	55	89089	1103485.54
Plastic	A2	45	67544	43337.2
Metal	A3	98	199	3355.08

TABLE 7.4 DATA FILE=WAREHSE.BILLSUM

Again, experienced SAS users will be very familiar with such techniques. This simple example shows how, by using SAS it is possible to avoid re-reading vast amounts of data to update summary (or metadata) data. The example above is very trivial, involving less than ten rows. In a medium size Data Warehouse implementation, this same file could contain 5 million rows and, in a large implementation, over 20 million rows. In these situations, it is essential to find as many resource-saving techniques as possible.

7.7 Scheduling the Loading of the Data Warehouse

The scheduling of Data Warehouse loading has already been discussed in relation to Client/Server implications. The scheduling of the Data Warehouse loading should be constructed with two major goals in mind:

- To complete the process in the quickest time possible, which is why in a Client/Server environment jobs should be scheduled so that they do not cause a network problem.
- To load the data in the correct order. This will ensure, for instance, that the detail data has finished loading before the summarized tables are created.

Scheduling is largely a matter of common sense. It can be controlled in many ways: putting all the programs in a job stream so that one job cannot run out of order, or by using a scheduling package. SAS programs can be scheduled on virtually any of the commercial scheduling packages, including CA-7 on the OS/390 platform and cron under UNIX. Even if the scheduling of the loading process is not implemented using a scheduling package, the order and expected running times of each task within the loading process must be managed in some way. This will help in future planning and in estimating the impact of making changes to the Data Warehousing process. In the short term, when the size of the loads in terms of the size of the jobs and the number of jobs might be small, it might work not to formalize the schedule of the loading process. In the long term, however, loading will soon become unmanageable. Like other aspects of the Data Warehousing process, it is best to initiate a formal process to schedule the loading.

Chapter 8:
Data Warehousing Using Client/Server Technology: The Role of SAS/CONNECT® and SAS/SHARE® Software

8.1 What is Client/Server Computing?

Client/Server is a phrase that is used a great deal when the topic of computers is discussed. This is no exception in the Data Warehousing environment. It is very unusual for a Data Warehouse implementation to be entirely devoid of at least a single aspect of Client/Server. This means that to efficiently design a Data Warehouse a thorough understanding of Client/Server is required.

In the excellent book, *The Essential Client/Server Survival Guide, Second Edition*,[1] by Orfali, Harkey, and Edwards, they put forward nine characteristics that encapsulate a Client/Server system. Whether or not a system needs all nine characteristics to be truly Client/Server is not necessary to question because, in terms of Data Warehousing, we are going to simplify the definition. It is worth outlining the nine characteristics, however, to help put the architecture in perspective:

---

[1] Orfali, R., Harkey, D., and Edwards, J., *The Essential Client/Server Survival Guide, Second Edition*, John Wiley & Sons, Inc. 1996, p11.

1) **Service:** Independent processes run on independent computers that are related: because one computer (Client) requests (consumes) a service that is run on another computer (Server).

2) **Shared Resources:** The computer that is providing the service (Server) can do so to many requesters (Clients).

3) **Asymmetrical protocols:** The requesters (Clients) always are the initiators of the service from the otherwise passive server.

4) **Transparency of location:** The physical location of the Client and the Server is immaterial. They can be on different computers or on the same computer.

5) **Mix and Match:** Not only is the physical location of the Client and Server computers immaterial, but they should be independent of hardware or Operating System software.

6) **Message-based exchange:** The initiation of the service is started by a message passed from the Client to the Server.

7) **Encapsulation of services:** Based upon a message sent to the Server from the Client (see 6), the Server will respond by determining how the requested service will be best expedited. This means that the Server can be upgraded without changing the Client, as long as the Server can still interpret the message sent as meaning the same thing.

8) **Scalability:** Clients can be added to a system with little overall impact, or the Server can be enhanced without any comparable changes being needed for the Clients.

9) **Integrity:** The Server code and data reside centrally, making maintenance easier and ensuring data integrity for all of the Clients.

The above nine points are all outlined and discussed in great detail in *The Essential Client/Server Survival Guide*, and for those especially interested, this is a fantastic source of Client/Server information. For our purposes, the preceding nine points are enough for us to understand Client/Server as it relates to Data Warehousing.

In fact, these nine points can be made clearer, for those who either do not have a technical background (but are still qualified to design a Data Warehouse) or those who find concepts easier to understand by allegories, by considering the following analogy. The relationship between a waiter and a diner can be considered a Client/Server relationship. This can be illustrated by taking each of the nine points presented earlier and putting them into a familiar situation.

1) **Service:** The diner and the waiter co-exist independently of each other, but they are related because the diner will request a service from the waiter. Never will the waiter (server) ask the diner (client) for a

service until the bill needs to be paid. Then the waiter becomes the client and the diner becomes the server.

2) **Shared Resources:** A waiter can serve many diners at the same time, independently of each other.

3) **Asymmetrical protocols:** The diners (clients) always are the initiators of the service from the otherwise passive waiter (server)— although it could be argued that many waiters are not quite passive enough!

4) **Transparency of location:** Theoretically, the diner (client) and the waiter (server) could be the same person. Although not advisable, it is possible for the diner to send a message to himself to order the tuna.

5) **Mix and Match:** It should not matter if the diner (client) and the waiter (server) do not speak the same language, as long as the waiter (server) understands what the diner (client) is ordering.

6) **Message-based exchange:** The diner need only say: "Number 42" for the waiter to understand the process he needs to go through to get the Chicken Tandoori to the table.

7) **Encapsulation of services:** It is up to the waiter to determine the best way to get the correct food to the table. This means that the diner can order Number 42 on consecutive days, and because the waiter has changed his technique, the method by which the food arrives on the table may have changed. There is no reason for the diner to worry about this. His only concern is that he is getting what he ordered.

8) **Scalability:** More diners (clients) can attend the restaurant with little impact to the waiter (server). As with a computer system, there comes a point where the waiter (server) will no longer be effective, and this will mean getting another waiter (server) or improving the current one.

9) **Integrity:** The waiter (server) not only has a good knowledge of the menu, but if it changes, all the diners (clients) should be aware of the fact.

Obviously, this analogy runs a little thin at times, but it helps to illustrate the relationship between a Client and a Server computer. There is no mystery to the architecture on a conceptual level, although the technicalities can become very complex. This is the reason we have software such as SAS. To a large degree, we are given the tools to build the above relationships, without having to understand how much of it works. This is an incredible advantage because it means that we can concentrate on ensuring that it will help us architecturally build an effective Data Warehouse, rather than becoming 'bogged-down' in the nitty-gritty technicalities. Users of SAS have SAS/CONNECT and SAS/SHARE software plus a variety of associated tools that can allow the Warehouse designers do what they are meant to be doing, instead of spending time and energy on the technicalities of Client/Server computing.

8.2 Client/Server Architecture within the Data Warehouse Process

No amount of powerful software will allow us to incorporate a Client/Server aspect to our architecture without a firm understanding of what we are trying to achieve. It is necessary to include a design of where data should start (at the extraction from the source system), to where it should end (in a detail or a summary table). It is then possible to fully appreciate the options in terms of movement and processing of data.

Example: Understanding the Client/Server Requirements for a Data Warehouse

Summarized information is designed to help a Marketing Department track its projects. This information might be summarized on the company mainframe and then physically moved to the departmental UNIX machine that is directly accessed by the marketing analysts. This location is selected because the heavy usage will result in a network bottleneck if the summarized data were to remain on the mainframe. On the other side of the world, the company director occasionally likes to look at this same summarized information. The company director accesses this data from a PC that runs Windows.

This example illustrates some classic requirements of Data Warehouse design. There are two very important factors: first of all, to locate the information (the summarized data in this case) as close to the principal users as possible. This is sensible design because it will reduce the amount of network traffic and make the request response time as fast as possible. The second important factor is that in locating the information close to the principal users, other less frequent users will not be limited.

Where in this situation is the Client/Server architecture? First of all, let us assume that the Data Warehouse is administered from a Windows platform using the SAS Data Warehouse Administrator (see Chapter 9). At a given time, the Warehouse Administrator (the Client) requests of the mainframe (the Server) that it starts a job to extract data from the Data Warehouse and create a summary file (maybe in the form of a Multi-Dimensional Database). The data is duly summarized. Then the mainframe (now the Client) requests of the UNIX computer (the Server) that it upload the summarized file. When the company director accesses the summarized file, his PC (the Client) requests that the UNIX machine (the Server) perform some operation (maybe a breakdown of sales increases by Product and by Region) and return the results to his PC.

This process, given the way this particular company works, is very efficient. To actually perform this apparently complex set of interrelationships is not as hard as it might seem. In fact, the experienced SAS user might wonder why it should ever be considered difficult. To achieve the circumstance just described, the following diagram illustrates what will be needed, from a SAS software perspective, on each of the four computers:

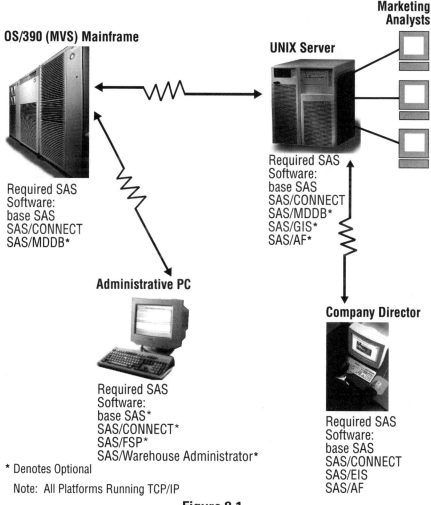

Marketing Analysts

OS/390 (MVS) Mainframe

UNIX Server

Required SAS Software:
base SAS
SAS/CONNECT
SAS/MDDB*

Required SAS Software:
base SAS
SAS/CONNECT
SAS/MDDB*
SAS/GIS*
SAS/AF*

Administrative PC

Required SAS Software:
base SAS*
SAS/CONNECT*
SAS/FSP*
SAS/Warehouse Administrator*

Company Director

Required SAS Software:
base SAS
SAS/CONNECT
SAS/EIS
SAS/AF

* Denotes Optional

Note: All Platforms Running TCP/IP

Figure 8.1

What is common to all the platforms is that both base SAS software and SAS/CONNECT are running. These two software products are the driving engines behind the SAS Client/Server tools. The SAS/Warehouse Administrator is required in a situation where central and structured control of the Warehouse is desired. (See Chapter 9 for a discussion about this product.)

In the case of the MDDB Server, SAS/EIS and SAS/AF will be required in the circumstance just outlined because a Multi-Dimensional Database is the form of the summary information. There are enough tools using just SAS/CONNECT and base SAS software for the above architecture to work.

The situation, as outlined above, illustrates the creation of a Data Mart (an extract from the Data Warehouse that is designed for a specific purpose). This exact situation might well exist where the loading of the physical Data Warehouse is taking place. For instance, the files on the mainframe might be a General Ledger that resides in a DB2 relational Database Management System. From this General Ledger, monthly data is extracted to refresh the Data Warehouse that is located on the UNIX platform. The summary files could be created on the UNIX platform and then accessed from PCs by using a very similar architecture to the one outlined in the preceding example.

Another option would be that the company Director accesses the data through the Internet. This would mean that he would not have SAS installed on his computer, but he would use a Browser to find out the information he needs. This is another Client/Server option that is more than feasible. It would mean, from a SAS perspective, that the SAS/IntrNet product would be installed on the UNIX computer, but the same Client/Server design questions would have to be answered.

The point, however, is the same: to take advantage of Client/Server architecture, it is essential to understand both the strengths and the weaknesses of the physical computer architecture (both in terms of the network and the computers themselves) and the needs of the users. In our example looking at the Marketing Department's summary information, it was understood that the principal users had immediate access to their departmental UNIX computer, so this was the obvious place to put the data.

 The success of Client/Server architecture within a Data Warehouse environment is based upon a thorough understanding of:

- *The computer infrastructure*

- *The user's needs.*

These two must be assessed together to fully design the Client/Server component of the overall Data Warehouse design.

In many situations, the design of the Client/Server relationship is not so clear cut. Many organizations try to implement Client/Server architectures without thinking ahead-of-time. In these situations, there is a great risk of designing an inefficient process that potentially leads to a failed project. Either the network cannot handle the amount of data that it has to transport, or the physical location of either the data or the programs that run are not well thought-out. The blame is put on Client/Server architecture in general, instead of the design of the system. Data Warehouses usually deal in large amounts of data, which means that there is a likelihood of large volumes passing across a network. Therefore, this means that it is essential to assess the network capabilities thoroughly in the design of the Data Warehouse when looking at the Client/Server component. Inefficient transfer of data can cause a very slow response time to user requests. This can lead to a disenchantment with an otherwise well-designed Data Warehouse.

How Client/Server Fits into the Data Warehouse Process

As discussed in Section 8.1, Client/Server computing is not a topic that is specific to Data Warehousing. There are, however, many reasons why, as a separate topic, it is worth careful consideration within a Data Warehouse environment. The reason that it is being specifically addressed here is that understanding the options available, on both a conceptual basis (for the users and the managers of the Data Warehouse) and a technical basis (for the Technology groups), will open an unbelievable set of alternatives for the delivery of data. In this case, *delivery* means getting the data (or information) to the business units that need it to fulfill their roles.

Another reason for SAS users to understand Client/Server architecture is that the software is extremely rich in all of the tools that can lead to both performance and cost advantages, which can potentially ensue if well managed. Client/Server architectures have been both heralded and despised as a solution, and, as usual, most of the opinions are based upon simplistic reasoning. As with all technology, Client/Server architecture has its place. If results are negative, then it is the fault of the designers, not the architecture itself. To utilize a Client/Server architecture and then have it fail is a very expensive mistake. Client/Server technology cannot be undertaken lightly.

The view has also been purported that the growth of the Internet as a tool to distribute information will make Client/Server architectures redundant. On the contrary, the alternatives that the Internet gives the Data Warehouse designer will increase the Client/Server options, rather than limit them. The hard part of instigating Client/Server is not the technology (which is more awkward than difficult due to all the disparate pieces having to coordinate exactly) but ensuring that it is well-planned. Its success will be based on the 'weakest link' in the system.

Special Topic:
SAS MultiVendor Architecture™ (MVA)™

One of the major benefits to using SAS software is the MVA (MultiVendor Architecture) approach taken to the design of the product. This is central to the Client/Server capabilities of SAS software. What this means is that code or commands within SAS on one platform (e.g., UNIX, Windows NT, etc.) and another is as identical as possible, given the differences between the Operating Systems. Why is this important to Data Warehousing? This opens up vast flexibility because it means that when designing a Data Warehouse, it does not have to be platform specific. For instance, if a company is currently running a Data Warehouse on a Windows NT platform, but, for whatever reason, needs to move it to a UNIX platform, all the SAS software will be compatible.

8.3 Ensuring a Portable Data Warehouse When Using SAS

The approach to looking at Client/Server architecture when using SAS is to consider each of the applicable SAS modules. Look at how the modules fit into both Data Warehousing and Client/Server, and then describe their usage with examples of code and techniques. Although the designers (as opposed to the implementers) of the Data Warehouse need not be very concerned about the code, it is very simple and can be easily understood. By understanding some of the code, the capabilities and options open to the designer of the Data Warehouse will become more apparent. Therefore, there are potential benefits to all those involved in the Data Warehousing process to reading about the specific SAS components.

Example: Changing Platforms with a Minimal Change in Corresponding Code

Due to the MVA capabilities of SAS, usually, all that will need to change to move processing from one platform to another will be the references to specific files.

Consider this snippet of simple SAS code:

```
LIBNAME saslib 'c:\mkt\data';
 PROC SQL;
 CREATE TABLE newfile
 AS SELECT * FROM saslib.oldfile
 WHERE age > 85;
QUIT;
```

All this code does is to create a new SAS data set named **newfile** by reading an existing data set named **OLDfile** which is permanently stored in a

SAS library referenced by the alias `saslib`. This snippet of code will run on any platform that SAS runs on. All that would need to be changed would be the first statement because the physical location of the existing SAS library will be Operating-System dependent, not SAS dependent. Therefore, the above code would work for any flavor of Windows, but it would change as follows for either OS/390 (MVS) or UNIX:

OS/390: `LIBNAME saslib 'MVS.STYLE.MKT.DATA';`
UNIX: `LIBNAME saslib '/mkt/data';`

These are minimal changes to make and might not even be necessary (given a design that allows for automatic substitutions to be made) based upon the Operating Systems. Indeed, if all such file references were made based upon substitutions, then the applicable changes could be made by placing the physical references in a file.[2] For instance, consider the following simple example of a very powerful concept:

The SAS data set **whdata** has been created with three columns as follows:

LIBNAME	WIN	OS/390
Mktdata	F:\mkt\data	Whse.mkt.data
Findata	F:\finance\data	Whse.finance.data

Table 8.1 TABLE=*whdata*

This snippet of code could then be used on any Operating System without any changes:

```
❶  %MACRO crtlibs;
❷  DATA _NULL_;
❸    SET whdata(RENAME=(&SYSSCP=libspec)) END=EOF;
❹    x+1;
❺    LIB='L' || TRIM(LEFT(PUT(x,3.)));
❻    PHYSLOC='P' || TRIM(LEFT(PUT(x,3.)));
❼    CALL SYMPUT(lib,libname);
❽    CALL SYMPUT(physloc,QUOTE(libspec));
❾    IF EOF THEN CALL SYMPUT('maxlib',_N_);
❿  RUN;
⓫  %DO I=1 %TO &MAXLIB;
⓬    LIBNAME &&L&I &&P&I;
⓭  %END;
⓮  %MEND crtlibs;
⓯  %crtlibs
```

---

[2] The use of table-driven strategies using SAS software see: Kolosova, Tanya and Berestizhevsky, Samuel, *Table-Driven Strategies for Rapid SAS® Applications Development*, Cary, NC: SAS Institute Inc., 1995. 259pp.

Although making use of the SAS macro language,[3] this short piece of code will allow for the correct physical libraries to be referenced by SAS LIBNAMES based upon the Operating System that the code runs under. There are many other ways to achieve this same goal, but in designing a Data Warehouse, it is definitely worthwhile to set up a similar platform-dependent option. The preceding code can be explained as follows:

❶ Create the SAS macro `crtlibs`. For users who are not SAS users, this can be considered as a stored routine that can be called by an application or a SAS program at any time.

❷ Create the SAS data set `_NULL_`. Using the `_NULL_` data set name saves on resources by not creating an intermediate work file. This is best used when the data set is not needed again during the life of the SAS session or program.

❸ Read in the existing data set `whdata` and rename one of the variables corresponding to the current Operating System to `libspec`. The `&SYSSCP` is a SAS generated macro variable that will resolve to the current Operating System. Therefore, it is important that the column names in the file `whdata` correspond to the potential resolved value of the macro variable `&SYSSCP`.

The variable `EOF` is created, which will have a value when the last record in the data set `whdata` is read

❹ A counter set to `X` is set. It will increase with every new row read from `whdata`.

❺ The column `LIB` is created that will equal `L` concatenated with the value of `x`. The PUT function is used to avoid numeric-to-character conversion messages.

❻ The column `PHYSLOC` is created that will equal `P` concatenated with the value of `x`.

❼ A macro variable is created and named whatever the current value of the column `lib` is. This variable is equal to the current value of the column `libname` from the data set `whdata`. For example, on the first iteration of the DATA step, when `libname=MKTDATA` and `lib` will equal `L1`, then a macro variable `L1` will be created that will resolve to `MKTDATA`.

❽ The same will happen as in ❼, except that the macro variable will start with `P` and will resolve to the value of the variable `libspec`

---

[3] SAS Institute Inc., *SAS® Macro Language: Reference, First Edition*, NC: SAS Institute Inc., 1997. 304pp. for a complete overview of the Macro Language.

(which is the variable that has been renamed based on the current Operating System in ❸.) In the first iteration, a macro variable `P1` will resolve to `f:\mkt\data` if the program were running under a Windows environment.

⑨ If the last row in `whdata` is being read, then create a macro variable named `maxlib` that will resolve to the number of rows in `whdata`.

⑩ Run the DATA step.

⑪ Begin a loop that will go from 1 to the number of rows in `whdata`.

⑫ Assign a library that will have as its alias (its LIBNAME) when I=1 the resolved value of the macro variable `L1 MKTDATA`) and as a physical file reference the resolved value of the `P1` macro variable (`f:\mkt\data`.)

⑬ End the loop after all iterations (in this case it will be two).

⑭ End the SAS macro named `crtlibs`.

⑮ Run the macro variable named `crtlibs`.

Just this small amount of work at the beginning of a project can save an enormous amount of time and resources later on. This system will be of use if either there is a platform change or if new sources of data are created. There will be no necessary changes in the program itself, but only to the file `whdata`.

From a Client/Server perspective this approach has tremendous appeal because

- The Data Warehouse will have the flexibility of a Client/Server approach that will allow the processing to take place where it is best suited.
- If the selection of platforms is changed at some juncture, then it can be done easily with little impact to the code that is involved in the Data Warehousing process.

As mentioned above, Data Warehouses by their inherent nature change over a period of time, and therefore the more anticipation of change the designer can make, the easier the task will be of keeping the design in line with the enterprise requirements. At every point in the design of the Data Warehouse, it is essential that the question be asked: *How will the current design adapt to changes?* If the answer to the question is something along the lines of: *Not very easily*, then it is time for a re-think.

Although the small example shown here could be beneficial beyond just a Data Warehousing environment, it certainly gives the designers a degree of flexibility that is essential. Remember that a successful Data Warehousing project is one that is always developing. Therefore, the need for change is greater than in the vast majority of Operational Systems. It follows that the likelihood that there will be the need to change platforms will also be more likely in an Operational environment where the rules and scopes tend to be more fixed.

8.4 Communicating between Different Hosts (Computers) Using SAS

The basis of the SAS Client/Server options is SAS/CONNECT. This enables services to be initiated by one SAS session (*the local client*) that will be implemented on another SAS session (*the remote server*). Although the vast majority of the time, the remote SAS session will reside on a different computer, indeed running under a different Operating System, this does not necessarily have to be the case. A simple example of using SAS/CONNECT would be if a Data Warehouse were to reside on a UNIX computer, but the Operational Systems from which it is populated is on an OS/390 (MVS) based mainframe. A SAS/CONNECT session could be initiated from the UNIX computer (Client) to the mainframe (Server), then the UNIX computer could request of the mainframe that it extract data, manipulate it, and then physically download the resultant data. Hence, the Client has asked for a variety of services from the Server.

Some Notes about Installing SAS/CONNECT

SAS/CONNECT is a middleware product. It is not a standalone product that will allow interoperability between two SAS sessions residing on different computers or platforms. It needs an underlying communication method upon which to run. The computers upon which SAS/CONNECT will run will need the ability to communicate in some way before SAS/CONNECT is installed. For instance, TCP/IP has become a standard communications access method over the past few years. If SAS/CONNECT is required to run using a TCP/IP access method, then it must be possible to TELNET between the two computers for SAS/CONNECT to work. SAS/CONNECT after installation will then begin a session by using TELNET. After the session is established, then it will use TCP/IP as its communication protocol.

Problems with the installation of SAS/CONNECT are usually not due to the SAS software, but due to the multitude of other factors that make up the successful connection. For instance, there are different 'flavors' of TCP/IP from different vendors. Some of these flavors don't taste quite as good as some of the others. Problems are known, for instance, with the TELNET service being automatically made available. When SAS/CONNECT looks for the service, it is not there unless explicitly asked for, and therefore a session cannot be established. Communication software is still in its infancy and although great strides have been made, there is still a long way to travel. There is extensive documentation both in manuals and in online facilities that cover most of the situations that SAS/CONNECT might encounter during installation, all of which is worthwhile investigating.[4]

How to Start a SAS/CONNECT Session

In most cases, to start a SAS/CONNECT session, three parameters have to be established. We will concentrate on TCP/IP because it is as standard as the industry will allow, however, SAS/CONNECT supports many other communication protocols. The three parameters that are needed for TCP/IP are:

1. The communication protocol (set using a COMAMID= option within SAS).

2. The name of the connection (set using a REMOTE= option within SAS).

3. A script that is used to emulate the way one would use the communication protocol in a native fashion (i.e., if one were connecting without using SAS/CONNECT).

An example using SAS code would be as follows:

```
%LET MVSBOX=199.55.160.22 23;
OPTIONS COMAMID=TCP;
OPTIONS REMOTE=MVSBOX;
FILENAME RLINK 'physical.script.file.name';
SIGNON;
```

It is not always necessary for every communication protocol to use a script. For instance, if the NetBIOS (Network Basic Input/Output System) communication method is used, then it works by the *Server computer* listening for a message. This listening technique is established by using a *spawner* program that is supplied with SAS software. After the spawner has received the message it is listening for, it knows to start SAS as a CONNECT session. This technique is becoming less popular because it only works well for smaller networks. It is considered a 'chatty' protocol that has too much superfluous messaging travelling along the network.

---

[4] Within SAS, help on specific problems can be used by selecting the Tech Support options from the Help pull-down menu and following the directions. Further information can be found by accessing the Technical Support World Wide Web pages at www.sas.com.

The REMOTE= value is interesting in this case, because it is set to MVSBOX which resolves to the IP address of the OS/390 (MVS) computer (in this case `199.55.160.22`). The 23 after the IP address references the port that should be used to access the OS/390 computer. This is standard across all TELNET accesses. Specifically referencing the IP address, as is done here, is not always necessary, because if the value of the REMOTE= value is set to a known IP alias, then this address will be automatically substituted. This latter method is preferable, because if there is a change in an IP address, the code will not need to be changed, so long as the change is made to the host files that contain the IP aliases. This will be the case if domain name services (DNS) or a host file within TCP/IP is used.

The scripts that are needed to access remote machines vary by machine and communication method. These scripts are supplied with the SAS/CONNECT software and often work without much modification. The exception to this is where a connection to an OS/390 (MVS) mainframe is being established. It is very unusual for the access to such a computer to be consistent across organizations, so consequently the scripts need adjusting. The scripting language used by SAS is very easy to understand and is outlined in great detail in the documentation.[5] It is easy to become caught up in scripting, but there are two underlying rules to follow: first of all, the two computers must be able to communicate using the access method without SAS/CONNECT and secondly remember that all the script does is to emulate the native communication access method. This means that a rubric already exists for the script to be based upon.[6]

Using SAS/CONNECT

There are three major capabilities that SAS/CONNECT gives to the Data Warehouse designer.[7] All three are Client/Server in nature but are different in their use and application. A combination of all three opens up a variety of options that allow for a more flexible and responsive Data Warehouse design. These three major capabilities are as follows:

- Compute Services
- Data Transfer Capabilities
- Remote Library Services (RLS).

---

[5] SAS Institute Inc., *SAS /CONNECT® Software, Usage and Reference, Version 6, Second Edition*, Cary, NC: SAS Institute Inc., 1994. 368pp., Chapter 17.

[6] A useful option when installing SAS/CONNECT with the use of a script, is the TRACE ON or ECHO ON option, which will display the messages sent from the host. SAS Institute Inc., *SAS /CONNECT® Software, Usage and Reference, Version 6, Second Edition*, Cary, NC: SAS Institute Inc., 1994. 368pp., p161

[7] For a superb outline of using SAS/CONNECT see: Horton, Susan, "Maximum Performance Utilization for SAS/CONNECT ® Processing," *Observations*, 4th Quarter 1995, SAS Institute Inc.

Compute Services

Compute Services allows for an application to perform its processing across different SAS sessions. Although the code for the application might reside on one computer, using SAS it is very simple to request for the code to be submitted on a remote computer. In a Data Warehousing environment, this is a very powerful tool because it gives the designer the power to decide which computer (or platform) is best suited to perform which tasks. This means that when the user or the application decides to use a remote computer, the application logic (the code) is passed to that machine for processing. The results of the processing are then passed back through the network to the Client machine.

For example, extensive Compute Services will be required in a situation where an analyst is constructing a query to run against a Data Warehouse that resides on an OS/390 mainframe, in a DB2 database structure, using the SAS Query window under Windows. The query would need to be constructed using information from the DB2 catalog tables on the mainframe.[8] After constructed, the query would have to run using application logic on the mainframe. The code would therefore be moved to the mainframe, submitted, and the resulting set would be sent back to the Windows computer.

This technique uses the best resource for the processing. The down side is the amount of network usage in both the moving of the logic to the processing machine and moving the results back to the Client. Unfortunately, there are no hard-and-fast rules for deciding where processing should take place. For example, it might be advantageous to have a mainframe (the remote SAS session, the Server) process a piece of logic early in the morning when usage is very low (and CPU cycles very cheap). At a busy time later in the morning, as the coffee is poured and the workers roll in, it might be more practical to run the same logic locally (on the Client) after downloading the required data. This is because the usage of the mainframe will increase and, with it, the cost of running the specific piece of code. It is therefore necessary to understand not only the physical architecture and its limitations, but also the pertinent usage patterns. To make a Client/Server decision, it is necessary to understand all the options. Decisions can then be made based upon knowledge of both the technology available and the particular set of

---

[8] This overhead could be removed by copying the relevant DB2 system tables to the Windows system (using PROC DOWNLOAD) and then changing the SAS Query window profile accordingly. See: SAS Institute Inc., *SAS® Guide to the SQL Query Window: Usage and Reference, Version 6, First Edition*, Cary, NC: SAS Institute Inc., 1995.

restricting circumstances. Very often, a Client/Server approach runs into problems because elementary common sense is not used. Decisions are based only upon the technology rather than the particular set of operating circumstances.

To use the Compute Services options within SAS is very simple. Consider the following code:

```
RSUBMIT unixbox;
 PROC SQL;
  CREATE TABLE work.test
  AS SELECT * FROM whse.data
  WHERE date > MDY(01,01,1997);
 QUIT;
ENDRSUBMIT;
```

This simple code creates the temporary SAS data set **test** from the permanent data set **whse.data** only if the date is after 1, January 1997. The data file **work.test** physically resides on the computer, **unixbox**. The interesting part of the code is the '**rsubmit unixbox**' and '**endsubmit**'. These two commands tell SAS to submit the code contained between them, not to the local SAS session, but to a remote SAS session named **unixbox** . The **unixbox** reference corresponds to the value specified in a REMOTE= option that was specified during initialization of the remote session.

The actual principle of using Compute Services is very simple indeed. As long as there is a remote SAS session, the mechanics of actually submitting code either locally or remotely is very easy. Remember that a Client SAS session is not restricted to a single SAS/CONNECT session but could have multiple sessions associated with it. In a Data Warehousing environment, it is usual to have multiple platforms and also have the need to process in a variety of places.

A good example of using SAS/CONNECT in an imaginative way is the following situation. An administrator who uses a Windows PC needs to

- extract data from the enterprise-wide Data Warehouse that physically resides on an OS/390 (MVS) mainframe
- create a Multi-Dimensional Database for the Marketing Department
- move this data structure to the departmental UNIX computer.

This is actually a very simple process: the Windows SAS session will connect to an OS/390 SAS session. The logic to create the multi-dimensional structure will then be *remote submitted* to the OS/390 SAS session using the Compute Services option of SAS/CONNECT. After the data structure has been created on the OS/390 computer, code will be remote submitted to the OS/390 machine, which will allow it to connect to the departmental UNIX machine. The data strucure will then be uploaded to the UNIX machine using the *Data Transfer* capabilities of SAS/CONNECT, which are outlined below.

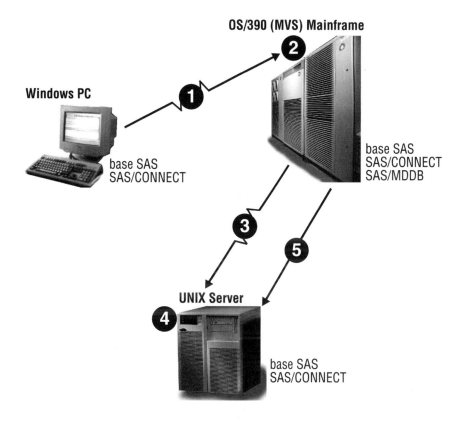

OS/390 (MVS) Mainframe

Windows PC

base SAS
SAS/CONNECT

base SAS
SAS/CONNECT
SAS/MDDB

UNIX Server

base SAS
SAS/CONNECT

Figure 8.2

1. A SAS/CONNECT link from the Windows PC (Client) to the mainframe (Server) is established.
2. SAS code is remote submitted from the Windows PC to extract detail data from the warehouse and create the MDDB using Compute Services. (Note that it is not necessarily essential to extract the data before creating the MDDB.)[9]
3. The mainframe remote connects to the UNIX server.

---

[9] See Chapter 4 for details on creating SAS MDDBs.

4. Code is remote submitted from the mainframe to the UNIX server to establish a LIBNAME through Remote Library Services.[10] This code physically resides on the Windows PC and is submitted by using nested remote submits.

5. The MDDB created on the mainframe is moved to the UNIX server using PROC COPY.[11]

Data Transfer Capabilities

As mentioned previously, it is often necessary to bring the data to the logic, rather than the logic to the data. Again, there are no hard-and-fast rules as to when one or the other is preferable. Very often, the choice is obvious. For instance, if a file that contains a million rows resides on a UNIX computer and analysis is required on only 3,000 of these rows, then the decisions are easy. It makes sense to submit the query on the UNIX machine and move the resultant 3,000 rows to a Windows machine for the complex analyses. Not only is this using each machine optimally, but it also means that the software to perform the analyses will only be needed on the Windows machine. This is another reason to use a Client/Server approach intelligently.

SAS/CONNECT software will easily allow the movement of data between computers and platforms. This is done through the use of the two SAS procedures UPLOAD and DOWNLOAD. One of the major advantages to the movement of data is that processing can be off-loaded from a remote computer and distributed across Clients. It logically follows, however, that to move data means network traffic, which is a key factor in deciding where processing should take place.

One of the major weaknesses of many Data Warehouses is the inability to put the information into the control of those that are going to need it. It is no good having a marvelous central store of data that represents everything the enterprise is ever going to need from a decision support perspective, if the tools are not in place to allow the users to access it. This is a problem that is very common in a lot of Data Warehouses, which is why a tool that allows movement of data easily is essential.

---

[10] See the Section, "Remote Library Services (RLS)" in Section 8.4.

[11] To move an MDDB from one platform to another if the releases of SAS are not synchronized means that PROC COPY must be used. This means that moving an MDDB between a Windows PC and a UNIX server (both running SAS Release 6.12), PROC UPLOAD and PROC DOWNLOAD data transfer capabilities of SAS/CONNECT can be used. Version 7 will ensure possible synchronization of releases across platforms.

Given that the movement of data is a prerequisite for a successful Data Warehouse, it also follows that network performance concerns will follow. One way that this can be helped is by giving the users the ability to move only the information they need. Both the DOWNLOAD and UPLOAD procedures have the ability to restrict the information that is moved. This is done by selecting only the columns and rows of information that are needed. Consider the following snippet of code:

```
RSUBMIT unixbox;
 LIBNAME whse '\whse\data';
 PROC DOWNLOAD DATA=whse.data(KEEP=date sales)
              OUT=analysis;
 WHERE date > mdy(01,01,1997) AND product='CK';
 RUN;
ENDRSUBMIT;
```

Note that if using either procedure, UPLOAD or DOWNLOAD, the procedure has to be submitted on the remote SAS session. In other words, it is always the prerogative of the Server and not the Client to supply the service.

The code shown above requests that the permanent file (**whse.data**) be downloaded to the Client computer, but not in its entirety. The data has been restricted by the request that only asks for two columns (**date** and **sales**) and only where the date is after 1, January, 1997 if the product is **CK**. If the file **whse.data** has 2 million rows and 120 columns, then this DOWNLOAD request will save a great deal of network load and make the analyst's role far easier by only supplying the information needed.

The previous example is a very simple example of downloading a file. This can become far more complex and powerful, without Data Warehouse users needing to be able to understand any SAS code at all. For instance, the SAS Query Window (part of the base SAS software) will allow for the inclusion of a profile that will automatically start a SAS/CONNECT session. As mentioned above, it will also allow for queries to be built against file structures beyond SAS by specifying alternative access modes. In this way, through a 'point-and-click' interface, Data Warehouse users can not only access data, but easily construct requests that will be specific to their needs. The users can then select to create a file either on the local computer or on the remote computer that will be the result set from the constructed request. Indeed, it is even possible to move the result set into file structures other than SAS if that is needed. Data Warehouse users need not know one line of code, yet they will be performing complex Client/Server processing, accessing multiple file structures across platforms.

The most important factor in this architecture, however, is that users can actually concentrate on performing the work, and not have to focus on the behind-the-scenes technicalities. In Data Warehousing, there is always a balance needed between giving the users complete flexibility in accessing pertinent information and not requiring them to become technical experts. Many successful Data Warehouses have been designed to shield the users from needing to understand anything about the structure. This is fine, as long as the resources to build front-end applications are there, or, if the needs for the Data Warehouse are so specific, that it is easy to anticipate the users' needs. Very often, this is not the case, which is where a tool like the SAS Query Window comes in very useful.

So the transferring of data from one location to another is usually an essential part of Data Warehouse design. It is important to understand two things: what the user is going to do with the data and the limitations of the computer architecture. One of the frustrations that the technical community, which is traditionally used for building an Operational System, has with Data Warehouse design, is the degree to which the requirements change. If this is indeed the case, then the wrong people are designing the Data Warehouse. Changes are going to be requested all the time; it is the nature of business. Given that these changes are needed, it is then essential that flexibility be an integral part of the design, and part of the design is the use of Client/Server architectures.

As mentioned earlier, the movement of information is dependent upon the underlying communication method. SAS/CONNECT cannot move the data any faster than the method will allow, but there are possibilities within SAS to help optimize the process. One of these is the TBUFSIZE option, which must be set when starting the remote SAS session and not during the session itself. The TBUFSIZE option controls the amount of data that SAS sends at a given time to the communication software's buffer. The only way to find out the optimum TBUFSIZE is to test it and see. It is easy to change the size, so testing is not a difficult process. The default TBUFSIZE is 32K, so to change this to 64K, the following code will work:

```
%LET MVSBOX=199.55.160.22 23;
OPTIONS COMAMID=TCP;
OPTIONS REMOTE=MVSBOX;
FILENAME RLINK 'physical.script.file.name';
SIGNON TBUFSIZE=65536;
```

Note that there are some potential problems with adjusting this option,[12] but the performance gains are well worth the time spent with up-front experimentation.

In looking at SAS/CONNECT up to this stage, we have considered two situations.

- Where we take the logic to the data (with Compute Services)
- Where we take the data to the logic (Data Transfer).

Often the situation arises where neither of these potential solutions actually fits the situation. Something in-between is needed. In this case, Remote Library Services often fits to solve the problem.

Remote Library Services (RLS)

RLS has less of an impact and use within Data Warehousing than it does in applications that have a less static data source. It is, however, a very useful option because it allows an application to recognize a data source that physically resides remotely as a local source. It is especially useful in situations where the remote data source is small (because RLS can be a network intensive solution) or if the remote data source is frequently changed (not usually a situation in Data Warehousing). Note also that RLS can only be used if SAS/CONNECT is running over a program-to-program communication access method (e.g., APPC, DECnet, NetBIOS, TCP/IP).

The best way to explain how to use RLS is by example. Suppose on an OS/390 mainframe, there is a table contained in a DB2 RDBMS. A SAS View exists on the mainframe that enables the SAS user to access the DB2 table as though it were a SAS data set (using SAS/ACCESS for DB2).[13] This table needs to be combined with a table that is stored in an ORACLE RDBMS on a UNIX computer and finally with a SAS data set on a Windows NT computer, where the local SAS session is running.

One option would be to extract both the DB2 and ORACLE table into a SAS format and then download this information to the local PC. The three tables could then be combined, as the user needs require. The code to do this would be as follows:

---

[12] See: Horton, Susan, "Maximum Performance Utilization for SAS/CONNECT ® Processing," *Observations*, 4th Quarter 1995, SAS Institute Inc., p33. Not that the TBUFSIZE option is only of use in peer-to-peer (program-to-program) communication access methods (e.g., TCP/IP), as opposed to terminal-based access methods (e.g., EHLLAPI).

[13] See Chapter 5 to find out how to access data not physically stored in SAS data sets.

1. Sign-on using SAS/CONNECT to the OS/390 Mainframe.

```
%LET mvsbox=199.55.160.22 23;
OPTIONS COMAMID=TCP;
OPTIONS REMOTE=mvsbox;
FILENAME RLINK 'physical.script.file.name';
SIGNON TBUFSIZE=65536;
```

2. Remote submit to the OS/390 mainframe and download the DB2 table to the local (client) Windows NT server.

```
RSUBMIT mvsbox;
LIBNAME14 db2acces 'db2.to.sas.views' DISP=SHR;
PROC DOWNLOAD DATA=db2acces.db2table
               OUT=work.db2table;
RUN;
ENDRSUBMIT;
```

3. Sign-on using SAS/CONNECT to the UNIX server.

```
%LET unixbox=199.55.160.24 23;
OPTIONS COMAMID=TCP;
OPTIONS REMOTE=unixbox;
FILENAME RLINK '\whse\data\';
SIGNON TBUFSIZE=65536;
```

4. Remote submit to the UNIX server and download the ORACLE table to the local (client) Windows NT server.

```
RSUBMIT unixbox;
LIBNAME oraacces '/oracle/sas/views/';
PROC DOWNLOAD DATA=oraacces.oratable
               OUT=work.oratable;
RUN;
ENDRSUBMIT;
```

5. Process files extracted from the OS/390 and the UNIX computers locally.

```
LIBNAME saslocal 'c:\sas\files';
PROC SQL;
 SELECT * FROM work.db2table db2, work.oratable ora, saslocal.sastable sas
 WHERE db2.date=ora.date and db2.date=sas.date;
QUIT;
```

The preceding code will connect to two remote computers, download data from two entirely disparate database engines (DB2 and ORACLE), and then combine them with a third source on the Windows NT server, that just so happens to be in SAS.

---

14 For a description of using LIBNAME within SAS, see: Delwiche, Lora D., and Slaughter, Susan J., *The Little SAS Book: A Primer*, Cary, NC: SAS Institute Inc., 1995. 228p, p56-57.

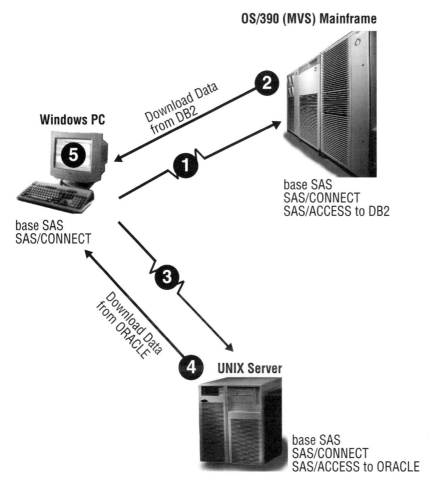

OS/390 (MVS) Mainframe

Windows PC

Download Data from DB2

base SAS
SAS/CONNECT
SAS/ACCESS to DB2

base SAS
SAS/CONNECT

Download Data from ORACLE

UNIX Server

base SAS
SAS/CONNECT
SAS/ACCESS to ORACLE

Figure 8.3

The preceding example **does not** illustrate the use of RLS. Exactly the same process could be completed using RLS as follows:

1. Sign-on using SAS/CONNECT to the OS/390 mainframe.

```
%LET mvsbox=199.55.160.22 23;
OPTIONS COMAMID=TCP;
OPTIONS REMOTE=mvsbox;
FILENAME RLINK 'physical.script.file.name';
SIGNON TBUFSIZE=65536;
```

2. Sign-on using SAS/CONNECT to the UNIX server.

```
%LET unixbox=199.55.160.24 23;
OPTIONS COMAMID=TCP;
OPTIONS REMOTE=unixbox;
FILENAME RLINK '\whse\data\';
SIGNON TBUFSIZE=65536;
```

3. Assign local LIBNAME to remote libraries through Remote Library Services.

```
LIBNAME oraacces remote '/oracle/sas/views/' SERVER=unixbox;
LIBNAME db2acces remote 'db2.to.sas.views' DISP=SHR
@lastcode:SERVER=mvsbox;
```

4. Combine the remote files using local processing through the use of Remote Library Services.

```
LIBNAME saslocal 'c:\sas\files';

PROC SQL;
 SELECT * FROM work.db2table db2, work.oratable ora, saslocal.sastable sas
 WHERE db2.date=ora.date and db2.date=sas.date;
QUIT;
```

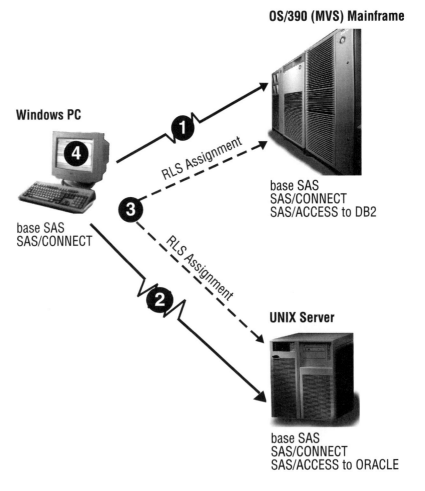

Figure 8.4

Note that the two major differences are first of all that no data is actually downloaded to the Windows NT (client) computer, and that the LIBNAME statements to access the remote files use the SERVER= option to let SAS know where the files are physically located. This code is a little simpler than the code where a physical download took place.[15]

From a Data Warehouse perspective, especially when looking at front-end access by users, both of the techniques above can be achieved through the use of the SAS Query window without the user having to write a line of the code. If a less generic tool than the Query window was required, then the above could be easily written using SAS/AF (Application Facility) software which could be customized to the particular Data Warehousing circumstance.

The RLS example is simple to understand, but it is not magic. Data has to move along the network at some point, so for an SQL join as illustrated in the previous example, the full table will, at some point, have to be moved to the local SAS session because this is where the physical join will take place. However, if a subsetting WHERE clause is applied to the remote tables, then this will take place on the Server level, and only the results from the clause will have to be moved to the local SAS session. RLS does, however, make the Client/Server architecture completely transparent because the user does not have to know where the files are physically located. SAS takes care of that through the SERVER= option in the LIBNAME statement. The example illustrating RLS outlined above will only be efficient if the number of rows in both the DB2 and the ORACLE tables is very small.

It is often advantageous to have a library referenced both in the local and the remote session. For example, maybe the remote SASUSER library (the permanent library automatically created by SAS for each individual user) needs to be accessed using RLS from a local Client. The problem is that it will already be referenced automatically in the remote session. The same goes for the temporary library (WORK), which is automatically created at the initiation of a SAS session. This can be done quite easily as follows:

```
LIBNAME rsasuser SLIBREF=sasuser SERVER=mvsbox;
```

This statement simply tells the local SAS session that it should have access to a remote library that is already referenced in the remote SAS session. The SLIBREF= option specifies the explicit reference to the remote LIBNAME=

---

[15] For several more complex examples of using Remote Library Services, Compute Services, and Data Transfer Services see: SAS Institute Inc., *SAS/CONNECT® Software: Usage and Reference, Version 6, Second Edition*, Cary, NC: SAS Institute Inc., 1994. 368pp., Chapter 3.

statement. This can be illustrated more readily by looking at the following example:

```
/* The DB2 views are referenced in the remote SAS session */
RSUBMIT mvsbox;
 LIBNAME db2acces 'db2.to.sas.views' DISP=SHR;
ENDRSUBMIT;

/* The DB2 views are also referenced in the local SAS session through RLS */
LIBNAME db2views SLIBREF=db2acces SERVER=mvsbox;
```

The user or the local application then has the option to access the data within the views either through RLS using code submitted locally or through Compute Services using code submitted remotely.

As already mentioned, the use of RLS is best utilized when the remote files are small. A way to also control network traffic is through the TOBSNO= option, which will explicitly tell SAS the number of rows that will be transmitted to the local computer by the SAS server. This option will have an effect when the Server is performing *multi-observation* buffering, in other words when it is trying to send more than one observation at a time. Whether or not this option has any effect depends on the open mode of the remote data. If the remote file is opened in UPDATE mode, then only one observation will be transmitted at a time, otherwise, the TOBSNO= option will have some effect.

If you are using multi-observation buffering and you do not specify the TOBSNO= option, then the number of observations sent across the network from the remote SAS session to the local SAS session will be dependent upon:

- The size of the observation (the record length).
- The buffer size (usually defaulted to 32K).

From a Data Warehousing perspective, the use of the Remote Library Services capability of SAS/CONNECT will usually have limited value. This is because the amount of data usually being handled is greater than the amount that is advisable to use with RLS. Another reason is that usually (but not always) the physical organization of the data within a Data Warehouse will be optimized to prevent the use of RLS. This is probably the case in the Data Warehouse back end (the extraction, cleansing, and manipulation of data). It is not necessarily the case in the front end where the flexibility that Client/Server architectures give the user means that RLS might be an applicable solution.

SAS/CONNECT Summary

SAS/CONNECT is the backbone of the SAS Client/Server solutions. It is a flexible product that can give the designer of the Data Warehouse a set of options that can lead to a flexible Data Warehouse. It allows the designer to place the data close to the predominant user, without restricting the less-frequent users from access for example, when a Data Mart is created for a Marketing Department and is physically located on the department server. Ninety-five percent of the time, the analysts within the department use this machine directly to analyze their data, and so network traffic is kept to a minimum. The other five percent of the time, the data is used as part of a company-wide information system, and to enable this, the data is used via SAS/CONNECT sessions from remote Windows based computers. This is a simple and very sensible Client/Server approach, which has been well thought-out from a strategic level.

8.5 Using SAS/SHARE for Concurrent Access to Data

SAS/CONNECT is a product that allows one SAS session (a Client) to initiate another SAS session (a Server). The key point to this arrangement is that one session spawns another session. In very many cases, this arrangement is ideal. Processing can be completed by the most suitable SAS session and data can be conveniently located where it is deemed most fit (where it will reduce network traffic, in many cases). This is a very powerful option for the Data Warehouse designer because it adds flexibility, performance, and control over the data. All of these three benefits can lead to an enterprise responsive Data Warehouse that will grow with its needs. Certain instances, however, might lead to a situation where it is not advisable for each user to be able to spawn more than one SAS session (maybe for resource reasons) or where a file needs to be updated concurrently by more than one user. The latter is an unusual situation in a Data Warehousing environment, due to it usually being *read-only*, but concurrent updates might well arise in the maintenance process. Both of these situations can be accounted for by using SAS/SHARE.

SAS/SHARE enables the running of a single SAS session that brokers requests on potentially shared data from a variety of users. A single initiation of a SAS session running under the control of SAS/SHARE is often referred to as a Server, but this should not be confused with *file servers* common on networks. There are three major differences between a SAS/SHARE server and network file servers:

1. Network file servers are usually designed to transfer vast amounts of data across a network, which is not what SAS/SHARE servers are designed to do.

2. Network file servers are not aware of the contents of the data that they are moving, whereas a SAS/SHARE server can enable multiple users concurrent update access to the same file. This means that the SAS/SHARE server has to understand the internals of the files it is controlling.

3. Network file servers are usually not capable of data translation. If a SAS/SHARE server is a Server to a Client that has a different representation of data, then the Server will automatically perform the translation. For instance, if a SAS/SHARE server is running on an OS/390 mainframe and the Client is a SAS session running under Windows, there has to be a degree of data translation for access to make any sense. A network file server would not usually care about this difference, but would move the data *as is*.

So, the advantage of a SAS/SHARE server is that because it is, in effect, a single SAS session being a Server to multiple Clients, it can reduce the system overheads. The SAS/SHARE server can also allow for multiple Clients to concurrently access and update a single file.

SAS/SHARE in a Data Warehousing Environment

Data Warehousing is not just a question of talking to a few key users, building a few programs to extract data, performing a piece of perfunctory data modeling, and giving the user a report-writing tool. It is the process of building a process that will keep in line with future requirements, and part of that building is putting the pieces in place to anticipate those requirements. Every part of the process is strategic, and therefore every product that is used must also be so. SAS/SHARE is a strategic product that must be viewed not in terms of its immediate use, but in terms of how it will fit into the long-term picture.

From a Data Warehousing perspective, SAS/SHARE can, like SAS/CONNECT, add a level of flexibility to the process. Again and again, we reference the fact that a successful Data Warehousing process never remains static. There are continual changes and enhancements that require a methodology and process to be completely adaptable to whatever the enterprise needs require of it. The more options that will allow the architecture to be adapted to the enterprise requirements, the more they will lead to a successful long-term Data Warehouse project. SAS/SHARE is another of those products that allows for a Data Warehouse design that can adapt to change.

Features of SAS/SHARE Relevant to the Data Warehousing Process

The following features of SAS/SHARE might well be very useful in a Data Warehousing environment:

- If security is an issue in the Data Warehouse, then SAS/SHARE can optionally create secure Servers.
- If some form of concurrent update is going to be needed (this is more likely on the maintenance side of the Data Warehouse with metadata update) then SAS/SHARE will afford this capability.
- If part of the physical Data Warehouse is only likely to be accessed by a limited number of users but it is located on a computer that is otherwise highly utilized, then the option of a single SAS session handling multiple users might make perfect sense.

Differences between SAS/SHARE and SAS/CONNECT

There are some fundamental differences between SAS/SHARE and SAS/CONNECT that mean each of them can play a distinct role in the Data Warehousing process. Although both products might not be necessary in any particular Data Warehousing project, it is important to understand the differences between the two. These differences include the following:

- SAS/CONNECT does not allow for multiple update accesses to the same file.
- SAS/SHARE does not give Compute Services availability.
- SAS/SHARE is manifested as a Server, which is a single SAS session that users can share. The Server acts as a broker for the data that is defined to it.

In some ways, the two products can perform similar types of tasks:

- Both products allow for transparent access to data across computers and Operating System platforms.
- Both products automatically perform any data translation that is required between disparate Operating Systems.

One of the major operational differences between SAS/CONNECT and SAS/SHARE is that the former has to be started during initialization of a SAS session or during that session. In other words, it is an action by the user (the initiator of the local session) that allows a remote SAS session to be invoked. This is usually different in the case of SAS/SHARE because the Server is not started from within an existing SAS session, but from outside one. This means that someone has to be responsible for starting it. For this reason, there is usually a SAS/SHARE administrator who is responsible for the invocation of the server and the maintenance thereof. This maintenance role is fairly trivial, but necessary nevertheless.

Using SAS/SHARE Software

To start a SAS/SHARE server, a SAS session is established on the computer where the Server will be running. From within this SAS session, the following code is submitted:

```
OPTIONS COMAMID=tcp;
 PROC SERVER SERVERID=servname;   RUN;
```

This section of code tells SAS, first, that the TCP/IP access method will be used for connection to the Server, and second, to start the Server SERVNAME running. Note that after the above code has been submitted, there can be no direct interaction with this SAS session. Any subsequent action must be performed from within another SAS session through the use of the SAS procedure OPERATE (see the next section).

This snippet of code raises two major questions:

- What data does the Server broker, or how is data defined to the SAS/SHARE server?
- How does a user access and use this Server?

How Is Data Defined to a SAS/SHARE Server?

There are three principal methods by which data can be defined to a Server. The first two are defined by the Server administrator and the last one by the user of the Server.

1. A data library can be defined to the SAS session before the Server is actually started. In the snippet of code above, if the following line were added at the top, then this library would be under the control (brokerage) of the Server:

   ```
   LIBNAME servlib 's:\server\brokered\data';
   ```

2. A data library can be defined to the Server after it has been initialized. This can be done by the administrator who will be running another SAS session that has the capabilities to link to the Server. The following code submitted from within this parallel SAS session will add a library to the Server:

   ```
   PROC OPERATE SERVER=servname;
   ALLOCATE LIBRARY newlib 's:\new\server\brokered\data';
   ```

PROC OPERATE is the means by which the Server administrator can control the Server or obtain information about the Server. This action of the administrator, allocating a library after the Server has been invoked, is fairly unusual because libraries defined to a server remain fairly constant.

3. A data library can be defined to a Server by a user (as opposed to an administrator), as long as the Server was initialized with the ALLOC option (which is the default). This can be done by the following code from within a user's SAS session.

```
LIBNAME userlib 'c:\users\data' SERVER=servname;
```

This statement will associate a library with the Server's SAS session, not the user's SAS session, and will automatically connect the two sessions. Note that before this LIBNAME is valid, the user must state the correct communications access method by using the COMAMID= option. Any reference to this library during the existence of the user's SAS session will be handled by the Server's SAS session.

How Does a User Access the Data Brokered by the SAS/SHARE Server?

Using the data that is brokered by a SAS/SHARE server is a simple task for the user or the application that is done via the LIBNAME statement. Let's suppose that a Server is running on a UNIX computer, and the user is requiring access to data from a Windows based computer. Again, in this case, TCP/IP will be the communications protocol. The LIBNAME statement will be as follows:

```
LIBNAME shrdata '/warehse/shared/data' SERVER=unixnode.shrsvr;
```

This is very much the same as previous LIBNAME statements we have looked at in this chapter. There is one difference. That is the **unixnode** part of the SERVER= value. In this situation, where we are using the TCP/IP communications access method, **unixnode** refers to a known IP alias. In other words, the network recognizes **unixnode** as a remote computer (in this case, the particular UNIX computer where the SAS/SHARE server is running). To illustrate this further, consider the following snippet of code:

```
%LET unixnode=199.23.190.22;
OPTIONS COMAMID=tcp;
LIBNAME shrdata '/warehse/shared/data' SERVER=unixnode.shrsvr;
```

In this case, we are defining the **unixnode** value to a SAS macro variable named **unixnode** and then referencing it in the SERVER= option. The value for `unixnode` will be substituted and the correct computer will then be known. **Note that this two-part SERVER= value is only needed in a situation where the SAS/SHARE server is running on a different computer.** If the Server and the user's SAS session are on the same computer, then only the `shrsver` portion of the SERVER= parameter needs to be referenced.

The `shrsver` portion of the SERVER= parameter references a defined SAS/SHARE TCP/IP service, which must be contained in both the *services* file[16] on the computer where the user's SAS session is running and on the computer where the SAS/SHARE server is running. One of the problems with being able to use multiple communications access methods and operating systems is that there can be no standard configuration that will work for all SAS/SHARE configurations.

We have been using TCP/IP as an example because it is an industry standard and is commonly used; however, it is important to ensure that in the design of the Data Warehouse, the infrastructure is completely considered. From a SAS perspective, it doesn't really matter what operating system or communications access method is used. From a Data Warehousing perspective, however, it matters a great deal. The phrase, *Keep it simple, stupid!*, comes to mind. It is possible to operate with more than one communications access method (for instance, sites often run both TCP/IP and NetBIOS), but this means having the overhead to support both, and when something does go wrong (....and it will), what has caused it? Resolving problems in communication networks is like trying to solve a problem with a car's electronics: finding the problem is very difficult, but solving it is usually easy. The more options that are used, the harder the diagnosis will be.

A single SAS/SHARE server will allow for more than one communications access method. This is done with extensions to the COMAMID= option. These extensions are COMAUX1= and COMAUX2= which are specified in the user's SAS session. These should be placed in the SAS configuration file, as opposed to being set after the session has begun.[17] The SAS/SHARE servers also have extensive security options that restrict or allow use of their services. This has particular benefits in a Data Warehousing environment when the content of the data is very sensitive. Instead of individual SAS

---

[16] The *services* file contains a name for a service (SHRSVR) and a TCP/IP port. As with all TCP/IP services, the port must be unique on both the Server and the Client but must be identical on both.

[17] Technical details for SAS/SHARE servers can best be found in the SAS/SHARE Technical Reports for the applicable operating system. For instance, for the Windows environment, see: SAS Institute Inc., *SAS/SHARE® Technical Report for the Microsoft Windows Environment, Release 6.11*, Cary, NC: SAS Institute Inc,. 1995. 75pp.

sessions handling the allocation of sensitive data so it can be used, it would be possible to allocate that information to a restricted SAS/SHARE server. The Server can then handle the security and the usage can be monitored through the log of the Server.[18] If the sensitive data were handled by a SAS/CONNECT session, even if the data itself were password protected, then there would be no audit of who had actually accessed the data and when.

SAS/SHARE Summary

As already mentioned, any decision made on products when designing an architecture is strategic. For this reason, no single decision can be taken lightly. With SAS software, these decisions can be easier to make than with many other vendors, due to the ability when using SAS to change the architecture without having to make vast changes to the underlying code. The decision whether to use SAS/SHARE within the Data Warehouse environment can be answered using the following questions:

1. Do you ever have a situation where a single source of data needs to be updated concurrently?

2. Do you have a situation where it is beneficial to the entire Data Warehouse to have certain data physically located on a computer that cannot handle multiple SAS sessions?

3. Do you have a situation where a single point of control is necessary for access to specific data?

If the answer to any of these three questions is *yes*, then SAS/SHARE might well be of use to the Data Warehousing architecture.

Unlike SAS/CONNECT, it is unlikely that SAS/SHARE will be absolutely integral to any Client/Server requirements that a Data Warehouse might need. There are features of the software that might well come in use, but none that are likely to make it the cornerstone of the architecture. SAS/SHARE was originally designed as a tool to allow for concurrent updates to data within a low-to-medium load transaction-based system. Data Warehouses do not come under this classification of systems. As such, SAS/SHARE is a product that should be looked at when solving specific problems, rather than as a strategic product.

---

[18] For methods of controlling access to a SAS/SHARE server, see: SAS Institute Inc., *SAS/SHARE® Software: Usage and Reference, Version 6, First Edition*, Cary, NC: SAS Institute, Inc., 1991. 111 pp.

Chapter 9:
Managing the Implementation:
The SAS/Warehouse Administrator™

9.1 The SAS/Warehouse Administrator and the Data Warehouse

This chapter will give an overview of the SAS/Warehouse Administrator and how it relates to the process of data warehousing. Details about the product in terms of how it can aid in the implementation process will be outlined. This chapter is not intended to replace any usage documentation that is currently available. It can certainly be used as a precursor to reading the available documentation and does not presuppose that the reader has any experience with the SAS/Warehouse Administrator. As with the rest of this book, this chapter is intended to guide the reader through the SAS software tools in relation to data warehousing, not to give an in-depth nuts-and-bolts description of any product. Note that the SAS/Warehouse Administrator product has been developing rapidly. For information about the latest developments, see the SAS World Wide Web page (www.sas.com).

To effectively utilize the SAS/Warehouse Administrator it is first necessary to thoroughly understand exactly where it fits into the Data Warehousing process. The process of building a Data Warehouse involves three predominant phases:[1]

- The building of the Conceptual Data Warehouse.
- The Transition Phase moving the Conceptual Warehouse to the Implemented Warehouse.
- The Implementation Phase.

The SAS/Warehouse Administrator is primarily a tool to help control the implementation and maintenance of the Data Warehouse. It will be a valuable and beneficial tool to pull a potentially vast process (the implementation of the Data Warehouse) under a single manageable umbrella. With a process as large and complex as the building of a Data Warehouse, any help in the coordination and management of change is invaluable.

The key to using the product successfully is to understand its positioning within the Data Warehouse process, and this can be best recognized by the name of the product itself. It is an *administration* tool, and not a *design* tool. The product will **not**, therefore help you in the following tasks:

- Create or assess the enterprise needs.
- Automatically recognize the source data that is needed.
- Model the Data Warehouse.

If the underlying design of the Data Warehouse is flawed, the best the SAS/Warehouse Administrator can do is to ensure that the flawed Warehouse is produced efficiently. It might make the flaws in the process apparent, and can certainly help in effectively making the changes that will be required to make the Data Warehouse successful, but it cannot participate in the design process, except in the Implementation phase.

Although there are major benefits to the users of the Data Warehouse to have the SAS/Warehouse Administrator as an underlying basis for the implementation of the Warehouse, it is not directly an end-user tool. The metadata that is stored within the SAS/Warehouse Administrator can be extracted and therefore incorporated into applications that might benefit the business users. Starting with Release 1.2, the product includes an API (Application Program Interface) that allows direct access to the metadata. (See the Special Topic, "Introduction to the Metadata API Available in Release 1.2 of the SAS/Warehouse Administrator" at the end of this chapter for more information.

---

[1] See Chapter 2 for an overview of these three phases.

It is important to keep in mind exactly why an administration tool can be of use in a Data Warehousing process:

- It allows for continuity in an ever-changing process. People come and go (both from the business and technical side), and rules will adjust to meet the changing needs of the enterprise. An administration tool will not only hold the underlying rules that the Data Warehouse will be based upon, but will also, just as importantly, contain and help maintain the process that is essential to a successful implementation.

- In situations where a Data Warehouse is made up of a number of Data Marts, an administration tool can be invaluable in the coordination of the design. The concept of *reverse engineering*[2] the Data Warehouse by creating smaller, more enterprise need receptive Data Marts and then altering them to be of a more generic, enterprise wide use is becoming more common. This is because there can be more immediate return on investment by targeting specific department's needs. The problem arises when these generic *islands* of information must be incorporated to meet the wider needs of the enterprise. In this situation, an administration tool can be the means by which the enterprise wide Warehouse may be designed. Note that the administration tool should be used as the underpinning for the Data Marts, even before they are brought under an enterprise wide umbrella.

- An administration tool will add structure to the Data Warehousing project. One of the problems in the implementation phase of the Data Warehousing process is the multitude of overlapping tasks that have to be performed. This means that it is easy to either forget, or duplicate, these tasks. An administration tool can help in the avoidance of such a problem.

- The administration tool can help in the creation of consistent code (as the SAS/Warehouse Administrator will do). Although each Data Warehouse implementation is likely to have specific needs outside the limits of a generic administrator, using a single tool for code generation will result in a single understandable approach in the extraction of the source data and the loading of the transformed data.

9.2 The SAS/Warehouse Administrator Basics

The SAS/Warehouse Administrator runs on three different platforms: UNIX, OS/2 and Windows (3.1, 95 and NT). This does not mean that either

---

[2] See Chapter 3, Section 3.2 where there is a *special topic* discussing the *reverse engineering* of Data Warehouses.

the source data or the final Data Warehouse itself need be on these platforms. Only the underlying processing of the administration of the Data Warehouse has to take place on these three platforms. In fact, it is not even necessary for the metadata that will be generated within the Administrator to physically reside on the same platform as the product itself. For performance reasons, this is advisable, but is not essential.

To run the Administrator on any platform, the following SAS products will be needed:

- Base SAS software
- SAS/FSP

These two products are required as a minimum. However, if these were the only two products licensed, then for the Administrator to be used effectively, all of the data that will be required within the Data Warehouse would have to be on the same computer as the Administrator itself. This would mean that the source data and the Warehouse itself would be on the same computer. This is a highly unlikely situation on a practical level and not advisable on an intellectual level. In Data Warehouses where the use of the Administrator product can be cost justified (see the next section), it is likely that a variety of computers and data sources external to SAS will be used in the entire process. This means that extra products will be required:

- SAS/CONNECT[3]
- SAS/ACCESS[4]

It is also likely that in most Data Warehouse implementations of a reasonable size, there will be multiple people who have responsibility to update information contained within the scope of the Administrator. This will mean that there must be the ability for many users to concurrently update data within the Administrator. This will require the following product to be licensed:

- SAS/SHARE

Of the five products mentioned above, only SAS/SHARE will be required because the Administrator is licensed. In other words, all the other products will probably be needed to implement the Data Warehouse using SAS software even if the Administrator is not used. SAS/SHARE will be essential if

---

[3] See Chapter 8 for a description of SAS/CONNECT and its role in the Data Warehousing process.
[4] See Chapter 5, "Data Storage within the Warehouse: Effectively Using SAS/ACCESS® Products" for outlines of SAS/ACCESS. This is not a single SAS module, but is licensed dependent upon the external data format that needs to be accessed or written to.

more than one person is likely to be using the Administrator and working on the same metadata at one time. It is possible to avoid the need for SAS/SHARE, but the danger of corrupting the metadata exists if more than one person concurrently tries to update the metadata. Alternatively, coordination is required to ensure that concurrent updates are not made.

Note that the SAS Scalable Performance Data Server[5] in release 2.0 will have record level locking. This means that it will potentially be possible to use the SPDS as a store for the metadata. In this case, if the SPDS is licensed, it will work as an alternative to SAS/SHARE. The SAS/Warehouse Administrator also supports the creation of multi-dimensional databases,[6] but the SAS/MDDB server will, in this situation, be required.

An aspect of the Administrator that can be confusing is where it actually runs: what host should it be on? It would be a very unusual situation for the Administrator to run on the same host (computer) as the operational systems used to populate the Data Warehouse. It is also unlikely that it would run on the same host(s) as the Data Warehouse reside upon. If the entire data warehouse implementation process is spread across hosts, then it means that it will be essential to have SAS/CONNECT on the host upon which the Administrator is installed. If concurrent updates to the metadata held within the Administrator are to occur, then SAS/SHARE is required. Therefore, it may be economical to install the Administrator on a small server to keep the cost of additional products to a minimum. Careful consideration needs to go into the choice of host for the Administrator, but to be absolutely clear, it does not have to be installed where either the data for the Warehouse exists, or where the processing to create and maintain the warehouse will take place.

Is the SAS/Warehouse Administrator Necessary to Implement a Data Warehouse?

The necessity of the Administrator to a successful Data Warehouse implementation is dependent upon the approach taken to the process. Metadata is the heart of a Data Warehouse and therefore it is essential to have some form of control over necessary updates to current data, or modifications that are needed from a structural standpoint.

---

[5] See Chapter 5, the section "The SAS Scalable Performance Data Server" for a description of the SAS SPDS product and how it fits into a Data Warehousing process.
[6] See Chapter 4 for a discussion of multi-dimensional databases and their part in the Data Warehouse process.

For instance, part of the metadata might be a definition of a source system that feeds product numbers to the Data Warehouse. This will be a simple process if only one system contains definitions for product numbers. If, however, more than one system contains product numbers then there is the potential for two completely different coding schemes. This situation could occur when a new company is purchased. Both source systems will need to be incorporated in the extraction and transformation process. The Administrator in this situation will visually display the current process of moving the product numbers from the source system into the Data Warehouse. It will also show exactly which programs/methods are employed for that part of the process. From this, it will be apparent exactly what needs to be changed for the new data source to be incorporated into the Data Warehouse process. It will then be possible to make these changes, understanding exactly the impact that will be made upon the process.

Without a tool to control the metadata, changes such as that illustrated above will become increasingly difficult to manage. An isolated example is not difficult to deal with, but as the number of changes increase, so will the problems of administration. It might not be necessary to the SAS/Warehouse Administrator, but in its absence, some form of other control will be needed. Building such a control will be an immense project, and one that will take resources away from the real aim of the Data Warehouse: to fulfill enterprise requirements defined in the first of the three phases of the process.[7]

The answer to the question of whether the SAS/Warehouse Administrator is necessary to build a Data Warehouse using SAS is no. SAS has all the tools necessary so that the Administrator is not an absolute necessity. If, however, the Data Warehousing process is thoroughly understood as both perpetual and ever changing, then a control tool will be necessary. The SAS/Warehouse Administrator will fulfill this role and as such, should always be considered in any situations where the Data Warehouse process is even vaguely complex. The cost of building a Data Warehouse can be immense, and any control over the process could potentially result in vast savings. As with many software tools, justifying the cost of purchase (or license in the case of all SAS Institute software) is tied not so much to what it will do for you but what will happen if you don't use it. It is not necessary to have the SAS/Warehouse Administrator to build a successful Data Warehouse, but without it the chances of successful implementation and maintenance will be reduced.

---

[7] See Chapter 2 for an outline of these three phases.

9.3 How the SAS/Warehouse Administrator Views the Data Warehouse

No two Data Warehouse implementations are similar. Because of this, any product that is designed to help in the implementation will have to be very flexible. Within this flexible construct, however, a framework is needed for the implementation to work within. This section describes that framework.

SAS/Warehouse Administrator Terminology

Some key terms within the Administrator are important to understanding its usage. Three terms are outlined below. In reading through these terms, it is not necessary to thoroughly understand them all. Later on in the chapter, they will be referenced in context and will therefore make more sense.

Environment Level

The following terms relate to items that are defined at the environmental level. Note that one of these terms is *Data Warehouse*. It is possible to have multiple Data Warehouses for each environment that is defined. This is beneficial because the metadata defined to the *environment* can be used across each Data Warehouse. If each Data Warehouse were its own environment, then the *high level metadata* would have to be redefined for each implementation.

Environment: the environment is the highest level of information that the Administrator will store. The environment is a directory that stores metadata that can be used by any Data Warehouse. In the vast majority of cases, there will only be one *environment* created. A single Data Warehouse can only get metadata from one environment, so there are no real benefits to creating more than one.

Shared Metadata: this is information that is stored on an environmental level. This will include global level information about operational data stores (see the next section), host definitions, library definitions, warehouse storage options, owner and administrator information and links to external computers.

Operational Data Definitions (ODD): The Administrator defines an ODD as a definition of a data source that will be used for inclusion in one or more Data Warehouses. The ODD can be a SAS data set, SAS view, SAS/ACCESS view or an SQL pass-through view descriptor. Logical groupings of ODDs are grouped into *ODD Groups*.

Data Warehouse: a Data Warehouse is a collection of data made up of read-only data and can be used on an enterprise-wide basis for decision support. It is made up of a series of elements that are connected through metadata stored within the Warehouse. These elements include detail tables, summary tables, information marts and data marts.

Data Warehouse Level

The Data Warehouses themselves are nested within an environment. Within each Data Warehouse, the following terms are important to understand.

Subject: a *subject* is one way to dissect the Data Warehouse into manageable sections. A subject is a logical and distinct area of interest to the enterprise. Although it is often difficult to discern where a subject starts and ends, it helps in the organization of the Data Warehouse to think in terms of subjects. For instance, a subject might be Sales, or Population. This is not to say that the Data Warehouse will not require data across subjects (it invariably will), but that it is a way to logically store the data.

Detail Logical Table: a *detail logical table* is either a physical or a virtual definition of one or more *detail tables/views*. A subject can have only one detail logical table. It might happen that the detail logical table is also a detail table, but it is more likely to be a view of more than one detail table.

Logical Tables/Views: a *logical table/view* is the actual store of the data making up the lowest level of granularity that the Data Warehouse requires. These are the storage elements that contain the data that have been extracted and transformed from the operational source systems.

Nested within the Data Warehouse level are the more targeted elements of the Data Warehouse. These elements are targeted toward specific enterprise needs, or broader departmental needs. The first step to these elements is usually, although not necessarily, the creation of summary level information. Summary level information is nested within the subject areas. This means that each subject could have summary level information created within it. This makes perfect sense, because, for example, if a subject is sales, then it might be prudent to create a table of sales by month.

Summary Groups a subject can have multiple *summary groups*. These *summary groups* are made up of related summary level information (that could be stored in any format accessible to SAS, including the SAS/MDDB[8]). Each summary group defines a series of parameters that are to be included as defaults in creating the *summary levels* (which are actual data tables). The summary group therefore contains the ways that detail data should be sum-

---

[8] See Chapter 4 for a full discussion on SAS/MDDB.

marized. If it is required that there are many different ways the detail data should be summarized, then it follows that there need to be multiple summary groups.

Summary Levels: summary levels make up the summary groups. They are actual tables of data that are summarized to all the levels defined within the summary group. These tables are time-base summaries. This means that the subject information is summarized by time period. There are six time periods available (day, week, half-month, month, quarter, and year), not all of which need to be defined and created. Each of the different time levels requested will be stored in a separate physical table if a SAS or DBMS format is selected.

This means that for each subject, it is possible to use the Administrator to create one or a series of summary level tables, creating statistics (sum, mean, standard deviation etc.) by any of the categorical variables contained within the detail data (e.g., salesman, plant, region). It is further possible to create different levels of summarization based upon the six time dimensions mentioned above.

There are two further ways that the detail data can be used to more specifically address the specific enterprise needs, or the more vague departmental need. It is easy to become confused between the two, but although they can be nested within each other, they are very different. These two Data Warehouse elements are *data marts* and *information marts*.

Data Mart Groups: a *data mart group* is made up of any number of data marts or information marts.

Data Marts: *a data mart* is an individual, or series of tables that give the users a subset of the data available to them in the full Data Warehouse. Although a data mart is usually made up of tables, they can also contain the results of queries or analyses performed across subjects in the Data Warehouse.

Information Marts: *information marts* are logical groupings of *information mart items*.

Information Mart Items: *information mart items* are more related to the exploitation of the Data Warehouse than are Data Marts. The difference between the two can be understood by their names. A data mart contains data that is a subset of that in the Data Warehouse. Although closely tied to the needs of a department, or an enterprise need, it is still one step away from being information. The information mart item, however, is most likely to contain items such as graphs, charts or reports, or executable items that will directly create specific information.

How Do the Administrator Tasks Relate to the Data Warehousing Process?

The Administrator will help build and monitor several tasks in the implementation phase of the Data Warehouse process. To understand the Administrator, a clear definition of the tasks it will perform is essential. Each of these tasks should then be viewed in terms of the entire Data Warehousing process, and as such, the Administrator can therefore feature heavily in the design process. To fully utilize the capabilities of the Administrator, it is therefore necessary to fully understand each of the separate tasks it can fulfill and how each of these fits into the entire process.

Although the following list is not a full description of every feature of the Administrator,[9] it will act as a means to understanding how the product is positioned within the Data Warehouse process:

- Definition of *high level* metadata. This is termed *shared* metadata in the product documentation. This is information that is common across the entire Data Warehouse architecture and will therefore be shared by any designer or user that needs to access the information. For instance, an example of this high level metadata would be the definition of an external database, or the parameters needed to create a SAS/CONNECT link to the computer upon which the external database resides. This is information that is standard across any part of the entire Data Warehouse.
- Definition of Data Warehouse *elements*. An element within the Data Warehouse can be considered an attribute. It is best understood by use of a few examples. The following can be considered elements in the Data Warehouse:
  - summary tables
  - detail tables
  - a Data Warehouse
  - a subject within a Data Warehouse
  - a multidimensional table
  - a definition of a source table
  - a Data Mart

Each of these elements are actual objects that exist within the data warehousing process. Each one of them is a *something* that has to exist for the Data Warehouse to become a viable source of business information.

---

[9] This chapter is not meant to replace the documentation that specifically relates to the SAS/Warehouse Administrator. For a full description of features and usage, see: SAS Institute Inc., *SAS/Warehouse Administrator™ User's Guide,* Cary, NC: SAS Institute Inc.

- Definition of Data Warehouse *processes*. A *process* can be described as something that happens to link together two or more elements. It is very important to fully understand that a process cannot exist before the elements have been defined. It is not possible to define the way that a summary table is created before fully defining the summary table itself.

These are the three major tasks in the implementation of the Data Warehouse. It is necessary to create information (high level metadata) that will contain the details to allow for the Administrator to understand the architecture (both hardware and software). It is then necessary to define what will actually exist (the elements) in each of the stages in the implementation of the Data Warehouse. After this is completed, then it is necessary to link (the processes) each of these elements so they can be created.

Although this is the basic underlying basis for the Administrator, key points should be made:

- The definitions in each of the three steps outlined above are not final. One of the major reasons to use the Administrator is not to initially create the Data Warehouse, but to allow continual updates. The high-level metadata, the elements and the processes will be in a continual state of flux, which if well controlled will not detrimentally affect the performance of the Data Warehouse. The Administrator is the tool that will allow for that control. One of the principal challenges of a Data Warehouse implementation is to keep in line with current enterprise needs. This can only be done in a fluid and dynamic environment that the Administrator can help create.
- The Administrator will fulfill many more tasks than those outlined above. It will generate code, schedule jobs and allow for metadata analysis among many other things. Although these features are of great importance to the Data Warehouse, they are the icing on the cake, albeit the icing that makes the cake palatable.
- The Administrator will also allow for the metadata to be exported to data exploitation tools (e.g. SAS/EIS) for analysis and presentation. Starting with Release 1.2, the Administrator makes the metadata even more accessible and extendable by containing an API (Application Program Interface). (See the Special Topic, "Introduction to the Metadata API Available in Release 1.2 of SAS/Warehouse Administrator," at the end of this chapter for more information. This will make the metadata easily accessible to both developers and users.

Given this three-stage process in the implementation of the Data Warehouse, the physical organization of the warehouse environment is as follows:

- There can be multiple Data Warehouses under a single environment. Although in many cases, a single warehouse would suffice for any organization, if it were decided that the enterprise would benefit from more than one warehouse, then the Administrator will allow for this. A Data Warehouse cannot be defined before an environment is established.

- Each of these Data Warehouses will share information (metadata) that has been defined to the environment. This will include the information that defines a link to an external computer or database, or a definition of a source operational data file. This information, the *shared metadata* can be viewed as objects of information that can be used by any Data Warehouse defined to the environment, or any part of that Warehouse. This shared metadata can optionally be created before a Data Warehouse is defined. It is also possible, and often essential, to define the environmental metadata as the Warehouse itself develops. One of the most important pieces of the shared metadata are ODDs *(Operational Data Definitions)* which are the basis for extracting data from operational sources.

- Each Data Warehouse will have its own *mappings* and *data transfers*. The mappings will define how an operational data source will be transformed so that they can create detail tables/views. Data Transfers are required when data needs to be moved.

9.4 What Information Is Needed to Use the SAS/Warehouse Administrator Effectively?

Sections 9.1, 9.2 and 9.3 have explained some of the background in understanding how the SAS/Warehouse Administrator interacts with the implementation of the Data Warehouse. What is quite clear, and explicitly stated in Section 9.1, is that the Administrator is not a tool that can replace the designer of a Data Warehouse. Before the product can be used effectively, a great deal of work in terms of the design process needs to be completed. It is therefore logical to question as to what design work should be completed before the Administrator becomes an effective tool. In other words, what information does the Administrator need to know to effectively implement the Data Warehouse?

A very important point to make is that a successful Data Warehouse is rarely the result of a single process that results in a data store that will fulfill the needs of the enterprise for many years. It is more likely to be an iterative, spiral approach that requires constant changing and tuning. Most successful Data Warehouses have been built with very targeted results in mind, and have slowly evolved from there. In other words, it is unusual (and inadvisable) to try the *big bang*[10] approach to building a Data Warehouse from both a business and technological perspective. They become expensive follies very quickly. Given that the approach should be iterative and controlled, the SAS/Warehouse Administrator is a flexible tool that allows for an incremental design process. Certain pieces of information are needed to begin to use the product. These are outlined below.

Environmental Level

1. All computers that will be used throughout the Data Warehousing process must be known. This includes the computers upon which the source data systems are located and those upon which the Warehouse itself, or any extracts (Data Marts) from the Warehouse reside.

2. The owners of both the data and the elements within the Data Warehouse. There are two different types of owners: those that own the data from a technological level, and the business owners. Note that an owner can be defined upon an element level. This means that it is not possible to have ownership on a column level, but it is on a table level.

3. Details with regard to any external Database Management Systems that will be accessed.

4. SAS libraries that will be used during the implementation of the Data Warehouse. It is very important that these libraries be thought out ahead of time, because there will be multiple internal references to them in generated code. In other words, although it is possible to change library references, this is not an advisable thing to do. These library references will include the location of metadata stores, SAS files, SAS views, etc.

5. ODDs must be defined outside the Administrator. That is to say that the Administrator will not generate the definitions for accessing the source data. Links within the product allow the user to create an ODD using existing SAS tools (e.g. the Import window, the Query window), but they have to already exist to be registered in the metadata. This means that the source data and an access method to extract data (this can be a SAS data set, a SAS/ACCESS view descriptor, an SQL view or a DATA step view) must be known.

6. The overall structure of the Data Warehouse environment. Although most organizations will only have one Data Warehouse, it might be necessary to have more than one. Although it is not necessary to know

---

[10] See Chapter 2, the section "Why Data Warehousing Requirements Change Over Time" for a discussion on the *big bang* approach to Data Warehousing.

all of these structures at the beginning of the project, it could be expensive and time consuming to break out portions of an existing Data Warehouse to create a second one at a later date.

Data Warehouse Level

It is advisable to complete the *environmental level* metadata before proceeding to the *warehouse level* metadata. This is not absolutely essential, because the environmental level metadata can be revisited at any time. If, however, there is a constant revisiting of the environmental metadata as the *warehouse metadata* is being created, then this indicates that the process has not been thoroughly thought through. This does not mean that the environmental level metadata will never be revisited, but that the marginal information required to create the Data Warehouse should be understood and registered before starting the Warehouse.

1. It is essential that the detail table information be thoroughly understood to use the Administrator. These tables will be defined based upon the ODDs registered in the environmental level. The data transformations necessary to create the detail tables will also be known.

    Although this cannot be completed within the Administrator, the ODD should be designed with the detail table it will feed in mind. This is easiest when an ODD is only used to populate a single detail table. In other words, it is sensible to revisit the design of the ODD based upon the detail tables it will feed. This is especially important when the ODD represents an expensive data extraction that might, for instance, include multiple table joins.

2. The subjects for each of the Data Warehouses will have to be known. This is because a detail table is nested within a subject. A detail table cannot be defined unless the subject is already known.

After the information above is known, then the Administrator can be used. To only include the information outlined above would mean that there would be no summary level information or any Data Marts have been created, but these can be developed over time. Indeed, these additional levels of the Data Warehouse will probably be the most volatile part of the entire process, being very dependent upon the changing needs and whims of the enterprise. This means that by their very nature, they will be undergoing constant modification. The definition of the environment, the ODDs, the subjects and the detail tables should be far more stable (although certainly not stagnant). The Administrator will allow for changes in this level of metadata, although the repercussions will be more far reaching.

> *A situation might arise where a single ODD could feed multiple subjects. If this is the case, and the ODD is complex enough to use extensive computer resources, there is nothing to stop the situation where the operational data is extracted only once, and then the different subjects are fed off this extracted file.*
>
> *This would mean that an ODD would be defined for the extraction of source data and then another would be created to feed the different subjects. This second ODD would effectively be built off pseudo-operational data. There is an argument that this initial extract would be a detail table within the Data Warehouse but it is likely that it would be deleted after the loading process and would therefore never be used in the exploitation process.*

9.5 How Does the SAS/Warehouse Administrator Work?

The SAS/Warehouse Administrator is a graphically based software product that allows for the implementers of the Data Warehouse to visually see how it is constructed. It is designed by storing metadata that pertains not only to the individual elements that have been defined, but how and when these elements hang together. The metadata therefore does more than describe the source data tables, the detail tables, the summary tables, graphs that are produced for an information mart or Multi-dimensional tables. It also holds information about how and when each of these elements is created. In other words, it contains metadata about the Data Warehouse implementation process. Every chapter in this book refers to designing a Data Warehouse not based upon its contents so much as the process needed to reach the final product. Although the Administrator is only part of the implementation phase of the data warehousing process, it adheres to this overall premise, that the success of an implementation is based upon understanding *how*, rather than *what*. The what part of data warehousing is constantly changing, especially if the project is a success, and these changes are easy to implement so long as the *how* of the process is thoroughly understood and built.

To understand how the Administrator works, it is necessary to step through the conceptual process to implement a Data Warehouse using the product. The following sections cover a large portion of the data warehousing implementation process, as performed by the SAS/Warehouse Administrator. It is used primarily to look at the process, rather than the details of the product itself.

9.6 Defining Elements to the SAS/Warehouse Administrator

Several steps define the elements to the Administrator. The following sections explain several of the elements that must be defined to use the Administrator. The actual interface to the product is covered both in the User's Guide and in the course notes for Building a Data Warehouse using SAS/Warehouse Administrator software and will not be duplicated here.

Creating a Data Warehouse Environment

Before anything else can be done, an *environment* must to be created. The SAS/Warehouse Administrator works under the desktop environment, which first became a production part of the base product in Version 6.12. To use Administrator it is necessary to understand the desktop environment which is well described in the SAS online documentation. Very briefly, the desktop environment is described as follows:

"The SAS desktop is an interface to the SAS System and has two primary components: folders and the SAS Explorer.
Folders are the primary containers on the SAS desktop. They enable you to create your own SAS environment by dragging and dropping items. You can fill the folder with several different types of items, which can represent files, applications, or commands.

The SAS Explorer provides a hierarchical view of the SAS files in the current SAS session as well as any external files that are defined to SAS.

The SAS desktop is a part of base SAS software. You can access the desktop by selecting Desktop from the Globals menu."

An environment is defined by opening a SAS desktop folder and adding a new *data warehouse environment* item into that folder. If the SAS command *dw* is entered, then the default SAS/Warehouse Administrator folder is opened. After this new item is defined, then it is necessary to complete the *properties* of the item. In this case, this will be the storage location associated with the environmental metadata. This libname and pathname will refer to the physical location of the environment's metadata repository. Note that after this libname has been established, it **cannot** be changed.

> *Do not assign a similar pathname for the metadata to more than one environment, or more than one warehouse. It is important to organize where the physical metadata will be stored. If the same pathname is used in more than one environment or warehouse, then the metadata will be comingled. After this occurs, it will be very difficult to undo.*

Not only is it important to ensure that the organization of metadata is well distinguished in terms of separate pathnames, but also there are advantages to having the metadata stored on the same computer as the SAS/Warehouse Administrator. This is for performance reasons.

It will also be necessary to assign a name and a description to the environment. After these pieces of information have been entered they **cannot** be changed.

> *Throughout the entire warehouse definition process, opportunities exist to enter names and descriptions to elements. Also the ability to insert notes allows for detailed explanations of the definition process. It is highly advisable to use all of these description and note options as the warehouse is being defined. In the excitement to implement the warehouse these descriptions are often overlooked. This leads to incomplete metadata definition and potential confusion at a later date.*

Creating the Shared Metadata

After the environment has been created, then it is possible to create the *shared metadata*. One metadata element must be entered and three elements are optional:

- SAS libraries (required).
- Local and remote host definition (optional).
- DBMS connections (optional).
- Data Warehouse contacts (optional).

The product itself does not make any of these compulsory, but without SAS libraries, the warehouse implementation process will be unable to find any of the pieces it needs to create the Data Warehouse. Note that it is not necessary to define the shared metadata at this stage. It can be done when defining the individual warehouse elements, but it is probably best done at the environmental level for control purposes and for simplicity's sake. Even if the metadata is defined during the definition of the individual warehouse elements, it will still be stored at the environmental level.

SAS Libraries: the SAS libraries defined on the environmental level will reduce any confusion that could occur by having similar pathnames referenced by different *librefs*. These librefs will reference the following:

- The environment and warehouse metadata.
- The ODDs (Operational Data Definitions).
- The detail logical tables.

- The data marts and information marts.
- The summary files (MDDBs or SAS files).

Every time that an element is defined, it will be necessary to specify the librefs. Also, an option allows for the libref to be assigned by SAS itself, rather than the Administrator user having to assign them every time. This should be the default, unless there is a good reason not to do so. One other important point about the libraries is that the pathnames have to physically exist before they can be defined as part of the environmental metadata.

Local and Remote Host Names: as each of the Data Warehouse elements is defined, it will be necessary to point to the location where it resides, or where any processing needs to take place. For this to occur, it is necessary to define how to connect to each of the remote hosts. These connections are made using SAS/CONNECT software.[11] Although it is possible that the elements that make up the Data Warehouse might reside on the same computer as the Administrator (the local host), it is fairly unlikely. This means that most probably at least one remote host is defined to the environmental metadata.

When setting up a remote host, all the information needed to make the connection must be stored as part of the metadata. This means that when the remote host is needed, the correct information will already be part of the metadata and will therefore not need defining every time the host is required as part of the warehouse process. Because links to remote hosts will have to be possible both in interactive and batch mode (because processes will take place in batch mode), then any passwords that are required to connect to remote hosts will have to be stored in the metadata. These are stored in an encrypted SAS file and are automatically retrieved using a supplied SAS macro (GETUSRPW).[12]

Defining DBMS Connections: in most Data Warehouse implementations, access to an external relational database management system usually is required. This is because either the source data or some of the actual warehoused data resides in a format outside that of a SAS data file.[13] Metadata needs to be created for each of these external file locations. If the external system is in IBM's DB2, then each SSID (Sub System ID) needs to be defined as a separate item within the environmental metadata. If the product is

---

[11] Setting up the remote hosts is part of the Client/Server considerations of the Data Warehouse. This is covered in detail in Chapter 8.

[12] See SAS Institute Inc., *SAS/Warehouse Administrator™ User's Guide*, Cary, NC: SAS Institute Inc. for specific information on setting up remote hosts and using the GETUSRPW macro.

[13] See Chapter 5 for a detailed description of using external file formats from SAS software.

ORACLE, then each *schema* needs to be defined. Each of these different formats requires slightly different information and this is accounted for in the Administrator front-end.

As each of these connections is defined, the opportunity also exists to insert specific SQL or DBLOAD options that pertain specifically to the external file structure. These are fully explained in the SAS/ACCESS documentation that corresponds to the particular relational database being defined.

Defining DBMS connections under Version 6 of SAS requires a good knowledge of the SAS/ACCESS product, along with a firm familiarity with the external file software product. The implications of ignoring or putting incorrect options in the metadata could result in inefficient loading or transferring of data.

Defining Data Warehouse Contacts: one of the important aspects of implementing a successful Data Warehouse is to know who in the enterprise is responsible for different aspects of the data. This is from two different perspectives: the business and the technological side. Sometimes, but not usually, this might be the same person. The Administrator allows for owners to be assigned on an element level. Of all of the four different types of *environmental metadata* this is the one that could best be handled as the elements are being defined, instead of up-front. As noted above, however, it is very important that there is ownership to each of the elements in the Data Warehouse, because ownership brings with it responsibility. This in turn leads to overall ownership, which means that there is a commitment from those involved in the project. For this reason, it is highly advisable to associate contacts with each of the particular elements.

Setting up the contacts in the Administrator is a very simple process, but it should include more than just the names of the person. Other information that can be stored includes: position, address, e-mail address, and telephone number.

All of the four different types of environmental metadata are entered through the desktop environment into clear screens. The key to successfully creating this metadata is to fully understand the environment in which the Data Warehouse is being created. After this is understood, then creating the metadata is a simple process.

Creating Operational Data Definitions

The Operational Data Definitions (ODDs) are defined at the environmental level. This is to allow any Data Warehouse that might be created within the environment to share these definitions to avoid them having to be re-created for each Data Warehouse. If only one Data Warehouse is going to be defined, then the implications of this are minor. If many Data Warehouses are going to be created within the same environment, then storing ODDs at the environmental level will save extra definitions being created and ensure that there is consistency in the definition of operational tables. There are two major stages to registering ODDs within the Administrator. First is to specify ODD Groups, and second to create the actual ODDs that are nested within the groups.

The concept of an ODD can be a little confusing. It is easy to think about it as a definition of a source file from which the Data Warehouse will be populated. This means that it is usual to have one ODD for every source table that feeds the Data Warehouse. These ODDs are defined outside the Administrator (although there are links from within the Administrator to SAS tools that aid in the definitions), but exist as part of the metadata. For example, a SAS view into an ORACLE operational table could be an ODD. The Administrator does not create this view, but it is stored as an ODD in the metadata.

Operational Data Definition Groups

Before registering an ODD, an ODD Group must exist. An ODD Group is a logical grouping of ODDs. What constitutes a logical group is at the whim of the designers of the Data Warehouse. This could be done in several ways:

- Define the ODD Groups based upon the host the source files reside on.
- Define the ODD Groups based upon the operational system the ODD definitions relate to.
- Define the ODD Groups based upon Data Warehouse subjects.

There is no right or wrong way to decide upon a logical grouping of ODDs. It depends purely upon the way the data warehousing process is defined in the particular enterprise. After they are defined however, it is important to ensure that the ODDs are correctly located within them. In other words, decide upon a logical grouping and stick to it!

Actually defining an ODD Group is very simple. Very little information is stored on the group level. This is restricted to:

- The name of the ODD Group.
- A description of the group.
- The designation of an owner.
- The designation of an administrator.

As would be expected, the owner and administrator names come from the *contacts* metadata stored at the environmental level. After an owner and administrator are designated, then these will be inherited by default to all the ODDs that are nested within the group.

Operational Data Definitions

There are two major features that are important to remember about ODDs:

- The objects (e.g. views, physical files) that an ODD represents must be created outside the Administrator environment. Although the ODD itself is part of the metadata that exists within the Administrator, the ODD references an object (e.g. a view) that cannot be created by the Administrator. This is why links are available to SAS tools (e.g. the Query window within base SAS software) that make this creation easy.
- They are one of the following:
  - A SAS/ACCESS view
  - An SQL procedure view, which could include those using the pass-through facility.[14]
  - A DATA Step View.

If the ODD has not already been defined before it is being registered in the Administrator, then it is possible to directly link to the following SAS tools to create the definition:

- The SAS Query Window.
- The External File Interface (part of the Import Window).
- The SAS/ACCESS Window.

The first two options above are part of the base SAS product, but the third requires the pertinent SAS/ACCESS product to be installed on the same host as the administrator. In most situations, the external database format that requires a SAS/ACCESS view will not reside on the same host as the Administrator. This means that if a SAS/ACCESS view is to be registered as an ODD to the Administrator, then it will have to be created upon the host where the external source resides. For example, suppose that an external data source is contained in a DB2 table on an IBM OS/390 host, the SAS/ACCESS view into that table will have to be created on the host itself, not on the platform where the Administrator resides. This is the primary reason why it is necessary to create an ODD outside the Administrator environment.

---

[14] See Chapter 5, the section "Using SQL" in Section 5.3 for a discussion on the pass-through facility.

Another important concept to understand at this stage is that all of the allowable formats for an ODD can be referenced through using SAS librefs. This means that the librefs that point to an ODD must be registered with the Administrator at the environmental level before the ODD itself can be registered.

When defining an ODD to the Administrator, several pieces of information are required:

■ A name and description for the ODD
■ An owner and an administrator (which by default will be those assigned to the ODD group into which the ODD will be registered).
■ The name of the host where the ODD resides.
■ The SAS libref that points to the ODD.
■ The table or view name of the ODD definition within the SAS library. Note that this SAS table or view does **not** have to exist in the library at the time the ODD is registered. This table or view is considered to be the ODD's *data location*.
■ The column definitions of the ODD. It is possible to create the column definitions at this stage, but more likely, they will be imported from the table or view name. This column information will be stored with the metadata itself, rather than just as part of the data location.

> *It is very advisable to ensure that every single piece of information within the metadata has a description, if allowed. For instance, when defining an ODD, make sure every column has a label associated with it. This might seem like a tedious task, but will pay dividends over time. The rule is not to shortcut when defining metadata.*

ODDs and ODD groups can be added as they are needed. Each new ODD usually represents a new external data source that needs to be included within the data warehouse environment. This means that new ODDs will be registered with the Administrator as the Data Warehouse addresses additional enterprise needs. There is obviously an economy of scale to the registering of ODDs. As the scope of the Data Warehouse expands, the likelihood is that the pertinent ODDs will already be registered.

Creating Data Warehouses

After the environmental level information is registered with the Administrator, then comes the time to actually begin to create the Data Warehouse.

There are four major steps in the SAS/Warehouse Administrator to fulfill this task:

1. Create a Data Warehouse environment (which will be nested within an environment).
2. Define the subjects for the Data Warehouse.
3. Define the detail logical tables.
4. Define the logical tables.

Creating the Data Warehouse within the Warehouse Administrator

For most enterprises, a single Data Warehouse will suffice. The point where an extra Data Warehouse is needed is likely to be based on business organizational reasons as opposed to technological reasons. There might be a good case to create multiple Data Warehouses, but from an administration perspective, overhead will be increased. Each of the Warehouses will have a completely different set of metadata (although they do have the option to share environmental level metadata) which cannot be consolidated without a great deal of work. The decision to create more than one Data Warehouse must therefore be thought out very carefully. It is best to default to only creating one Data Warehouse, unless there are reasons not to do so.

A Data Warehouse within the SAS/Warehouse Administrator is nested within an environment. A Data Warehouse is added as an item nested within an environment. A Data Warehouse is considered an element within the Administrator and must therefore have a name, description, owner, and administrator. A physical location must also be assigned where the metadata must be stored. This physical location should not coincide with the metadata stored on the environmental level or for another Data Warehouse. As with the environmental level, the Administrator will reserve a libref name (*dwmd*) that will be used internally to reference the metadata.

After the Data Warehouse has been registered with the Administrator, then it is possible to start creating the elements contained within it.

Creating Subjects for a Data Warehouse

The definition of subjects is a function of the design rather than the implementation of a Data Warehouse. It is a means of logically organizing the Data Warehouse into different categories that will coincide with the needs of the enterprise. A subject is usually defined at a Data Warehouse, rather than a Data Mart level, because the business abstraction is at a higher level. Examples of subjects could be sales or customers. This does not mean that it will not be possible to use the contents of the Data Warehouse across subjects, but that the internal logical organization is based upon a set of rationales that make sense to the way the Warehouse will be used.

Within the Administrator, a subject is a logical grouping. This means that when it is defined as a nested item within a Data Warehouse, all it needs is the standard name, description, owner and administrator. Each of these logical groupings can have many other elements located within them. These elements included a detail logical table, information marts and summary groups. An important fact to remember is that there can only be **one** *detail logical table* for each subject. This single detail logical table will in most likelihood be made up of multiple detail tables.

For a logical detail table to exist there must be detail tables. The creation of detail tables will therefore be addressed in the next section.

> *It is important to realize exactly what is being done at this stage. We have not created any of the actual Data Warehouse during this process. No loading has actually been performed. All that is being done is the creation of metadata pertaining to the elements within the Data Warehouse. Based upon this metadata, the Data Warehouse can be built, but that is another stage in using the Administrator.*

Creating Detail Tables

Detail tables contain the data for the Warehouse at the lowest possible level. It is the *common denominator* information that can be used to create any summary information. They can be one of two different types:

- A SAS data file or view.
- A DBMS table or view.

Note that if the detail table is in the form of a DBMS table (e.g. an ORACLE or a DB2 table), then a SAS/ACCESS view into that table must be created.

Detail tables are nested within a logical detail table (see the next section). There can be multiple detail tables within any single logical detail table. Multiple logical detail tables can, however, reference a single detail table. This means that assigning a detail table to a logical detail table is not an absolute commitment. It does not preclude the detail table from being used by multiple subjects.

To create a detail table, many items of information are needed. Alongside the generic information required of all elements within the Administrator (name, description, owner, administrator), the following should be addressed:

- The columns that make up the detail table.
- The physical storage of the detail table. This can be in a SAS or a DBMS format.
- The load technique for the table: this is either append or refresh.[15]
- The physical location where the detail table will be stored (this will include the host).
- The location of a view of a detail table if it is stored in a DBMS format.
- Other information including indexes, password protection, encryption, etc.[16]

At this stage in using the Administrator, there is a move from defining what could be called high-level metadata to more basic metadata. A detail table will actually be used as part of the exploitation of the Data Warehouse. The design of the detail tables should reflect their expected usage and as such, should be well defined before it is entered into the Administrator.

Creating a Logical Detail Table

There are two different ways that a logical detail table can be defined:

- Only as a grouping element.
- As a view to multiple detail tables.

The simplest of these two is when the logical detail table is purely a grouping element. This means that its only function is to logically group together a set of detail tables. In this case all that is needed is the basic element information (name, description, owner, and administrator) and the names of the detail tables that are nested within it. This more accurately groups all the detail tables under a single subject. This is because there can only be one logical detail table for every subject.

If the logical detail table is to be defined as a view of multiple detail tables, then additional information will be needed. First of all, columns must be selected from the list of all columns from all the nested detail tables. Secondly, a storage location for the view must be designated. This will include not only the name of the view, but the host and libref where it will be stored.

---

[15] See Chapter 7 for details on loading techniques for the Data Warehouse.
[16] The details can be found in *SAS/Warehouse Administrator™ User's Guide*.

9.7 Defining Processes to the SAS/Warehouse Administrator

At this stage in the process of setting up the Data Warehouse within the Administrator, the structure has been defined. Multiple elements have been defined to the Administrator, but no loading of any data has been done. No processes have been defined: the relationships between the source systems and the tables that exist within the Data Warehouse have not been established.

The elements defined up to this point will result in a working Data Warehouse. There have been no Data Marts, or Information Marts, but these are not necessarily required to have a successful, functioning Data Warehouse.

The stage is reached where the input sources and the target sources for the Data Warehouse have been defined, but no information has been created to determine how one will become transformed to the other. This information is defined within the Process Editor feature of the Administrator. There are three major tasks that need to be completed:

- Defining the *input sources* for the ODDs.
- Defining any data transfers that are required.
- Defining the *operational mappings* that take ODDs and convert them to the detail tables.
- Define any *user exits* that require additional code outside the domain of the Administrator.
- Define *record selectors* that will filter out the unwanted rows from the source operational systems.

Defining Input Sources for ODDs

From the perspective of the Administrator, an ODD is purely a definition of an input source to the Data Warehouse. It does not, in itself define the actual physical file(s) from which it will pull the data. This means that as part of a process, the input source must be defined for each ODD. Also, as part of the definition of the process, the input source for each ODD must be defined.

To define the external file sources for each ODD, it is necessary to use the Process Editor that graphically shows the set-up of the external files that satisfies the ODD definition. In some situations, this will be a very simple one-to-one map, where a single ODD requires a single input source. The ODD could well be a view that requires several input sources, in which case, each of these will need to be defined.

The step can be difficult to understand unless what is actually being defined is thoroughly understood. This can best be described using an example.

Suppose that a simple SAS view into an external file is as follows:

```
DATA oddloc.customer / view=oddloc.customer;
 INFILE custref;
 INPUT @1 custname $30
      @31 custnum;
RUN;
```

A view is created, but as far as the Administrator is concerned, it does not know anything about the data file that is referenced by the `custref` file reference. If this view had been used as an ODD, there is a missing piece of information. This is exactly what is being completed within the input source for the ODD process.

If the source file is a SAS data file (including SAS Views) then it will be necessary to give information so that the libref can be assigned. For instance, suppose the following SQL view is used as an ODD:

```
PROC SQL;
 CREATE VIEW oddloc.customer AS
 SELECT * FROM oper.cust;
QUIT;
```

This is a very simple SQL view. The only problem is that at this stage, the `oper` libref is unknown to the Administrator. Information that will allow for this libref to be created must be entered so that when the data is extracted, all the information as to its location is known. Note that in both cases above, it is important to coordinate the fileref or libref with that in the views.

Defining Data Transfers to the SAS/Warehouse Administrator

An integral part to virtually every Data Warehouse implementation is the Client/Server aspect of the design. At some point in the process, it is likely that data will have to move from one place to another. The simplest example of this is when the source data and the target source within the Data Warehouse are on different hosts. Somewhere in the process, data will have to be transferred between one host and another. The Administrator uses SAS/CONNECT to perform this task.

Two options are open to perform data transfer.

- Incorporate user-written programs that will transfer the data between one host and another. This will mean that the data can move directly between the two hosts.
- Use Administrator generated code. The problem with this process is that the Administrator only sees remote hosts as they relate to its own host. For example, suppose that the Administrator resides on a Windows NT server, the source data is on an OS/390 mainframe and the Data

Warehouse is on a UNIX host. For the data to move from the mainframe to the UNIX host, it would first have to move through the NT server. This is because the Administrator does not know how the mainframe will link with the UNIX host directly, but only as it relates to itself. A way around this limitation is described below.

> *Although the Administrator views the movement of data as it relates to the host upon which it is installed, it is possible to directly move data between two other computers. In other words, it is not essential, when moving data between, for instance an OS/390 mainframe and a UNIX server, to use the Administrator to physically pass the data through the Windows PC upon which the Administrator resides.*
>
> *The technique used would be, in the situation outlined above, to define the program that moves the data to run on the OS/390 mainframe. This job will itself connect to the UNIX server and move the data through the UPLOAD procedure, thus removing the need for it to pass through the PC.*

A data transfer can be included in any part of the Data Warehouse implementation process. The following information is needed to create a data transfer:

- The name, description, owner, and administrator of the transfer.
- How the source code for the transfer is to be created. If the user creates the source code, then the location of the program must be specified.
- Where the code is to run. Because the Administrator uses SAS/CONNECT, it will always have to be processed on the remote host.
- The location of the transferred data after it has been moved.

Defining Operational Data Mappings to the SAS/Warehouse Administrator

One of the key pieces to creating a Data Warehouse up to this point has been that there is no link between an ODD and a detail table. In other words, what hasn't been described is what has to happen between the ODD being used to extract the source data and it being loaded into the detail table. This step is performed using operational data mappings. Every detail table that is fed by an ODD must have at least one operational data mapping.

Stepping outside the Administrator environment, when a detail table in a Data Warehouse is loaded, the data must come from one or many source operational systems. The data from these source operational systems are modified in such a way that they are consistent when loaded into the detail tables. Furthermore, the way that the source data is incorporated into the detail table must be specified. These steps are exactly those that take place using an operational data mapping within the Administrator.

The operational data mappings can be a very complex process. This is especially true when a single detail table is populated using multiple ODDs that need to be both joined and transformed on a column basis. It is very important not to use the Administrator as the tool to help design this process. As already mentioned, the Administrator is an implementation, not a design tool. The process of mapping data should take place outside of the Administrator environment and then the logic should be defined to the Administrator.

The following information will be needed by the Administrator to implement an operational data mapping:

- The name, description, owner, and administrator of the mapping.
- Whether the Administrator or the user will create the source code for the mapping. If the user creates the code, then the location of the program must be specified.
- Which host the processing will take place on.
- The location where the mapped and transformed data will reside.
- A definition as to how each of the columns involved in the mapping should be transformed.
- An optional WHERE clause that will build in any subsets or join criteria between the incoming source tables.

The Administrator uses many tools to help easily define the above steps. For instance, there is an Expression Builder window that will help to build derived mapping transformations. This means that it is possible to specify all the transformations that each column must undergo and also the option to create derived fields. These derived fields can also be transformed.

This stage is probably the most complex in the entire process. It has only been covered above insomuch as how the Administrator can fit into the Data Warehousing process. Two good examples of operational data mappings can be found in the SAS/Warehouse Administrator course notes in section 8.4. The key to successfully using the SAS/Warehouse Administrator is to fully appreciate where it fits into the implementation of the Data Warehouse. To do this, it is essential to sometimes step back from the very detailed and involved process of defining each of the elements and processes so that the bigger picture can be appreciated.

Incorporating User-Written Programs into the SAS/Warehouse Administrator

Although the Administrator is capable of generating most of the code to extract, transform and load the Data Warehouse, a situation will sometimes occur that requires an external program to be incorporated into the process. These are called user exits in the Administrator and can be inserted virtually anywhere in the process.

Inserting a user exit is a very simple task. Only the following information is needed:

- The name, description, owner and administrator of the user exit.
- The location of the program. The program must reside as a *source* entry in a SAS catalog. Note that this entry need not be SAS code. It could, for instance, be a CALL MODULE that allows for COBOL routines to be used within the Data Warehouse.

Some warnings about using a user exit are as follows.

- Any global SAS options that are set during the user exit should be reset at the end of the program. A good example of this would be if the SAS global option OBS= is set to anything but MAX. If this were not reset, then it would mean that any subsequent programs would be subject to the same option.
- Thorough testing of the program should be done to ensure that it does not in any way detrimentally affect the running of the Administrator to generate code. As soon as a user exit is used, effectively the control on the Data Warehouse process is moved outside the Administrator. Although the program runs as part of the Data Warehouse metadata, there is no internal knowledge of what the program actually does.
- If the user exit does not generate any output, then this should be specified when it is defined.

There might be a variety of reasons to incorporate user exits. One of these might be the execution of a complex validation program that runs a series of tests against the incoming source data.

Filtering Out Unwanted Records from the Loading Process

An ODD will define an input source table that is required in populating the Data Warehouse. There is nothing inherent in this ODD as it extracts only the records needed for each refresh/update of the Warehouse. This is achieved by using a record selector. This can be seen as a filter that usually acts before the mapping in the process. The actual code that performs the record selection can be generated by either the Administrator or it can be included from an external source. Information that will be needed includes the following:

- The name, description, owner and administrator of the record selector.
- Whether the administrator or the user has responsibility for the code generation.
- On which host the code will be processed.
- Where the filtered data will be stored.
- A WHERE clause that will actually perform the filtering of the incoming records.

It will sometimes be necessary to use a program generated by the user because selection criteria can become very complex. This is especially the case if the selection criteria is not *hard coded*. For instance, if the Data Warehouse is refreshed monthly, and it is known that only data that has a date of the previous month should be loaded, then the following WHERE clause could be used:

```
WHERE MONTH(date)=MONTH(&today)-1;
```

This would work if it were known that the Warehouse would only be loaded in from the month previous to the current one. This would be quite simple for the Administrator to generate. If however, the extract is to be based upon information from an external file, then this would be more complex:

```
PROC SQL;
 CREATE TABLE filter AS
 SELECT * FROM source.data
WHERE date > (SELECT max(date) FROM
           existing.data)
;
QUIT;
```

This code will subset the incoming data **source.data** where the **date** column is greater than the maximum date column in the **existing.data** file. Selection of whether to use the Administrator or some user written code is therefore based upon the complexity of the selection criteria.

Overview of the Process Definition

It is important to understand exactly what the Administrator is trying to achieve during the process definition. Although each of the above steps are performed independently of each other, using a different series of input screens, they are in fact very closely tied. This is because each step will generate code that will be part of a larger unified stream. As the Data Warehouse designer, it is important to remember this fact. The way that the information is entered can affect the overall performance of the Data Warehouse load after the process is run.

One of the options open to the user is to view the code. This can be done on a piece by piece basis, but makes more sense when the entire process is viewed. It is well worth having the code looked over by experienced SAS programmers to see if any performance improvements can be made. If changes are necessary, then it is possible this can be done by changing the information in a particular step. For instance, if the data transformations has an inefficiency, then this could be adjusted from within the Administrator. It might also be necessary to include a user exit. Either way, efficient loading of the Data Warehouse is a key part of the successful implementation of the project and, as such, should be optimized as far as is possible.

The different steps outlined above when taken individually can seem confusing. The key to effectively using the process editor within the Administrator is to fully understand the steps necessary to load the particular Data Warehouse **before** using the product. The Administrator will not design the process of loading the Data Warehouse, but can help implement this process. This means that it is necessary to fully understand all the steps in the process to effectively use the Administrator. This does not mean that every detail has to be known ahead of time, but that the basic flow of data, and the actions performed upon that data at every point in the process should be fully thought out to use the Administrator.

9.8 Supplying Attributes to Each Loadable Warehouse Element

Several of the elements defined in Section 9.6 will be loaded as part of the Data Warehouse process. These include the following:

- Operational Data Definitions (ODDs).
- External Files.
- SAS data files.
- Detail Logical Tables.
- Detail Tables.

Several elements have not been discussed up to this point. These include:

- Data Marts.
- Summary Tables (including any Multi-dimensional data base structures).
- Information Mart items.

These elements will be discussed later in the chapter. Each one of these elements listed above must have load process attributes assigned to them. In this stage, we are adding attributes to the elements as opposed to the processes in Section 9.7. These attributes include the following:

- Whether the source code is Administrator or user generated.
- Whether there will be a union of data from several input sources during the load process.
- Which host the processing will take place on.
- Whether there will be any post-processing after the element is loaded. This code will be generated by the user and must be stored as a source entry in a SAS catalog.

One important attribute that should be specified at this time is whether a time stamp will be added to the element during the loading process.[17] If it is decided to add a time stamp, then a column called _LOADTM will automatically be added to the element. Adding a time stamp is a very fundamental decision to make.[18] As a default it is probably advisable to add this time stamp, because it will not be possible to retroactively add it if the option is declined.

9.9 Loading the Tables Using the SAS/Warehouse Administrator

After the load process attributes have been specified, then enough information has been supplied to the Administrator to begin loading the tables. Up to this point, the following information is known to the Administrator:

- The attributes and location of all the source tables needed to populate the detail tables.
- The attributes and location of all the detail tables required within the Data Warehouse.
- At what point and how any data transfers will need to take place between different hosts.
- All data mappings and transformations that are needed to convert the source tables to the detail tables.
- On which host the different parts of the processing should take place.

---

[17] See the *SAS/Warehouse Administrator™ User's Guide*.
[18] See Chapter 6, the section "PROC SGL or Match-Merge?" for a discussion on time stamping Data Warehouse data.

It is now possible to generate source code that will be needed to create any detail table or logical detail table. After this source code is generated, it can be run interactively, or can be stored as an external file and submitted as a batch process as needed, or as a scheduled job. These tasks are defined during the *loading table* stage of the process.

Loading Detail Tables

To load the detail tables, several pieces of information have to be known by the Administrator. This information includes the following:

- Whether the code needed to generate the detail table will be run interactively or in batch mode.
- Whether the code needs editing.
- The scheduling information if the code will be run in batch mode.

All of the information needed to generate the code is already entered into the Administrator. At this stage it is just a case of deciding how the tables should be created. One of the determinants of when the code should be run is based on the environment in which the Data Warehouse is being created. It might not be possible to schedule a particular load stream to run because it will be based upon the source systems being both available and ready. In many situations, the source systems will have to undergo a series of operational based programs (*month-end programs*) before the data can be extracted into the Data Warehouse. This means that somehow, the Warehouse load stream will have to be started after this process has ended.

One factor in whether the Warehouse job stream can be scheduled is whether the code that loads the detail tables will need to be modified each time a load takes place. This might occur in a situation where the record selection is manually changed each load cycle. There are two principal ways of scheduling a load cycle. First of all, a one-off schedule that will run the load cycle only after at a specified time (probably during the night when usage of the Warehouse is nonexistent). Secondly on a schedule that will run the load cycle at many preset times (every second Wednesday in a month). The first situation is probably the safest. One of the keys to Data Warehouse design is the acceptance that if things can change, they probably will. This means that it is advisable to force a situation where the parameters behind the loading process are checked before every load cycle. In the second situation, the code will be run at a given time, whether necessary changes have been made or not.

Loading Detail Logical Tables

When defining a detail logical table (see the section "Creating a Logical Detail Table," earlier) for a subject, it was configured as a logical grouping or as a view of detail tables. Each subject can only have one detail logical table. If the detail logical table was configured as a view, then this will need to be loaded. This is performed by defining the load process attributes for the detail logical table. In every situation, the source code for the detail logical table is created by the user. The location of this code (which must be stored in a SOURCE entry in a SAS catalog) must be defined to the Administrator.

Alongside the actual location of the source code, the host upon which the processing will occur should also be defined. Additionally the location of code that will perform any required post-processing will also be registered with the Administrator.

> *Having only one **detail logical table** for each subject has its advantages. It means that the users have a single view of each subject and so can easily understand the contents without the need to comprehend multiple **detail tables**.*
>
> *However, having the **detail logical table** defined as a view has a potential downside. Depending on the complexity of the view, in terms of the joins, and the size of the **detail tables** using the view might be very expensive. It might be beneficial, therefore to store the **detail logical table** as a physical table. This will, of course, take up more storage space and could be considered redundant (see Chapter 3, the section, "Weaknesses of a Normalized Structure for Data Warehousing"). This decision is based upon resource availability, user performance expectations, size of data and processing power available.*

9.10 Creating Summary Level Information with the SAS/Warehouse Administrator

After the definitions for the loading of the detail logical tables are complete, then all the pieces for implementing the Data Warehouse are complete. This does not mean that all the necessary pieces to effectively respond to the enterprise needs are complete, but that the raw data needed to satisfy these needs can be loaded into the Data Warehouse.

In many Data Warehouse implementations, the detail level data is all that is used. Many enterprises prefer to create Data Warehouses that contain large amounts of detail data and give the users a tool so they can then perform their own extraction, summarization and analysis. In some situations this might work. If the users of the Data Warehouse are technologically sophisticated then this essentially ad-hoc approach can be an effective use of resources. In most situations, however, this leads to an inordinate amount of time spent in the process of obtaining the required information, as opposed to using that information. For this reason, it is usual and advisable to take the Data Warehouse design to the next stage, the creation of summary level data.

Deciding upon the summary data that should be created and how it should be created is a very important decision. This was covered in Chapter 6, Section 6.7. The Administrator will support both types of summary data creation, a full refresh where the summary data is completely re-created every time a load cycle is complete, or an incremental approach, where summary data is recalculated based only on the new detail data.

Creating Summary Groups

A summary group is defined to the Administrator as part of a subject. It is considered an element within the process. There are no limits to the number of summary groups that any individual subject can have. Within each summary group there can be up to six summary tables, or an unlimited number of SAS MDDBs (see Chapter 4). Note that the summary tables do **not** have to be in a SAS format, they can be stored in any format that SAS can access.

At the summary group level, the following information will be registered:

- The data from which the summary data will be created. This is likely to be either the detail logical table or one of the detail tables that are contained within the subject.
- The hierarchies (class columns) of the summary.
- The analysis columns and their associated statistics.
- Any ID columns required.
- A time column that will be the basis for breaking out the summary into different tables.

All of the above *terminology* complies with either the generation of an MDDB, or the use of the SAS SUMMARY procedure. Note however, that it is not the SUMMARY procedure that is actually used to create the summary tables. A SAS DATA step, supporting incremental updates is employed as the method to create these summary tables.

It is important to understand that it is at the summary group level that the above parameters are defined. Any summary tables, whether they be MDDB or otherwise will adhere to these parameters and cannot deviate from them.

Also the users have an option to write their own summarization code. If this is the case, then new columns that are not part of the input detail data can be created. If the Administrator is selected to produce the code for the summarized tables then it will also handle all of the naming conventions of the columns in the summary tables. In some situations, where a duplicate name would be created for columns in the output summary table, the Administrator requires that the name be explicitly assigned.

The time column, if the Administrator is to create the tables, has to be in a SAS datetime format. Each of the tables within the summary group will be based upon a different level of this time column. For instance, one table might summarize the data annually, another monthly, another daily, and so on.

To actually define a *summary group* the following information needs to be registered with the Administrator:

- A name, description, owner and administrator.
- Class, analysis, time and id columns.
- A start time for each day, week, month and year.

This final piece of information, the start time for the different periods is necessary so that each row of detail information can be correctly assigned to the correct time period.

Creating Summary Tables

Every summary table is part of a summary group. These can either be stored in a relational format (as a SAS file, or a Relational database table) or as a SAS/MDDB. Most of the parameters for each of the summary tables will already have been defined at the summary group level. Each of the summary tables corresponds to one of the following time dimensions:

- Day
- Week
- Half-month
- Month
- Quarter
- Year

In creating each summary table, an element within the Administrator structure, the following information will be registered:

- The name, description, owner, administrator, and aggregation level of the table. Note that this is slightly different from other elements in that an extra piece of information is needed.
- The storage format of the summary table.
- The load technique for the summary table (merge or refresh).

- If the summary table is to be stored in an external relational database table format, then the location of a SAS view into that table must be specified.
- The physical storage location of the summary table.

Other information about the physical storage of the summary table is also specified. This includes information about passwords, encryption options and data compression.

After this information has been entered, then the definition of these particular elements is complete. As with other parts of the Administrator, defining the element and the process for loading the element is done separately.

Loading the Summary Tables

Specifying the load process for the *summary tables* is almost identical in technique to that used with the *detail tables*. Basic information must be given, including:

- Whether the user or the Administrator is responsible for generating the source code to create the table.
- The source code location if the user is responsible.
- The host upon which the processing will take place.
- Whether the table will be created interactively or in batch.
- Scheduling information if the table is generated in batch mode.

> *Many steps are involved in defining a full Data Warehouse implementation to the SAS/Warehouse Administrator. As already mentioned, these should be well thought out ahead of time. The Administrator should not be used to design this process, only to implement it. The process editor will allow the user to see the entire process graphically represented as a flow of elements and processes, which will help in visualizing the entire implementation.*

If the summary tables are in the form of SAS MDDBs, then there must be a thorough understanding of how MDDBs are generate. The information that the Administrator will need to generate the MDDBs will correspond to that needed to generate an MDDB outside of the Administrator environment. An important note is that by default the Administrator will generate code that will create a hierarchy statement for every combination of the columns defined as *class* columns in the *summary group element*. This can be overridden by editing the source code the Administrator generates.

9.11 Creating Data and Information Marts

To this point, the detail data has been created within the Data Warehouse, and summary data has been generated from this detail data. In most implementations, however, the information contained within the Data Warehouse is still too generic for many of the users. Very often, departmental needs require access to only a small portion of the data. This portion could be small either because it is a subset of the data within the Data Warehouse, or could be small because it is more highly summarized. The data might be needed across Data Warehouse subjects and so they might require data delivered in a form that is more conducive to departmental needs. If this is the situation, then either Data or Information Marts needed.

Creating Data Mart Groups

The first step to creating data marts is the creation of a data mart group. A data mart group is defined at the Data Warehouse level. Each Data Warehouse can have multiple data mart groups. A data mart group is an element within the Data Warehouse implementation. To create the data mart group, only the name, description, owner and administrator need to be known.

Creating Data Marts

Within each of the data mart groups there can be a multitude of data marts. A data mart is considered to be a single SAS table or a SAS view. This table or view can be data pulled from a variety of subjects. To create a data mart the following should be specified:

- A name, description, owner and administrator of the data mart.
- The host, SAS library, and SAS data set where the data mart will reside.
- A command to view the data mart. This already has a default entry, but can be changed as needed.

Loading a Data Mart

The elements have already been created. The actual load process must now be defined. This is similar again to defining the load process of any other loadable element of the Data Warehouse except that the source code to create the data mart **will always be user created**. As with other processes, it can be run either interactively or in batch mode. If run in batch mode, then it is possible to schedule the execution of the code.

◗ *The scheduling of the load process of both data marts and information marts is of prime importance. The data marts and information marts must be synchronized to run after the detail or summary data has completed its load cycle. The users must not be allowed to generate information from one part of the Data Warehouse that contradicts that in another part.*

Creating an Information Mart Group

An *information mart group* is a logical grouping of information mart items. An information mart item includes the following:

- A stored query.
- An application.
- Pregenerated graphs, reports or charts.

The key to understanding an information mart item is that it must stored as a SAS catalog entry. This means that virtually any type of information that can be stored in this way can be recognized as an information mart item. For example, an application within SAS can be stored as one, or a series of FRAME catalog entries, a graph can be stored as a GRSEG entry or a report definition can be stored as a REPT entry. All of these can be registered as information mart items. An information mart group is nothing more than a logical grouping of these items.

An information mart group is an element that can be nested within a subject, data mart group, or ODD group. Wherever it is located, the way it is defined remains the same. The information mart group only needs a name, description, owner and administrator to be assigned to it for registration within the Administrator.

Creating an Information Mart Item

After the information mart group has been defined, then items can be added. These will need the following information:

- A name, description, owner and administrator.
- The host, SAS library and SAS catalog entry where the item exists.
- A means by which the item can be viewed.

Loading an Information Mart Item

Information mart items can be divided into two broad types:

- Data dependent items that require code to be run. For example, if a graph is defined as an item, then there must be a program to create this graph. In this case, load process attributes must be assigned to the graph element.
- Data independent items. An application will not be dependent upon any data to exist. This does mean that it will not use data in the Warehouse, but it is not, in itself, a data dependent item. In this case, no load process attributes are needed.

If the item requires load process attributes then as with other loadable elements there is basic information required:

- The source of the code that generates the information mart item. This source code will always be generated by the user and will be stored in a SAS catalog entry of type SOURCE.
- The host upon which the code will be run.
- Any post-processing options.
- Whether the code will be run interactively, or in batch. If the code is to be run in batch, then scheduling the job is an option.

9.12 Using the Metadata Stored within the SAS/Warehouse Administrator

One of the key aspects to successfully using the SAS/Warehouse Administrator is to realize that the metadata it needs to implement a Data Warehouse is, in itself, a valuable source of data. If the metadata could only be used for the implementation process, then this would represent a serious weakness in the product. This is fortunately not the case. It is possible to search and browse any of the metadata contained within the Administrator. Additionally, the metadata can be exported from the Administrator and manipulated and analyzed with all the tools available within SAS, or any other software.

Because the metadata itself is a source of data, it too could be defined as an input source for the Data Warehouse. It would be possible to create an ODD that would define the metadata structure within the product. This would mean that a Data Warehouse could be created within the environment that would contain detail data that is actual metadata that is generated by the Administrator.[19] This would be a useful tool in large Data Warehouse implementations, where analysis of the metadata would be of use. It would

---

[19] Release 1.2 of the Administrator contains a Metadata API (Application Program Interface) that can also be used to easily access metadata. (See the Special Topic, "Introduction to the Metadata API Available in Release 1.2 of SAS/Warehouse Administrator" at the end of this chapter for more information.

also be useful in a situation where a Data Warehouse user wanted to know which source system the data they use comes from and all the transformations that take place before it is loaded into the Data Warehouse.

In many situations, the tools that come with the Administrator will suffice. It is possible to search the metadata for specified strings that exist within specified elements. It is also possible to browse any of the metadata. Additionally, the metadata can be exported out of the Administrator into SAS data files for further use. One of the powerful and important options is the ability to directly take the metadata and export it to a SAS/EIS metabase. The following tables can be directly loaded into an SAS/EIS metabase:

- Detail logical tables (if they represent a single view of detail tables)
- Detail Tables
- Summary Tables
- Summary MDDBs

It is not necessary to export all of the tables, but they can be optionally selected by:

- Table.
- All tables within a *detail logical group.*
- All tables within a summary group.
- All tables in a subject.
- All tables in a Data Warehouse.

Note that it is not possible to import data into the Administrator. Even if it were, this would probably lead to an unreliable process and therefore an unpredictable Data Warehouse.

Special Topic:
Introduction to the Metadata API available in
Release 1.2 of SAS/Warehouse Administrator

What is a Metadata API?

A metadata application program interface (API) is a set of software tools that enable users to write applications that access metadata. The SAS Metadata API allows you to export the metadata in an open format, which makes the metadata accessible to many SAS products, as well as to non-SAS products. Using the SAS Metadata API, you can write programs that read and write the metadata maintained by a number of SAS products. Starting with Release 1.2 of SAS/Warehouse Administrator, the Metadata API enables you to write applications to access metadata maintained by the SAS/Warehouse Administrator application.

What Can I do with the SAS Metadata API?

Using the SAS metadata API, you can write programs that read, add, or update the metadata in the SAS/Warehouse Administrator — without going through the application's interface. Examples of applications you can write include:

- publish HTML pages containing the current metadata for a SAS application
- import DDL (Data Definition Language) from industry-standard modeling tools
- change path names in metadata
- copy a table's metadata (in order to create a similar table, for example)
- add columns to a table
- update a column attribute
- add tables and other objects defined by metadata
- use the API in a SAS macro to generate a LIBNAME statement.

For more information about the Metadata API available in Release 1.2 of SAS/Warehouse Administrator, see *SAS/Warehouse Administrator Metadata API Reference, Release 1.2*.

Why is the SAS Metadata API important?

Different Data Warehouse implementations collect varying amounts of metadata. A general rule is that the more extensive the scope of the Data Warehouse, the more important the collection of metadata becomes. The reason is that as the scope increases, the control of both the Data Warehousing process and the contents becomes more difficult. Metadata is therefore a very important source of information so that not only the developers, but also the users, understand fully what is contained within the Data Warehouse, *and how it got there*. It therefore follows that the more options that exist to control and query this metadata, the more effectively the Data Warehouse can be used. The SAS Metadata API extends access and update to the metadata so that it is possible for Data Warehouse developers to use it in an almost limitless number of ways. This can directly benefit both the users and the developers of the Data Warehouse.

9.13 SAS/Warehouse Administrator Summary

The overview of the SAS/Warehouse Administrator above has been given so that the process of implementing a Data Warehouse using the product can be appreciated. Many details have not been discussed, including the graphical interface, navigation, and scheduling of batch jobs. All of this information is readily available within the existing documentation.

The key to this chapter is that to fully appreciate the design of a Data Warehouse, the process must be understood. The Administrator uses a process that involves the creation of elements and processes that link these elements. The two, although linked, are treated separately of each other. For a process to exist, the element that is a result of the process must already be defined to the Administrator. In this way, the Administrator forces the Data Warehouse designer to think carefully about every stage of the process. It is easy to slap together a few programs that extract data, modify it and then write it out to a detail data source that is the end result of the Data Warehouse process. This method is often the way Data Warehouses start, but they do not last long that way.

The best Data Warehouse designers have a detailed understanding of the reasons it is being developed. This is of great importance, because a Data Warehouse is always being *developed*. This means that having control over the process is essential. The control is needed because of the constant changes that are being made. For this reason, tools like the SAS/Warehouse Administrator can be of invaluable help. It means that the designers can concentrate more on the vision of the Data Warehouse, by removing a lot of the work from the nitty-gritty implementation. This is not to say that using the SAS/Warehouse Administrator is not time and resource consuming, but in comparison to the alternatives (a rogue Data Warehouse project) it is time and effort well spent.

Chapter 10:
Design and Implementation
of the Data Warehouse:
A Case Study

10.1 Case Study

The case study used in this book is an example of building a Data Warehouse. This study illustrates all of the major points made about building a successful Data Warehousing process outlined in this book. Each of the different decisions made during the design of the process will be related back to specific sections in the book in order to tie them together. This case study is designed to keep the mechanics of the process simpler than might be addressed in the real world by avoiding the over-explanation of business processes. It is a skeleton with the barest of flesh. It can certainly, however, be used as a foundation upon which larger scale Data Warehousing processes could be built.

Company Background and Structure

World Furniture is a privately held importer and retailer of specialty furniture from around the world. Their business is essentially a very simple one:

- Buy furniture in foreign countries.
- Import it into the U.S.
- Store the furniture in warehouses located close to the port of entry.
- Distribute the furniture to fifty retail outlets located across the U.S.
- Sell the furniture to the general public.

Although the complexities within these five steps could be many, the business does not have to worry about the manufacturing process or purchasing raw materials. World Furniture's success lies in several key components of the business:

- purchasing furniture in demand at the best possible price
- timing purchases to maximize the benefits of exchange rates
- minimizing shipping costs
- minimizing warehouse storage costs
- getting furniture to the retail stores quickly
- attracting and selling to retail shoppers.

The company has five warehouses, all located at ports of entry in the U.S.:

- Los Angeles (where the company has its headquarters)
- Seattle
- New York
- Miami
- New Orleans

The 50 retail stores are located around the U.S. and are predominantly located in upscale shopping malls because the products are high quality, expensive items. They also have a 'bargain' store at each of the warehouses to sell items that have been in stock beyond an acceptable time. These items are sold at discounted prices. The company does not sell any of the furniture anywhere except in the retail stores.

There are five regional offices, each with their own profit and loss structures, which are geographically located with the warehouses. The warehouses are not part of the profit and loss structures but are paid for on a company level. Each of the sales regions will buy the furniture they need to populate the retail stores from the warehouses and will be responsible for the shipping costs of the furniture. The shipping costs are a function of the weight of the furniture. Therefore, an incentive is offered for the regions to use the furniture in the warehouse located closest to them to reduce transportation costs.

Operational Computer Systems

The operational computer systems for the company are based in the headquarters in Los Angeles. Each warehouse and retail store has a UNIX server that locally runs the operational systems. Data is then transferred to a central OS/390 (MVS) mainframe, located in Los Angeles. This transfer is made overnight, when the retail stores are closed and work is minimal in the warehouses. All the operational systems use the IBM product, DB2, as the relational database.

As mentioned earlier, each retail store has Point-of-Sales systems that are tied to a central database on the mainframe by overnight downloads. Each warehouse has its own inventory system. As a region requires furniture, a request is made to the warehouse located closest to the retail store. If the request cannot be fulfilled, then each of the other warehouses is queried in turn. If the required furniture is not already in inventory (or on order), the request will automatically be made to the purchasing system to obtain more.

The operational systems are therefore a mixture of OS/390 (MVS) mainframe and UNIX systems, using a variety of client/server techniques, with DB2 as the underlying relational database.

SAS® Software Products Licensed

Under OS/390 (MVS) and UNIX, World Furniture had base SAS, SAS/CONNECT and SAS/ACCESS to DB2 licensed. Under Windows on the PC platform, the following products are licensed: base SAS, SAS/CONNECT, SAS/STAT, SAS/AF, SAS/EIS, SAS Enterprise Reporter, SAS/FSP and SAS/GRAPH. World Furniture was also fortunate to have the SAS/MDDB product available on one of the UNIX servers.

Data Warehousing Background

Although the operational systems work very well for World Furniture, the Corporate Level Management felt frustrated that the analysis of the business was not being performed adequately. Analysis was primarily completed at the spreadsheet level, with data being imported from extracts made into flat files from the operational systems. There were pockets of more sophisticated users, who used SAS software to perform more advanced statistical and Operations Research analysis, but these uses of SAS software were limited to looking at current operational patterns of business, rather than those related to decision support.

The regional managers reflected this corporate level frustration from the lack of business analysis on a more tangible level. They felt that their business was reactive, rather than proactive. There was no real tool to anticipate buying patterns at the retail level, and no way to incorporate trends in business found in other regions. In addition to this problem, the regional managers also felt that the profit margins could be improved if the cost to the company of selling any single item, at any single store was better understood.

The Drivers Behind the Instigation of the Warehouse Process: Creating the Vision

The major driving force for a Data Warehouse initiative was the increase in sales in the five bargain stores associated with each of the warehouses. At an annual general meeting, the Chief Executive Officer of World Furniture asked the regional managers to explain why the largest increase in sales occurred in the bargain stores, rather than the retail stores. This led to a discussion about the lack of information available on the buying patterns of customers at the retail level. Because of the lack of information, the regional managers felt the marketing campaigns were off target.

Having attended a marketing conference where the topic was discussed, one of the regional managers suggested that the company consider a Data Warehousing initiative. The company's CEO, after reading general material on Data Warehousing, suggested that a proposal be written on the structure of a project. The responsibility of developing the proposal was given to the regional manager who first mentioned the potential benefits of a Data Warehousing initiative at the annual general meeting. The Data Warehousing initiative began, with minimal investment by the company, as a request for a high-level, strategic document that would outline the steps World Furniture would have to follow to create their own Data Warehouse.

This start to the Data Warehousing initiative by World Furniture follows many of the points outlined in Chapter 2. Already, without being aware of the fact, the CEO of World Furniture has set the tone for the design of the entire process:

- A commitment to the project is made at the very highest level (the CEO of World Furniture). He actually suggested that the document be produced. This means that if it is to be accepted, then he will have effectively set the *vision* for the project.
- World Furniture is very fortunate to have the project instigated by the CEO. Very often, this is not the case. A situation that commonly occurs is having the project started by people within an organization who have less influence. What invariably happens then is that the project must be sold to the executive level at some point in the process. This 'after the fact sale' can become a political hurdle rather than a business hurdle. Ideally, there needs to be executive level buy-in and *commitment* from the beginning of the project.

The vision *of the data warehouse serves two purposes:*

- *It serves as the check against which decisions within the process can be made.*
- *It defines the scope of the process.*

The vision is more than just a mission statement. *It should be a document (formal or informal) that is accepted by the designers and the users of the warehouse alike. This document should contain high-level descriptions of the problems and needs to be addressed and details about the approach that will be taken. This information will give the designers guidance on both the content and the methodology that should be used.*

- This step has been started with minimal investment. Every step of a Data Warehousing project faces changes and unexpected problems. Building a Data Warehouse is an iterative process that should be mirrored by an iterative approach to committing resources. Although it is necessary to plan, a key part of effective resource utilization within a Data Warehousing project is to only plan as far ahead as is absolutely necessary. Commit resources at the latest possible time.

- A very important part of this first step in the initiative is that a good tone has been set for the entire project; the Data Warehouse initiative has been designated first and foremost as a *business* rather than a technological process. Many Data Warehouse projects start with the immediate incorporation of some form of technology, either by:
  - Requesting that the Information Systems group lead the project—a move that may increase the chances of failure. Information Systems groups can play a leading role in the implementation of the Data Warehouse but are not necessarily equipped to handle the design of a business process.
  - Approaching the project from the wrong direction by loading the Data Warehouse with data that is available, rather than data that is needed to solve explicit enterprise needs.

10.2 Starting the Project

World Furniture took the first step in their Data Warehousing project by putting together an executive overview of the scope and benefits that could be expected. This document included several sections:

- the need for a Data Warehouse at World Furniture
- the strategic approach to Data Warehousing that World Furniture would take

- the resources that would be needed for the project
- the expected benefits from the project

This executive overview was not intended as an exhaustive project plan, but as an overview to educate the executive level on the topic of Data Warehousing as it specifically pertained to World Furniture. The desired outcome would be the buy-in of executives so that the project could be started.

Because executives tend to be wary of indiscriminently allocating resources to projects, it was important that the document show an adverse risk approach to Data Warehousing. The document addressed these issues:

- **The need for a Data Warehouse at World Furniture**. This section outlined who the document was designed for, why it was written and a high-level overview of how the lack of information is preventing World Furniture from the growth that is expected.
- **The strategic approach to Data Warehousing**. This section specifically addressed how a Data Warehousing project would be conducted at World Furniture. There were two key point made in this section:
  - Business rather than technological forces would drive the project.
  - The design of the process would be based inherently on using minimal resources for each step in the process. In other words, marginal cost for each additional unit of resource needed would be minimized. This meant that the *big-bang*[1] approach to Data Warehousing would not be considered. This also meant that to gauge the worth of incurring marginal costs, the worth of additional benefits would have to be assessed. Tightly tying costs to benefits would mean that it would be necessary to fully understand enterprise needs that would be met for every given increase in resources. *This does not necessarily mean that a Data Warehouse process should be undertaken with the intent of only using minimal resources, but that in allocating resources, each incremental addition of resources should be carefully considered.*
  - **The resources that would be needed**. The point was made that most of the resources needed for the project would be dedicated to Data Warehousing. For the project to be a success, it would be necessary to have people working only on Data Warehousing. What often happens in situations where individuals are assigned to work on a Data Warehouse on a *part-time* basis, is that their other

---

[1] See Chapter 2, Section 2.3 for an overview of the *big-bang* approach to data warehousing.

responsibilities (often operational) take priority. Some resources on the project could be part-time but the designers of the Data Warehouse should not have other operational duties.

Ensuring that the Scope Is Realistic

This document was presented to the CEO of World Furniture, who was concerned enough about the performance of the company to give it his immediate consideration. The CEO decided that the project should go ahead on a limited scale. The CEO was sufficiently interested in the project to have some influence in its development, and the CEO placed three main conditions on the project:

- The project should bring results within six months.
- No major purchases of either hardware or software should be made before the CEO was fully convinced of the benefits that the Data Warehouse could bring.
- A process would be fully designed, including checks and balances, to ensure that the development of each part of the Data Warehouse would directly address the needs of World Furniture.

The CEO cleverly defined these conditions. One of the main misconceptions of Data Warehousing is that the project should take a long period of time before results can be realized. As long as the scope and priorities are well-defined, it is possible for tangible results to be realized within a short period of time.

The CEO also realized that an investment in new hardware and software would lead to confusion in the development of the process. The lengthy process of deciding upon software and hardware would take away valuable resources from the real goals of the project. Most companies that start a Data Warehousing initiative have many of the hardware and software resources readily available to them to start the project. If, at a later date, it can be shown that alternative software or hardware would be needed, the hardware and software can be evaluated based on their impact to the Data Warehouse process.

The final condition shows that the CEO had obviously been involved in large-scale technological projects that lost their way. This final condition would keep the *Data Warehouse* honest. Every decision made about the design of the Data Warehousing process, including the contents of the Data Warehouse itself, would directly address the enterprise needs of World Furniture.

Empowering the Main Participant in the Process

The regional manager who prepared the executive summary was given the responsibility of running the project. This responsibility would last for a period of six months, after which the decision would be made to develop the project further or drop it. During this period of time, this project would be the regional manager's only responsibility. It was not expected that an entire Data Warehouse would be completed within that time period, but that there would be tangible results from all the effort and resources put into the project.

Other resources would be available to the project, as they were needed, but only if they could be justified. The project would be fully supported by all divisions or departments, including the Information Systems group. This support would be explicitly enforced from the CEO level. For the length of his involvement in the project, the regional manager was designated as Data Warehouse Manager, reporting directly to the CEO. One reason the CEO selected this person was that she had a broad experience within the company and was therefore in a position to understand enterprise-wide needs, instead of just departmental requirements. It was intended that this would lead to a Data Warehouse that would benefit the entire company, rather than a warehouse of limited scope that only catered to the few.

World Furniture was very lucky in having a CEO who realized that a project of this importance could not be done in someone's spare time. The direction of the project had already been set early on. There would not be a large-scale budget allocated to the project, yet resources were dedicated. Support for the project would be from the very highest level (the CEO himself). This example shows how a Data Warehousing project should be run. Very often, in real projects, the allocation of resources becomes very confusing; the budget is larger than it needs to be to begin the project, and resources are rarely dedicated. This is a potentially wasteful combination, leading to expenditure without results! World Furniture was very fortunate to have a CEO that understood the business implications of starting a Data Warehousing project and a project leader who understood that designing a Data Warehouse is essentially a business, rather than a technological process.

10.3 Phase 1: Building the Conceptual Data Warehouse

The warehouse manager began the process by making a list of all the most immediate needs of World Furniture. These needs were based upon informal discussion with the key members of each of the different divisions within the company. These needs were only considered on a very high level. Although the warehouse manager thought about devising a questionnaire for each of the departments, she decided that at this stage, this was unnecessary and would take too much time. The list was therefore defined based upon semi-formal consultation with key people in each of the divisions. Each of the different needs was taken at face value. There was no attempt to read behind the needs. All that she needed was a broad understanding of the problems that were faced by every facet of the business. She knew that there were six months to actually obtain positive and tangible results from the Data Warehouse and therefore her main aim was to understand the basic shortcomings in the current analyses capabilities of the company. These could then be categorized. Given that the major shortcomings were outlined, business decisions could be made as to which should be initially addressed.

This approach is consistent with that outlined in Chapter 2 in the building of the conceptual warehouse. The building of a list of enterprise requirements should not be part of a long and drawn out process, but a gathering of information based upon input from key personnel. Although the approach of using a questionnaire or lengthy needs analysis meetings can work, they take a long time to coordinate and the analysis of the results themselves can be very complex. This part of the process should be a simple as possible (which is not to say that requirements can be fabricated). The process will have opportunity to become complex at a later date. One of the tricks to ensuring that this stage is kept simple is to ensure that the warehouse manager has a good overall understanding of as many facets of the business as possible.

Effectively Assigning Resources

Early on in the process, the data warehouse manager co-opted the support of a business analyst from the marketing research department. This person had a firm grounding in both the business, and technological issues. This person was used, not to begin any implementation of the Data Warehouse, but as business support for the warehouse manager. It was decided very early on that all the details behind every step of the process should be electronically stored. In this case, the business analyst was a SAS user and so it was decided to store all the pertinent information in SAS files. This decision was consistent with the CEO's initial decision that only existing products were to be used.

> *It is important that the technological issues raised do not cloud the business issues. For example, it is easy for the designers to worry about which computer(s) should be used to hold the implemented warehouse. This issue could undermine the development of the entire warehouse process. Although it is important to decide upon the right computer, this is a technological issue and should not act to confound the development of the process. There is often the feeling that the right computer will solve all the problems. This is, of course, not true. The selection of the hardware (if not predetermined due to practical reasons), can only be made after there is a full understanding of the business process.*

Creation of the Business Need Metadata

The business analyst decided that it would be a good idea to create a series of files in which key information would be stored regarding the enterprise needs expressed by the departments. The following code was used to create these files:[2]

```
LIBNAME whmeta 'w:\warehouse\metadata\programs';
PROC SQL;

 /* This table contains a list of unique departments */

 CREATE TABLE wh.depts(LABEL='Table of Unique Departments')
 ( dept       NUM          LABEL='Associated department number',
 dpt_name     CHAR(30 )    LABEL='Department Name',
 contact      NUM          LABEL='ID of Contact'
 );

 CREATE UNIQUE INDEX dept ON whmeta.depts(dept);

 /* This table contains a list of unique contacts */

 CREATE TABLE whmeta.contacts(LABEL='Table of Unique Contacts')
 ( contact    NUM          LABEL='ID of Department Contact',
 contname     CHAR(30 )    LABEL='Name of Contact'
 cont_ph      NUM          LABEL='Contact Phone Number'
 );
 CREATE UNIQUE INDEX contact ON whmeta.contacts(contact);

 /* This table contains a list of categories into which needs will be
    placed */
 CREATE TABLE whmeta.category(LABEL='Table of Unique Need Categories')

 ( category   NUM          LABEL='Category Number',
 catdesc      CHAR(200)    LABEL='Description of Category'
 );
 CREATE UNIQUE INDEX category ON whmeta.category(category);
```

---

[2] Note that in Version 7 of SAS, the 200 character fields corresponding to descriptions would be larger than specified. This is because Version 7 allows character columns to be up to 32K in size. SQL was used to create the tables because it is a standard for the industry. Many other techniques within SAS could have been used.

```
/* This table contains data about each of the enterprise needs */

CREATE TABLE whmeta.needs(LABEL='Table of Data Warehouse Needs')
( need          CHAR(200)    LABEL='Short definition of need',
  needdesc      CHAR(200)    LABEL='Description of need',
  need_num      NUM          LABEL='Unique need identifier',
  dept          NUM          LABEL='Associated department number',
  category      NUM          LABEL='Category of needs',
  selected      NUM          LABEL='Date need accepted for inclusion'
                             INFORMAT=mmddyy7.
);

/* SQL View to see a denormalized version of the above four tables */

CREATE VIEW whmeta.metaview AS
 SELECT n.need, n.needdesc, n.need_num, n.dept, n.category, d.dpt_name,
        c.catdesc, co.contact, co.contname, co.cont_ph
 FROM whmeta.needs n, whmeta.depts d, whmeta.category c, whmeta.contacts co
 WHERE n.category=c.category AND n.dept=d.dept AND d.contact=co.contact;
QUIT;
```

After these four tables were created, then they were used to store the results of the initial enterprise needs investigation. Initially, the contents of these tables are as follows:

Category Number	Description of Category
1	Sales Analysis
2	Shipping Analysis
3	Competitive Analysis

TABLE 10.1 whmeta.category (Table of Unique Categories)

Associated Department	ID of Department Contact	Department Name
1	1	Marketing
2	3	Purchasing
3	2	Pricing

TABLE 10.2 whmeta.depts (Table of Unique Departments)

ID of Contact	Name of Contact	Contract Phone Number
1	Bob Barber	5553415151
2	Rachel Heyhoe-Flint	5553415218
3	Fred Rumsey	5553419763
4	Billy Ibadulla	5559871232
5	David Brown	5559765432
6	John Jameson	5557645432
7	Tom Cartwright	5557534325

TABLE 10.3 whmeta.contacts (Table of Unique Contacts)

Short Definition of Need	Description of Need	Unique Need Identifier	Associated Department Number	Category of Need	Date Need Accepted for Inclusion
Analysis of Sales Compensation	Create an analysis to explore the potential of a commission structure	1	1	1	
Sales Forecasting	Forecast sales by store to improve buying knowledge	2	2	1	
Time of Shipment by Shipper	Analyse different shipping companies to find time taken to ship goods	3	2	2	
Analysis of Prices Charged by Competitors	Look at how competitors structure their pricing of furniture	4	3	3	

TABLE 10.4 whmeta.needs (Table of Data Warehouse Needs)

These four very simple tables were built to provide a basis for analyzing the enterprise needs of World Furniture. Although these tables might seem trivial when starting a Data Warehousing project, they will become increasingly important over time. These lists of needs, contacts, departments, and categories will become the gauges against which the success of the Data Warehouse will be judged. The more of these needs that are addressed by the Data Warehouse, the more the Data Warehouse will be serving the requirements of the company.

Avoid Confusing Enterprise Needs with Technological Capability

There are a couple of interesting points in the above tables:

- The *whmeta.needs* table does not include the date the need was accepted for inclusion into the Data Warehouse. These values will be known and entered during the second phase (the Transition Phase) of the Data Warehousing Process. What will go into the Data Warehouse at this point is totally irrelevant. This is part of the building of the conceptual Data Warehouse and as such is just an enterprise wish-list of what is not currently being addressed in terms of business needs.[3]

- The *whmeta.categories* table although very small at this stage shows an interesting development. The contents of the columns could well correspond to *subjects*[4] that would mean that from a very early stage, the construct of the Data Warehouse is already being developed.

This part of the development of the Data Warehousing process is very often based upon a document. The approach taken above is far more analytical in nature. Each of these tables above could become quite extensive, so the early categorization of needs is essential to control the warehouse development.

These four tables *not only* are used during the initial design of the warehouse process, but also are important for the entire life span of the Data Warehouse. Every business changes over time, and as these changes occur, modifications should be made to the Data Warehouse. Having a technique for the Data Warehouse to incorporate these changes is essential to the process. Creation of metadata, as illustrated in the above four tables, will allow for the evolving as opposed to static Data Warehouse. One of the weaknesses of many data warehouse processes is that there is no place for incorporating change. The Data Warehouse is seen as an information source (which intrinsically needs not to respond to change), as opposed to a tool to help meet enterprise needs (which will intrinsically mean that it has to change as the needs alter).

The four tables can act as a benchmark for the Data Warehouse. Benchmarking the Data Warehouse is addressed in Chapter 2, Section 2.3. In summary, how well a Data Warehouse performs is a function of the enterprise needs it meets. Unless those enterprise needs are documented on a continuing basis, it will not be possible to truly gauge how good the Data Warehouse is.

Do Not Stifle Progression with Over Complication

The four tables were populated with pertinent information. The Data Warehouse Manager was very careful at this stage to ensure that this process was

---

[3] See Chapter 2 for a discussion on the development of a Conceptual Data Warehouse.
[4] The development of subjects is key to the implementation of a Data Warehouse if the star-schema (see Chapter 3, Section 3.5) design is used or when using the SAS/Warehouse Administrator (see Chapter 9).

completed quickly because of the time limitations imposed by the CEO. Fully populating these tables with every enterprise need of the World Furniture would not occur at this time. These tables could be populated as the Data Warehouse developed. Because the process the manager had designed was based around anticipated change, it was not necessary to create an exhaustive list of all the enterprise needs at the beginning of the project.

The list of enterprise needs could be far larger than illustrated above. This case study is primarily concerned with the illustration of the development of a data warehousing process, and so only the bare minimum of detail will be included. The four tables could contain far more columns depending on the depth of metadata that is felt necessary. This technique of documenting enterprise needs as part of the warehousing process is completely scalable. In fact, it makes more sense when done on a very large scale, because this is when the warehouse *vision* can be obscured by detail.

> *It is best to collect as much metadata as possible during the warehouse process. If it is found that some of this metadata is unnecessary to the process later, then it can be dropped. It is far harder to collect data after the fact. This is also true of data that will be the implemented Data Warehouse. If in doubt, collect it!*

At this stage in the process, there were two different ways that the Data Warehouse Manager could take the process. This decision as the direction was based upon business pressures, rather than any personal preference or technological involvement. These business pressures are going to be a driving force behind the entire data warehousing process and are based upon the vision set by the CEO. At this time, this vision included time limits that required that there be tangible results within the period of six months from the start of the project. The collection of the very basic enterprise needs of World Furniture had already taken three of these weeks, so there was a considerable time constraint that was acting as the major driving force behind the project.

> *A useful technique in making decisions with regard to the data warehousing process is to assess at each step exactly what the key driving forces are. This can be a useful process in helping to make the decision. It might turn out that there are no driving forces, in which case the vision has not been adequately defined. It could also be determined that the driving forces behind the decisions are not in line with the vision of the data warehouse project, in which case a reassessment will be required.*

Breakdown of Business Needs to Business Need Detail

The next stage for the Data Warehouse Manager was to take the needs and break them down into business details. The three choices available to the manager were as follows:

- Select specific needs that will be addressed in the Data Warehouse before breaking these needs into business details. The advantage to this approach would be the time saved by only working on needs that were going to be addressed in the Data Warehouse. The disadvantage is that at this stage, it is not known whether there are the resources or data necessary to fulfill the need.
- Break all of the needs down into their business details and then decide which should be addressed in the Data Warehouse. This is a much lengthier process than pre-selecting needs, but less risky. In Chapter 2, this technique is the recommended approach. The decision about the enterprise needs that will be addressed is part of the *Transition Phase* of the Data Warehouse process, outlined in Section 2.5.
- Combine the previous two choices. In most situations, this will probably be the most practical approach. Some enterprise needs, due to their critical nature will be automatically included. After these selected needs have been broken down into their business details, other needs that can be easily addressed will become apparent, because of the similar content.

The first option was selected in this situation because of the time constraint set by the CEO. This option was also selected because the Data Warehouse Manager was also a knowledgeable business person. It is a great advantage to have people who are very business knowledgeable involved in the development of the Data Warehouse process. They have insight that will lead to decisions that could save a great deal of time and resources.

Selecting the Needs to Be Addressed

After consulting with the CEO the Data Warehouse Manager decided to concentrate the available resources on two of the enterprise needs documented in the `whmeta.needs` table. The two needs that were chosen for initial incorporation into the Data Warehouse were:

- Create an analysis to explore the potential of a commission structure.
- Forecast Sales by store to improve buying knowledge.

These two were chosen for two major reasons:

- They were seen as absolutely essential to the business based upon the *vision* set by the CEO.

- They were seen to have a lot of overlap in terms of the data they require. By initially addressing needs that have this overlap, it is possible to leverage the maximum amount of benefit from the minimum amount of work.

These needs would be evaluated from a business perspective. Exactly what information, on a business level, will be needed to allow for the analyses required to meet the enterprise needs? The Data Warehouse Manager, along with the department representatives concerned for the particular need, broke each need down as far as possible.

Note that the Manager checked with the CEO before making any final decision. This was not because she could not make the decision herself, but because it is essential to check-back to the *vision* of the Data Warehouse at every point in the process. Because the CEO was setting the vision, this is where the check had to be made.

The decisions made above were very sensible. As pointed out, the two needs not only are of absolute top priority but also overlap to a great extent. From a project perspective, these decisions were also very important because the needs came from different departments, Marketing and Purchasing. Addressing the needs from different departments will give the impression that the Data Warehouse is for the good of the entire enterprise. More departments will feel ownership and therefore be likely to actively participate in the design of the process and the Data Warehouse itself.

Data Warehousing projects are often started because of very specific needs. As the project begins, the focus on the specific needs is often lost in the attempt to make the Data Warehouse the answer to everything. This loss of focus leads to a Data Warehouse that does not directly address enterprise needs and is consequently under-utilized. Focus is of primary importance in building a successful Data Warehouse.

The following two tables were created to cross-reference business information with the needs (**whmeta.needs**) table.

```
PROC SQL;

CREATE TABLE wh.bus_item(LABEL='Table of Unique Business Items')
   ( bus_item      char(200)        LABEL='Short definition of Business Item',
   bus_desc       char(200)        LABEL='Long description of Business Item :
Business Rule',
   bus_num        num        LABEL='Unique Business Item identifier'
   );

CREATE UNIQUE INDEX bus_num ON whmeta.contacts(bus_num);
```

```
CREATE TABLE wh.need_brk(LABEL='Table of Business Need Breakdowns')
( need_num      NUM              LABEL='Unique Need Identifier',
 bus_num       NUM       LABEL='Unique Business Item Identifier'
 );
QUIT;
```

In making the decision as to the enterprise needs to address, the `selected` column in the `whmeta.needs` table could then be completed. This field is important from a business standpoint because it will give a history of the development of the Data Warehouse. It will also be a document for the departments to know which of their needs have been or are being addressed.

Each of the two departments evaluated their respective needs. The breakdown was based on the lowest level of business detail. Each item represents a piece of business information that will be needed if the larger *need* is to be addressed.

Create an Analysis to Explore the Potential of a Commission Structure

The items needed to address this business need include:

- The sales person.
- The sales amount of each item purchased.
- The purchase cost to World Furniture of each item.
- Returns made to the store.
- The retail store.
- Current salary levels.
- Date of sale was made.
- Date of return.
- Furniture Item identifier.

Several decisions were made related to the data gathered for this business need:

- The time the item was in storage (a cost to the company) would not be a part of the commission structure.
- The shipping cost of each item would not be part of calculating the commission structure. The commission structure would be based upon factors that the sales people could actually control. For example, if an item is shipped from Seattle to Miami, the sales person cannot control this transfer and his or her commission should not reflect the shipping costs.
- The commission should be based upon the actual price the item was sold for, rather than the list price.

Forecast Sales by Store to Improve Buying Knowledge

The items needed to address the business need include:

- Sales levels of each item.
- Store each item was sold in.
- Time each item was sold.
- Furniture Item identifier
- Originating Warehouse (port of entry) of each item.

The Purchasing Department was essentially interested in a predictor to help anticipate future need, not only to ensure that there would be stock to meet the needs of the customers, but also to reduce the overstocking of items. Overstocking created the stock for the bargain stores, where items were sold for a reduced profit margin to the company.

Each of these items was entered into the two tables, `whemeta.bus_item` and `wh.need_brk` (created earlier.) The two tables then contained the following data:

Short Definition of Business Item	Business Rule	Unique Business Item Identifier
Sales Person	The Retail store sales person	1
Sales Amount	Actual Purchase price of each item	2
Purchase Cost	Cost of each item in $	3
Returned Item	Amount returned to customer in $	4
Retail Store	Retail Store Code	5
Retail Sales person salary	Monthly salary of each Sales Person	6
Date of sale	Date the sale was made	7
Return date	Date the item was returned	8
Originating Warehouse	Originating Warehouse of Each item sold	9
Item Stock code	Item Identifier	10

TABLE 10.5 whmeta.bus_item (Table of Unique Business Items)

Unique Need Identifier	Unique Business Item Identifier
1	1
1	2
1	3
1	4
1	5
1	6
1	7
1	8
1	10
2	8
2	10
2	5
2	7
2	9

TABLE 10.6 wh.need_brk (Table of Business Need Breakdowns)

Again it is important to understand that this case study is demonstrating how to build a Data Warehousing process. For the case study, only two business needs are being addressed. The number of enterprise needs that are initially incorporated into the Conceptual Warehouse is as many as the *vision* requires, or the available resources allow. In many cases, a Data Warehouse project will start with a very limited number of needs. In fact, starting with a limited number of needs could be a very good idea because limiting needs will allow for the development of a Data Warehouse process that suits the particular enterprise, with the minimum of resources.

Understanding the Goals of the Warehouse Will Lead to an Efficient Implementation

Documenting enterprise needs and breaking them down into business items is probably the hardest part of the Data Warehouse process. What is being built is a Conceptual Warehouse, which will be the business basis for the implemented warehouse. This Conceptual Warehouse is an important tool in itself. It is the documentation for the future direction of the enterprise as set by the *vision* of the Data Warehouse. The Conceptual Warehouse is a list of enterprise-wide requirements that will be used both to help define the Implemented Warehouse and to act as the test against which the warehouse will be measured. (See Chapter 2, Sections 2.3 and 2.4 for more information.) If this section is completed successfully, the implementation process is much easier.

> *The implementation phase of the Data Warehousing process may be very difficult if the Conceptual Warehouse is not fully developed. What often happens is that the implementation process begins before the needs that the Warehouse will be addressing are thoroughly thought out. This leads to a 'build it and they will come' Data Warehouse, which is rarely successful.*

The process of developing business items that match enterprise needs should be very carefully thought out. It demonstrates the importance of having a centralized data warehouse metadata store, and a controlled method to add new items. After an enterprise need has been broken down, the business items that are already registered (in the `whmeta.bus_item` table) should be carefully examined to find a similar entry before any new additions are entered. This part of the process requires an in-depth understanding of the business and a willingness to further define the business rules associated with the business items to reduce confusion.

At this point in the process, the Data Warehouse Manager has six tables containing business metadata. It would be possible to build a moderately-sized system using SAS/AF as a front end to these tables to help input the new data and reduce the possibility of duplication of business items. The tables are already normalized which helps in the development of this system. The system would benefit from a search facility that would, for example, extract all business items that have the word *sales* in the description. This search would help identify similar business items. This system could be incorporated with the metadata contained within the SAS/Warehouse Administrator, which does not, at this time support the development of business needs analysis or their incorporation into the Data Warehouse process.

At this stage, the Data Warehouse Manager had developed a small-scale Conceptual Data Warehouse. She realized that not only were the needs fully defined, but that they were also broken down into business items that could be readily transformed into a technological lexicon. What she had cleverly developed, however, was a process for the business community to register their needs with the Data Warehouse.

10.4 Phase 2: The Transition Phase—Moving from Concept to Reality

The World Furniture Data Warehouse has had absolutely no involvement from a technological implementation perspective. What is now known is:

- **The needs of the business community**: This list is not fully developed but does not have to be at this stage. In some Data Warehouse implementations, this list of needs could be very large (hundreds of items), but many of them overlap in terms of the information they require. In any case, these needs are explicit and have the backing of the business community.
- **The business items that make up each of the needs**: This unique list of business items is the key piece of information needed to begin the design of the physical Data Warehouse.

The Data Warehouse Manager already had a good idea of the needs that were to be addressed initially by the Data Warehouse. World Furniture, at this stage, has made the Transformation Phase much easier than it often is. This is because of the explicit *vision* set by the CEO and his involvement in the process. By this stage, the decision has been made to address only two needs initially:

- Create an analysis to explore the potential of a commission structure.
- Forecast Sales by store to improve buying knowledge.

The decision to incorporate these two needs was made earlier in this warehouse process than is often advisable because of the limited time-span and resources available to the project. In most processes, the business items would be documented for each of the needs before a decision is made about which needs would be addressed. The decision would be based, in part, on trying to meet as many needs as possible with the least amount of work. Therefore, it would be logical to select needs that had the most business items in common. This analysis could be easily performed using SAS and the six tables created earlier.

Managing User Expectations

After these needs were identified, the next step would be to balance the needs that have the most business items in common with the overall vision for the Data Warehouse. This discussion, or set of discussions, should be made with the departments that are working together. One of the main goals of the Transition Phase of the Data Warehousing process is to manage user expectations. Making rational and agreed upon decisions about the needs that will be addressed is a major part of managing those expectations. Involving the business departments in the decision process will promote the ideas that the Data Warehouse is an enterprise wide resource and that it is designed for everyone, not just for an isolated business unit.

Now that the enterprise needs and their associated business items were defined, the Data Warehouse Manager, for the first time, had to interact with a technological department. For the duration of the pilot project, two technicians were assigned to the Data Warehousing project. Both of these two people were SAS programmers with a background in both the manipulation and analysis of data. Neither of these two people had been contacted up to this point, because the warehouse manager considered that until this time there were no technological issues.

Many Data Warehouses have been designed entirely by technological staff (Information Systems Groups). Although this approach can work, it is usually better to assign technological staff to the warehouse effort, so effectively their line of report is to the warehouse manager. This technological staff can come from either Information Systems or from the user community so long as they are working full-time on the warehouse project. What does not work is having technological staff working part-time on the warehouse project.

Another key point is that the technological staff should be skilled and experienced in the design of systems because the extraction, transformation, and loading of the data can become very complex. A Data Warehousing project differs greatly from the design of an operational system, however, so the technological staffing should also be adept at handling constantly changing situations.[5]

Establishing the Source Operational Systems

The two technologists were brought up to speed with the project. Each one of them knew that a time limit on implementing the warehouse had been set, but they also realized that the important part of their work was to establish a process that could be used to develop the warehouse. The next part of the process was to take each of the business items and cross-reference them

---

[5] See Chapter 2, Section 2.1 for a brief discussion on the differences between Operational and Data Warehouse applications.

to existing systems. After the systems were identified, the tables and columns required could be documented. This required the existence of three more tables:

- A table for the systems
- A table for the table names
- A table for the columns required.

The code to create these tables is outlined below:

```
/* Create Table for Systems */

PROC SQL;
CREATE TABLE whmeta.systems(LABEL='Table of Unique Application Systems')
 ( system     CHAR(200)    LABEL='Short description of Application System',
   sys_desc   CHAR(200)    LABEL='Long description of Application System',
   sys_num    NUM          LABEL='Unique Application System Identifier'
   contact    NUM          LABEL='ID of Contact',
 );
 CREATE UNIQUE INDEX sys_num ON whmeta.systems(sys_num);

/* Create Table for Tables */

CREATE TABLE whmeta.tables(LABEL='Table of Unique Tables')
 ( table      CHAR(32)     LABEL='Table Name',
   tab_desc   CHAR(200)    LABEL='Long description of Table',
   tab_num    NUM          LABEL='Unique Table Identifier',
   sys_num    NUM          LABEL='Unique Application System Identifier'
 );

 CREATE UNIQUE INDEX tab_num ON whmeta.tables(tab_num);

/* Create Table for Columns */
CREATE TABLE whmeta.columns(LABEL='Table of Unique Columns')
 ( column     CHAR(32)     LABEL='Column Name',
   col_desc   CHAR(200)    LABEL='Long description of Column',
   col_num    NUM          LABEL='Unique Column Identifier',
   tab_num    NUM          LABEL='Table Identifier'
 );

 CREATE UNIQUE INDEX col_num ON whmeta.columns(col_num);

QUIT;
```

Each of the business items in the **whmeta.bus_item** table was considered and the corresponding system, table, and columns were documented. This process was actually performed by the two technical people working with the people in charge of the operational systems and the people responsible for the enterprise needs.

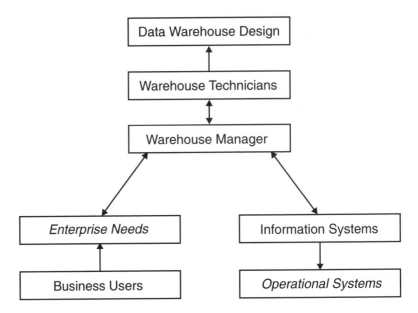

Figure 10.1
Design of World Furniture's Key Warehouse Personnel Interaction

There are some very interesting points to be made here:

- At no point is it necessary to have the business users communicate directly with the information systems people. This does not mean that they won't be in the same meetings but that both sides are buffered by the warehouse manager and the full-time warehouse technicians. This organization will reduce the likelihood of confusion in translation that might be needed between the enterprise need definitions and the actual column definitions in the operational systems.
- For the first time in the process, the SAS/Warehouse Administrator could be used.[6] If this tool is to be used, the metadata collected so far should be leveraged so that it can be used. For example, it is likely that the `whmeta.tables` table will be used as the basis for understanding all the Operational Data Definitions (ODDs) that the SAS/Warehouse Administrator will be requiring.
- Until this part of the process, it has not been known if the enterprise need could actually be met by extracting and transforming data from current operational systems. This would not preclude the enterprise need from being included in the Conceptual Warehouse.

---

[6] See Chapter 9 for a full description of the SAS/Warehouse Administrator and how it can be used within the data warehousing process.

■ Note that the `whmeta.system` table uses the column, contact. This will join with the table `whmeta.contacts` created already. There is no differentiation between types of contacts, for example, that has been between a *technical* and *business* contact.

Ensuring that the Granularity of the Warehouse Is Designed to Meet Long Term Goals

The granularity of the data needed to fulfill the two selected enterprise needs was also discussed. The outcome for each of the needs was that analysis would have to occur at a sales transaction level. This means that data will have to be collected by every item sold. The warehouse manager, although wary of a short-term objective with the Data Warehouse, was adamant that the granularity should be kept at the very lowest level. The reason was that she wanted to avoid unnecessary changes in the warehouse design would be required to allow for lower-level granularity when it could have been planned for and collected from the start of the warehouse.

Granularity of the data collected within the Data Warehouse is actually a much easier decision to make than often thought. The default should be to collect data at the lowest-level of granularity possible. Arguments can then be made against this decision and, only if these arguments are valid, should the decision be revoked. Nothing is more frustrating than to have to collect the same data again because of lack of foresight or planning.

Over the period of time that the meetings to determine the requirements from the different applications were held, the three tables (created in the previous section) were populated. The three tables ended up being populated as follows.

Application System	Long Description of Application System	Unique Application System Identifier	ID of Contact
Point of Sale System	Point of Sale Systems on UNIX systems at each Warehouse	1	4
Inventory System	Inventory System on UNIX systems at each Warehouse	2	5
Payroll	Payroll and Human Resource system on UNIX system in Los Angeles	3	6
Purchasing	Purchasing System on OS/390 mainframe	4	7

TABLE 10.7
whmeta.systems (Table of Unique Application Systems)

Table Name	Long Description of Table	Unique Table Identifier	Unique Application System Identifier
pos.sale	Table containing sales amounts by individual furniture item	1	1
pos.return	Table containing sale return amounts by individual furniture item	2	1
pur.amounts	Table containing purchase amounts by stock item	3	4
hr. salary	Table containing Payroll Details by employee	4	3
inv.invent	Table containing inventory by Warehouse	5	2

TABLE 10.8 whmeta.tables (Table of Unique Tables)

COLUMN	COL_DESC	COL_NUM	TAB_NUM
employee_id	Employee ID Number	1	1
employee_id	Employee ID Number	2	2
emp_id	Employee ID Number	3	4
sales_$	Sales Amount of Transaction	4	1
sale_#	Unique Identifier for Sale	5	1
return_$	Return Amount of Transaction	6	1
return_#	Unique Identifier for Return	7	1
store_#	Store Number	8	1
store_#	Store Number	9	2
emp_salary	Employee Monthly Salary	10	4
sale_date	Date and Time of Sale	11	1
return_date	Date and Time of Return	12	2
stock_#	Stock Number of Sold Item	13	1
stock_#	Stock Number of Returned Item	14	2
stock_#	Stock Number Item	15	5
warehouse_#	Originating Warehouse	16	5
purchase_amount	Unit Purchase Price	17	3
stock_#	Purchase Stock Number	18	3
purchase_date	Date Stock Purchased	19	3
product_group	Product Group Based on Stock	20	5

TABLE 10.9 whmeta.columns (Table of Unique Columns)

These three tables defined the systems, the tables, and the columns within the tables that would be required to meet the enterprise needs that had been selected. However, the warehouse manager realized that without being able to tie the data to the need, most of this work would become redundant. She had two main goals in the design of this process:

- To build business metadata that would be the key information source for extracting information from the operational systems. This goal was met by the creation of the tables above.

■ To be able to identify the columns of data from the operational systems with the need. From the current set of tables, no link exists between the operational systems and the business needs.

Linking the Operational Data to the Enterprise Needs

This second goal was satisfied by creating an additional table that simply linked the unique column identifier from **whmeta.columns** to the enterprise need identifier, **need_num** in **whmeta.needs**. This table was created as follows:

```
PROC SQL;
CREATE TABLE whmeta.col_need(LABEL='Table to Link Columns to Enterprise
Need')
  ( col_num      NUM          LABEL='Column Identifier',
    need_num     NUM          LABEL='Need Identifier',
  );
QUIT;
```

It was then populated as follows:

Column Identifier	Need Identifier
1	1
2	1
3	1
4	1
5	1
6	1
7	1
8	1
9	1
10	1
11	1
12	1
13	1
14	1
4	2
5	2
6	2
7	2
8	2
9	2
11	2
12	2
13	2
14	2
15	2
16	2
17	1
18	1
19	1
20	1

TABLE 10.10
whmeta.col_need (Table of Columns Linked to Enterprise Needs)

This table enables the contents of the physical implemented warehouse to be analyzed by column. This information only has value to the Data Warehouse designers. One of the main problems of assessing the use of a Data Warehouse is that after it is populated, there is no direct way of understanding how the data is being used. There are two main benefits to breaking down each defined enterprise need into component business elements:

- Although not as dynamic as the make-up of the Data Warehouse, operational systems do change. This means that if the definition of a column of data in the operational system changes, it is possible to immediately understand the impact to the Data Warehouse. This understanding can be especially important if additional data is being added to the Data Warehouse. For example, if World Furniture were to purchase another retail company, there would probably be new operational sources to add to the Data Warehouse. Knowing the existing columns used to address that need would also mean that the business rules associated with each of the columns would also be known. It would then be possible to match existing business rules to the new ones in the additional operational systems.
- Enterprise needs can be reported using a single program. The following example shows how this data can be used to obtain a useful report showing all needs:

```
PROC SQL;
 SELECT n.need, c.column, t.table
 FROM whmeta.col_need cn, whmeta.needs n, whmeta.columns c,
 whmeta.tables t
 WHERE cn.need_num=n.need_num AND cn.col_num=c.col_num
 AND t.tab_num=c.tab_num;
QUIT;
```

If this view were printed, it would look like this:

NEED	COLUMN	TABLE
Analysis of Sales Compensation	Employee_id	pos.sale
Analysis of Sales Compensation	Employee_id	pos.return
Analysis of Sales Compensation	Emp_id	hr.salary
Analysis of Sales Compensation	Sales_$	pos.sale
Analysis of Sales Compensation	Sale_#	pos.sale
Analysis of Sales Compensation	Return_$	pos.sale
Analysis of Sales Compensation	Return_#	pos.sale
Analysis of Sales Compensation	Store_#	pos.sale
Analysis of Sales Compensation	store_#	pos.return
Analysis of Sales Compensation	emp_salary	hr.salary
Analysis of Sales Compensation	sale_date	pos.sale
Analysis of Sales Compensation	return_date	pos.return
Analysis of Sales Compensation	stock_#	pos.sale
Analysis of Sales Compensation	stock_#	pos.return
Analysis of Sales Compensation	purchase_amount	pur.amounts
Analysis of Sales Compensation	stock_#	pur.amounts
Analysis of Sales Compensation	purchase_date	pur.amounts
Analysis of Sales Compensation	product_group	inv.invent
Sales Forecasting	sales_$	pos.sale
Sales Forecasting	sale_#	pos.sale
Sales Forecasting	return_$	pos.sale
Sales Forecasting	return_#	pos.sale
Sales Forecasting	store_#	pos.sale
Sales Forecasting	store_#	pos.return
Sales Forecasting	sale_date	pos.sale
Sales Forecasting	return_date	pos.return
Sales Forecasting	stock_#	pos.sale
Sales Forecasting	stock_#	pos.return
Sales Forecasting	stock_#	inv.invent
Sales Forecasting	warehouse_#	inv.invent

TABLE 10.11 VIEW=work.needanal

In situations where more resources are available than with World Furniture, it would be possible to fully analyze all of the needs before deciding upon those that should be addressed. In this situation it would be possible to leverage the minimum number of columns to address the maximum number of needs. More realistically, rather than selecting specific columns, it would be more feasible to select the fewest operational tables that would address the most enterprise needs. Either way, the above technique would supply the data that could easily be analyzed using SAS tools.

The data created in all the tables illustrated above *only* specify operational sources. They include no information about transformations of the data or the model of the final implementation of the Data Warehouse. This has been a process that has been designed to ensure that the Data Warehouse is responsive to explicit enterprise needs, not a process to define the final model of the Data Warehouse. That part of the process comes in the third phase of the process, the actual implementation of the Data Warehouse.

Using the Vision to Control the Scope of the Data Warehouse

The temptation for the Data Warehouse Manager at this time was to push for more enterprise needs. The process of defining both the needs and the constituent parts took less time than it could have because the scope of the project was determined by the *vision* of the Data Warehouse. The vision stopped any project creep at this point in the development process. This is not to say that the vision will not change over time. In fact, with World Furniture, if the initial design process outlined in the case study is a success, the vision will automatically change to incorporate more enterprise-wide needs.

The Data Warehouse Manager, however, understood two more key points in the transformation of the Conceptual Data Warehouse to an Implemented Data Warehouse.

- If columns of data are not currently documented as being directly associated with the enterprise needs, they should not necessarily be ignored during the actual implementation phase. One of the most important parts of designing a Data Warehouse is to anticipate change (or additions). This is why it is essential to have the decisions about the contents of the Data Warehouse made by business users, not those involved with the technology aspects of the project. Any elements of information that are not necessarily needed immediately, but are expected to be needed in the future, should be included in the implementation of the physical warehouse.

- Knowing the sources of the data is important in designing the Data Warehouse, but understanding the data and how it relates to the enterprise needs is equally important. This point is the driving force behind the transformation process[7] that transforms data that is organized for the operational system into data that will address the enterprise needs from a decision support perspective.

10.5 Phase 3: The Data Warehouse Implementation

After the Conceptual Data Warehouse was built, the first step that the Data Warehouse Manager at World Furniture had to address was the definition of the source operational systems. This step had to be completed before the transformations could take place. For efficiency, the transformation of the data was designed to take place at the same time that the data from the source operational system was extracted. This timing helped to avoid unnecessary multiple reads of the data. However, each of the five operational tables that were currently required had to be defined first. These tables are itemized in the `whmeta.tables` file. Each of these tables is in DB2 format. Because World Furniture already had the SAS/ACCESS to DB2 product, SAS/ACCESS would be used.

Extraction of Data

The actual definitions of the five basic tables were as follows:

```
/* Definition for Sales table */
/* Stored in whmeta.db2cat as sales.source entry */

PROC SQL;
 CONNECT TO DB2(SSID=pos);
 CREATE VIEW whdata.sales AS
 SELECT * FROM CONNECTION TO DB2 AS
 (SELECT   employee_id,
           sales_$,
           sales_#,
           sales_date,
           stock_#
  FROM pos.sale)
  AS t1(emp_num, sale_amt, sale_num, sale_dt, stck_num);
 DISCONNECT FROM DB2;
QUIT;

/* Definition of Returns table */
/* Stored in whmeta.db2cat as returns.source entry */

PROC SQL;
 CONNECT TO DB2(SSID=pos);
 CREATE VIEW whdata.returns AS
```

---

[7] See Chapter 6.

```
SELECT * FROM CONNECTION TO DB2 AS
(SELECT  employee_id,
         return_$,
         return_#,
         return_date,
         stock_#
FROM pos.return)
AS t1(emp_num, ret_amt, ret_num, ret_dt, stck_num);
DISCONNECT FROM DB2;
QUIT;

/* Definition of Purchase Amount table */

/* Stored in whmeta.db2cat as pur_amt.source entry */

PROC SQL;
 CONNECT TO DB2(SSID=pur);
 CREATE VIEW whdata.pur_amt AS
 SELECT * FROM CONNECTION TO DB2 AS
 (SELECT  purchase_amount,
          stock_#,
          purchase_date
 FROM pur.amounts)
 AS t1(pur_amt, stck_num, pur_dt);
 DISCONNECT FROM DB2;
QUIT;

/* Definition of Inventory table */

/* Stored in whmeta.db2cat as invent.source entry */

PROC SQL;
 CONNECT TO DB2(SSID=inv);
 CREATE VIEW whdata.invent AS
 SELECT * FROM CONNECTION TO DB2 AS
 (SELECT  warehouse_#,
          stock_#,
          product_group
          FROM inv.invent)
 AS t1(stck_num, whse_num, prod_grp);
 DISCONNECT FROM DB2;
QUIT;

/* Definition of Payroll table */

/* Stored in whmeta.db2cat as salary.source entry */

PROC SQL;
 CONNECT TO DB2(SSID=hr);
 CREATE VIEW whdata.salary AS
 SELECT * FROM CONNECTION TO DB2 AS
 (SELECT  emp_id,
          emp_salary,
          store,
          month,
          department
          FROM hr.salary)
 AS t1(emp_num, emp_sal, store,date, dept);
 DISCONNECT FROM DB2;
QUIT;
```

Centralization of Metadata

The Data Warehouse Manager decided that she wanted all the code that extracted the data from the operational sources to actually be located on the same platform as the metadata. This platform was a Windows-based PC that had all the licensed SAS products loaded, including SAS/CONNECT. Each of these extracts would be considered a separate part of the warehouse process. The extract programs were separated for two reasons:

- The extract process for each operational source is not dependent upon any other extract process. This means that the extract processes are not required to be part of one program.
- As new enterprise needs are addressed, it may become necessary to extract data separately. The two enterprise needs being addressed required monthly data; future needs may require weekly or daily data to be loaded into the Warehouse. Therefore, each item should be treated in isolation.

These programs were stored in a SAS catalog in the same library in which the metadata is stored. The catalog was called PROGRAMS. This decision to use SOURCE entries in the SAS catalog was made because of the flexibility in the way they can be used by SAS. They would be easy to store and modify, as well as move between different hosts. If these different programs are stored as individual files, an explicit reference to each one is needed if they are to be moved around.

These five basic definitions (defined in the previous section, "Extraction of Data") extract data from the operational DB2 formats. (The techniques for extracting data from formats external to SAS are discussed in detail in Chapter 5.) These extracts are very generic. They do not specify anything but how the data is to be defined to SAS. In these cases, they are defined as SQL views. These views can then be used in whatever way the different parts of the Data Warehouse require. If each of these extracts had been written only to address the two enterprise needs, then it is unlikely that they will be scalable to other needs. This concept is directly in line with the use of the SAS/Warehouse Administrator, where each one of these definitions would be an Operational Data Definition (ODD).

At this point in the process, the enterprise needs have been converted to required columns of data from operational source systems. In the case of World Furniture, this was a fairly straightforward process. In many Data Warehousing processes, the data required to meet a specific business need might not be so easy to identify and extract. Many tables from a single operational system might be needed to create a single column of data for the warehouse. For instance, it is unlikely that the salary of an employee could be obtained from a single column in a single table. More likely, this salary would be made up of a number of different values, representing both wages and benefits. In other words, this salary more likely would be represented by the cost to the company of employing that person, which is very different from just the monthly salary.

World Furniture is also fortunate to have a purchase cost for each stock item readily available in the `pur.amounts` DB2 table. This purchase amount for an item of furniture would be a function of the amount paid to the manufacturer, the exchange rate at the time of purchase, the shipping costs, and the storage costs. Another example of the ease of data extraction is that the product group is available in the inventory DB2 table. In a normalized operational system, this value typically would be in its own table, along with the stock number.

Use Operational System's Definitions whenever Possible

Having the operational systems define and calculate columns has benefits to the Data Warehouse:

> The Data Warehouse will avoid the responsibility of having to calculate this value. It would still be necessary, however, to document the business rules contained within the operational systems so that the users of the warehouse would understand fully what they were actually using.

- The Data Warehouse will always tie back to the operational sources. This is a great benefit because operational and warehouse reports will correspond to each other.

The storage of programs needed for Data Warehouse is quite an important decision. It is essential to break each of the programs up into components. It would not, for example, be advisable to store the code to create each of the SQL views in one physical location. At the same time, the programs should be grouped into logical sets. In the case of World Furniture, the programs would be stored in different SAS catalogs. For example, all the programs needed to access remote DB2 data would be stored in a DB2-related SAS catalog, all the programs needed to transform the sales data would be stored in a *Sales* related catalog, and so on. There is no right or wrong way to determine how many catalogs to use or how they should be organized. The number of catalogs and their organization should help minimize the number of explicit references to physical files.

> One of the confusing aspects of building a new Data Warehouse is that the initial code will be designed to extract multiple time periods (maybe the previous 36 months). This code, however, will only be needed once. The Data Warehouse update code will then be required for the periodic refreshes and updates. These two different sets of code are related but are not

necessarily similar. For example, if the historical data is no longer stored as part of the operational system, it is possible that it should be retrieved from a series of flat files on a tape. The extraction code in this case will be different than the periodic refresh code that might extract the data from a relational database.

In this situation, it is important that the initial load code be treated almost as if it were disposable. If a metadata tool (like the SAS/ Warehouse Administrator) is being used, registering all the initial load code as elements might be a waste of resources. Perform the initial extract as an isolated project, and concentrate on the periodic update code as part of the Data Warehouse process.

10.6 The Modeling of the Data

Now that the operational sources, tables and columns have been recognized and code has been created to perform the extracts, it is no longer possible to ignore how the data should be organized within the physical Data Warehouse. The transformation of the data is to some degree dependent upon how the information is to be organized, both in terms of the actual changes that will be made to the information and the timing of these changes.

Model the Data to Reflect the Enterprise Needs Being Addressed

To determine the model of the Data Warehouse, the manager returned after again to the enterprise users. She realized the one point that distinguishes an excellent Data Warehouse from a merely adequate one: the data should be organized to directly meet the needs. She wanted a pattern that would allow for the creation of a more generic base of detail data, with specific summary data created as needed. She also realized that it might be necessary in some cases to organize the detail differently in order to meet different enterprise needs. She understood that this apparent redundancy[8] might be necessary if the Data Warehouse was to meet the enterprise needs for which it was created.

This process of modeling the data could have been performed during the earlier discussions with the departments on the columns of data that are required to meet each need. It is always advantageous, however, to revisit requirements as often as possible. Expanding in the amount of information known could result in a change to the needs. No attempt

---

[8] See Chapter 3, Section 3.3 for a discussion on data redundancy and the Data Warehouse.

should be made to freeze the needs because this will lead to a data warehouse that will not suit specific purposes.

The Data Warehouse Manager did not want to leave anything to chance. Only two business requirements were selected:

- Analysis of Sales Compensation
- Sales Forecasting

The Data Warehouse Manager wanted to make sure that both needs would be satisfied. Together with the business departments concerned (Purchasing and Marketing), she looked at the ways in which the different needs would require the data. Her evaluations are discussed in the following sections.

Enterprise Need: Analysis of Sales Compensation

This analysis should be designed to determine the impact of placing sales people on a commission. To do this, any analysis has to be performed on an employee level. The really important aspect of the analysis is to find out how each store will be affected by the change in salary structure of its employees.Therefore, the following hierarchies of data will be needed:

STORE	DATE	PRODUCT
Store	Year	Product Group
Department	Month	Stock item
Employee	Day	

TABLE 10.12

There are three different hierarchies of information that are required called *store, date,* and *product.* The final data will have to be created so that the analysts can access the information easily across any of the hierarchies. In addition to these dimensions,[9] the key facts that need to be analyzed are sales, returns, and purchase amount. There is no real reason why there would be an analysis on the transaction level for each purchase, but there might be reason for the analyst to need to access this data for purely informational purposes.

Enterprise Need: Sales Forecasting

The need to anticipate future sales was driven by the purchasing function. Although it could have an associated benefit of increasing sales, the main

---

[9] See Chapter 3, Section 3.5 for a discussion on formulating dimensions for a Data Warehouse. This topic is also addressed in Chapter 4, which discusses the SAS/MDDB (Multi-Dimensional Data Base) and how it can be used to impact the model of a Data Warehouse.

issue is to reduce unnecessary purchases (that lead to an increase in stock in the discount stores) and ensure that stock is available to meet demand. The Data Warehouse Manager realized the importance of really understanding the driving force behind the enterprise need. There are subtle, but important, differences in analyses to increase sales and to improve purchasing patterns.

The breakdown into dimensions was as follows:

STORE	DATE	PRODUCT
Warehouse	Year	Product Group
Store	Month	Stock Item
	Day	

TABLE 10.13

To forecast the sales, by any of the crossing from any of the dimensions in the above table, it is necessary for both **sales** and **returns** to be the facts that will be analyzed.

Creating the Model

The Data Warehouse Manager wanted simplicity to be a key driving force behind the design of the detail data in the warehouse. This was for two main reasons:

- The simpler the design, the more generic it will be. This means that as new enterprise needs are addressed, it is very likely that the current detail data structure can be used as the basis for the analyses.
- The simpler the design, the easier it will be to load and maintain.

The main reason these two enterprise requirements were selected in the first place was the commonality between them. Therefore, the first step is to create the way that the detail tables will look before any of the dimensions outlined above are incorporated. The business departments and the technology group decided upon the detail tables. (See Tables 10.14 and 10.15.) The detail tables should be denormalized[10] by default. If, at a later date, performance or other issues make this decision questionable, it would be possible to normalize the tables.

---

[10] See Chapter 3, Section 3.3 for a discussion on the implications of using normalized data within the Data Warehouse.

> ### *Normalization of Data in a Data Warehouse Does Not Necessarily Lead to an Optimal Data Design*
>
> This approach of having denormalized tables as the default goes against the predominant approach which is to have normalized tables by default. This is the predominant approach because of the incorporation of classic relational theory. There is no overwhelming reason why Data Warehouse data models should conform to this classic relational theory and therefore Data Warehouse models do not need to be encumbered by it. Fast sequential access to data is at the heart of a successful data model within a Data Warehousing environment, which points toward denormalization of data as the most efficient model, by reducing the number of complex joins.

An interesting discussion that occurred at this time in the model development was the approach that a `return` is also a `sale` and can be treated as such. A return is nothing more than a negative sale. This allows return amounts to be incorporated as a sales amounts, thus making the model easier to understand.

Creation of the Detail Tables

Two detail tables were decided upon, based on the five operational source tables:

Column Name	Description
emp_num	Unique employee id
amount	$ amount of sale/return by item
tran_num	Unique sale identifier
date	Date of sale/return
stck_num	Stock Number
pur_amt	Amount Stock cost by item
pur_dt	Date stock purchased
orig_whs	Originating Warehouse
store	Store where item sold
dept	Department of employee

TABLE 10.14 Sales Detail Table (whdata.sales)

Column Name	Description
Emp_num	Unique employee ID
Emp_sal	Employee Salary
Date	Date of salary record

TABLE 10.15 Payroll Detail Table (whdata.payroll)

The final organization of these two detail tables was not without much discussion and debate from both the technological and business users. The issues listed in the next section were discussed in detail before the final decision was made.

Deciding on the Data Model Requires Considered Discussion

- Some participants from the business departments wanted a single table, so that the employees' salaries were easily available. This would have meant physically joining `whdata.payroll` with `whdata.sales`. The major proponents of this design were the business users in the marketing department who were to responsible for the analysis of sales compensation. The final decision to keep that data separate was twofold:
  - The data was too sensitive to store with the rest of the sales information. Security at the table level is much easier to control than at the column level and this would make it desirable to keep any sensitive salary information in its own table.
  - The employees' salaries, although essential for the sales compensation project, were not likely to be a common piece of information required for other enterprise needs. The assessment was therefore made that the extra cost of the join between the two tables for the sales compensation project was justifiable.
- The technology representatives on the project argued that it was unnecessary to store the originating warehouse data for every single transaction. They argued that a third table was needed to cross-reference stock item and originating warehouse (as it was stored in the `inv.invent` table). After much discussion, this proposal was turned down because for World Furniture, the originating warehouse (and therefore port) was a key part of the way the business operates. It is likely that the originating warehouse would be key part of addressing many enterprise needs. The extra cost of storing the data on a transaction level would be more than made up for by the savings from the continual joins that would be necessary if the data were stored in a separate table.

The discussions outlined above are essential during the Data Warehousing process. If they do not take place, the design may not consider the overall needs of the enterprise. This approach can work in the short term, but does not usually lead to a scalable warehouse that will suit the needs of the enterprise over time.

The approach taken here by the Data Warehouse Manager is interesting for two reasons described below.

- **The data model should reflect the needs of the users**. Modeling of the data moved away from the technological group to the business users. This reinforces the underlying solidarity between the data warehouse process and the vision of the project: the process should be driven by the enterprise needs, not by technology.
- **The final look of the data is assessed before the design of the warehouse**. This approach is contrary to many data warehouse implementations that create the data and then expect the users to adapt their needs to the model of the detail data instead of vice-versa.

> *Note that much of the design of the Data Warehouse process has been completed, but not after has the question of where (on what host) the actual implemented warehouse will reside been addressed. Any code or design up to this point is completely platform independent. In other words, there has been no commitment to the hardware.*
>
> *In some Data Warehouse processes, it is impossible to avoid the hardware question. Even if it is addressed, however, this does not mean that the code should become platform specific. The entire warehouse design should be built around flexibility and lack of commitment to any single hardware platform.*

Again, note that the entire process so far has been designed to fall in line with the process that would be used if the SAS/Warehouse Administrator[11] were used. Elements have been defined that would be directly applicable to the Administrator. The elements are Operational Data Definitions and Detail Tables. Although some of the other aspects of the Administrator have not been directly discussed (the logical detail tables, or the subject areas), these would not be difficult to incorporate. All of the work performed up to this point would have to be done whether the SAS/Warehouse Administrator were to be used or not.

---

[11] See Chapter 9 for full details on the role of the SAS/Warehouse Administrator in the data warehousing process.

Involve the Business Users in the Modeling Process

The final detail tables were therefore designed and **approved** by the business users and the technology group. Any differences in opinion were discussed and resolved. The *vision* of the warehouse was the determining vote in any situation where the structure of the data was in question. The two detail tables were then created using the following code.[12] In each situation, each of the DB2 tables was extracted into a SAS format before the detail tables were created. This was done for efficiency and because the DB2 installation did not allow for tables to be joined across SSIDs. From a non-DB2 perspective, this means that DB2 was not configured to allow tables from different systems to be joined directly within DB2. Each one had to therefore be moved to a SAS format and then joined.

```
/* Extract the DB2 tables to a SAS format */
/* Code stored in whmeta.transfrm as sas_ext.source entry */

PROC SQL;
 CREATE TABLE sales(INDEX=(stck_num emp_num)) AS
 SELECT * FROM whmeta.sales;

 CREATE TABLE returns(INDEX=(stck_num emp_num)) AS
 SELECT * FROM whmeta.returns;

CREATE TABLE pur_amt(INDEX=(stck_num)) AS
 SELECT * FROM whmeta.pur_amt;

CREATE TABLE invent(INDEX=(stck_num)) AS
 SELECT * FROM whmeta.invent;

CREATE TABLE salary(INDEX=(emp_num)) AS
 SELECT * FROM whmeta.salary;

QUIT;

/* Create the whdata.sales Detail Table */
/* Stored in whmeta.transfrm as sales.source entry */

PROC SQL;
 CREATE TABLE whdata.sales AS
 SELECT  s.emp_num,
         s.sale_amt AS amount,
         s.sale_num AS tran_num,
         s.sale_dt AS date,
         s.stck_num,
         p.pur_amt,
         p.put_dt,
         i.whse_num as orig_whs,
         sa.store,
         sa.dept
```

---

[12] For this case study, it is assumed that the initial load of the Data Warehouse is similar to those that would be needed during refreshes. This assumption was made to ensure that the Data Warehousing process would not be disguised by overcomplicating the loading process.

```
    FROM    sales s,
            pur_amt p,
            invent i,
            salary sa
    WHERE   s.stck_num=i.stck_num
            AND s.stck_num=p.stck_num
            AND s.emp_num=sa.emp_num
            AND s.sale_num ne .
    UNION
    SELECT  r.emp_num,
            r.sale_amt AS amount,
            r.sale_num AS tran_num,
            r.sale_dt AS date,
            r.stck_num,
            p.pur_amt,
            p.pur_dt,
            i.whse_num as orig_whs,
            sa.store,
            sa.dept
    FROM    returns r,
            pur_amt p,
            invent i,
            salary sa
    WHERE   r.stck_num=i.stck_num
            AND r.stck_num=p.stck_num
            AND r.emp_num=sa.emp_num
            AND r.sale_num ne .
    ;
ALTER TABLE whdata.sales
 ADD year char(5)
 ADD month char(5) ;
UPDATE whdata.sales
 SET year=year(date)
 SET month=put(date,yymmd5.);
CREATE INDEX stck_num ON whdata.sales(stck_num);
CREATE INDEX emp_num ON whdata.sales(emp_num);
CREATE INDEX orig_whs ON whdata.sales(orig_whs);
CREATE INDEX date       ON whdata.sales(date);
QUIT;

/* Create the whdata.salary Detail Table */
/* Stored in whmeta.transfrm as salary.source entry */

PROC SQL;
 CREATE TABLE whdata.salary AS
 SELECT emp_num,
        emp_sal,
        date as month /* Note month in MM-YY format */
 FROM   salary s;
 CREATE INDEX emp_num ON whdata.salary(emp_num);
 CREATE INDEX date ON whdata.salary(month);
QUIT;
```

This above code is written using simple SQL, which might not be the most efficient way of creating the `whdata.sales` or `whdata.salary` data files. Using SAS, many different techniques could be employed to perform the same task. Finding the most efficient is a function of hardware, data size, and structure of data. The best way to find the most efficient technique for any situation is trial and error.

The code was stored in a new catalog `whmeta.transfrm` in source entries. The Data Warehouse Manager realized that early in a warehouse project, it is easy to keep track of all the different components of the process, but over time, keeping track of the components becomes far more complex. The earlier the metadata, code, and tables are logically organized, the easier it will make the process scalable.

> The model of the detail in the Data Warehouse is very loosely based around a denormalized star-schema model. This is the case in many Data Warehouse implementations. As an approach to looking at the business, the dimension/fact combination can be very useful. When it comes down to actual implementation, this approach has influence. World Furniture unknowingly used a very loose star-schema approach by looking at the dimensions that would be needed to satisfy each of the enterprise needs being addressed. They then used this as a basis to formulate the model for their detail data, but without ever going through a formal data modeling process.

Creation of the Summary Tables

The structure of the detail tables was decided upon to directly reflect the enterprise needs that were being addressed, along with any wider implications to World Furniture. The detail tables could not be designed with only the immediate enterprise needs in mind, because this would be shortsighted. At the same time, it is not always possible to anticipate all the future requirements. These detail tables were, therefore, very generic.

The next step was to model the final structure of the data that would be accessed to directly meet the two enterprise needs being addressed. Two main points were outlined during the discussions with the departments responsible for the enterprise needs:

- The detail data, which was at the sales transaction level, would be far too detailed, and therefore would require the analysts to perform more data summary than would be desirable.
- Simple summary tables would meet most of the needs; however, to provide the flexibility needed to navigate the data, a multi-dimensional structure would be preferable.

Ensure the Summary Tables Specifically Meet the Needs of the Enterprise

Given these two points, it was decided that both needs would be addressed on a summary level by using the SAS/MDDB and the detail data as input.[13] Indeed most of the design work had already been completed, with the dimensions of the data already known to the warehouse manager. (See tables 10.12 and 10.13.) Based upon the design work already completed, two multi-dimensional tables were designed. The code for these tables was stored in two more SAS catalogs. The reason for the extra catalogs is that this part of the design is absolutely specific to the enterprise needs. A new SAS catalog was therefore created in the `whmeta` SAS library to contain enterprise need specific information.

```
/* Code to create MDDB for the Sales Compensation Project */
/* Stored in SAS catalog whmeta.slsecomp as mddb.source entry */
/* Create MDDB */

PROC MDDB DATA=sales OUT=whdata.salesmdb(label='Sales Compensation MDDB');
 CLASS date year month store dept emp_id stck_num prod_grp;
 VAR amount / sum;
 HIERARCHY store dept emp_id / DISPLAY=YES NAME='Store Drill';
 HIERARCHY year month date / DISPLAY=YES NAME='Date Drill';
 HIERARCHY prod_gp stck_num /DISPLAY=YES NAME='Product Drill';
RUN;

/* Code to create MDDB for the Sales Forecasting Project */
/* Stored in SAS catalog whmeta.slsefore as mddb.source entry */


/* Create Data Step View with merge of Sales and Salary tables */

DATA forecast / VIEW=forecast;
 MERGE whdata.sales whdata.salary;
 BY emp_id month;
RUN;


/* Create MDDB */

PROC MDDB DATA=forecast OUT=whdata.foremdb(label='Sales @code:Forecasting
MDDB');
 CLASS orig_whs store date year month stck_num prod_grp;
 VAR amount / sum;
 HIERARCHY orig_whs store / DISPLAY=YES NAME='Warehouse Drill';
 HIERARCHY year month date / DISPLAY=YES NAME='Date Drill';
 HIERARCHY prod_gp stck_num /DISPLAY=YES NAME='Product Drill';
RUN;
```

The summary tables were designed with just the individual enterprise needs in mind. They could be described as data marts, but the distinction

---

[13] See Chapter 4 for the details of creating a multi-dimensional database using the SAS/MDDB product, and how it can fit into the data warehousing process.

would be purely academic. As far as the Data Warehouse process is concerned, the creation of these summary files is just another step. The distinction between the Data Warehouse and the data marts does not matter, because they are part of the same process. If separate data mart processes were created outside of processes used to design the Data Warehouse, then this would be an important distinction. This would also be more risky, because summary data is dependent upon the detail (in most cases) and being part of the same process makes more sense.

World Furniture, at this stage, has developed the model of it's Data Warehouse. Other steps are needed to complete the process. World Furniture has taken a full refresh strategy at this time to create its Data Warehouse. It is likely that this will change as the amount of data increases. It would mean that modification would be needed to the extract programs, and the creation of the MDDBs. The extract programs would contain logic that would incorporate only data that had changed because the previous refresh. It is likely that the MDDBs would not be fully created from the detail data every refresh cycle, but using the drip feed[14] approach, which means that it would not be recalculated except where new detail data was involved.

10.7 The Transformation Process

Much of the transformation process was automatically included in the modeling process. Modeling of the data, by its very nature of outlining the structure of the data, naturally incorporates much of the transformation process. Outlined in Chapter 6 are the stages of the transformation process:

- Data Validation
- Data Scrubbing
- Data Integration
- Data Derivation
- Data Denormalization
- Data Summarization
- Metadata Creation

Of these steps, only the first two, the validation and scrubbing of the data, have not been addressed by World Furniture. This is also a typical occurrence in the design of a Data Warehouse. Much of the transformation

---

[14] See the section, "MDDB within the Data Warehouse" in Chapter 4, Section 4.3. for a brief discussion on the *drip-feed* technique to updating SAS multi-dimensional data structures.

process occurs during the extraction process and is often logically addressed during this stage. For the Data Warehouse, because all of the above steps have been addressed already, only validation and scrubbing remained. As mentioned in Chapter 6, these two steps in the transformation process also tend to be merged together; if it is possible to scrub data as problems are found, the amount of overhead will be reduced.

Validation is Primarily a Business, not Technological Issue

While modeling the data, several questions were raised about the quality of data being created in the operation source systems. Both the marketing and purchasing departments were not convinced that all the data could be trusted, and they decided that they would be more comfortable if there were some form of validation in the process. They initially saw validation as being a technological issue. They thought that internal checks on the data could be made through building programs with minimal input from them. The Data Warehouse Manager had to explain that the way the data was to be validated should be based upon:

- Business rules that would allow for data to be *flagged* based upon some form of expectation. For example, an item of furniture could not be returned before it was sold, or items with similar stock numbers could not originate from different warehouses.
- Internal inconsistencies in the data. For example, a single style of furniture should not vary much in its sale price either across stores or within a store.

Validation and Scrubbing of the Data

The basis for the validation and what should be done with invalid data became a responsibility of the business departments. They were given the task of creating a list of validations that would make them comfortable with the quality of the data.

The process for the validation and scrubbing of the data was determined by the Data Warehouse Manager. All validation would take place on the `whdata.sales` detail data table, after data were extracted from the source operational systems, but before any summary tables were created. Every refresh period (i.e. every month), the data would undergo a series of tests to ensure the validity of the data. The scrubbing of the data (the changes that were made based upon the validation) was to be performed on the same table. The warehouse manager realized the implications of doing this:

- The possibility that the Data Warehouse would not match with the operational systems.

- The potential problem of the source data being updated after the fact and therefore not being in line with the Data Warehouse.

One of the most difficult Data Warehousing issues that has to be addressed is what the relationship between the operational systems and the Data Warehouse should be.[15] In most cases, it is not possible to update source systems due to problems found in the Data Warehouse. If this were so, then after the updates were made, a new reload would have to occur. If the changes are made to the Data Warehouse directly, auditing problems would appear, because it is unlikely that a record of all the changes made would be stored.

> *One of the misunderstandings about a Data Warehouse is that the data is frozen. In certain circumstances, this might be the case, but it should not be the rule (unless there are explicit reasons to do so). For instance, most companies undergo reorganizations periodically. The historical data stored in the Data Warehouse should reflect the current organization of the company. This means that the Data Warehouse would have to be restructured to allow for any changes to the organization of the company.*
>
> *Beware of operational systems that claim also to be Data Warehouses. Due to their very nature, they are not afforded the liberty of restructuring historical data based upon current organization.*

Consider Carefully Where the Scrubbing of Data Should Take Place

World Furniture made some decisions about the scrubbing of the data based upon consultation between the business departments and the CEO:

- Data would be scrubbed before the final load into the Data Warehouse. The CEO decided that the purpose of the Data Warehouse was as an analytical source of data, rather than as an operational reporting tool. This meant that the users of the Data Warehouse had to be aware that an absolute match to the operational systems would not be present.
- Going forward, the Data Warehouse would be refreshed on a 'changed data capture'[16] basis. This would require that only the data that had changed because the last update would be incorporated. The main data source for the current Data Warehouse implimentation was the point-of-sale system, which held sales data on a transaction level. Changed data

---

[15] This topic is discussed in detail in Chapter 6, Section 6.3.
[16] See the section, "SAS Software and the Transformation Process," in Chapter 6, Section 6.1.

would be relatively easy to find, because each record in the `pos.sale` DB2 table are time-stamped for their last update.

It was decided that validation and scrubbing of the data would be broken down by column in the detail tables. Every column that was validated would be a separate piece of code that would be stored independently of other validatation tests. A separate SAS catalog would be created for each of the detail tables to handle all the validation code. This organization helped avoid long programs that would, over time, require a great deal of maintenance. The Data Warehouse Manager realized that compartmentalizing validations by column would not, in itself, reduce maintenance; however, if the rules of validation for a specific column were needed, they would be easily accessible in a SAS catalog entry, rather than hidden in a long program. Storing these rules and their associated code as separate SAS catalog entries requires very careful control of naming conventions.

Consider Each Validation Technique Carefully Before Making Final Decisions

To do this, each column in the detail tables was considered by the business departments, who decided from a business perspective how they should be validated. To help in the process of defining different validations, the four major validation techniques were explained to the business users:[17]

- Exploratory Validation
- Finite Validation
- Derived Validation
- Statistical Validation

The business groups put together quite an extensive list of options with the help of the SAS programmers associated with the project. The following are some examples of the validation tests that were created.

```
/* CHECK ON THE AMOUNT FIELD BASED ON THE STOCK NUMBER */

PROC FORMAT LIBRARY=library;
  VALUE amt_grp;
  0-50 = '0-50'
  50.01-100='50-100'
  100.01-150='100-150'
  150.01-200='150-200'
  OTHER='Other';
RUN;

PROC FREQ DATA=whdata.sales;
  TABLES stck_num * amount;
```

---

[17] See Chapter 6, Section 6.2 for a full explanation of these four techniques.

```
FORMAT amount amt_grp.;
 WHERE amount > 0;
RUN;
```

The above code performs a form of *exploratory validation* that is using a format (**amt_grp**) to logically group the amount of sales for each item and the amount the item cost to purchase. The actual breakdown of these groups is not very important. What is important is that similar items should fall within the same groupings. For example, if a chair with a stock number of 676767 is sold, and its price is in more than one of the groups, then there is a possibility that the data has a problem. An individual stock item should only fall within one, or at the most, two groups categorized by the **amt_grp** format.

```
/* CHECK ON THE ORIG_WHS COLUMN */

PROC FORMAT LIBRARY=library;
 VALUE whse
 1='SEATTLE'
 2='LOS ANGELES'
 3='MIAMI'
 4='NEW YORK'
 5='NEW ORLEANS'
 OTHER='UNKNOWN'
RUN;

DATA bad_whs;
 SET whdata.sales;
 IF PUT(orig_whs,whse.)='UNKNOWN'
 ;
 RUN;
```

The above code performs *finite validation* check, to ensure that the warehouse number is valid. This is a very simple test using PROC FORMAT. As outlined in Chapter 6, there are many ways to perform this same test.

```
/* CHECK ON THE STCK_NUM COLUMN */

DATA stck_prb;
 SET whdata.sales;
 IF stck_num IN: ( 56 97 24) AND orig_whs NOT IN(2 4);
RUN;
```

This code performs a *derived validation* where a stock number will be included in the **stck_prb** temporary data file if it begins with either 56, 97 or 24 and does not have an originating warehouse of Los Angeles or New York. This in fact, checks the business rule that a stock number that begins with 56, 97 or 24, has to be imported into either Los Angeles or New York.

Keys to Successfully Validating Data

The key to successfully validating data within the Data Warehouse is threefold:

- Efficiently performing the validations with the minimum number of reads of the data. For example, the second and third of the three examples above could be combined into one DATA step to avoid multiple reads of the data.
- Having a process in place to handle the validation output/analysis.
- Having a process in place to handle scrubbing the data after the validation is completed.

The scrubbing of the data was to be performed on an organized ad-hoc basis. This meant that after the validations were analyzed, either programs would be written (if there were a pattern to the invalid data), or the file would be updated directly (for specific or minor changes). The Data Warehouse Manager understood that the process for the validation and scrubbing of the data would not stay constant from month to month. This meant that it was important to ensure that there was a check in the process to ensure that the scrubbing was complete before the data was loaded into the warehouse. This check took the form of human, rather than technological intervention. The loading of the warehouse could only be performed each month after each department involved in the project signed that their particular part was complete.

By involving each of the departments in every part of the process, the warehouse manager ensured that there was a continuing commitment from the business departments. One important piece of the warehousing process is to ensure that the business departments always stay involved. They should be continually encouraged to add more needs to the Conceptual Warehouse. They should go through the process of analyzing the enterprise needs and their constituent business rules and elements so that they can be incorporated into the Implemented Warehouse when the resources allow. As the World Furniture Data Warehouse Manager realized, it is not always possible during the transformation process to exclude the business departments. In fact, it is necessary to build a process to deal with the transformation rules, and the way that incorrect data should be handled. This is principally a business, as opposed to technologically-based set of decisions. Two broad groups of decisions have to be made:

- What the actual changes should be. This will be based upon business rules and knowledge, laid down by the business departments. There will always be more situations that have to be handled, so the process to handle this must be based on the same cycle that upon which the warehouse is refreshed.

- Where the changes should be made. This set of decisions is based upon both a business and technological basis. This is because the business basis might request for the changes to be made where it is not, from a technological perspective, possible (e.g. in the operational source system). It is the role of the technological participants to work with the business groups to find a mutually agreeable decision.

10.8 Client/Server Considerations

World Furniture has three principal computer platforms upon which the company works:

- Mainframe (OS/390)
- UNIX
- Windows

Although in the design of the Data Warehouse process, the operational source data was defined, as was the detail and summary data, no mention was made of where processing should take place, and therefore how the data should be moved. One of the key decisions that was made by the CEO early in the project was that there would be no purchases of hardware, therefore the Client/Server options had to be based upon existing computers. There are several factors that the data manager considered in the decision:

- The amount of spare capacity on each machine.
  - Processing (cpu) capacity
  - Data storage (disk) capacity
  - Data accessibility (Input/Output) capacity
- The networking capability between each machine
- The operational restrictions on each machine.

Balance Client/Server Decisions Against Potential Changes in Architecture

It was decided that only minimal work could be performed on the mainframe. This was because of its operational importance to the company and the lack of spare capacity. For this reason, only the extraction of data could take place on the mainframe. Any subsequent processing would be performed on other computers.

The Windows-based machines did not have the potential capacity, both in storage and processing terms to handle the amount of work that would be required. This left the UNIX platform, by default, as the main platform to handle the initial Data Warehousing requirements. Note that the Windows platform had already been assigned as the platform upon which the warehouse metadata would be stored.

A great deal has been written about hardware within the Data Warehousing process. In some projects, the warehouse designers have the resources to purchase hardware. Very often the important points are obscured behind the basic performance issue of each hardware option. The important points include the following:

- Purchasing the theoretically most powerful machine is less important in a situation where the Data Warehouse will be dependent upon a network to deliver the information. The entire architecture should be looked at in its entirety, rather than each isolated piece.
- As mentioned several times in this book, one of the keys to designing a successful Data Warehouse is to incorporate flexibility at every stage, because the Data Warehouse needs to be able to change. Decisions about the hardware configuration should reflect this approach. Whatever hardware is selected, it may be outgrown in a fairly short period of time. It is therefore important to ensure that the hardware can be upgraded. Because hardware may change, it is essential for every step in the warehousing process to be designed so that it is platform independent (as much as possible).

After discussions with the computer systems department, it was decided that in the short term, there was spare capacity on the UNIX computer in the headquarters in Los Angeles. It was also understood that this computer would not be a long-term solution to the location of the Data Warehouse, but would be an effective way to really understand what the needs will be. The Data Warehouse Manager didn't mind at all that there was not a dedicated computer. The design of the process, including the extraction and transformation of the data was already platform independent and could be readily changed to run on virtually any computer.

Benchmarking the Data Warehouse is not as straight-forward as with an operational system. The underlying reason for this is that it is not always possible to emulate the real load and variety of usage that the computer will undergo. It is possible to take typical activities and run these as multiple concurrent processes. This will give an idea of the performance that can be expected, predicting the usage of a system (the Data Warehouse) that will be undergoing constant change, is very difficult to do. It is therefore better to perform benchmarking using typical activities and assume that the selection of hardware will not be sufficient in the long-term. It is very important, therefore, to thoroughly understand what the next upgrade will be at the time the initial computer is selected.

World Furniture was very sensible in their approach to hardware. They did not spend a great deal of money at the start of the project, but waited until they were in a position to more thoroughly understand the usage patterns before committing to expenditure on hardware. The rule of thumb is to use the *'just-in-time'* concept to purchasing hardware. Only purchase hardware at the last possible moment, so that the most up-to-date changes have been made to the Data Warehouse and the new hardware will therefore reflect the most recent warehouse needs.

The World Furniture Data Warehouse needed a Client/Server configuration because the source operational data was not located on the same computer as the Data Warehouse. The configuration is shown in Figure 10.2.

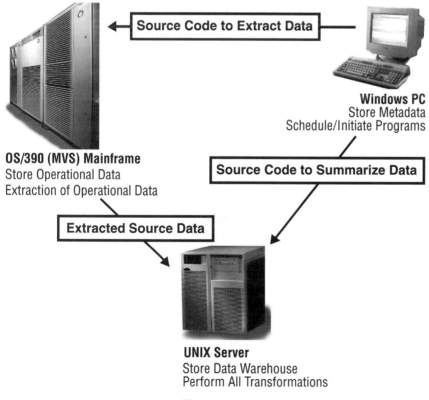

Figure 10.2

Keep Client/Server Decisions as Simple and Flexible as Possible

The basis of the Client/Server strategy was to keep it as simple as possible. The arrangement shown in Figure 10.2 keeps all the metadata (including the code required to create each part of the Data Warehouse) on one computer (the Windows PC). The relevant code is then moved to the mainframe whenever the extraction of data needs to take place. This code includes the connection from the mainframe to the UNIX Server and the upload of the extracted source data.

> The arrangement shown in Figure 10.2 can be easily performed using the SAS/Warehouse Administrator. This is thoroughly explained in Chapter 9. In Figure 10.2, the Warehouse Administrator will be located on the Windows PC. The only part of the above configuration that is not absolutely apparent in the set-up of the metadata would be the movement of the extracted source data to the UNIX Server. The source data is moved by using nested connections. This would be performed by the code that actually extracts the data, which would include a section that would connect to the UNIX server and perform the upload. The other alternative would be to download the extracted information to the PC and then connect from the PC to the UNIX Server and perform an upload to the server.[18]

To complete the configuration in Figure 10.2, SAS/CONNECT was needed on each of the three platforms. On the mainframe, base SAS software and SAS/ACCESS to DB2 was also required.

The configuration shown in Figure 10.2 is really for the exploitation of the Data Warehouse. One additional consideration for this client/server configuration would be determining what would happen to the summary data after it had been created on the UNIX Server. The World Furniture Data Warehouse Manager realized that the implementation of the warehouse, and the exploitation are two different processes, requiring different software (although possibly overlapping software) and entirely different needs. The World Furniture implementation of a Data Warehouse was based on a model where the data was made ready within the warehousing process, but the final exploitation was the responsibility of the buiness departments themselves. For this reason, the exploitation of the Data Warehouse was

---

[18] The techniques and implications of connecting and moving data from computer to computer using SAS software is fully discussed in Chapter 8. The process of using SAS/CONNECT can be fully automated so that the entire Data Warehouse refresh or creation can be initiated from one computer (in this case, the Windows PC).

based upon multiple PCs running SAS under Windows to access the UNIX Server, using SAS/CONNECT.

Train the Users to Exploit the Data Warehouse

One of the main parts of the design of the Data Warehousing process for World Furniture was the realization that the judgement as to the success of the project would not be based upon the actual creation of the Data Warehouse, but on the ability for it to be used. This ability not only was based upon the users being given easy access to the data, but also was based on their having the necessary skill required to do something with that data. For this reason, while the Data Warehouse was being designed, the users were being trained in the use of SAS software within their own environment. For the World Furniture business users, the data would be in a summarized form that suited their particular needs, with the ability to view the detail if necessary. The concept of using the multi-dimensional model works very well in this situation because of the inherent reach-through abilities of the SAS/MDDB product.[19]

At some point in the design of a Data Warehouse, it will necessary to address the actual use of the data. Some Data Warehouse implementations hide the end-users from the structure of the data through the creation of front ends. This is a perfectly valid way to implement a Data Warehouse, but resources would be needed to build and maintain the front-end applications. Alternatively, the access and exploitation of data can be less structured, by allowing users to use non-customized tools. In either case, training is needed. This training *is not* a one-time event, but a continuing process that should match the development of the warehouse itself. As with all training, little benefit results unless the new skills can be used immediately. This means that the timing of the training is of paramount importance.

The particular client/server model that World Furniture selected was dictated by three main factors:

- **External factors which included the external restrictions imposed by the CEO and the needs of the operational systems.** In the case of the former, it meant that the Data Warehouse could only operate on existing systems. The latter restricted the Data Warehouse Client/Server configuration by dictating that there was little capacity on the mainframe.

---

[19] Reach-through allows the user to request the detail data that makes up the particular view of the multi-dimensional structure. This is discussed in the section, "MDDB within the Data Warehousing," in Chapter 4, Section 4.3.

- **The need to stay simple.** A complex Client/Server configuration would mean that the control of the architecture would require more resources. The more complex the configuration, the more pieces would have to be both developed and maintained.
- **The need for change.** In the very short term, the World Furniture Data Warehouse was limited to addressing very few enterprise needs (only two). In the longer term, there was a good chance that due to additional scope, it would be necessary to add extra pieces to the Client/Server configuration. Because of this, the entire process had to allow for easy adaptation in a very short period of time, with the least amount of resources. The Client/Server configuration was platform independent as far as possible. With the addition of a new server, for example, all that would need to change would be the actual connection between the computers. This change would not affect the code itself.

10.9 Loading the Data Warehouse

There were two different circumstances that the Data Warehouse Manager had to deal with in the loading process. The first of these was an initial load, and the second was the periodic refreshes. Each situation involves a slightly different process, although to a large degree they overlap.

The distinction between the intial and subsequent loads is very important. The initial load typically *does not* extract data from the same source as subsequent loads. For example, in the case of World Furniture, if 36 months of data were required within the Data Warehouse, it is highly unlikely that this data would still be in the point-of-sale system. It is more likely that the data would reside on some other medium than disk (usually tape) and will not still be in a similar format to the data that resides on the opertional system. Typically, an extract is made from the operational systems, which is stored in a *flat-file* format. This is what would be accessed to initially load the Data Warehouse. It normally bears little resemblance to the structure of the periodic load. This means that it is necessary to create the *one-off* code to initially load the warehouse separately from the periodic load. It is generally not worth spending the time to incorporate the initial load code into a fully-formed system, because it is generally disposable.

The initial load of the World Furniture Data Warehouse was performed against historical data. The programs were run *manually* on the mainframe. They were run manually as opposed to being part of the general Data Warehouse process. The Data Warehouse Manager decided upon this approach for two reasons:

- It would have been a waste of resources to set up the initial load within a system.
- Because this was the initial load, the process would have to be monitored very carefully. This monitoring would ensure that the transformation process was working correctly.

No matter how much planning goes into the Data Warehouse process, the data will always hold surprises. Try to capture as many surprises as possible early on in the process. The initial load is a good time for this. Involve as many people as possible in this process. Each column of data needs to be explored thoroughly to test the assumptions that have been made. Each of the transformations should be tested to ensure that they are valid and are going to produce what is wanted to meet the business needs it will address. This is why it is necessary to breakdown each enterprise need into its corresponding columns of data. The needs that each of the columns of data will meet through the data files is stored in the metadata and illustrated in Tables 10:9 through 10.11.

The World Furniture initial load is comprised of the historical data, in addition to any data that still existed in the operational systems. It was decided that any data that was still stored in the operational systems would be used, even if it was also stored in on the historical files. For instance, the point-of-sale operational system kept twelve months of data, but each full month was stored on tape. All of these twelve months were extracted from the live operational data rather than the historical backup, in order to test the efficiency of the extraction process.

After the data was extracted, the transformation process was initiated. The Data Warehouse Manager realized that this initial load would require an extended transformation process for several reasons:

- The volume of data.
- The adjustments to the process that would be needed due to unexpected data.
- Little experience with the process which meant that the process would take longer than usual.

She realized, however, that this part of the process was very important and could not be rushed. If problems were not discovered and solved at this stage, they could spill over into the Data Warehouse in the long term. Every resource the manager could find was used at this stage to address the performance of the extracts, the data itself, and the transformations. Time was put aside to make changes to the transformations so that subsequent loads would be as smooth and account for as many quirks as possible.

This is a difficult phase of the Data Warehouse process because it is not typical of the usual extraction process. There is no formula to make it a success except to ensure that both business and technical departments are involved as much as possible. The success of this process, however, will go a long way to ensure that future extractions and loadings will occur with minimal work. It is therefore worthwhile to spend as many resources as possible upon this part of the process.

After the transformation of the data was complete, the summary data was created. In this creation of summary data, further metadata was created. SAS formats[20] were created for key columns of data, and other information like minimum and maximum values for all the numeric columns were obtained. The needs at this stage of the Data Warehouse development were fairly rudimentary but would be developed as the warehouse needs expanded.

10.10 World Furniture Data Warehouse: Summary

After loading the Data Warehouse, the users were in a position to utilize the data. This was done by connecting from their Windows-based PCs to the UNIX server. Although the users were sophisticated analysts, the training they obtained in efficiently using SAS software to analyze data located on different computers came into use. They used the UNIX server to perform most of the data manipulation and analysis, and their PCs for smaller analysis and presentation of results. The two main factors for the successful use of the information contained within the Data Warehouse were as follows:

■ The data was organized to suit their needs, which meant that they could spend their time analyzing the business.
■ The users were trained to use the information in the Data Warehouse. The users were trained in the specifics of the Data Warehouse and how to access the data. Users did not attend generic technical training to teach them how to use a software product (although this might also be desirable). Usually, generic training alone does not suffice. Knowing how to use a product does not necessarily lead to successfully accessing and analyzing data contained within a Data Warehouse.

---

[20] See the section, "Finite Validation," in Chapter 6, Section 6.2 for a outline of the format procedure.

At this stage, the Data Warehousing process for World Furniture was developed. The first extraction and creation of summary data was completed and was ready for the users to fulfill their needs. This does not mean that the Data Warehouse is complete. Indeed there are two ways that it will develop from this point:

- **The scope will expand.** The scope of the Data Warehouse is defined as the number of defined enterprise needs that it addresses. As the scope increases, the number of external file definitions will increase as more data is required. This means that the volume of data within the warehouse will increase, leading to new problems (possibly those associated with very large databases).[21]
- **The process itself will develop.** The process for creating the Data Warehouse will not remain static. The first attempt at defining a process will probably not result in an ideal process. The process will have to be developed because it does not meet the needs of either the business or technological groups involved. Nothing is wrong with the process changing. What is more damaging is a process that does not change with the needs. This will lead to a Data Warehouse that is out of step with the enterprise it is meant to be serving.

10.11 The SAS/Warehouse Administrator and World Furniture

The case study outlined in the previous sections illustrates the flow (the process) of a Data Warehousing project, rather than how each particular item or element in the process should be constructed or programmed. Every Data Warehousing project will need a process to act as the underpinning for the creation of each of the corresponding parts. While the processes used to develop different Data Warehouses may be similar, the actual elements involved in the projects may be very different. The SAS/Warehouse Administrator can be used to help formalize the process of the implementation of a Data Warehouse. It views the implementation of a Data Warehouse as a combination of elements (definitions of operational source systems, definitions of detail tables, etc.) and a series of processes that pull those elements together.

World Furniture could have used the SAS/Warehouse Administrator either during the initial phase of their Data Warehousing project or after the intial phase was completed. Because the company did not already have the

---

[21] See the section, "Installing SAS/ACCESS," in Chapter 5, Section 5.3 for details on the SAS Scalable Performance Data Server that can be used to handle large data in a SAS environment.

Special Topic:
How do I know if my Data Warehouse is Successful?

Measuring the success of a Data Warehouse is very difficult. There are no real standard measures. The methodology contained within this book does allow for a basic measure of success. This measure can be adapted by any enterprise to more readily suit their purposes.

To measure the success of the Data Warehouse, it is necessary to rank (or weight) the importance of each of the enterprise needs that must be addressed. The following set of factors will make up the success measure of the Data Warehouse:

1. The sum of the ranked (or weighted) enterprise needs.
2. The sum of the ranked (or weighted) enterprise needs actually addressed.
3. The average amount of time spent accessing or manipulating data as a percentage of the total amount of time spent using the Data Warehouse.
4. The average amount of time spent analyzing or reporting on the data as a percentage of the total amount of time spent using the Data Warehouse.

Example:

In the case of World Furniture, there were only four enterprise needs documented. Assume that each of these were ranked 1 to 4 in importance. The following parameters would be parts of the algorithm:

1. 10 (the sum of the ranks of the four needs .... 1,2,3,4 where 1 is most important).
2. 3 (The sum of the ranks of the needs addressed .... 1,2).
3. .3 (The users spend 30% of their time accessing and manipulating the data.)
4. .7 (The users spend 70% of their time analyzing and reporting upon the data.)

The measure of success is based upon a completely successful Data Warehouse being 100%, and is therefore:

$(1-(.3/1.0) * .7) *100 = 49\%$

This measure is based on the enterprise needs being fully defined. This is not always possible, so the measure of success will be more accurately defined as the success of the Data Warehouse based upon documented needs. The rankings of these needs could be categorized (e.g. 1=very important, 2=important, etc.)

This measure is, of course, a rough guide, and not a thoroughly scientific measure. However, as an indicator, this measure could be very revealing. To gauge the average amount of time that users spend using (a good thing) as opposed to accessing (a bad thing) could be difficult to do. Remember, however, that this measure is an indication of the success of the Data Warehouse, rather than a definitive statistic. The indicator is useful, however, because it is sensitive to both the scope of the Data Warehouse (that is, as new enterprise needs are discovered and documented, the success will fall) and the effectiveness of the model (that is, as users are able to spend more time analyzing rather than accessing data the indicator will improve).

The ideal situation would be where every single enterprise need is addressed and that the users spend all of their time analyzing rather than accessing data. In this case, the indicator will be 100%. This situation is very unlikely to happen for two reasons: the changing nature of business will cause new enterprise needs to be continually produced, and a successful Data Warehouse will raise as many questions as it solves, thereby automatically increasing its own scope.

One other option to include in the above algorithm could be ROI (Return on Investment). This measure is hard to calculate since it involves both an understanding of the costs involved in the entire warehouse process. Very often, these costs are only considered from a pure I.S. (Information Systems) standpoint. This means that only costs directly attributable to I.S. are considered. The benefits to the entire business are hard to gauge since there is little real assessment on the impact of the Data Warehouse. In the model described in this book, it will be easier to assess benefits, since every need that the Data Warehouse will be documented. It will then be far easier to put a monetary value on each of the addressed needs, leading to an overall figure on the benefit to the enterprise of owning the Data Warehouse.

Warehouse Administrator available and the company CEO did not want any additional software purchased before the Data Warehouse proved itself as a viable proposition, the process was fully developed without the aid of specific metadata tools. Some metadata was created to store data about the enterprise needs and the columns of information that would be created from the operational source systems. Although the way that the metadata, the code and the data stored was very organized, no management tools were involved in the process. In a situation where a Data Warehouse or a Data Warehouse process becomes very large and complex, the management of the extraction and transformation of data can become very difficult without the availability of a tool like the Warehouse Administrator. In the case study outlined in this chapter, the need for a management tool was not absolutely necessary. However, if this Data Warehouse grew, control over the process would become increasingly difficult, even though the organization of the project contents was well constructed.

How Could World Furniture Have Used the SAS/Warehouse Administrator?

As outlined in detail in Chapter 9, the Warehouse Administrator is not a **design** but an **implementation** product.[22] World Furniture could have used the Warehouse Administrator after the all of the following had been completed:

- The definition of the enterprise needs
- The mapping of enterprise needs to business elements
- The mapping of business elements to operation systems, tables, and columns
- The modeling of the Data Warehouse

At this point, the elements of the Data Warehouse could be defined to the Warehouse Administrator. Chapter 9 outlines the process to utilize the Warehouse Administrator within a Data Warehousing project. Each of these steps is referenced below followed by how World Furniture could have incorporated their own process.

Defining Data Warehouse Elements to the Warehouse Administrator

Creation of a Data Warehouse Environment

A single Data Warehouse Environment would have been created for the entire World Furniture organization.

---

[22] See Chapter 9, Section 9.1 for an overview of how the SAS/Warehouse Administrator fits into the data warehousing process.

Creation of the Shared Metadata

The shared metadata that World Furniture would assign to the Warehouse Administrator would have included the following:

- The names of all the hosts (computers), including the mainframe, the UNIX Servers and the Windows-based PCs involved in the process. In all, there would have been seven hosts defined (one mainframe, five servers and one PC).
- The libraries involved in the process. These will have included the **whmeta** and **whdata** libraries that were used throughout the process.
- Information about the DB2 databases that were located on the mainframes and the servers. This would loosely be correlated with the entries in the **whmeta systems** file. (See Table 10.7.)
- The contacts included in the **whmeta contacts** data file. (See Table 10.3.)

The Warehouse Administrator does not require that all this information be added ahead of time. Optionally, it can be entered as it is addressed during the creation of the actual Data Warehouse.

Creation of Operational Data Definitions

For World Furniture, the creation of Operational Data Definitions (ODDs) would have been a very simple because of the process that was used. The recognition of the relevant operation source systems and the component tables within each system was part of the process of addressing specific enterprise needs. This meant that the ODDs were already defined during the Transformation Phase of the Data Warehouse process.

ODDs that World Furniture would have defined to the Administrator would be all those that relate to the entries in the **whmeta tables** file. (See Table 10.8.) As more enterprise needs are addressed, additions will probably be made to the **whmeta tables** file. Every addition to this file would mean the creation of an additional ODD.

World Furniture had several options available to them about how to group the ODDs. The Warehouse Administrator requires that the ODDs be grouped into ODD groups. These ODD groups might have corresponded to the operational systems that contain each of the tables. This means that the ODD groups would correspond to the definitions of the database connections. This is not necessarily the way that an ODD group has to be constructed, but would make the World Furniture implementation more logical.

The ODDs that would be registered for World Furniture will already exist. They are stored as source entries in the SAS catalog **whmeta.db2cat**. (See the section "Extraction of Data" in Section 10.4 of this chapter.) The process World Furniture went through to define their process complements the use of the Warehouse Administrator.

Creation of a Data Warehouse

The Warehouse Administrator requires at least one Data Warehouse be defined for each Environment. World Furniture would only need one Data Warehouse for the Environment created above. This Data Warehouse would be the container for subjects, detail logical tables and logical tables.[23]

Creation of the Data Warehouse Subjects

The subjects that World Furniture would have in the Data Warehouse would be related to the enterprise needs to be addressed. The two enterprise needs are both related to sales. This means that it is sensible to have *sales* as a subject. Defining subjects can be a very difficult task, because different items of data could be used across subjects, but can only be physically stored as one. For this initial Data Warehouse implementation, World Furniture could have decided upon several subjects. For instance:

- *Personnel* could have been created using the data from the payroll operational system.
- *Inventory* could have been created using data from the inventory system.
- *Sales* could have been created using the data from the point-of-sale system.
- *Purchasing* could have been created using the data from the purchasing system.

The Warehouse Administrator allows detail data from different subjects to be cross-referenced, so there is no real disadvantage to having multiple subjects. In some ways, there are advantages to having many subjects, because it allows the data to be logically divided. However, most Data Warehouses are used in a cross-subject fashion. This means that dividing the Data Warehouse into artificially-created subject areas goes against the actual way it will be used.

Creation of Detail Tables[24]

The registering of detail tables again illustrates how the World Furniture Data Warehousing process complements the usage of the Warehouse Administrator. All of the detail tables for World Furniture are defined and

---

[23] See the section, "Creating Data Warehouses," in Chapter 9, Section 9.6
[24] See the section, "Creating Detail Tables," in Chapter 9, Section 9.6.4

stored in a SAS catalog as source entries (`whmeta.transfrm`). Although minor modifications might be needed to incorporate these definitions, the process of designing the detail tables has already been completed. Therefore, the Warehouse Administrator is best used on the back of a well-constructed Data Warehousing process and does not substitute for one. All of the logical tables are described in Section 10.4.

Creation of a Logical Detail Table[25]

The Administrator needs a single Logical Detail Table for every subject. This table can either be a physical detail table, a view of multiple detail tables, or a grouping of detail tables. In the case of World Furniture, the Logical Detail Table would merely group together the corresponding detail tables within each of the subjects. There is no real need for either a physical table, or a view of multiple tables to be used as the Logical Detail Table.

Defining the Processes of the World Furniture Data Warehouse to the SAS/Warehouse Administrator

At this stage, the elements of the Data Warehouse have been defined. All of the work that World Furniture put into the design of their Data Warehouse, including the modeling process, would not have been wasted if it was decided to use the Warehouse Administrator. In fact, not having the Warehouse Administrator could well have worked to World Furniture's advantage, because it forced them into organizing their process without having the crutch of a management tool.

Now, the pieces that need to be defined are how each of these elements that have been defined are related and what processes link them together.

Defining the Input Sources

As far as the Warehouse Administrator is concerned, it does not know the physical file location of each of the tables defined in the ODDs. It is now necessary to specify where the source operational files are located, and on which host. This is again a very simple process for the World Furniture implementation because all of this information is well documented. All of this information has already been entered as environmental-level metadata.

For example, one of the ODDs will be the following definition for the extraction of data from the point-of-sale system.

---

[25] See the section, "Creating a Logical Detail Tables," in Chapter 9, Section 9.6

```
/* Definition for Sales table */
/* Stored in whmeta.db2cat as sales.source entry */

PROC SQL;
 CONNECT TO DB2(SSID=pos);
 CREATE VIEW whdata.sales AS
 SELECT * FROM CONNECTION TO DB2 AS
(SELECT employee_id,
        sales_$,
        sales_#,
        sales_date,
        stock_#
 FROM pos.sale)
 AS t1(emp_num, sale_amt, sale_num, sale_dt, stck_num);
DISCONNECT FROM DB2;
QUIT;
```

This ODD would have been registered already. The only problem is that without further information it will not be of much use in the creation of the Data Warehouse. The host computer where the `pos.sale` table is located needs to be associated with the ODD, as does the definition for the `whdata` SAS libref.

Defining Data Transfers to the Administrator

The Client/Server strategy of the Data Warehouse implementation was well considered during the construction of the process. This strategy must now be defined to the Warehouse Administrator, so that the data that should be moved between computers and when it should be moved is understood. Using the ODD above, it was decided that the data would be extracted on the host machine and then immediately moved, as is, to the UNIX server where the Data Warehouse would be located. This meant that it would be necessary to build code that would move the data. This code would essentially be a PROC UPLOAD from the computer upon which the DB2 point-of-sale system resides, to the UNIX server.

The next choice open to World Furniture, with the Warehouse Adminstrator running on a Windows PC, is how the data transfer should take place. Within the Warehouse Administrator, it is easy to define all the information related to the movement of data to (download) and from (upload) the PC. In this case, the `whdata.sales` data that is defined by the view will be moved from one UNIX server (where the point-of-sale system resides) to another (where the Data Warehouse will reside). To do this as a two-stage process would probably be inefficient,[26] but it would be possible to have user-written code move the data directly. This user-written code would contain the code not

---

[26] See the section, "Defining Data Transfers to the SAS/Warehouse Administrator," in Chapter 9, Section 9.7 for a full explanation of data transfer options available within the SAS/Warehouse Administrator

only to move the data but also to create a SAS/CONNECT session from the host where the operational system resides to the host where the Data Warehouse resides.[27]

For World Furniture, defining the Client/Server configuration to the Warehouse Administrator is a fairly easy process, because the Data Warehouse is already fully designed. Some additional source code might have to be constructed (see the above paragraph). Because the underlying rules of the Client/Server strategy for World Furniture are very straight-forward, all that is needed is to put these rules into place. The underlying rule for World Furniture is that no intensive processing will be performed on the mainframe. Whenever possible, processing will be performed on the UNIX server that the Data Warehouse resides upon.

Moving the Operational Data to the Detail Tables

A very important part of the task of the Warehouse Administrator is to have all the rules that will allow an operational data source (ODD) to be mapped to a detail table. This process is equivalent to creating the `whdata.sales` detail table, illustrated in the section "Establishing the Source Operational Systems" in Section 10.4. In creating `whdata.sales`, two input data sources are used and are concatenated together (using the SQL UNION option). Two options are open to World Furniture: they could use the code as a user-exit in the process,[28] or they could go through the process of actually defining all the mappings to the Administrator. In this situation the mappings should be defined to the Warehouse Administrator, because the Warehouse Administrator is designed to handle such transformations of data. User-exits, although often very useful, should only be used when the code is of a type that is best generated outside the Warehouse Administrator.

As with the previous steps in using the Warehouse Administrator, World Furniture is very well placed. All of the work in the design of the process is being incorporated into the use of the Warehouse Administrator. Although some of the code might not be needed, because the Warehouse Administrator will actually create the code itself, the process has not been invalidated. Redesigning the process has not been necessary to incorporate the use of the SAS/Warehouse Administrator. It has been necessary to adapt specific details to allow the Warehouse Administrator to take over managing the warehouse process, but none of the resource investment has been wasted.

---

[27] See Chapter 8, Section 8.4 for details on the code required to connect between SAS sessions on different hosts.

[28] See the section "Incorporating User-Written Programs into the SAS/Warehouse Administrator," in Chapter 9, Section 9.7 for a description of user-exits in the SAS/Warehouse Administrator.

In other words, in a well-designed Data Warehouse process, the SAS/Warehouse Administrator can be incorporated after the initial design, without compromising any of the resources expended.

Ensuring that Only Desired Data is Extracted from the Source Operational Systems

The record selector options within the SAS/Warehouse Administrator will allow World Furniture to extract only the data that is needed for the particular update cycle. Most of the discussions within this case study have related to building a process, and starting a new Data Warehouse. The record selecter will allow for conditional extraction of source operational data. For World Furniture, this subsetting of the operational data will be based upon a particular time period. This will be manifested as a WHERE clause defined to the Warehouse Administrator. This WHERE clause will be applied to each of the ODDs on the hosts where the operational data resides. Remove unneeded data as early in the refresh cycle as possible to avoid processing data that will not be required.

Loading the Data Warehouse

All the details behind the different parts of the World Furniture Data Warehouse will have been entered in the preceding steps. Nothing has actually been done up to this point. Only after the loading information is defined to the Warehouse Administrator can the Data Warehouse be loaded or refreshed.

> *When to actually begin using the SAS/Warehouse Administrator can be confusing. Because the initial load of a Data Warehouse inevitably varies from subsequent cyclical loads, resources might be wasted in defining the initial process to the Administrator. Instead, use this initial process as the basis for subsequent loads. The process will remain very similar, but the code might well differ (e.g., the ODDs will probably not refer to the same operational source).*
>
> *Using this technique, the initial load will be performed without the Warehouse Administrator. Defining the process subsequently to the Warehouse Administrator will be far easier, because the process will already be thought through. One of the main points of Chapter 9 is that the Warehouse Administrator is not a design tool, but is an implementation tool. The design of the Data Warehouse, therefore, should not take place within the Warehouse Administrator environment.*

Because all the details of the Data Warehouse are defined to the Warehouse Administrator, the loading information is very easy to define. All that is needed is whether the code will be run using batch (which would be the case with World Furniture), or interactive mode, and the associated scheduling information. This again, would be very simple for World Furniture, because their **design has already been completed.** If the Warehouse Administrator were used before a design is complete, it would be far more difficult to successfully define all the relevant information.

Creating Summary Information

At this stage, World Furniture has completed the immediate configuration of their Data Warehouse within the SAS/Warehouse Administrator. The next step is to create the necessary summary files. The code to perform this step can be created by the Warehouse Administrator. The creation of summary files within the Warehouse Administrator can take place as part of a subject, or as part of a Data Mart. If the summary file is part of a subject, only detail tables that are defined as part of that subject can be used. (Remember, however, that detail tables can be registered across subjects.)

For World Furniture, the immediate need was for a Data Mart, although there might be a need to create summary groups within each subject[29] at some point. In the case of World Furniture, two different departments (Purchasing and Marketing) require summary information in a slightly different form. A single Data Mart could be established for the two enterprise needs being addressed, but for strategic reasons this was decided against. The Data Warehousing Manager wanted to structure the current configuration so that it would be compatible with future needs. She recognized that there might be reasons in the future, as the Data Warehouse grows, to physically locate each department's specific data on separate servers. To logically separate the organization at this point would therefore be compatible with this long-term expectation.

Therefore, World Furniture created two Data Mart Groups.[30] Each of these Data Mart Groups was defined for each of the different departments. Both of these Data Mart Groups are part of the single defined Data Warehouse. For a Data Mart, the code used to generate the tables **is always** user-written. This means that the current code for creating the SAS multi-dimensional databases that were already created would also be used to define the Data

---

[29] See the section, "Creating Summary Groups," in Chapter 9, Section 9.10 for a description of Summary Groups.

[30] See Chapter 9, Section 9.11 for details regarding the creation of Data Marts using the SAS/Warehouse Administrator.

Mart. This code would comply to the SAS source code to generate the MDDBs in Section 10.5.

After the Data Marts have been registered with the SAS/Warehouse Administrator, additional loading information is required (where the processing will take place, whether the code is to run interactively or in batch mode, etc). Then, the Data Mart registration will be complete. Again, this activity illustrates how a Data Warehousing process, when well-designed, can easily be adapted to fit into the Warehouse Adminstrator. Again, the process is more important in many ways than the details.

Using the Metadata

The metadata from the SAS/Warehouse Administrator can be particularly useful to the designers of the World Furniture Data Warehouse because the Warehouse Administrator allows individual columns of data to be traced from operational source systems back to the enterprise needs they help address. Because the data can be traced to the needs, it is possible to understand, from a business perspective, how important certain data from source systems actually is. By understanding this importance, it is then possible to understand how crucial different operational systems are, beyond just their immediate function of keeping the enterprise running.

For example, in the case of World Furniture, the sales amounts from the point-of-sale systems are critical to address the two enterprise needs selected. This means that the sales amount is therefore a key factor in the decisions that will affect the company's future. Because it is a key factor, relative changes in the distribution of its domain will have a major influence on the company. If the sales amounts increased, for example, the results of the analyses relating to the two selected enterprise needs will be directly affected. This means that a relationship exists between columns of data in the operational systems and the decision making process. It helps in the overall understanding of the business to know the columns of data that greatly affect the business. Although in this example, sales amount will affect the decision support process, it might well become apparent that columns of data have a far greater influence than was thought as the Data Warehouse increases in size.

One very important development in the use of the metadata from the SAS/Warehouse Administrator is the addition of the SAS Metadata API (Application Program Interface) starting with Release 1.2. This API will allow for metadata to be easily used in applications outside the Warehouse Administrator itself. One of the main benefits to using the API is that if the metadata is changes in structure over time (as it inevitably will), the API will remain constant. The structure of the tables that contain the metadata are complex, both internally and in terms of their relationships with each other. Using the API rather than DATA steps or SQL to process the information is highly recommended. The API will keep in line with these complex relationships as they change over time and will ensure that the use of metadata from the Administrator can be easily supported.

Glossary

aggregation
the act of creating a statistic across columns in the same row of a table.

class
in object-oriented methodology, the template or model for an object, which includes data that describes the object's characteristics (instance variables) and the operations (methods) that it can perform. See also subclassing.

client/server architecture
a computer architecture that allows for more than one logical entity to work together to perform a specific task. Usually, but not necessarily, this task is completed over a computer network, and each logical entity is physically located on different hosts (computers).

data cleaning
the process of analyzing data values (to determine whether they conform to pre-defined criteria for completeness, consistency, and accuracy) and transforming any undesirable values. This process is also called data scrubbing.

data extraction
a step within the transformation of the Data Warehouse that involves moving data from source (usually operational) systems typically in a staged region, where it is converted into the form required within the Data Warehouse.

data integration
the process of combining data elements from different operational sources into a single representation for use in the Data Warehouse. See also denormalization.

data-implementation approach
an approach to building a Data Warehouse that ignores the definition of enterprise needs. This form of building a Data Warehouse is best described as the 'build it and they will come' approach, which assumes that if there is a physical implementation of a Data Warehouse, then someone, somewhere will find a use for it.

data mart
in SAS/Warehouse Administrator, tables that provide easy access to a subset of the data in a warehouse. Typically, data marts store information of interest to a specific department or individual. They can also be used to store the results of ad hoc queries or cross-subject analyses.

data mining
the process of searching for patterns, trends, or correlations in operational or Warehouse data. Data mining uses statistical analysis techniques or pattern recognition technology or both.

data model
a set of entities (objects), their attributes (characteristics), and a description of the relationships between those entities or objects. See also logical data model and SAS data model.

data scrubbing
See data cleaning.

data staging
the process of validating, transforming, and integrating data. See also data cleaning, data integration, data validation, denormalization, and transformation.

data storage
the amount of space on disk or tape that is required to keep your data.

data structure
1) a group of related data items stored in memory. In FORTRAN, data structures are called COMMON blocks; in IBM 370 Assembler, data structures are called DSECTs. C and PL/I use the term data structures.
2) in SAS/CONNECT software, a collection of data declarations that is used to pass information between a user-written procedure and the SAS System.

data transformation
the process of changing a data value from one form to another (for example, a calendar date to a SAS date value or vice versa).

data validation
the process of analyzing data values to determine whether they conform to pre-defined criteria for completeness, consistency, and accuracy.

Data Warehouse
a collection of data that is organized into subjects and to which time values have been added. A Data Warehouse is designed to hold a large volume of read-only data and is used by an entire enterprise for decision support. A Data Warehouse can also be thought of as a container for metadata shared among the elements of a given Warehouse: subjects, detail tables, summary tables, information marts, and data marts.

Data Warehouse Administrator
an individual who is responsible for the day-to-day functioning of the Data Warehouse and for its on-going maintenance.

Data Warehouse Architecture
the broad phrase used to describe the design of the entire Data Warehousing process. This architecture includes not only the process but any associated hardware, software, and data structures.

Data Warehouse element
a distinct component of a Data Warehouse such as a subject, data mart, or information mart.

denormalization
the process of organizing normalized or standard data, which are typical of online transaction processing (OLTP) systems, into subject form by combining data from separate tables. Denormalization optimizes the performance of a Data Warehouse and frequently results in some data redundancy.

extraction
the process of selecting data from an operational data source.

inheritance

in object-oriented methodology, the structural characteristic of class definitions in which all methods and instance variables of a class are automatically defined in all its subclasses.

logical data model

a model of a specific business process or concept from an end-user's perspective. A logical data model identifies the subjects and relationships among data elements but does not describe the functional or physical characteristics of the data elements.

match-merging

a process in which the SAS System joins observations from two or more SAS data sets according to the values of the BY variables.

metadata

data or information about the entities, such as tables and columns, in a Data Warehouse. Metadata includes business and technical metadata. Business metadata defines how an entity is used by business users. Technical metadata defines the physical characteristics of an entity such as, which online transaction processing (OLTP) table the data was extracted from, which transformations were applied to the data, when the data was loaded into the Warehouse, and so on.

multi-dimensional database (MDDB)

a SAS database format for summary tables that optimizes access and retrieval times for the data that the tables contain by storing data in a pre-summarized format. An MDDB also requires less physical storage space than standard database formats.

normalization

in the analysis of test scores, the process of converting each set of original scores to some standard scale. One method in common use is to determine percentiles of the scores and then express them as corresponding deviations from the mean of a normal distribution.

object

in object-oriented methodology, a specific representation of a class. An object inherits all the characteristics (instance variables) of its class as well as the operations (methods) that class can execute. For example, a push button object is an instance of the Push Button class. The terms object and instance are often used interchangeably.

object-oriented programming (OOP)

a form of programming that concentrates on the building of reusable components, which can be combined at will to create entire systems. Although having many facets, one of the unique capabilities of an object-oriented approach is the concept of inheritance, where a component (object) that is based upon another object will automatically take with it all of the behaviors of that object.

OLAP (Online Analytical Processing)

a broad term to describe a type of processing that allows for unlimited views of multiple relationships within summarized data. It is typically, although not necessarily, associated with multi-dimensional databases where this pre-summarized data can be efficiently stored.

online transaction processing (OLTP) systems

the systems that an enterprise uses for processing business transactions on a day-to-day basis.

Open Database Connectivity (ODBC)

an industry de facto standard that allows for one software product to view and use the data that is native to another.

operational data definition (ODD)

the name of a SAS data set, a SAS view, a SAS/ACCESS view descriptor, or an SQL view descriptor that identifies an operational data source. To access operational data stored in flat files, you define a SAS DATA step view that functions as the SAS/Warehouse Administrator ODD. To access operational data stored in DMBS tables, you define either a SAS/ACCESS view or a PROC SQL view that functions as the ODD.

parallel processing

the ability, through a combination of hardware and software, for the work required for a single task to be divided between different computer processors.

pass-through SQL

the ability for SQL (Structured Query Language) code to be processed by the database engine that is native to the data being processed. For example, it is possible within SAS to write SQL code to extract data from an ORACLE data table by using the ORACLE database engine.

relational database management system (RDBMS)

a database management system that organizes and accesses data according to relationships between data items. The main characteristic of a relational database management system is the two-dimensional table. Examples of relational database management systems are DB2, INGRES, ORACLE, and SQL/DS.

SAS data file

1) a SAS data set that is implemented in a form that contains both the data values and the descriptor information. SAS data files have the type DATA.
2) a form of a SAS data set that contains both the data values and the descriptor information associated with the data, such as the variable attributes. In previous releases of the SAS System, all SAS data sets were SAS data files. SAS data files are of member type DATA. In the SAS System, a PROC SQL table is a SAS data file.
3) a SAS data set that contains both the data values and the descriptor information.

SAS data model

the framework into which engines put information for SAS processing. The SAS data model is a logical representation of data or files, not a physical structure.

SAS data view

a SAS data set in which the descriptor information and the observations are obtained from other files. A SAS data view contains only the descriptor and other information required to retrieve the data values from other SAS files. Both PROC SQL views and SAS/ACCESS views are considered SAS data views. SAS data views are of member type VIEW.

SAS/ACCESS views

See SAS data view.

Scalable Performance Data Server

a SAS product that exploits the use of parallel processing to increase the speed with which data can be extracted and exploited.

schema

a map or model of the overall data structure of a database. A schema consists of schema records organized in a hierarchical tree structure. Schema records contain schema items.

scrubbing

part of the transformation of the Data Warehouse where incoming data is cleansed before being loaded into the Data Warehouse. Scrubbing always follows some form of data validation.

star schema

an arrangement of database tables in which a large Fact table that has a composite, foreign key is joined to several Dimension tables. Each Dimension table has a single primary key.

star-join schema

an approach to modeling the Data Warehouse that was made popular by Ralph Kimball. It is based around the Data Warehouse being made up of 'facts' and 'Dimensions'. Facts are the information that will be analyzed (e.g., sales) and the Dimensions are the categorical variables by which the facts might be viewed (e.g., region, manager).

subclassing

in object-oriented methodology, the process of deriving a new class from an existing class. A new class inherits the characteristics (instance variables) and operations (methods) of its parent, and it can contain custom instance variables and methods. See also class.

summarization

the act of creating a statistic (sum, mean, standard deviation, etc.) across rows in a table. See also aggregation.

transformation

the act of changing physical data into subject data. The reason for the changing is to integrate operational data formats into a consistent format within the Data Warehouse. Transformation can be at the variable level or the table level. Table-level transformation is sometimes referred to as summarization.

Index

Quick Start to Data Analysis with SAS®
by **Frank C. Dilorio**
and **Kenneth A. Hardy** ....Order No. A55550

Reporting from the Field: SAS® Software
Experts Present Real-World Report-Writing
Applications ....Order No. A55135

SAS® Applications Programming: A Gentle Introduction
by **Frank C. Dilorio** ....Order No. A55193

SAS® Foundations: From Installation to Operation
by **Rick Aster** ....Order No. A55093

SAS® Programming by Example
by **Ron Cody**
and **Ray Pass** ....Order No. A55126

SAS® Programming for Researchers and
Social Scientists
by **Paul E. Spector** ....Order No. A56199

SAS® Software Roadmaps: Your Guide to
Discovering the SAS® System
by **Laurie Burch**
and **SherriJoyce King** ....Order No. A56195

SAS® Software Solutions
by **Thomas Miron** ....Order No. A56196

SAS® System for Elementary Statistical Analysis,
Second Edition
by **Sandra D. Schlotzhauer**
and **Dr. Ramon C. Littell** ....Order No. A55172

SAS® System for Forecasting Time Series,
1986 Edition
by **John C. Brocklebank**
and **David A. Dickey** ....Order No. A5612

SAS® System for Linear Models, Third Edition
by **Ramon C. Littell, Rudolf J. Freund,**
and **Philip C. Spector** ....Order No. A56140

SAS® System for Mixed Models
by **Ramon C. Littell, George A. Milliken, Walter W.**
Stroup, *and* **Russell W. Wolfinger**......Order No. A55235

SAS® System for Regression, Second Edition
by **Rudolf J. Freund**
and **Ramon C. Littell**............................Order No. A56141

SAS® System for Statistical Graphics, First Edition
by **Michael Friendly** ....Order No. A56143

SAS® Today! A Year of Terrific Tips
by **Helen Carey** *and* **Ginger Carey** ......Order No. A55662

The SAS® Workbook and Solutions
(books in this set also sold separately)
by **Ron Cody** ....Order No. A55594

Selecting Statistical Techniques for Social
Science Data: A Guide for SAS® Users
by **Laura Klem, Kathleen B. Welch,**
Terrence N. Davidson, Willard L. Rodgers,
and **Patrick M. O'Malley** ....Order No. A55854

Statistical Quality Control Using the SAS® System
by **Dennis W. King, Ph.D**....................Order No. A55232

A Step-by-Step Approach to Using the SAS® System
for Univariate and Multivariate Statistics
by **Larry Hatcher**
and **Edward Stepanski** ....Order No. A55072

Survival Analysis Using the SAS® System:
A Practical Guide
by **Paul D. Allison** ....Order No. A55233

Table-Driven Strategies for Rapid SAS® Applications
Development
by **Tanya Kolosova**
and **Samuel Berestizhevsky** ....Order No. A55198

Tuning SAS® Applications in the MVS Environment
by **Michael A. Raithel** ....Order No. A55231

Univariate and Multivariate General Linear Models:
Theory and Applications Using SAS® Software
by **Neil H. Timm**
and **Tammy A. Mieczkowski** ....Order No. A55809

Working with the SAS® System
by **Erik W. Tilanus** ....Order No. A55190

Your Guide to Survey Research Using the
SAS® System
by **Archer Gravely** ....Order No. A55688

Audio Tapes
100 Essential SAS® Software Concepts (set of two)
by **Rick Aster** ....Order No. A55309

A Look at SAS® Files (set of two)
by **Rick Aster** ....Order No. A55207

*Welcome * Bienvenue *Willkommen *Yohkoso * Bienvenido*

SAS® Publications Is Easy to Reach

Visit our SAS Publications Web page located at www.sas.com/pubs/

You will find product and service details, including

- **sample chapters**
- **tables of contents**
- **author biographies**
- **book reviews**

Learn about

- **regional user groups conferences**
- **trade show sites and dates**
- **authoring opportunities**
- **custom textbooks**
- **FREE Desk copies**

Order books with ease at our secured Web page!

Explore all the services that Publications has to offer!

Your Listserv Subscription Brings the News to You Automatically

Do you want to be among the first to learn about the latest books and services available from SAS Publications? Subscribe to our listserv **newdocnews-l** and automatically receive the following once each month: a description of the new titles, the applicable environments or operating systems, and the applicable SAS release(s). To subscribe:

1. Send an e-mail message to **listserv@vm.sas.com**

2. Leave the "Subject" line blank

3. Use the following text for your message:

> **subscribe newdocnews-l** *your-first-name your-last-name*

For example: subscribe newdocnews-l John Doe

Please note: newdocnews-l ◄——— that's the letter "l" not the number "1".

For customers outside the U.S., contact your local SAS office for listserv information.

Create Customized Textbooks Quickly, Easily, and Affordably

SelecText™ offers instructors at U.S. colleges and universities a way to create custom textbooks for courses that teach students how to use SAS software.

For more information, see our Web page at **www.sas.com/selectext/**, or contact our SelecText coordinators by sending e-mail to **selectext@sas.com**.

You're Invited to Publish with SAS Institute's User Publishing Program

If you enjoy writing about SAS software and how to use it, the User Publishing Program at SAS Institute Inc. offers a variety of publishing options. We are actively recruiting authors to publish books, articles, and sample code. Do you find the idea of writing a book or an article by yourself a little intimidating? Consider writing with a co-author. Keep in mind that you will receive complete editorial and publishing support, access to our users, technical advice and assistance, and competitive royalties. Please contact us for an author packet. E-mail us at **sasbbu@sas.com** or call 919-677-8000, then press 1-6479. See the SAS Publications Web page at **www.sas.com/pubs/** for complete information.

Read All about It in *Authorline*®!

Our User Publishing newsletter, *Authorline*, features author interviews, conference news, and informational updates and highlights from our User Publishing Program. Published quarterly, *Authorline* is available free of charge. To subscribe, send e-mail to **sasbbu@sas.com** or call 919-677-8000, then press 1-6479.

See *Observations*®, Our Online Technical Journal

Feature articles from *Observations*®: *The Technical Journal for SAS*® *Software Users* are now available online at **www.sas.com/obs/**. Take a look at what your fellow SAS software users and SAS Institute experts have to tell you. You may decide that you, too, have information to share. If you are interested in writing for *Observations*, send e-mail to **sasbbu@sas.com** or call 919-677-8000, then press 1-6479.

Book Discount Offered at SAS Public Training Courses!

When you attend one of our SAS Public Training Courses at any of our regional Training Centers in the U.S., you will receive a 15% discount on any book orders placed during the course. Each course has a list of recommended books to choose from, and the books are displayed for you to see. Take advantage of this offer at the next course you attend!

SAS Institute Inc.
SAS Campus Drive
Cary, NC 27513-2414
Fax 919-677-4444

E-mail: sasbook@sas.com
Web page: www.sas.com/pubs/
To order books, call Book Sales at 800-727-3228*
For other SAS Institute business, call 919-677-8000*

* Note: Customers outside the U.S. should contact their local SAS office.